Hiking

Grand Staircase–Escalante and the Glen Canyon Region

Ron Adkison

FALCON®

HELENA, MONTANA

A FALCON GUIDE®

Falcon® Publishing is continually expanding its list of recreation guidebooks. All books include detailed descriptions, accurate maps, and all the information necessary for enjoyable trips. You can order extra copies of this book and get information and prices for other Falcon® guidebooks by writing Falcon, P.O. Box 1718, Helena, MT 59624 or calling toll free 1-800-582-2665. Also, please ask for a free copy of our current catalog. Visit our website at www.falconguide.com

©1998 Falcon® Publishing, Inc., Helena, Montana
Printed in the United States of America.

1 2 3 4 5 6 7 8 9 0 MG 03 02 01 00 99 98

Falcon and FalconGuide are registered trademarks of Falcon® Publishing, Inc.

All photos by author unless otherwise noted.
Cover photo by Larry Carver.

Library of Congress Cataloging-in-Publication Data
    Adkison, Ron
            Hiking Grand Staircase–Escalante and the Glen Canyon Region/ by Ron
        Adkison.
                p. cm.
            Includes bibliographical references.
            ISBN 1-56044-645-5
            1. Hiking—Glen Canyon Region (Utah and Ariz.)—Guidebooks.
        2. Hiking—Grand Staircase-Escalante National Monument (Utah)—
        Guidebooks. 3. Glen Canyon Region (Utah and Ariz.)—Guidebooks.
        4. Grand Staircase-Escalante National Monument (Utah)—Guidebooks.
        I. Title.
        GV199.42.G54A35 1998
        917.92'59—dc21   98-22584
                                                                                    CIP

CAUTION
Outdoor recreational activities are by their very nature potentially hazardous. All participants in such activities must assume the responsibility for their own actions and safety. The information contained in this guidebook cannot replace sound judgment and good decision-making skills, which help reduce risk exposure, nor does the scope of this book allow for disclosure of all the potential hazards and risks involved in such activities.

Learn as much as possible about the outdoor recreational activities in which you participate, prepare for the unexpected, and be cautious. The reward will be a safer and more enjoyable experience.

♻ Text pages printed on recycled paper.

Contents

Acknowledgments

Writing a guidebook to the canyon country of the Glen Canyon region was an enormous but unforgettable task. Although I hardly scratched the surface of hiking opportunities in this vast region, I learned much more than I had known previously about this fascinating landscape, one that I began exploring many years ago.

A number of extraordinary people not only helped me to complete this book, but they also offered generous support and guidance, helping to make the book more informative and useful.

Foremost among them was Neil Stufflebeam, the BLM ranger at Kane Gulch Ranger Station. Few people know more about the backcountry and cultural history of Cedar Mesa than Neil, and over the course of many visits, Neil and I became good friends. He taught me more about the region than I would have thought possible.

Phil Gezon of the BLM office in Monticello, who is unquestionably one of the authorities on the Cedar Mesa area, was most gracious in answering an endless barrage of questions. Phil shared many documents and helped fill in the gaps in my knowledge of Cedar Mesa.

While in the Escalante region, I met ranger Jeff Lauersdorf, who generously offered time out of his busy schedule to answer questions and to share insights and documents. If Jeff couldn't provide the answer to a question, he introduced me to someone who could. Without Jeff's help, many aspects of the Escalante region would have remained a mystery to me.

Mike Salamacha, whose knowledge of Paria Canyon and the Grand Staircase is equaled by few, was also very generous with his time and knowledge, answering questions and sharing documents.

Once again I must offer my thanks and gratitude to Phil Gezon and Mike Salamacha, and to Jim Bowman of the National Park Service and Jeanie Linn at the Escalante Interagency office, for reviewing the manuscript and passing it along for further review by other experts in their offices. Without their comments, suggestions, and corrections, this book would be incomplete at best.

While in Grand Gulch I met Tom Klein, and together we explored that beautiful canyon, taking a most memorable journey. It's hard to find a better hiking partner than Tom.

Countless others, both in BLM offices and in the backcountry, shared their knowledge and offered valuable insights, and they, perhaps unknowingly, contributed enormously to this book.

Finally, I could not have begun this project, let alone have completed it, without the love, support, and understanding of my wife, Lynette, and children, Ben and Abbey. It's not easy running a ranch and shouldering all the other responsibilities of work and family on your own, but Lynette did it well, and she deserves great credit.

Ron Adkison
February, 1998

USGS Topo Map Index
Cedar Mesa/Dark Canyon/
Hite

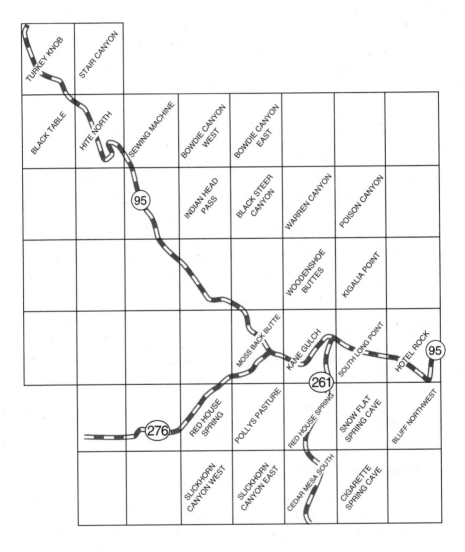

USGS Topo Map Index
Escalante Canyons

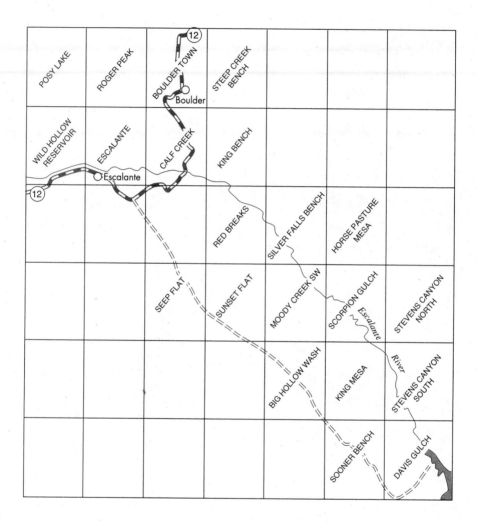

USGS Topo Map Index
Grand Staircase/Paria River

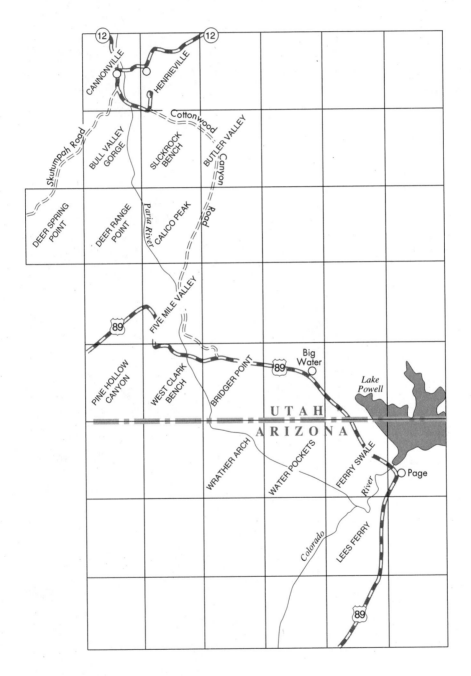

Map Legend

Interstate		Picnic Area	
U.S. Highway		Campground	
State or County Road		Bridge	
Forest Road		Cave/Alcove	
Interstate Highway		Cabins/Buildings	
Paved Road		Ruins	
Unpaved Road, Graded		Ranger Station	
Unpaved Road, Poor		Elevation	X 9,782 ft.
Trailhead		Butte	
Main Trail		Dome	
Secondary Trail		Cliffs	Top edge
Trailless Route, Wash Route		Falls, Pouroff	
River/Creek, Perennial		Pass/Saddle	)(
Drainage, Intermittent Creek		Gate	
Spring		Overlook/ Point of Interest	
Forest/Wilderness/ Park Boundary		Map Orientation	N
State Boundary	UTAH ARIZONA	Scale	0 30 60 Miles

ix

Locator Map #1

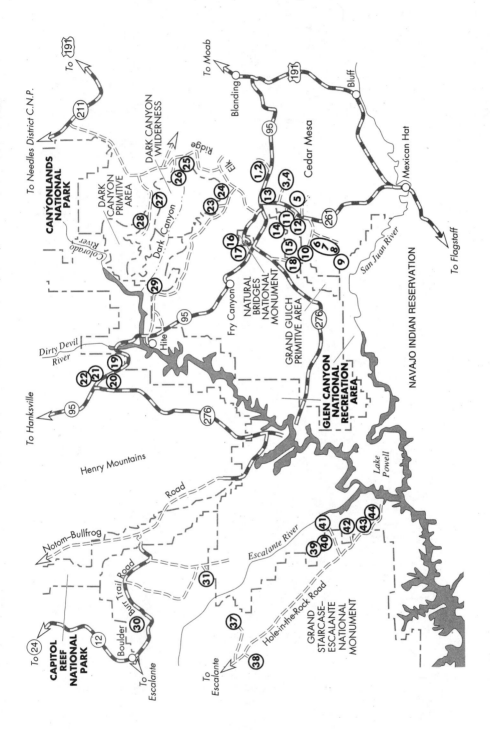

Locator Map #2

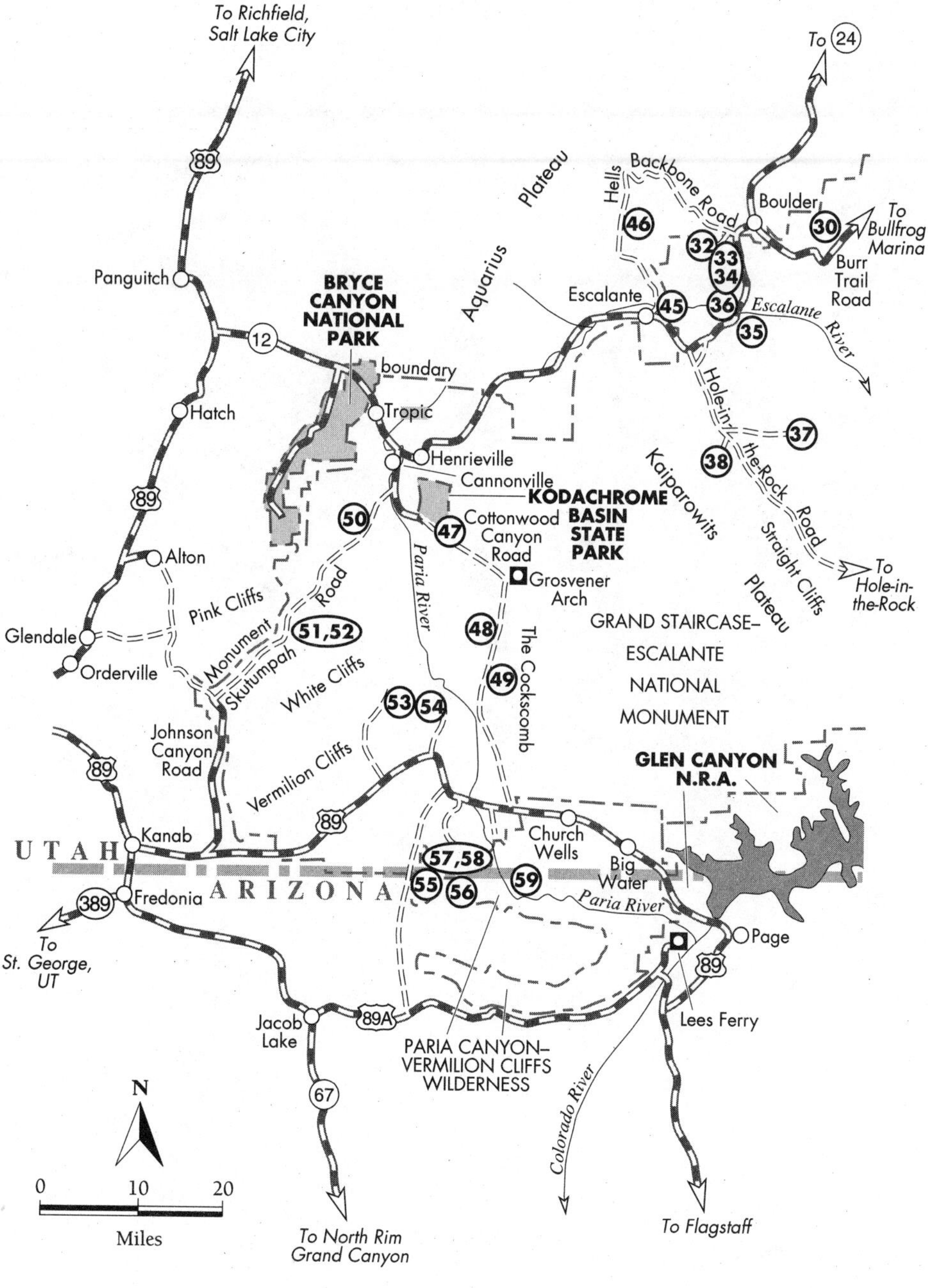

To Richfield, Salt Lake City
To 24
89
Panguitch
12
BRYCE CANYON NATIONAL PARK
boundary
Aquarius
Plateau
Hells
Backbone Road
Boulder
To Bullfrog Marina
Burr Trail Road
30
46
32
33
34
45
36
35
Escalante
Escalante River
Hatch
Tropic
Henrieville
Cannonville
Hole-in-the-Rock Road
37
38
To Hole-in-the-Rock
Kaiparowits
Plateau
Straight Cliffs
KODACHROME BASIN STATE PARK
Cottonwood Canyon Road
47
50
Grosvener Arch
Alton
Pink Cliffs
Monument Road
Skutumpah
51,52
Glendale
Orderville
Paria River
48
49
The Cockscomb
GRAND STAIRCASE–ESCALANTE NATIONAL MONUMENT
White Cliffs
53
54
Johnson Canyon Road
Vermilion Cliffs
GLEN CANYON N.R.A.
Kanab
Church Wells
Big Water
57,58
UTAH
ARIZONA
55
56
59
Paria River
389
Fredonia
To St. George, UT
Page
Lees Ferry
Jacob Lake
89A
PARIA CANYON–VERMILION CLIFFS WILDERNESS
67
Colorado River
N
0
10
20
Miles
To North Rim Grand Canyon
To Flagstaff

Overview Map

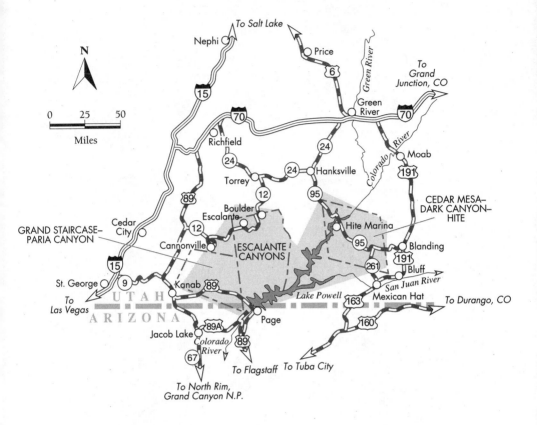

Nevills Arch in Owl Creek canyon.

Introduction

This guidebook focuses on the Glen Canyon region, an area which includes all of the major canyon tributaries to the Colorado River (Lake Powell) in southern Utah and many lesser canyons. It also includes several hikes from the newly established Grand Staircase–Escalante National Monument.

Glen Canyon, named by John Wesley Powell during his 1869 Colorado River expedition, begins at the confluence with the Dirty Devil River, near Hite, Utah, and extends down-canyon to Lees Ferry, where Marble Canyon and the Colorado River flow southward toward the Grand Canyon (see overview map, page vii). At its maximum water level, Lake Powell stretches upriver from Glen Canyon Dam for 187 miles, inundating Glen Canyon, Narrow Canyon, and the lower end of Cataract Canyon. The San Juan Arm of the lake reaches up the canyon of the San Juan River nearly to the mouth of Grand Gulch.

When the floodgates closed on Glen Canyon Dam in 1963, the waters of the Colorado steadily began to fill Glen Canyon and its tributaries, until the lake reached full capacity in 1980. Slowly, by increments, the alcoves, glens, amphitheaters, cultural remains, and the peaceful, undisturbed atmosphere of the idyllic canyon were lost. But the tributaries to Glen Canyon remain much as they did in Powell's day, and indeed have changed little since the Anasazi made their homes here.

The Colorado River carved an incomparable landscape in southern Utah, and erosion was the principal sculptor. The Glen Canyon region is a network of Colorado River tributaries, containing hundreds of all sizes. Only 10 to 12 miles separate the rims of the Grand Canyon, but the edges of the Colorado in the Glen Canyon region stretch 150 miles from the Pink Cliffs in the west to Elk Ridge and Cedar Mesa in the east. This is a raw land, stripped to its bare bones by erosion.

The Glen Canyon region is a national park that never was. Here visitors can find the incredible scenery of a national park without the crowds, developments, and excessive restrictions. Access here is a little more difficult than in national parks, but the region remains relatively undiscovered, and provides some of the finest backcountry recreation in canyon country.

The Bureau of Land Management (BLM) administers most of the trails in this book. More than 1 million acres in the Glen Canyon region are either protected as wilderness or primitive areas under the direction of the BLM or are managed as wilderness study areas. Other roadless areas in the region are managed by the U.S. Forest Service and the National Park Service. Nearly all of the hikes in this book are located within the boundaries of wilderness, primitive, or wilderness study areas.

Hiking opportunities are virtually unlimited in the Glen Canyon region. This book will lead you to both well-known and little used trails, and it will take you to some of the region's most interesting places. Included are several backpack trips and a wide variety of day hikes. Most of this land is seldom visited, and its backcountry affords excellent opportunities for solitude and unconfined wilderness recreation. Wherever you travel here, whether down remote desert roads or up lonely canyons, you will be rewarded at the end of your trip with vivid memories and a yearning to return.

The boundary of Glen Canyon.

How to Use This Guide

The Glen Canyon region is vast, with over 3 million acres of canyons, mesas, and plateaus. There are unlimited hiking opportunities in hundreds of remote canyons, and this guide focuses on many of the region's highlights. Difficult canyon routes that can be negotiated only by skilled veterans with advanced rock climbing skills were not included. The hikes covered in this guide should satisfy veterans and novices alike, and there are easy hikes that will appeal to parents with children and to hikers budgeting their time and energy.

Since the Glen Canyon region is a raw and often unforgiving desert canyon country landscape, hiking here requires some pre-trip planning. The hike descriptions in this guide give you all the information you need to inform and prepare you for your backcountry trip. Here are a few additional points to help you get the most out of this guide:

The **General description** and **Distance** headings tell if the hike is suitable as a day hike, a backpack, or both, and how far, in miles, a hike is. These listings also tell you if the hike is a *round trip*, in which you retrace your route to the trailhead after reaching your destination; a *loop trip*, in which you hike in on one trail and return to your starting point by another trail; or a *shuttle* (or *point-to-point*) *trip*, in which you hike in to a destination from one trailhead, and exit via a different trail to another trailhead.

The **Trailhead access** heading indicates the type of vehicle (two- or four-wheel drive) recommended to reach the starting point of each hike. Two-wheel drive is abbreviated 2WD, four-wheel drive is 4WD.

The **Difficulty** rating is based on the "average" hiker's ability, and may vary depending on your physical condition and state of mind, as well as the weather and trail or route conditions. This book focuses on more commonly used trails and routes leading to many of the region's highlights. Difficult canyoneering routes, where advanced rock climbing skills are required, were omitted. Still, many of the routes in this book are time consuming and arduous. Rudimentary rock climbing skills may be necessary, and the **Difficulty** section tells you when you encounter routes that require rock climbing skill. On most trails and routes the only skill involved is walking, and these are *Class 1* routes. On *Class 2* routes you will find scrambling and boulder-hopping. *Class 3* routes are often associated with pouroff bypasses, and these routes involve the use of hands and feet, usually with obvious hand and foot holds. *Class 4* routes involve climbing steep pitches with dangerous exposure, often with the aid of minor holds and cracks. If you are interested in rock climbing the canyonlands, see Falcon's *Rock Climbing Utah* by Stewart M. Green.

The **Trail conditions** listing tells you if you will be following a *constructed trail*; a *boot-worn trail*, where the path has been forged by the passage of other hikers; a *cow trail*, usually a well-defined path worn by cattle; a *well-worn trail*, which may be a constructed trail that is no longer maintained, but is easy to follow; a *wash route*, where there is no trail but you follow the path of a canyon's drainage, or wash; a *slickrock route*, where you follow a trailless way over bare, smooth sandstone, known as slickrock, and where there may be cairns, or piles of rocks, to indicate the course of the route; or a *road* or *4WD road*, usually a double track that is seldom used by vehicles. This listing also tells you if bushwhacking and routefinding, where there is no trail and you find your own way, will be necessary on the hike.

Average hiking times are based on the average hiker. Most hiking times listed are conservative estimates and many hikers will make a trip in less time. Keep in mind that on many of the region's trails and routes your pace will average about 1.5 to 2 miles per hour.

The headings **Elevation loss, Elevation gain and loss,** and **Elevation loss and gain** may appear confusing. The heading **Elevation loss** is used for hikes where the total elevation difference between the trailhead and the low point for a trip that only descends into a canyon, usually on a point-to-point, or shuttle, trip, or on a one-way trip that is intended as the first leg of an extended backcountry trip. **Elevation gain and loss** indicates a hike which only gains elevation between the trailhead and the destination, then loses that elevation on the return trip; or if there is some elevation gain en route to a descent into a canyon. The heading **Elevation loss and gain** is used for those hikes that descend from the trailhead and return the same way: first you lose elevation, then you regain it on the way back.

The **Optimum seasons** listing indicates the seasons providing the greatest probability of avoiding extreme summer heat and winter snow and cold. Of course you can hike in most of the Glen Canyon region year-round, but summer and winter hiking present challenges that can not be taken lightly.

Knowing a hike's **Water availability** is critical to a safe and enjoyable trip in the desert environment of the Glen Canyon region. Remember that conditions are changing constantly in these canyons, and springs can dry up. Always check with the appropriate BLM office for up-to-date information on water availability before heading into the backcountry.

Hazards indicates the dangers of a route such as flash flood danger or steep dropoffs; it also indicates trailless routes that should be avoided by an inexperienced hiker if there is a risk of becoming disoriented or lost. One thing that is *not* described here is the *remoteness* of a hike, since all of these hikes are in very remote areas, where help is far removed should you need it. Always be prepared and self-sufficient.

Permits for backcountry use are required for only a few areas covered in this guide. When necessary, this listing tells where to obtain them and if a fee is required.

Key points shows the cumulative mileage between prominent features and junctions. Unnamed features mentioned in the hike descriptions are referred to as "Point 6844," "Hill 5392," "Butte 5123," "Dome 6327," etc.

Elevation graphs accompany each hike description. Here, the ups and downs of the hike are shown on an elevation grid, with miles on the horizontal axis and elevation (in feet above sea level) on the vertical axis. Elevation increments are every 100, 200, or 500 feet, depending upon the hike's steepness. Elevation graphs also include some of the hikes key points. Some short dips and climbs (especially those less than 500 feet) may not show up on the graphs. Elevation lines are adjusted to fit onto the graph and do not necessarily reflect the actual trail slope angle.

HIKING IN THE GLEN CANYON REGION

The Glen Canyon region offers canyon country hiking at its finest, and perhaps the most notable feature of these hikes is the lack of trails. Indeed, most hikes covered in this book are trailless, but trails usually aren't necessary since most routes follow the well-defined avenues of canyon bottoms and washes. There are very few constructed trails, and fewer still that are maintained, though there are many paths forged by hikers and maintained simply by the passage of hiker's boots.

Hiking in this raw, rockbound landscape is far different than following trails in hilly or mountainous terrain. Trails are non-existent in most of the canyons of the Glen Canyon region, and it will be up to you to do the routefinding—with the occasional help of a boot-worn path.

There is minimal elevation change for the majority of hikes covered in this book, but don't let their gentle appearance on a map deceive you. Obstacles are hidden between the contours of topo maps, and many canyon routes are far more demanding and rigorous than maps might suggest.

Boulder-hopping, routefinding around pouroffs (dry waterfalls) and boulder jams, bushwhacking through jungles of riparian growth, scrambling, rudimentary rock climbing, and pitches over steep slickrock are routine on many canyon routes. Yet there are often indications of paths and routes that other hikers have forged to bypass obstacles. Experience will give you the ability to recognize indications of such routes. The challenges associated with hiking here are part of the attraction. They give hikers a greater probability of finding solitude and a feeling of accomplishment at their trip's end.

Most hikers will likely average only 1.5 to 2 miles per hour while hiking—seldom will you be able to set a steady pace. Hikers unaccustomed to the rigors of canyoneering should begin slowly and set modest goals as they gain more experience and adapt to routefinding in trailless canyons.

SEASONS AND WEATHER

Hikers come to the Glen Canyon region year-round, but most come during spring and autumn. Since the region is a desert environment, with daytime high temperatures often reaching 95 to 105 degrees F. almost daily from

June through August, summer is the most unfavorable time of the year to hike in the area. The exception is upper Dark Canyon, where elevations range from 5,800 feet to 8,600 feet, and summer temperatures can be hot but not intolerable.

The extreme heat of summer and the unrelenting sun pose serious hazards to hikers. Any seasoned desert hiker knows you cannot fight the desert heat, but you can adapt to it. In summer, hike from the pre-dawn hours until early morning, then rest in the shade during the hottest part of the day. Resume your travels after 5 P.M., when shadows begin to fill the canyons.

Spring and autumn are the best seasons for backcountry trips in the Glen Canyon region. Spring weather (March through May) can be highly variable, with daytime high temperatures ranging from the 50s to the 70s, and nighttime lows ranging from 20 to 50 degrees F. Occasional cold fronts from the west and northwest can bring cold, windy conditions, rain showers in the lower elevations, and perhaps snow on the higher mesas, particularly in March and April. Generally warm, dry weather prevails between storm systems.

Early spring is one of the best times of the year to hike in the canyons of the region. Springs and seasonal streams are likely to be flowing, and slickrock water pockets will hold rainwater longer at this time of year, providing more flexibility and a margin of safety in the backcountry.

The onset of searing summer heat usually begins in late May and can persist into mid-September. The monsoon season usually begins in mid-July and ends in mid-September. Moist tropical air masses over Mexico circulate an almost daily parade of thunderstorms over the region. Mid-summer weather over southern Utah is characterized by torrential rainfall, which is usually accompanied by strong, gusty winds and lightning.

Autumn provides some of the most stable weather of the year. Clear, warm, sunny days and cool nights make this one of the most delightful seasons to visit the Glen Canyon region. Expect daytime highs to range from the 70s and 80s in September to the 40s and 50s by November. Overnight lows are typically in the 20- to 50-degree range. Only the most active summer monsoon season will help recharge springs and streams, but the deepest water pockets often persist into early fall due to cooler temperatures and reduced evaporation. Cold fronts can sweep through the region as autumn progresses, and by mid to late October in some years, these fronts can drop temperatures significantly for several days or longer. Snowfall in the higher elevations above 5,000 to 6,000 feet is not uncommon.

Winter in the Glen Canyon region is cold and often windy, and deep snow sometimes covers the ground above 6,000 feet. Elk Ridge and upper Dark Canyon are closed by deep snows each year from November through the end of May. Other high elevation areas, such as Cedar Mesa and the Grand Staircase, may be rendered inaccessible by snow between December and mid-March each year. Cold weather experience is essential for winter hiking in the Glen Canyon region.

To stay up to date on weather conditions, listen to local radio stations while driving, and check with BLM offices for current forecasts. National

Oceanic and Atmospheric Administration (NOAA) weather radio broadcasts from a transmitter atop Navajo Mountain, allowing you to obtain current forecasts while in remote locations within sight of the mountain.

BACKCOUNTRY ESSENTIALS

The equipment for hiking in the canyon country desert is little different than that you would bring to other backcountry areas (see **Hikers' Checklist,** Appendix C). The most important things to bring with you are common sense, good judgment, a positive attitude, and an awareness of your limitations. Always carry a good map and compass and know how to use them. Also carry water, food, extra clothing, a first-aid kit, a flashlight, a pocket knife, matches, and sunscreen. Some obstacles, such as pouroffs or boulder jams, are impossible to negotiate while wearing a heavy pack, so carry at least 20 feet of nylon rope to raise or lower packs.

In many canyons you will spend a great deal of time wading through small streams and rivers, so you will need reliable footwear that will provide adequate ankle support. Some hikers wear sandals while wading, but sandals offer no support and no protection from abrasive sand. Running shoes are also popular, but these offer minimal support, and are unsuitable for an extended trip with a backpack. Whatever boots or shoes you wear, constant wading will shorten their life span. I recommend a pair of "sacrifice boots"— a sturdy, lightweight pair approaching the end of their usefulness.

Keeping your feet happy can be a challenge in hot desert canyons. Sweaty feet, combined with steep trails and difficult routes, are a good recipe for rubs and blisters. Wear well-broken-in boots, and pack along at least one change of socks, moleskin, and tape.

A walking staff is very useful for frequent wading, river and stream crossings, negotiating quicksand, and for an extra push in sandy terrain. Finally, an essential piece of equipment is a collapsible bucket. Since many streams and rivers are perpetually laden with silt, settling the water first before filtering it will greatly increase the life of your water filter and reduce the frequency of cleaning it.

MAPS

A good map is an essential piece of equipment for any hiker in the mostly trailless canyons of the Glen Canyon region, and there are several excellent maps available. The maps in this book, though they show the correct configuration of trails based on the author's field work, are designed to give a general overview of the trails, and are not intended for serious navigation in the backcountry.

The most popular maps are those produced by Trails Illustrated. These useful maps, printed on a tearproof plastic material, cover all areas of the Glen Canyon region except the Grand Staircase and Paria Canyon. They show a mostly accurate representation of trails, routes, trailheads, and access roads, making them useful not only for trip planning, but also for navigation en route to trailheads and in the backcountry. Each map covers the equivalent of at least 20 7.5-minute USGS quads.

The Grand Gulch Plateau map (#706) covers all of the Cedar Mesa backcountry on a scale of 1:62,500, the same scale as that of the old 15-minute USGS quads, with contour intervals of 80 feet. This map also highlights ruins and springs in Grand Gulch. The BLM produces a topographic map of Grand Gulch, showing most of the same features.

The Dark Canyon/Manti-La Sal National Forest map (#703) covers all of the Dark Canyon Wilderness and Dark Canyon Primitive Area, plus Natural Bridges National Monument. This metric map is on a scale of 1:90,000, with a contour interval of 50 meters (about 165 feet). The Dark Canyon map is highly recommended for navigation on the maze of forest roads on Elk Ridge en route to all of the upper Dark Canyon trailheads.

The Canyons of the Escalante map (#710) covers the entire Escalante River drainage, including the Box-Death Hollow Wilderness, the Circle Cliffs and Burr Trail Road, and the Hole-in-the-Rock Road. The map includes the eastern part of the Grand Staircase–Escalante National Monument and part of the Glen Canyon National Recreation Area in the lower Escalante canyons. This useful map is on a scale of 1:70,500, with a contour interval of 40 feet.

An excellent map useful for an overview of the Glen Canyon region is the Trails Illustrated Glen Canyon and Capitol Reef Area map (#213). This map, on a scale of 1:177,300, with a contour interval of 200 feet, shows the region from Lees Ferry in the west to Grand Gulch and Dark Canyon in the east, including most of the Escalante canyons and the Hite area.

The BLM produces 1:100,000 scale metric topographic maps that show an area roughly 35 miles by 55 miles. These maps are most useful for navigating remote desert roads and are recommended for anyone traveling in the Grand Staircase and Paria Canyon areas. The BLM also produces two other maps that are useful for Paria Canyon hikers. First, there is the inexpensive Paria Canyon-Vermilion Cliffs Wilderness map, which provides a good overview of the wilderness, though it is less useful for backcountry navigation. Anyone hiking Buckskin Gulch or Paria Canyon should obtain a copy of the BLM's *Hiker's Guide to Paria Canyon,* which is a booklet of detailed topographic strip maps.

A Utah highway map is a must for anyone visiting the area. Two detailed highway maps produced by the Utah Travel Council are very useful for navigating southern Utah's scenic but remote highways. The Southwestern Utah map includes the area between Kanab and Escalante, and the Southeastern Utah map includes the area between Escalante and Cedar Mesa. Also, DeLorme Mapping prints the *Utah Atlas & Gazetteer,* another excellent resource for finding trailheads (see **Finding maps** below).

The Glen Canyon region is also covered by 7.5-minute USGS topographic quadrangles. For the most part the fine detail of these maps is not required, since most routes are restricted to canyon bottoms and there is little chance of getting lost or turned around. The larger scale Trails Illustrated maps are sufficient for navigation in this country. Plus, the Trails Illustrated maps last longer, and their large area of coverage means you get more map for your money. However, in areas of the Grand Staircase and Paria Canyon, USGS quads are the only detailed maps available, and they are recommended for any backcountry travel in that region. You will rarely need more than two or three USGS quads for most of the trails covered in this book.

Finally, the BLM has produced a superb shaded relief map of Grand Staircase–Escalante National Monument that shows towns, highways, and major dirt roads in the monument and provides abundant recreation information. This map is available for a fee from the Kanab BLM office and from the Escalante Interagency visitor center (see **For More Information** in Appendix A).

FINDING MAPS

USGS topographic quadrangles (all maps listed in this book are Utah quads unless otherwise indicated) are available by mail from the USGS. They cost $4 each, with a handling charge of $3.50 on all orders. Order well in advance of your trip; orders often take one to two months or more to process. Send orders to: Distribution Branch, United States Geological Survey, Box 25286, Denver Federal Center, Denver, Colorado 80225.

You can order Trails Illustrated, Utah Travel Council, and USGS quads (quads available only for the Cedar Mesa, Dark Canyon, Hite, and the southeastern Escalante canyons) from the Canyonlands Natural History Association in Moab, Utah, by calling (800) 840-8978. Or you can fax your order at (435) 259-8263. To order Trails Illustrated maps directly, call (800) 962-1643.

In the Cedar Mesa region, Trails Illustrated and USGS quads are available at the Natural Bridges National Monument visitor center, and at the Kane Gulch Ranger Station, open from late March through October. In Escalante, region-wide BLM maps, as well as Trails Illustrated and USGS quads for the Escalante canyons, are available through the Dixie Interpretive Association at the Escalante Interagency visitor center at the west end of town, or by mail at P.O. Box 246, Escalante, Utah 84726, (435) 826-5499. Also in Escalante, an outdoor shop called Escalante Outfitters carries USGS quads for the entire Glen Canyon region covered in this book.

In Kanab, BLM maps and USGS quads are available at the BLM office, and at the Willow Creek Bookstore. The Paria Contact Station, located near the White House Trailhead to Paria Canyon, offers USGS and BLM maps for sale. You can also order BLM and USGS maps covering the Grand Staircase and Paria Canyon areas from the Arizona Strip Interpretive Association by calling (435) 628-4491, or fax your order at (435) 673-5729. Trails Illustrated and USGS maps are also available through the Glen Canyon Natural History Association at the Carl Hayden visitor center at Glen Canyon Dam. Order the DeLorme *Utah Atlas & Gazetteer* by calling (800) 452-5931.

DRIVING TO TRAILHEADS

Trailheads in the Glen Canyon region range from paved parking lots alongside major roads to remote turnarounds at the end of poor, rough, seldom-used dirt roads. Only eight hikes covered in this book lie alongside paved roads (see the **Trailhead access** heading at the beginning of each hike description). All others are accessed by dirt roads that range from good graded roads to unmaintained, rocky, or sandy doubletracks. These backroads not only offer access to trailheads, they also offer tremendous scenic driving potential. The Glen Canyon region is very remote, and once you leave paved highways, you are entering isolated country.

Nearly all of the trailheads covered in this book are usually accessible to cars in dry weather, though a four-wheel-drive (4WD) vehicle is recommended when traveling off the pavement in southern Utah. Keep in mind that **flash floods can deposit rocks and debris onto roads, so actual driving conditions can change quickly.** Nearly all of the trailhead access roads pass over clay beds, and during and shortly after rainfall, these roads become slippery, sticky avenues of mud. Avoid driving these unpaved roads when they are wet. The clay can become impassable when wet, even to 4WD vehicles. If you find yourself on a wet dirt road, be prepared to wait a day or two for the roadbed to dry out.

Most trailhead access roads are graded only twice a year: once in spring and again in autumn. Expect road damage following significant rainfall, and particularly following an active summer monsoon season. Flash floods and runoff from heavy rain will make desert roads impassable to all but high clearance 4WD vehicles. Always inquire about road conditions with the local BLM office prior to driving any unpaved road. Phone numbers for BLM offices are located at the beginning of each chapter in this book.

Unexpected storms, washouts, mud, rocks, and sand can stop you or strand you in the desert. I have seen drivers in cars stranded for days at a time on remote roads after only one afternoon of heavy rain. Travelers must come prepared to wait out inclement weather and impassable road conditions. Before setting out, be sure to have a full tank of gas, a tow rope or chain, a tool kit, jumper cables, a roll of duct tape, a tire pump, ample water to sustain your group for two to four days, and plenty of food, clothing, and other necessities, such as matches and fuel for your stove. Always carry a shovel when driving remote desert roads. A little road work with a shovel can save you hours of digging out should you become stuck or high-centered.

Several trailhead access roads in this book pass over deep, soft sand, where 4WD is required. Sandy roads will be much firmer when damp, and then may be passable to 2WD vehicles, but always remember to check first with local BLM offices. For the best traction, 4WD vehicles should be equipped with wide, deep-lug tires. Maintain your speed and forward momentum when driving sandy or muddy roads to avoid getting bogged down. Steering the wheels of your 4WD vehicle back and forth quickly will provide a better grip and help pull you through. If you do become stuck in the sand, first dig a path ahead of your tires, then deflate them to 10 to 15 psi. If you have extra water, wet the ground in front of your vehicle. This will provide a firmer tread. Use your floor mats under your tires for extra traction. If your 4WD vehicle has a winch, it will do you little good on the open desert where there are few anchor points. Always carry at least two winch pins—solid anchors with a flange welded to the bottom—and a sledge hammer to drive them.

Remember that you are far from assistance should you need it. When in doubt, stop your vehicle and scout ahead on foot. Walking an extra mile or two to the trailhead is far better than getting your vehicle stuck or damaged. Be prepared, travel-wise, and self-sufficient.

Cellular phone users will generally obtain a good signal from high ground in the region, particularly in areas which have a line-of-sight to Navajo Mountain. In case of emergency, phone numbers of sheriff's offices are listed at the beginning of each chapter.

Claret cup cactus displays one of the loveliest of all desert flowers.

Author's Hike Recommendations

Easy day hikes suitable for novice canyon country hikers and parents with children
Hike 1 (Mule Canyon); Hike 2 (North Fork Mule Canyon); Hike 10 (Government Trail to Grand Gulch); Hike 18 (Collins Spring Trailhead to The Narrows); Hike 20 (Hog Canyon); Hike 34 (Lower Calf Creek Falls); Hike 38 (Devils Garden); Hike 47 (Kodachrome Basin State Park, Panorama Trail); Hike 48 (Cottonwood Canyon Narrows); Hike 50 (Willis Creek Narrows); Hike 55 (Wire Pass).

Moderate day hikes
Hike 5 (Road Canyon); Hike 13 (Kane Gulch to The Junction); Hike 16 (Sipapu Bridge to Kachina Bridge); Hike 17 (Owachomo Bridge to Kachina Bridge); Hike 19 (Marinus Canyon); Hike 21 (Stair Canyon); Hike 22 (Butler Canyon); Hike 25 (Big Notch to Scorup Cabin); Hike 26 (Horse Pasture Trail to Scorup Cabin); Hike 27 (Trail Canyon to Dark Canyon); Hike 28 (Fable Valley); Hike 33 (Upper Calf Creek Falls); Hike 35 (Escalante River Trailhead to Maverick Bridge and Phipps Arch); Hike 36 (Escalante Natural Bridge); Hike 40 (Sunset Arch); Hike 42 (Willow Gulch Trailhead to Broken Bow Arch); Hike 43 (Fiftymile Creek); Hike 46 (The Box); Hike 51 (Lick Wash).

Strenuous day hikes recommended for experienced canyon country hikers only
Hike 3 (Nevills Arch); Hike 6 (Slickhorn Access #1); Hike 7 (Slickhorn Access #4); Hike 8 (Slickhorn Access #6); Hike 11 (Todie Canyon to Grand Gulch); Hike 12 (Bullet Canyon); Hike 29 (Sundance Trail; day hike to rim of Dark Canyon); Hike 32 (Boulder Mail Trail); Hike 41 (Fortymile Ridge to Coyote Gulch via Crack in the Wall); Hike 44 (Davis Gulch); Hike 49 (Yellow Rock/The Box of the Paria River); Hike 52 (Lick Wash to No Mans Mesa); Hike 53 (Mollies Nipple); Hike 54 (Starlight Arch); Hike 57 (Cobra Arch); Hike 58 (Middle Route to Buckskin Gulch).

Easy to moderate short backpacks of two to three days, for novice canyon country hikers or more experienced hikers with limited time
Hike 1 (Mule Canyon); Hike 2 (North Fork Mule Canyon); Hike 5 (Road Canyon); Hike 10 (Government Trail to Grand Gulch); Hike 13 (Kane Gulch to The Junction; or hike farther into upper Grand Gulch); Hike 18 (Collins Spring Trailhead to The Narrows; camp in lower Grand Gulch); Hike 23 (Woodenshoe Canyon; establish a base camp near Cherry Canyon); Hike 25 (Big Notch to Scorup Cabin; camp in Dark Canyon near Scorup Cabin); Hike 36 (Escalante Natural Bridge; camp along the Escalante River near the natural bridge); Hike 42 (Willow Gulch to Broken Bow Arch; camp in Wil-

low Gulch near the arch); Hike 46 (The Box; camp wherever you wish inside the canyon of The Box).

Moderate to strenuous short backpacks of two to three days, for experienced canyon country hikers
Hike 3 (Nevills Arch; camp in Owl Creek canyon near the arch); Hike 6 (Slickhorn Access #1; camp in Slickhorn Canyon between Access #2 canyon and Access #4 canyon); Hike 7 (Slickhorn Access # 4; camp in Slickhorn Canyon between Access #4 canyon and Access #6 canyon); Hike 8 (Slickhorn Access #6; camp at or near confluence with Slickhorn Canyon); Hike 12 (Bullet Canyon; camp near Jail House Ruin or at the confluence with Grand Gulch); Hike 11 (Todie Canyon to Grand Gulch; camp near confluence with Grand Gulch); Hike 26 (Horse Pasture Trail to Scorup Cabin; camp in Dark Canyon near Scorup Cabin); Hike 27 (Trail Canyon to Dark Canyon; camp in Trail Canyon or at confluence with Dark Canyon); Hike 28 (Fable Valley; camp below Fable Spring); Hike 29 (Sundance Trail to Dark Canyon); Hike 30 (The Gulch to Lamanite Arch); Hike 31 (Silver Falls Creek); Hike 32 (Boulder Mail Trail to Death Hollow); Hike 41 (Fortymile Ridge to Coyote Gulch via Crack in the Wall); Hike 43 (Fiftymile Creek); Hike 44 (Davis Gulch); Hikes 51 and 52 (Lick Wash and No Mans Mesa; camp in Lick Wash or on No Mans Mesa).

Extended backpacks of three or more days for hikers in good condition, preferably with previous canyon country hiking experience
Hike 4 (Owl Creek/Fish Creek Loop); Hikes 7 and 8 (enter via Slickhorn Access #4 and loop back to the trailhead via Slickhorn Access #6); Hike 9 (Slickhorn Access #6 to the San Juan River); Hike 14 (Kane Gulch Ranger Station to Bullet Canyon Trailhead); Hike 23 (Woodenshoe Trailhead to Dark Canyon); Hike 37 (Harris Wash); Hike 39 (Hurricane Wash to Coyote Gulch); Hike 45 (Upper Escalante River).

Long distance backpacks for experienced canyon country hikers
Hike 15 (Bullet Canyon Trailhead to Collins Spring Trailhead); Hike 24 (Woodenshoe-Peavine Loop); Hike 56 (Wire Pass Trailhead to White House Trailhead via Buckskin Gulch and the Paria River); Hike 58 (Middle Route to Buckskin Gulch and White House Trailhead or Lees Ferry); Hike 59 (Paria Canyon, White House Trailhead to Lees Ferry).

Backpacks to a backcountry base camp
Hike 4 (camp at Fish Creek/Owl Creek confluence); Hike 15 (camp between Bullet Canyon and Dripping Canyon); Hike 23 (camp near Cherry Canyon or at spring in lower Woodenshoe Canyon); Hike 28 (camp below Fable Spring); Hike 29 (camp between Lean-To and Lost canyons); Hike 30 (camp near Water Canyon or near Lamanite Arch canyon); Hike 32 (camp in Death Hollow); Hike 39 (camp between Jacob Hamblin Arch and lower Coyote Gulch below Cliff Arch); Hike 44 (camp anywhere in lower Davis Gulch); Hike 46 (camp anywhere in The Box).

Hikes Suitable for Children

Hike 1 (Mule Canyon; day hike or overnighter); Hike 2 (North Fork Mule Canyon; day hike or overnighter); Hike 10 (Government Trail; day hike or overnighter); Hike 13 (Kane Gulch Ranger Station to The Junction; day hike or overnighter); Hike 16 (Sipapu Bridge to Kachina Bridge; day hike to Sipapu Bridge, or take the entire loop); Hike 17 (Owachomo Bridge to Kachina Bridge; day hike to Owachomo or Kachina bridges, or take the entire loop); Hike 18 (Collins Spring Trailhead to The Narrows; day hike or overnighter); Hike 20 (Hog Canyon; day hike); Hike 28 (Fable Valley; overnighter); Hike 33 (Upper Calf Creek Falls; day hike); Hike 34 (Lower Calf Creek Falls; day hike); Hike 36 (Escalante Natural Bridge; day hike or overnighter); Hike 37 (Harris Wash; overnighter); Hike 38 (Devils Garden; day hike); Hike 40 (Sunset Arch; day hike); Hike 42 (Broken Bow Arch; day hike or overnighter); Hike 46 (The Box; day hike or overnighter); Hike 47 (Kodachrome Basin State Park, Panorama Trail; day hike); Hike 48 (Cottonwood Canyon Narrows; day hike); Hike 50 (Willis Creek; day hike); Hike 51 (Lick Wash; day hike or overnighter); Hike 55 (Wire Pass to Buckskin Gulch; day hike); Hike 59 (Paria Canyon; overnighter).

Lower Dark Canyon spreads out in all of its grandeur from the Sundance Trail.

Leave No Trace

The desert landscape of the southern Utah canyon country appears durable, but actually is very fragile. Once damaged, the recovery of the desert landscape is extremely slow, and it may not heal completely in a human lifetime, if at all. Soils in the rockbound canyon country are thin to non-existent. Plants and desert creatures have evolved in a delicate balance of survival. The simple acts of walking off-trail (even for short distances), crushing plants, or moving rocks can disrupt the balance that desert plants and animals have achieved.

There are far fewer regulations governing the use of the backcountry in the Glen Canyon region than there are in the national parks of Utah. This allows greater freedom and flexibility, but with that freedom goes a greater measure of responsibility for its preservation, and for your own personal safety. Consider the following ideas for no-trace travel as guidelines for preserving the wilderness resource, not only for the desert's native inhabitants, but also for those who follow in your footsteps.

In the Glen Canyon region, you may **camp** anywhere you wish in the backcountry. Where possible, choose a previously used site, thus concentrating your impact rather than distributing it to new locations. In pristine areas, where there are no previously used campsites, select a site on bare mineral soil, sand, or even slickrock, where minimal evidence of your passing will remain. A free-standing tent allows greater flexibility in campsite selection where soils are thin or where slickrock dominates.

Backpackers are drawn to desert oases such as springs, streams, and rivers. Backpackers should make an extra effort to camp at least 200 feet from springs, streams, and water pockets to prevent water pollution and allow undisturbed access for wildlife. Better still, tank up with water at springs or streams and move on to a dry camp, at least 0.25 mile away. Finally, avoid making unnecessary improvements at your campsite, such as rock walls or trenches around your tent. The goal is to leave no lasting sign of your passing.

Campfires are not allowed in many backcountry areas of the Glen Canyon region, including Grand Gulch, Paria Canyon, and the Glen Canyon National Recreation Area. The slow growth and limited vegetation in the desert make campfires inappropriate. Dead and down wood slowly recycles nutrients back into the poor soils, and provides habitat for many small creatures.

In washes where flood debris is present and campfires are allowed, keep your fire small, and don't build a ring of rocks: dig a sand pit instead. Always burn wood completely. Be sure your fire is cold before spreading the ashes—preferably in a wash, and never near campsites or trails. Don't build fires in alcoves or against slickrock or boulders; doing so will permanently blacken rocks, as soot stains in some 700-year-old Anasazi ruins attest. You may also be damaging hidden cultural remains in alcoves, and destroying chances for archaeologists to obtain accurate Carbon 14 dating at the site.

Fire danger in the tinder-dry woodlands, brush fields, and riparian areas is high, so only build a campfire if you feel it is really necessary, and then do so only during cool, calm weather, and when fuel wood is in obvious abundance.

The **scarce water sources** in the Glen Canyon region are the lifeblood of wildlife and hikers alike. Springs, water pockets, and sluggish streams are highly susceptible to contamination. Stirring up silt, using soap, or depleting a waterhole can have an adverse affect on water quality.

Do not dig in a water hole with a soil bottom to enlarge it. You may break the seal formed by fine silt and algae and thus the water may drain away into the ground. Using too much water from a limited source may deprive wildlife or other hikers of a much needed drink.

For bathing and dishwashing, take water only from large streams and rivers. Wash up and discard your soapy water at least 200 feet from water sources and drainages, preferably over sand or gravel. *Never* use soap in any water source. Do not swim or soak in precious water sources, particularly where there is no inflow or outflow.

One of the attractions of the region is that few regulations prevent you from bringing your **dog** into the backcountry, and many hikers do. Dogs are barred from trails only in Natural Bridges National Monument, in Slickhorn Canyon, and in Grand Gulch down-canyon from the mouth of Collins Canyon.

Be kind to your dog and avoid the hottest season, when slickrock will burn their paws and cause them to overheat quickly. Regulations in many areas require that your dog be leashed at all times, yet few hikers obey them. No one wants to be confronted by a barking or overly friendly dog while in the backcountry. Many dogs can't resist cooling off in precious desert water sources, stirring up silt and fouling the source for the hikers who follow. At archaeological sites, unleashed dogs can cause damage to the site by running and digging in the midden, by jumping over walls, and by climbing into ruins. It is therefore critical that dog owners either leave their dogs at home, or keep them leashed and under control at all times while in the backcountry.

Garbage and food scraps attract unwanted animals, ants, and flies. Pack out your garbage and leftover food scraps with the rest of your trash. Human waste must be deposited at least 200 feet from campsites, trails, water sources, and drainages. Choose a sunny spot (since heat helps break down waste) with organic soil and dig a cat hole about 4 to 6 inches deep, then cover the waste with soil.

Do not bury or burn your **toilet paper**. Fires caused by burning toilet paper have devastated parts of the Glen Canyon region, including areas of Grand Gulch and Paria Canyon. In most parts of the region you are required to *pack out* your used toilet paper, and it is likely that eventually all areas covered in this book will carry that requirement. So wherever you travel in the Glen Canyon backcountry, whether day hiking or backpacking, plan on packing out your used toilet paper. Zipper-lock bags are useful for this.

The passage of too many feet will create a lasting trail in the southern Utah canyon country desert. Short paths from campsite to water source as well as longer backcountry bushwhacks can evolve into a trail. Keep your group size to a minimum, since obviously the more hikers there are in your party, the greater the impact. Use established trails and routes where they are available. Remember that your boot tracks in trailless areas will induce others to follow. Although the majority of backcountry trails in the Glen Canyon region are unmaintained, hikers maintain them simply by using them.

When traveling **off-trail**, spread out to avoid concentrating the impacts of too many feet. However, in areas dominated by microbiotic soil crust, each member of your group should follow in the footsteps of the leader. Choose routes across slickrock or through washes and unvegetated areas as much as possible. Desert plants are stiff and spiny, yet they are fragile. Crushed plants may take many years to recover from damage, if they recover at all.

Restrain the urge to build more **cairns** (small piles of rocks). Some trails may be ill-defined, but there are almost always cairns to show the way. Unfortunately, there is a profusion of unnecessary cairns constructed by misguided hikers, and you could be led astray. On faint trails, consult your topo map and sight on the next cairn before proceeding, but please don't build any more cairns. Better still, use natural landmarks as your guide. Let the next person enjoy the challenge of route-finding as you did. If you need the guidance of cairns and other "handrails" to show the way, stick to well-defined trails instead.

Since many routes follow canyon bottoms, some with flowing water and a well-developed riparian area, you will be walking in streams and crossing them many times. The **riparian zone** is a specialized, water-dependent community of plants and animals. Here you will encounter pools brimming with tadpoles, and in late summer and early autumn, those tadpoles begin to transform into frogs and toads. In some canyons you will encounter thousands of these infant amphibians, and it is critical that you step carefully and avoid crushing them. You will also likely find garter snakes and whiptail lizards that feed on the young frogs and toads. Tread lightly to avoid disrupting the balance between predator and prey.

In some areas of the Glen Canyon region, particularly on the mesa tops, you will find large areas of soil covered by a black or gray lumpy crust. This **microbiotic soil crust** (which has also been called cryptobiotic soil) is a delicate assemblage of mosses, lichens, cyanobacteria, and fungus that forms a protective layer over the soil against wind and water erosion, and aids in the absorption and retention of moisture, allowing larger plants to gain a foothold. The passage of a single hiker can destroy this fragile crust, and it may take 25 years or longer to redevelop. In areas covered by microbiotic soil crust, choose your route carefully to avoid stepping on it. Follow routes through sandy areas, washes, or slickrock instead.

Many hikers seek out places like the canyons of southern Utah for the **quiet** and solitude they provide. Hikers should make an extra effort to allow ample distances from other parties, and keep loud noises to a minimum. During high use periods in certain places, such as Paria Canyon, Coyote Gulch, or Grand

Gulch, during which campsites may already be occupied when you arrive, don't force yourself on other campers. Ask others if they mind that you camp nearby before moving in and setting up camp.

ARCHAEOLOGICAL AND HISTORIC SITES

Evidence of ancient cultures, homestead cabins, cowboy camps, and oil drilling and uranium mining operations abound in the Glen Canyon region's backcountry. Particularly abundant are cultural remains. In the Cedar Mesa region for example, nearly every bend in any canyon reveals the ruins of dwellings, granaries, kivas, or rock art. Farther west, in the Escalante region, there are still ruins and rock art, though they are much harder to find. In the Grand Staircase and Paria Canyon areas, ruins are rare, but hikers may find potsherds, occasional rock art, and chipping sites, where ancient inhabitants fashioned tools from stone.

Keep in mind that these non-renewable resources offer archaeologists insights into past ways of life in the region and can be easily disturbed and damaged by curious hikers. Although federal and state laws protect cultural resources, ultimately it depends on each of us to walk softly and treat these resources with the respect they deserve. Excavation and stabilization of many sites has yet to take place. Over-visitation is threatening many cultural sites in the region. Most people don't intentionally damage cultural sites, but too many curious visitors invariably leads to site degradation. Although hikers are likely to encounter many sites, this book will lead you to only a few, preserving your sense of discovery. Finding ruins is one of the great rewards that is an added bonus to a backcountry trip through an incomparable southern Utah canyon.

The BLM, which administers the majority of the areas covered in this book, has classified cultural sites into 3 categories. This book will disclose the location of Class 1 sites only. In general, this category of sites has received an appropriate level of stabilization to sustain frequent visitation. Class 2 sites are more fragile and prone to damage by visitors. BLM personnel will direct you to these sites only if you ask about them specifically, and they will provide information and direction to reduce your impact while visiting the sites. The majority of backcountry sites are in the Class 3 category. These sites are completely vulnerable to visitor impacts, and their locations will not be disclosed. As you travel through the Glen Canyon region's backcountry, particularly in the Cedar Mesa area, you will likely find sites that fall into all three categories.

Ruins are best observed from a distance, perhaps with the aid of binoculars. Obviously, this will result in no impact to the site. If you do intend to inspect a site closely, before entering stop, look, and think how you can avoid damaging the site. Be aware of your presence and impact in the ruins. Avoid stepping on the "midden" area, a darkened, raised, refuse pile typical of ancient habitations. The midden provides archaeologists with a great deal of valuable information. Remember that these ancient structures are at least 700 years old, and though they may appear well-preserved, they are actually very fragile. Do not lean on walls or climb on roofs. They can collapse causing injury to you and extensive damage to the ruin. If you brought the family dog (or are equipped with packstock or llamas), keep it leashed and away from ruins.

If there is an established path leading to ruins, be sure to stay on it to avoid crushing the midden and any artifacts, either hidden or on the surface. Walk carefully around the slopes that support these structures. The passage of too many feet can undermine the foundation of rock walls, leading to their eventual collapse. Ruins are an interesting highlight of a hike, but are inappropriate places to make camp. After observing an archaeological site, move on before having meals. Food crumbs and garbage may attract rodents that could then nest in the site.

Leave all artifacts where you find them. Some people will take one or two potsherds, thinking that they will not be missed. Yet it is the cumulative effects of this practice that leads to fewer signs of the Anasazi culture each year. Artifacts have much greater significance to all of us when observed in their original setting, rather than gathering dust in your closet or on your mantle at home. Many well-intentioned visitors gather potsherds and other artifacts, placing them on display on so-called "museum rocks" at cultural sites. This may seem like a good idea, removing them from the ground where others may crush them, but removing artifacts from their resting place destroys clues needed by archaeologists gathering information about the site.

Pigments of ancient pictographs are easily destroyed by skin oils. Restrain the urge to touch them, particularly hand-print pictographs. Never add your own graffiti to irreplaceable rock art panels. Chalking, rubbing,

Well-intentioned hikers gather cultural artifacts for display at many archaeological sites. Once an artifact is removed from its resting place, its meaning to archaeologists is lost.

The delicate blooms of prickly pear cactus are beautiful but short lived, lasting only for a few days in early spring in the canyon country.

tracing, and touching leads to the eventual disappearance of rock art and can make methods of dating panels impossible. Enjoy rock art by photographing, sketching, or viewing only.

Cultural sites are not only protected by federal law, they are also places of great significance to Native Americans. These sites are preserved in what many have likened to an outdoor museum. Treat all sites you encounter as you would treat artifacts in any museum, with the care and respect that they deserve. Archaeological and historic sites are protected by the Antiquities Act of 1906, and the Archaeological Resources Protection Act of 1979. The Act of 1979 provides strong penalties, plus rewards for information leading to the arrest and conviction of vandals, pot hunters, or other illegal activity. Notify BLM rangers or the county sheriff if you observe any illegal activity at cultural sites. You can also call the BLM Law Enforcement Hotline at (800) 722-3998.

Being Prepared— Backcountry Safety and Hazards

Anyone who visits the backcountry of the remote Glen Canyon region must be aware of and prepared for the rigors of high desert hiking. Unexpected injury or illness, extreme heat, heavy rains or snow, flash floods, lack of water, dehydration, and encounters with poisonous creatures or spiny cacti can all stop you in your tracks.

Always obtain up-to-date information on trails, routes, road conditions, and water availability from the BLM offices listed in each chapter. Since conditions are constantly changing, this book is no substitute for updated information. Before you leave home for a backcountry trip, leave a detailed itinerary with a family member, a friend, or employer. Include your name, the trailhead where you will be parking, your vehicle make, model, and license number, the date the trip ends, and a detailed account of your route. Make arrangements so that if you do not return home or contact that person by a certain time, they will initiate search and rescue operations. Keep in mind that you will be held responsible for the costs incurred for the use of a helicopter during search and rescue operations. Upon returning from your backcountry trip, be sure to notify that person to avoid an unnecessary search. County sheriffs conduct search operations, and you will find the telephone numbers of each sheriff's office at the beginning of each chapter. And finally, always sign trailhead registers where available. Information from trailhead registers has helped to locate and save several overdue hikers.

Although **water** is responsible for carving Glen Canyon and its many tributaries, surface water, save for Lake Powell and a few modest, perennial streams such as the Paria and Escalante rivers, is scarce. Water is the single greatest limiting factor on travel in these high desert canyons—you must reach a water source each day, or carry all you will need until you reach that source. Some creeks and springs flow year-round, while others flow unpredictably, following favorable conditions of prolonged rainfall or snowmelt, or from late autumn to early spring when evaporation is reduced and some springs and streams resurface.

Hikers must always carry water on any trail or route and come prepared with enough water containers to carry a one- to two-day supply when necessary. Top off your water containers at every opportunity. Timing your hike to follow wet seasons—such as early spring, or an autumn that follows an active monsoon season—is important to insure an adequate water supply. Water requirements are based on heat, exertion, the time of day, and the time of year you hike. As a rule, and for a measure of safety, hikers should always carry at least 1 gallon of water on extended trips away from known water sources. When hiking in the desert, your water supply should be the heaviest item in your pack. **Running out of water in the backcountry of the Glen Canyon region is the single biggest mistake you can make.**

You will drink at least 1 gallon of water per day while hiking. If you are bound from your trailhead to a dry camp, you will need to pack at least 1.5 gallons, provided you can reach a reliable water source early on the following day. If you are hiking to a known water source, but the trip takes all day, you are still advised to pack a full gallon of water for the trip, in the event unforeseen situations develop that prevent you from reaching water.

Always pre-hydrate prior to your trip, and during your trip before your most strenuous hiking days. Drink large amounts of water over a period of several hours in the evening at camp and in the morning before leaving camp. Taking a water bottle into your tent at night prevents midnight dry mouth and helps you re-hydrate after a long day of hiking. It is essential, however, that you balance your water intake with electrolytes.

Adequate water intake is so critical to a safe and enjoyable trip in desert canyons that it is surprising that so many hikers carry their precious water supply in fragile containers, particularly thin plastic milk-type jugs. These jugs burst easily if dropped, and in summer when rocks are too hot to touch, the bottom will quickly melt if you set your jug down on one. Instead of large, flimsy jugs, transport your water supply in several smaller, more durable containers. Nalgene 1-quart and 2-quart bottles are best, and they take up little more room in your pack than larger jugs.

Water sources in the Glen Canyon region range from green, scummy pools brimming with tadpoles, to seeps, dripping springs, spring pools, cool and vigorous creeks, ephemeral slickrock water pockets, and silt-laden rivers. Springs, rather than flowing streams, are your primary sources of water. Very few springs in the canyons emerge from canyon walls. Most begin as seepage from the floor of washes. Wherever you obtain your water, it must be purified before drinking or even brushing your teeth.

Microscopic bacteria and protozoans may inhabit any surface water in these desert canyons. Boiling water for at least five minutes is the old standby for rendering water potable, but filters remove most organisms and make water safe to drink. For added insurance, choose a filter or attachment that eliminates viruses as well. Since filters can and do break down in the backcountry, always carry iodine tablets as a backup.

Filters can clog with silt easily, so choose a filter that you can clean in the field. When using silt-laden streams such as the Escalante River as your water supply, you will need to set water aside (a collapsible bucket is useful for this) and allow the sediment to settle before filtering. In mid to late summer, algae growth in water pockets and stagnant water holes will also quickly clog your filter. Pre-filter algae-rich water through a handkerchief or coffee filter.

Heavy rainfall and the resulting rise in waters or flash flooding can turn your water supply into a slurry of mud and debris that may not clear up for 1 to 2 days following a flood event. This soupy water cannot be settled adequately, and if you attempt to filter it, your filter will become instantly clogged. If heavy rains or thunderstorms are probable or in progress, expect that your drainage may flood. You should then draw an ample water supply (another reason to carry plenty of empty containers) to sustain your group until high silty flows subside and clear up.

The following information about **heat and dehydration** was compiled by Grand Canyon backcountry rangers. Following these guidelines will help make your hike much safer and more enjoyable.

Hiking in desert canyons, everyone sweats around 0.5 to 1 quart of water and electrolytes each and every hour that they are walking in the heat. This fluid/electrolyte loss can even exceed 2 quarts per hour if you hike uphill in direct sunlight, or during the hottest part of the day. Because the desert air is so dry and hot, sweat evaporates instantly, making its loss almost imperceptible. This evaporation allows our bodies to lose heat and keep cool. **Do not wait until you start feeling thirsty to start replacing these fluids and electrolytes. By the time you feel thirsty, you are already dehydrated.**

Even this mild level of dehydration makes your body approximately 10 to 20 percent less efficient, and this makes hiking a lot less fun. The more dehydrated you become, the less efficient your body becomes at walking and cooling. A slight to moderate fluid and electrolyte loss will lead to heat cramps and heat exhaustion (nausea, vomiting, headache, fatigue, fainting). A moderate to large fluid and electrolyte loss can lead to severe heat exhaustion (extreme dizziness, constant nausea and vomiting, shock, kidney damage), and possibly to heat stroke.

A normal hydrated adult should be able to urinate approximately 1 to 2 ounces of light yellow-colored urine every two hours. If you are urinating more frequently than this and your urine is clear in color, you may be over-hydrating and may need to cut back on your fluid intake. If your urine is dark in color (keep in mind that vitamins will turn urine yellow) and/or smells, you are probably dehydrated and need to drink more frequently. Your body can absorb only about 1 quart of fluid per hour, so drink 0.5 to 1 quart of some type of electrolyte replacement drink each and every hour that you are walking in the heat. Carry your water bottle in your hand and drink small amounts often. The average adult should drink approximately 4 quarts of electrolyte replacement drink for every eight hours spent hiking in the heat. Remember to at least double your normal intake of food to help meet your energy and electrolyte needs.

Your body uses an enormous amount of energy (food calories) keeping you cool in the heat. Eating is your most important defense against exhaustion and water intoxication. Heat will reduce your appetite; it seems all you crave is water. You must force yourself to eat adequate amounts of food to keep up with the demands of hiking in a desert canyon. You need to make sure that you eat a lot more than you normally do.

Eating adequate amounts of food will also help guarantee that you are replacing the electrolytes (salts) that you are sweating out. If you replace the water, but not the electrolytes that you have sweated out of your body, then you can develop a serious and dangerous medical condition known as *hyponatremia* (water intoxication) which, if left untreated, can lead to seizures and possibly death. Don't use salt tablets; they will make you nauseous. You need at least two to three times your normal food intake to meet your energy needs while hiking. If you have food, eat it. If you have extra food, share it. Eating well helps you hike well.

During conditions of **extreme heat**, walk in the shade during the early morning and late afternoon hours. You will quickly overheat if you hike in the direct sunshine. You will use up a lot of energy trying to stay cool, and you will sweat twice as much water/electrolytes hiking in the sunshine as in the shade. Your risk of heat-related illness increases dramatically. You will make better time and feel better if you wait until shade hits the trail before hiking.

If you must hike in the sunshine, keep yourself soaking wet to stay cool. This is one of the best things you can do for yourself. Whenever you are near water, make sure that you wet (actually soak) yourself down. If you hike while soaking wet, you will stay reasonably cool. Carry some extra water to wet yourself down again when your hair and clothing begin to dry. At the very least, keep your head gear wet. This will make a wonderful difference in how well you feel, especially at the end of the day. You will stay fresher longer, and you will reduce your fluid, electrolyte, and energy loss significantly.

Walking at a pace that allows you to be able to walk and talk will guarantee that your legs and your body are getting the oxygen that they need to function efficiently. Because your body will generate fewer metabolic waste products, you will be better able to enjoy your hike, and you will feel much better when you reach its end.

Flash floods are always a danger to be reckoned with, and as little as 0.25 to 0.5 inch of rain falling in a short period of time can result in a newborn stream coursing down a dry wash. A moderate rain lasting 2 to 3 hours can result in a significant flash flood. During the summer monsoon season (generally from mid-July through mid-September) torrents of rain are unleashed from towering thunderheads in hit-and-miss fashion throughout the region. Heavy rain pours off the slickrock, gathers in rivulets, and flows into larger side canyons. The result can be a flash flood. Although many canyon-bottom campsites are inviting, they can become a death trap in the event of a flash flood. **Avoid hiking in narrow canyons and camping in canyon bottoms and washes during stormy weather, and particularly during the monsoon season.** When scouting for a campsite in a canyon, you will likely see debris left behind by past floods, lodged on ledges above a wash. Always choose your campsite above that debris line. If you expect a flash flood, look for escape routes to higher ground immediately.

Lightning often occurs with summer thunderstorms. Keep your eye on the sky; dark cumulonimbus clouds herald the approach of a thunderstorm. If one is approaching, stay away from ridges, mesa tops, the bases of cliffs, solitary trees, shallow overhangs and alcoves, and open areas. Seek shelter in thickets of brush or in pinyon-juniper woodlands where the trees are plentiful, small, and of uniform size. Barring that kind of shelter, retreat to a boulder field or low-lying area. Keep in mind that, contrary to myth, lightning often strikes repeatedly in the same location.

Sticky mud and deep quicksand can also be a hazard in the Glen Canyon region. While mud is more of an inconvenience than a hazard, quicksand can really slow you down. Quicksand is super-saturated sandy ground that usually occurs above the water line, a short distance away from a flowing stream or in the bed of a wash where a stream or pools have recently evaporated. When hiking in dry washes, avoid walking in isolated areas of wet sand where quicksand may be present. In canyons with a flowing stream, you are better off walking in the stream itself, where the ground is almost always firmer. One rarely sinks more than knee-deep in this mire and extracting yourself, particularly with the help of a friend, is usually not too difficult. If hiking solo, remove your pack if you sink in more than knee deep; then you will be more able to extricate yourself.

The canyons have their share of **cacti, thorny shrubs, and biting insects** that can injure you if you are careless. Biting flies and gnats are common throughout the Glen Canyon region. Deer flies and sand flies are aggressive, carnivorous, and common in sandy areas of washes during the warmest months of the year, generally from June through mid-September. Midges or "no-see-ums" swarm from about mid-April through the summer months. These gnats inflict an itching bite—only the strongest insect repellents containing DEET will keep deer and sand flies at bay. The best defense is long-sleeved shirts and lightweight long pants. In my experience, the only effective product to repel no-see-ums is Skin-So-Soft, a bath oil spray from Avon. Only during the cooler months of the year will you encounter mosquitoes, and then usually only in limited numbers, primarily near seeps, springs, sluggish streams, and perennial water sources such as the Paria and Escalante rivers.

Various **spiders** (including the black widow and tarantula), **scorpions, centipedes, and vinegarones**—or whipscorpions—inhabit the region. Scorpions are the most common. Most can inflict a painful sting, but their venom is rarely life-threatening. Scorpions spend the day in the shade in dark crevices under rocks, logs, and bark. Be careful where you put your hands and feet and avoid picking up rocks. At night always wear shoes—not sandals—around camp, and look before you sit. Shake out your boots or shoes and clothing before putting them on, and either shake out your sleeping bag before retiring, or wait until bedtime before preparing your bed.

Ants are prevalent throughout canyon country. Red harvester ants can inflict a memorable sting, and tiny red ants may march toward your pack and food. Camp away from anthills and avoid discarding food scraps that will attract ants. Fortunately, ants and no-see-ums go to bed after dark. But then scorpions and vinegarones come out. Vinegarones are harmless, but their resemblance to scorpions and their fast movement can be startling.

Wasps and hornets are also common in canyon country. They nest on trees and shrubs, generally near areas with a reliable water supply. Particularly during autumn, these stinging insects will defend the area around their nests.

Rattlesnakes are uncommon in the canyons of southern Utah. I have hiked more than 1,500 miles in southern Utah and have seen only three. Snakes rest in the shade to avoid midday heat, so use caution when stepping over logs and boulders, and watch where you put your hands and feet. Throwing rocks down a descending route can sometimes warn rattlesnakes of your presence.

Beware of the spines of **cacti** and **yucca**. Although cactus spines are painful, they can usually be removed with tweezers. The glochids—those tiny hair-like spines—are more difficult to remove and cause painful irritation. Use adhesive tape to remove them, since probing with fingernails or tweezers often imbeds them deeper into your skin.

Yucca have large, stiff spines that can inflict a painful puncture wound. If one of these spines breaks off in your hand, leg, or arm, it can be very difficult to remove, and you may have to endure the discomfort until a doctor can remove it.

Mice are ubiquitous in the Glen Canyon region, and though they represent no direct threat to hikers they are potential carriers of the dangerous respiratory illness *Hanta virus*. The virus is spread by inhaling airborne particles of the droppings, blood, urine, and saliva of mice. Symptoms of the virus resemble the flu, but worsen as the lungs fill with fluid. If the virus is not detected and treated in its early stages, it can progress to coma, respiratory failure, and death.

Extra precautions are warranted when camping in a mouse-infested campsite. Sleep in a tent rather than on the ground. Protect your food supply from mice, and never keep food in your tent. If mice do chew into some of your food, don't eat it; pack it out and discard it. Mouse droppings are particularly abundant in caves and alcoves.

Also, when drawing water from springs, climbing, and hiking, beware of **poison ivy**, a plant growing 3 to 4 feet tall with woody stems and three large, shiny green leaflets.

Solar radiation is intense in southern Utah's dry desert air, and there is often little shade. Protect yourself from sunburn by using a sunscreen with a Sun Protection Factor (SPF) of at least thirty. Wear a light-colored long-sleeved shirt, a hat, and sunglasses with ultraviolet protection. Most canyon country hikers wear shorts, but long pants not only protect your legs from sunburn, they also afford some protection from rocks, stiff brush, and cactus.

Animal raids, both day and night, are a possibility at many campsites in the Glen Canyon backcountry. Mice, squirrels, skunks, ringtails, ravens, and even deer have grown accustomed to human food, particularly in more popular campsites. Unfortunately, many animals have learned to associate the smell of plastic with food, and they will chew through backpacks, and even tents, to reach it.

Some hikers suspend packs and stuffsacks from trees and shrubs with nylon cord, but mice and ringtails can easily walk the tightrope to your food supply. Instead, hang your food with fishing line (20- to 30-pound test works best). Put all of your food, plastics, toothpaste—anything you want to protect from damage—into a stuffsack and hang it at least 4 feet off the ground, high enough that a ringtail can't jump and reach it. Fishing line is slippery and thin enough to thwart the climbing efforts of the most determined mouse or ringtail. Hang your empty pack or leave it on the ground, with zippers open.

In upper Dark Canyon, where **black bears** are present, you must hang your food with nylon cord, far from their reach. Food raids by bears in Dark Canyon are rare, so to keep bears from developing a taste for backpacker's food, you must suspend it properly, and the counterbalance method works best. Fortunately there are usually tall trees in upper Dark Canyon from which to hang your food. See Falcon's *Bear Aware* by Bill Schneider for details on camping in bear country.

HANDLING EMERGENCIES

Hiking in the canyons of southern Utah can be dangerous. Help is far away anywhere you travel in this remote region. Solo hikers assume the greatest risks. Even a minor injury can become a life-threatening emergency when no one else is along to help.

BLM and Park Service rangers often patrol back roads, particularly following inclement weather. The more popular roads, such as Hole-in-the-Rock Road in the Escalante region, are patrolled frequently. In the backcountry, ranger patrols are frequent in the Escalante canyons, Paria Canyon and Buckskin Gulch, and in the Cedar Mesa area. Only occasionally do rangers patrol other canyons mentioned in this guide, so always be prepared to deal with emergencies yourself.

If you are hiking solo and become the victim of a mishap and cannot continue, try to find a shady place and remain calm. If you are on a trail, other hikers may come along and soon find you. Always leave your itinerary with a friend or family member. In case you don't return as scheduled, they should report your absence to the proper authorities (see Appendix A, **For More Information**). For more details on handling emergencies in the backcountry, see Falcon's *Wilderness Survival* by Suzanne Swedo.

General **deer hunting** season in the Glen Canyon region lasts for 5 weeks, beginning in late October. Expect to encounter hunters mostly on the wooded mesas and in the valleys, but seldom in the canyons. In the Grand Staircase is the Paunsaugunt Hunt, where hunters are in search of trophy-size bucks only. This hunt occurs from October 4 through October 15, in the area west of the Paria River and south of the Pink Cliffs, south to US 89 and the Arizona state line. This area is closed to hunting during the general deer hunting season. During hunting seasons, hikers are advised to wear blaze orange clothing, such as a hat, vest, or sweatshirt.

HIKING WITH CHILDREN

Hiking with children in the Glen Canyon backcountry has its limitations. The dry desert heat and intense sun, combined with bushwhacking, scrambling, boulder-hopping, fording rivers, and wading in streams quickly take their toll on children, and steep slickrock and dropoffs present a constant danger. Needless to say, parents must closely supervise their children near swift water and steep dropoffs.

Children need physical conditioning and hiking experience to prepare for the rigors of canyon country hiking, just as adults do. Start slow with short, easy day hikes, then progress to overnight trips with a modest goal in mind. As your children gain experience and confidence, your trips will be limited only by your time and imagination.

See the **Author's Hike Recommendations** on page 12 for a list of day and overnight hikes suggested for the entire family. Carefully read each hike description and study the maps to determine if a trip is suitable for your family.

CATTLE, OHVS, AND MILITARY AIRCRAFT AND YOUR BACKCOUNTRY EXPERIENCE

During your travels in the Glen Canyon backcountry, you will at times meet cows, off-highway vehicles, and in places, you will be startled out of your daydreams by low-flying military aircraft. The region as a whole provides much greater freedom than a national park, and although traditional uses such as cattle grazing occur here, you will likely pass your trip with few, if any, intrusions.

Cattle grazing is a concern among some hikers. You will seldom encounter cattle in the backcountry, but you may find evidence of their presence, including abundant cow pies and obvious trails. Much of the backcountry covered in this book does not sustain cattle grazing. On some routes you may be sharing the way with cows until fences or natural barriers prevent them from entering backcountry canyons.

Cattle grazing is a traditional use that in some places has occurred for more than 100 years. The BLM controls grazing in the region, and cattle grazing permits, predating the establishment of Federal wilderness preserves, will be allowed by law to continue in perpetuity. Many of the grazing permits for allotments in the Glen Canyon National Recreation Area have been acquired by the National Park Service, particularly in the lower Escalante canyons, and grazing in the canyons there no longer takes place. Within Grand Staircase–Escalante National Monument, the BLM, in cooperation with local ranchers, has begun to adjust seasonal grazing patterns and allotments in most of the region's backcountry are utilized from September through March.

Many of the trails in the region were blazed by cattlemen and their cows, and many of the backroads leading to remote trailheads would not exist but for the grazing of cattle. Cows blaze and maintain trails, helping hikers pass more easily through brush thickets and avoid obstacles. If cows were not present, parts of some routes covered in this book would be far more difficult to negotiate.

Hikers in the region should expect the possibility of finding grazing cattle, fences, gates, and water troughs. Respect the grazing permittee's facilities and livestock. Always leave gates open or closed, as you find them, and avoid disturbing livestock. Remember that beef comes from rangeland, not from the grocery store. Hikers who are disturbed by the presence of cows in the backcounrty have a choice: to enjoy the freedom and solitude the Glen Canyon region provides, and perhaps meet a few cows; or take a trip to a national park instead, where there are no cows, but greater restrictions and far more people.

If you believe your public lands are being abused by cattle, don't hesitate to contact the local BLM office. And if you observe stray cows, or cattle in areas where they probably don't belong, such as in Grand Gulch or in the lower Escalante canyons within Glen Canyon NRA, note the brand and the color of the ear tag and contact the BLM.

All vehicles, including mountain bikes, are prohibited from entering wilderness and primitive areas and wilderness study areas (WSAs). The exceptions are in WSAs where roads already exist, unless otherwise posted, and in the Dark Canyon Wilderness, where the Peavine Corridor 4WD road slices deep into the otherwise roadless canyon. Only parts of seven of the fifty-nine hikes covered in this book follow segments of 4WD roads where you may encounter four-wheelers, motorcycles, or dune buggies. Most of these poor roads are used very infrequently by vehicles, but do see some use by grazing permitees or by hunters during the late autumn deer hunt.

However, there is always the possibility that off-highway vehicle enthusiasts, for whatever reasons, may enter washes and canyons where they don't belong. If you observe violations of vehicle closures by OHVs, report your observations to a ranger as soon as possible.

Cattle are generally quiet, and OHVs are seldom seen in Glen Canyon region backcountry. Military overflights, by contrast, can provide a fleeting yet startling interruption to the natural quiet of the backcountry. Overflights occur in the region along a registered military flight path. Aircraft are allowed to deviate up to 10 miles from that path, which on occasion brings them over the Vermilion Cliffs, the Kaiparowits Plateau, and the lower Escalante canyons. In these areas you may see F-16s, A-10s, B-1s, B-29s, etc., engaging in low altitude exercises. You may be relaxing in a quiet canyon, perhaps in Coyote Gulch, when, for only a moment, a pair of screaming F-16s appear only 500 feet overhead.

With the help of abundant public comment, the National Park Service, which administers Glen Canyon NRA, is working with the federal government to adjust the occurrence of military overflights to daylight hours and during periods of lower use by backcountry recreationists. Address any concerns you have regarding military overflights and your backcountry experience to the NPS in Escalante, or write to: Superintendent, Glen Canyon National Recreation Area, P.O. Box 1507, Page, AZ 86040-1507.

GEOLOGY OF THE GLEN CANYON REGION

Although in-depth knowledge of the Glen Canyon region's rock layers is not prerequisite to hiking here, learning to recognize the rocks can help you better appreciate the landscape and anticipate features that affect backcountry travel.

Sedimentary rocks of the Glen Canyon region dominate the landscape and provide hikers with sheer visual delight. They also tell a silent history—

from the uplift, erosion, and metamorphosis of ancient mountain ranges to the ebb and flow of oceans and deserts. The Glen Canyon region is in the heart of the Colorado Plateau, an area dominated by horizontal layers of sedimentary rocks formed by wind and water.

Despite its name, the Colorado Plateau is not a single elevated plane. Indeed, many of its landscape features are flat, but the landscape is punctuated by many plateaus that have either been uplifted above the surrounding land by folding or faulting, or have been detached by erosion. Several isolated mountain ranges have domed the surface of the plateau, standing in stark relief above the mesas and canyons. Aside from the plateaus that characterize the Colorado Plateau landscape, this region is canyon country, containing some of the most notable canyons in the world.

The region is semiarid to arid, and precipitation often comes abruptly and violently, hammering the exposed rock layers, stripping away loose fragments, and transporting these materials downhill. Canyons are formed as running water erodes loose material. The transported sediments themselves have tremendous erosive power and they contribute to the formation of canyons by abrading and scouring drainages.

Rock layers on the plateau respond differently to the effects of weathering and erosion. Hard rock layers, such as limestone and sandstone, resist erosion and stand in relief, while softer layers, such as shale, siltstone, and mudstone, are subdued into slopes and terraces. In some areas of the Glen Canyon region, alternating hard and soft rock layers have formed a "stair-step" type of topography, where cliffs alternate with slopes and terraces colored in shades of red, tan, white, purple, green, and gray.

The oldest rocks exposed in the region are the marine sediments of the 345-million year old **Honaker Trail Formation**. The gray and red limestones, shales, and sandstones form the low cliff bands, ledges, and slopes that are exposed only in lower Dark Canyon near the Sundance Trail, in lower Slickhorn Canyon, and in the canyon of the San Juan River.

The limestones, shales, and sandstones of the **Elephant Canyon Formation** were deposited beginning 280 million years ago, just offshore from a retreating sea. Its gray and red cliffs embrace much of the inner gorge of Dark Canyon. The **Cutler Formation** is widely exposed in the Cedar Mesa, Elk Ridge, and Hite areas. It was deposited in three distinct layers during the Permian Period, between 225 and 280 million years ago. The first layer, **the Cedar Mesa Sandstone** reaches its maximum thickness of over 1,000 feet in the Dark Canyon area, which helps to make that canyon one of the most scenic attractions in the Glen Canyon region. The differential erosion of the Cedar Mesa Sandstone makes it one of the most challenging rock formations to traverse in the backcountry.

Capping the gentle surfaces of Cedar Mesa and Elk Ridge is the **Organ Rock Shale**, the second member of the Cutler Formation. The brick red and reddish brown siltstones and sandy shales of this formation were deposited in tidal flats in a freshwater environment. The Organ Rock typically erodes into the dramatic towers and hoodoos that surround Hite Marina, and form Browns Rim, which stretches from Hite to Dark Canyon's Sundance Trailhead.

White Rim Sandstone, the youngest memeber of the Cutler Formation, is a notable formation in Canyonlands National Park, but is present only as a thin layer of resistant white sandstone cutting through the red beds above Hite and in the upper reaches of Elk Ridge.

The most colorful of all the rock formations in the region is the **Chinle Formation**, comprised of sandstones, conglomerates, bentonitic mudstones, limestones, and siltstones, deposited in flood plains by meandering streams and in shallow lakes. The gray layers in the Chinle are composed of volcanic ash originating from eruptions in what is now Arizona. The formation creates barren badlands of red, green, lavender, yellow, and gray. It was the target formation for the uranium boom of the 1950s, and wherever the Chinle is exposed, you may find old prospector's roads, tunnels, and claim markers. One of the greatest exposures of the Chinle in the Glen Canyon region is found near the Vermilion Cliffs and upper Paria River surrounding the site of Old Pahreah and the Paria Movie Set. The Chinle also forms a colorful landscape in lower Paria Canyon, and is widely exposed in the Circle Cliffs basin in the northeast corner of Grand Staircase–Escalante National Monument.

The Glen Canyon Group of rocks—the Wingate, Kayenta, and Navajo— are the principal scenery producers throughout the Glen Canyon region, providing the most outstanding landscapes on the Colorado Plateau. In the eastern part of the region, extending from the Hite area west to the Escalante canyons, is the great cliff-forming **Wingate Sandstone**, laid down in vast deserts of drifting sand. The Wingate is a major barrier to travel wherever it occurs, forming sheer and often fluted cliffs that consistently rise 300 to 400 feet high. In the canyons, the Wingate forms slots and pouroffs that are often very difficult to bypass. Look for the Wingate in the Circle Cliffs, in North Wash between Hanksville and Lake Powell, and in the lower Escalante canyons.

The Wingate Desert did not extend into the western reaches of the region. In the Vermilion Cliffs of the Grand Staircase, and in Paria Canyon, you find the Moenave Formation in place of the Wingate. The Moenave forms ledges and cliffs and is composed of red siltstones and sandstones deposited in freshwater floodplains.

The **Kayenta Formation**, prominent in the walls of North Wash near Hite, in the canyon of the Escalante River, in the Vermilion Cliffs, and the lower Paria Canyon, forms reddish brown cliff bands and ledges. The Kayenta forms a distinctive break, often hosting abundant shrubs and trees, between the towering cliffs of the Wingate and the overlying Navajo Sandstone.

Of all the rock formations in the region, the **Navajo Sandstone** is the most widespread and the most dramatic. Deposited in vast deserts of drifting sand, this generally white formation displays prominent cross-bedding, the sweeping diagonal lines that record the advance of ancient sand dunes across the landscape. This porous formation is a vast reservoir of water, attested to by the myriad springs and seeps that issue from the contact with the underlying, impermeable Kayenta beds. The Navajo forms great cliffs, sweeping slopes, and most notably, domes, the petrified remains of ancient sand dunes.

31

The Navajo Sandstone provides the dramatic backdrop west and northwest of the Hite area on Lake Powell and dominates the landscape in the Escalante region. The White Cliffs of the Grand Staircase and the uplifted beds along the western margin of The Cockscomb are all composed of Navajo. Travel over the Navajo is both delightful and challenging. Vast expanses of gentle slickrock often give way to barrier cliffs, prominent domes, pouroffs, and slot canyons.

The **Carmel Formation**, composed of red and gray limestones, shales, and sandstones, forms ledges and slopes that cap the Navajo in the Escalante and Grand Staircase areas. This formation was deposited along the coastal margin of a retreating sea.

The **Entrada Sandstone** is widespread throughout southern Utah, most notably in the Moab area and in Arches National Park. In the Glen Canyon region, the Entrada is prominent as broad aprons of orange slickrock along the base of the Straight Cliffs above the lower Escalante canyons. Farther west in the upper Paria River drainage, and particularly around Kodachrome Basin State Park and along the northern 10 miles of the Cottonwood Canyon Road, three members of the Entrada are distinctive and unique in their coloration and erosional forms.

One of the unique features of the southern Utah canyon country is its isolated "island" mountain ranges. The Henry Mountains, Abajo Mountains, and Navajo Mountain are prominent features in a landscape dominated by canyons and mesas in the Glen Canyon region. The processes that resulted in the formation of these mountains began about 48 million years ago as columns, or stocks, of magma, or molten rock, forced their way toward the surface via fractures in the earth's crust. When the magma reached the horizontal sedimentary strata, it fanned out laterally in zones of weakness in the rock layers. For additional information on the geology of the Glen Canyon region, see Appendix B, **Further Reading.**

NATURAL HISTORY OF THE GLEN CANYON REGION

The flora of the Glen Canyon region reflects the diversity of environmental conditions here. Elevations in the region range from the 11,000-foot highlands of the Abajo Mountains to 3,700 feet on the shores of Lake Powell. Within the nearly 5,000 feet of vertical relief in the Glen Canyon region are plant communities ranging from cool forests to desert shrublands.

The high elevations of Elk Ridge at the head of Dark Canyon north of Cedar Mesa and The Box of upper Pine Creek in the Escalante area support well-developed conifer forests in the transition zone. Ponderosa pine dominates this transition zone, and in the most sheltered locations, Douglas-fir and the occasional white fir join the forest. In the microclimates that mimic much higher elevations, such as cool, sheltered draws, Engelmann spruce and blue spruce appear. These conifer forests reach well into the canyons, lending to their sandstones gorges an atmosphere of cool mountains. Quaking aspen are common in this zone, displaying golden foliage in early autumn.

Wildlife in this zone is typical of any high mountain region in the West. Black bear, elk, mule deer and mountain lions are common, and these large mammals extend their range into neighboring canyons on Cedar Mesa as well. Reptiles are almost absent in this zone, save for the short-horned lizard and the Great Basin rattlesnake, a rare sight in these forests.

Most of the Glen Canyon region lies within the Upper Sonoran Zone, and its pinyon-juniper woodlands are more widespread in the Southwest and Intermountain regions than any other forest type. It extends from about 4,500 feet to 7,000 feet and is characterized by the two-needled Colorado pinyon and the Utah juniper. Due to their small, uniform size, rarely exceeding 20 feet in height, the woodland has been dubbed the "pygmy forest."

The open brushlands of the Cool Desert Shrub and Sand Desert Shrub communities occupy the lower elevation mesas, canyons, and terraces, generally below 4,500 feet, but often mixing with the pinyon-juniper woodland at higher elevations. The Cool Desert Shrub community is dominated by big sagebrush in its upper elevations and by blackbrush in the warmer, drier, and lower elevations. Four-wing saltbush occupies sites where saline soils dominate. Mormon tea, yucca, and various cacti cover the landscape. Between the coarse, widely scattered shrubs in this community is a variety of native bunchgrasses.

Most desert plants are succulents and have fleshy leaves or stems that allow them to store water in their tissues. Cacti are the most obvious example. They have shallow but widespreading root systems that allow them to absorb moisture from even the lightest rainfall.

The Lower Sonoran Zone occurs in the lowest elevations in the region and is limited to areas surrounding Lake Powell and Lees Ferry. This is the hottest and driest part of Glen Canyon, and it is a true desert environment. Dominant plants include shadscale, blackbrush, mormon tea, and yucca. Rabbitbrush and arrow weed are common in open canyon bottoms, particularly along the Paria River near Lees Ferry.

A variety of lizards are frequent trail companions in this zone. Gopher snakes and striped whipsnakes inhabit dry areas, while garter snakes prefer riparian environments. The Great Basin and western rattlesnakes inhabit the western reaches of the region, while the midget faded rattlesnake is most common in southeast Utah. Amphibians are common in riparian habitats, and you will see the tadpoles and adults of the red-spotted and Great Basin spadefoot toads, western leopard frog, and canyon tree frog.

Large mammals include mule deer, which range well into many canyons and are sometimes followed by a mountain lion. Smaller mammals include the blacktail jackrabbit, rock squirrel, deer mouse, desert wood rat, antelope ground squirrel, chipmunk, coyote, and beaver in the lower canyons, particularly near Lake Powell. For additional information, including field guides and natural history references to the Glen Canyon region, see Appendix B, **Further reading**.

Cedar Mesa,
Dark Canyon, and Hite

CEDAR MESA

Cedar Mesa is a broad, seemingly featureless plateau in southeast Utah, stretching north from Monument Valley and the San Juan River to the lofty tableland of Elk Ridge. Utah Highways 95, 261, and 276 bisect this platform (see locator map, p. viii).

The canyons of Cedar Mesa offer some of the most outstanding hiking opportunities in the Glen Canyon region, yet most of these gorges are overlooked by hikers en route to better known destinations in southern Utah. All of the canyons are carved out of Cedar Mesa Sandstone, which forms great, bulging, often overhanging cliffs. Hoodoos and mushroom rock typically punctuate the rims of the convoluted canyon walls.

Because of the Cedar Mesa Sandstone's response to weathering and erosion, great slickrock amphitheaters, cavelike alcoves, and ledges dimple the canyon walls. Long ago, the Anasazi people built homes of rocks, sticks, and mortar, and stored their grain, in these hidden niches. Ruins of this ancient culture and its mysterious rock art abound in the Cedar Mesa region, and each canyon here is virtually an outdoor museum of the culture.

Lake Powell spreads out below Hite Overlook, near Hite Marina.

Although the Anasazi left their cliff-bound homes 700 years ago, many of their dwellings and granaries are so well-preserved it seems as if they left last week. An increase in visitation has led to the rapid deterioration of many sites, most often caused by the inadvertent impact of curious hikers. All visitors are urged to walk softly around these ancient archaeological sites (see "Leave No Trace" in this guide's introduction).

The nature of the Cedar Mesa Sandstone makes most hiking routes in the canyons very demanding and passable only to seasoned canyoneers. Yet there are exceptions, and some of the trails and routes described here are accessible to any hiker. All of these hikes visit ancient ruins, outstanding canyons, riparian oases, and natural bridges.

The hiking season in the Cedar Mesa area generally opens by the middle of March, depending upon snowpack and weather conditions. Summers are hot, but often briefly cooled by frequent thunderstorms during the monsoon. Autumn is an ideal time to visit, and periods of warm weather can extend the hiking season well into December.

DARK CANYON

The lofty, densely forested tableland of Elk Ridge rises between Cedar Mesa in the south and the Canyonlands basin to the north. Cleaved into this high plateau is Dark Canyon, one of the Glen Canyon region's most profound gorges. Stretching some 40 miles from its headwaters to its mouth in Narrow Canyon (beneath Lake Powell), this canyon spans 5,000 feet of vertical relief and contains all the life zones present in the region, ranging from forests of pine, fir, and aspen, to sun-baked, rocky deserts clad in a scattering of coarse shrubs. This tremendous elevation difference is equal to that from rim to river in the Grand Canyon.

Elevations in the upper tributaries and the main stem of the canyon near Elk Ridge exceed 8,000 feet, but the gradient of the canyon is gradual throughout its 40-mile course. Temperatures are consequently cooler in the upper reaches of Dark Canyon, making it comfortable to hike here even during summer. Unlike many canyons on nearby Cedar Mesa, Dark Canyon features a network of trails that is generally easy to follow, eliminating most of the delay and difficulty of routefinding. As if to compensate for the convenience of trails, a combination of deep, soft sand and very limited access to water sources make hiking in Dark Canyon demanding in different ways.

Although upper Dark Canyon and its tributaries are cut into the slickrock of the Cedar Mesa Sandstone, most of the canyon is a narrow gorge cut into the red and gray limestones and shales of the Elephant Canyon and Honaker Trail formations.

The trail network in the canyon began to evolve in the 1890s when herds of cattle were driven from Texas to the Great Sage Plain in southeast Utah, and eventually onto Cedar Mesa and the rich grasslands of Elk Ridge. Later, collective herds known as the "Bluff Pool," owned by the settlers of Bluff, grazed Elk Ridge during the summer season. Two of the cattlemen associated with the Bluff Pool, John Albert Scorup and his brother Jim, began gathering a herd of their own and also using Elk Ridge as summer range. In 1917, the Scorup's, in partnership with the Somerville brothers, acquired the Dugout Ranch holdings, with headquarters on Indian Creek near where the Needles District of Canyonlands National Park lies today. The ranch stretched south across Dark Canyon and Elk Ridge to White Canyon on Cedar Mesa and was the largest operation in Utah. Dark Canyon was at the heart of the ranch's range, and it was the Scorup's cows and cowboys who blazed the trails in Dark Canyon that hikers follow today. Cattle are still grazed in the area, though on a seasonal and three year rest-rotation basis. Hikers may find cows in early summer in upper Dark Canyon or Peavine Canyon.

Due to the high elevations of Elk Ridge, all of the upper Dark Canyon trailheads (those accessing Hikes 23 through 28) are inaccessible due to lingering snow and mud until late May each year. By late October, snows can once again render the Elk Ridge area inaccessible.

HITE

At the mouth of Dark Canyon at the Colorado River, Cataract Canyon ends where the river turns west and enters a confined gorge that John Wesley Powell's epic Colorado River expedition named Narrow Canyon on July 28, 1869. Narrow Canyon ends after only a few miles, where the Colorado was joined by a muddy stream members of the expedition thought was a "dirty devil." In the days that followed, as the party floated down-canyon from the mouth of the Dirty Devil River, they entered an idyllic canyon. Powell described it as "a curious ensemble of wonderful features--carved walls, royal arches, glens, alcove gulches, mounds, and monuments." They named this beautiful gorge Glen Canyon, and it begins at Hite. Yet most of what Powell observed in the canyon is now lost beneath the waters of Lake Powell.

The Hite area is set in a classic Glen Canyon landscape of colorful hoodoos, broad expanses of slickrock, bold cliffs, and towering domes. Lying in the hot, dry environment of the Lower Sonoran Zone, only sparse, stiff shrubs stud the colorful landscape. Daytime highs of 100 to 105-degrees are routine from late May through early September, making the lake's cold waters a Mecca for water-based recreation throughout the summer.

In 1883, Cass Hite settled at the mouth of White Canyon, and his camp grew with the gold rush to placer deposits in Glen Canyon during the 1880s and 1890s. Hite boasted a ferry and the only post office in Glen Canyon. The ferry operated until 1946, when UT 95 was completed. Not paved until 1976, "Utah's Bicentennial Highway" is today the premier scenic drive in the Colorado Plateau region.

UT 95 and Hite are the gateways to the few backcountry hiking routes in the region, including the incomparable Sundance Trail into Dark Canyon and the lonely slickrock gorges branching off from North Wash. The lower elevations here allow hikers to enter the canyons much earlier and later in the seasons than all other areas covered in this book. The debilitating summer heat should be avoided between late May and September.

THE ANASAZI

"Anasazi" is a Navajo word that has been variously translated to mean "ancient ones," "old ones," or "ancient enemies." Present day ancestors of the Anasazi, the Hopi, Zuni, and puebloan people of New Mexico, prefer to call their ancestors "pre-puebloan." The remains of this culture are scattered throughout southern Utah and the Glen Canyon region. The people who are called the Anasazi occupied the Cedar Mesa region as early as 200 A.D. Their name is derived from their finely woven baskets and this early period of the culture is known as the Basketmaker period. As the Anasazi evolved from strictly hunting and gathering, they developed horticulture and became more sedentary. They also chipped stone for tools and crafted various woven articles, including sandals. During this period the Anasazi constructed slab-sided cists for storage and lived in either upright structures fashioned from wooden posts, or in pit houses.

After about 700 A.D., the culture further evolved into what is called the Pueblo period. During this period, beginning about 900 A.D., the Anasazi population increased, they developed large villages in places, they became highly skilled at agriculture, and their ritualistic and social system became well developed. Also during this time, several culturally distinct branches of the Anasazi occupied various parts of the Four Corners region of the Colorado Plateau. In the Cedar Mesa and Dark Canyon areas were the Northern San Juan or Mesa Verde Anasazi, and this branch left behind the most visible remains of their presence. Farther west, reaching into the Escalante canyons, were the Kayenta branch, and though occasional rock art, granaries, and small dwellings are present there, those remains are much less conspicuous and harder to find than on Cedar Mesa. Finally, in the far western part of the region covered in this book, the Virgin River Anasazi occupied the Grand Staircase and Paria River areas. This branch is not known for elaborate architecture, and hikers will seldom find remains beyond chipping sites, potsherds, and rock art. Stone masonry, circular, ceremonial pit houses, or "kivas," and fine pottery, some of it highly decorated, are among the most abundant artifacts still remaining in the Cedar Mesa and Dark Canyon areas. At that time the Anasazi settled into their canyon homes in small family groups, cultivated crops of corn, beans, squash, and cotton, and raised turkeys, though they still utilized the native plants and animals for fiber, food, and raw materials.

For reasons that may never be determined, the Anasazi began to build their dwellings and storage structures in nearly inaccessible, defensible positions high on the cliffs of the canyons. By the late 1200s, the Anasazi abandoned southern Utah and northern Arizona, and archaeologists theorize the abandonment may have occurred because of drought. Drought did occur in the mid-1200s, but why then did the Anasazi retreat still farther from scarce water into remote cliff dwellings during that time? Some archaeologists believe that warfare developed among the Anasazi in response to competition for dwindling resources. To lend support to the theory of internecine warfare, hikers can find in Grand Gulch defensive walls with small loopholes pointing in strategic directions, large enough for defenders to aim and fire an arrow. A new theory suggests that the development of a new religion may have been responsible for the Anasazi abandonment of the region and the move south and east into New Mexico and eastern Arizona.

Descendants of this ancient culture still live in houses of stone and mortar and today occupy the Hopi mesas in Arizona, the Zuni pueblo in western New Mexico, and numerous other pueblos scattered along the Rio Grande River in northern New Mexico.

WILDERNESS AND ROADLESS AREAS

Cedar Mesa is part of a BLM management area known as an ACEC, or Area of Critical Environmental Concern, designated to protect both cultural resources and primitive recreational values. Within the Cedar Mesa area are four wilderness study areas (WSAs), which are managed to maintain their wilderness characteristics until Congress makes a final decision on whether to include them into National Wilderness Preservation System or to release them for other uses.

These WSAs encompass the majority of Cedar Mesa and its canyon network. The Grand Gulch Complex, which includes all of Grand Gulch, the existing Grand Gulch Primitive Area, Slickhorn Canyon, and Johns Canyon, encompasses 105,520 acres.

The Mule Canyon WSA is the smallest at 5,990 acres, and it includes both of the upper forks of Mule Canyon north of UT 95. The Fish Creek Canyon WSA contains 46,440 acres in the Fish Creek and Owl Creek drainages. The 52,420-acre Road Canyon WSA includes Road Canyon, Lime Creek and the West Fork Lime Creek, and extends into the low desert valleys of the Valley of the Gods north of Mexican Hat.

Dark Canyon contains a roadless portion of Glen Canyon National Recreation Area near its mouth, and two other wild areas protect the bulk of this incomparable gorge. In its upper reaches is the 45,000-acre Dark Canyon Wilderness, administered by the Manti–La Sal National Forest. Down-canyon from Woodenshoe Canyon, and including Fable Valley north of the Dark Canyon Plateau, the BLM administers the 62,000-acre Dark Canyon Primitive Area.

BACKCOUNTRY REGULATIONS

Grand Gulch/Cedar Mesa Regulations

1. All vehicles, including mountain bikes, must stay on established roads. No mountain bikes are allowed in the canyons.

2. Group size for the Grand Gulch Primitive Area, Slickhorn, Road, Lime, Fish, and Owl canyons is restricted to twelve individuals, and packstock parties are limited to ten animals.

3. All organized groups of eight or more people and parties using stock are

required to obtain a permit from the BLM office in Monticello at least three weeks in advance of their trip. No more than one stock party (commercial or private) will be allowed in each of the following canyons at a single time: Grand Gulch, Fish Creek, Mule Canyon, Road Canyon, and Johns Canyon.

4. Camping is limited to no more than two consecutive nights at the following heavily used campsites in Grand Gulch: Junction, Turkey Pen, mouth of Bullet Canyon, and Jailhouse areas.

5. All trash and garbage, including used toilet paper, must be packed out.

6. Campfires are prohibited.

7. Swimming or bathing in pools or streams pollutes these scarce water sources with body oils, lotions, and sunscreens. Never use soap, even if it is biodegradable, in or near water sources.

8. Latrines or shallow catholes for human body waste disposal should be dug no more than 4 to 6 inches deep and covered with soil after use. Pack out used toilet paper; never burn it.

9. Bathe, wash dishes, and dispose of human waste at least 200 feet from water sources.

10. There is a 14-day camping limit on Cedar Mesa.

11. Use of climbing gear to gain access to archaeological sites is prohibited.

12. All dogs must be on a leash and under physical control at all times.

13. Federal law prohibits disturbing Indian ruins or rock art panels and removing artifacts.

14. The Split Level Ruin and bench area surrounding it in Grand Gulch are closed to camping.

15. Dogs are not permitted in Slickhorn Canyon or in Grand Gulch down-canyon from the confluence with Collins Canyon.

(**Note:** Beginning in the spring of 1999, backpackers will be required to make reservations in advance for permits to backpack anywhere in the Cedar Mesa backcountry. As this book went to print in early 1998, the BLM's Monticello office was in the process of developing the reservation system. Contact the Monticello BLM office at the number listed on page 42 for current information on the reservation system.)

Dark Canyon Guidelines (recommendations issued by the U.S. Forest Service)

1. Organized groups and commercial parties are required to obtain a special use permit from the Forest Service and/or BLM.

2. Groups of ten or more people are encouraged to contact the Forest Service and/or BLM prior to their trip.

3. Groups are encouraged to restrict the number of people to no more than fifteen.

4. The Peavine Corridor Road is open to motorized, licensed vehicles and

mountain bikes. All other areas in the Dark Canyon Wilderness and Dark Canyon Primitive Area are closed to all vehicles.

CAMPING

Only one developed campground is located in the Cedar Mesa region, and that is the 13-unit campground in Natural Bridges National Monument. This fee campground is open year-round and is available on a first-come, first-served basis; it often fills by early afternoon in the spring and autumn. Arrive early if you wish to secure a site. Facilities include tables, tent pads, fire grills, and pit toilets. Water is available only at the visitor center, 0.25 mile from the campground.

If the campground is full or if your vehicle exceeds 26 feet in length, use the overflow camping area located 6.2 miles east of the visitor center. To get there, drive east of the monument to the UT 95/261 junction and turn right (south) onto UT 261. About 100 yards south of the junction signs direct you left (southeast) down a gravel road to the camping area.

A private campground with RV hookups is located at Fry Canyon Lodge, 19.8 miles west of the Utah 95/275 junction, the turnoff to Natural Bridges National Monument.

Most visitors to the Cedar Mesa region camp at-large, or wherever they wish, off of the network of San Juan County roads that criss-cross the mesa. Here, on public lands administered by the BLM, you will find almost unlimited opportunities to car camp in the pinyon-juniper woodlands. Most sites are short spur roads or pullouts, offering room enough to park and set up a tent. Always use established sites, and never drive off-road to create new sites. Extreme caution is advised if you choose to build a campfire. The use of portable toilets at vehicle campsites on Cedar Mesa is strongly advised and will likely become mandatory in the near future. Contact the BLM office in Monticello for current information.

On Elk Ridge there are no developed campgrounds, but there are unlimited opportunities for undeveloped camping in the cool conifer forests and aspen groves. In the Hite area there are many spur roads leading down to the shores of Lake Powell that offer popular undeveloped sites. Also, areas in North Wash along UT 95, outside of the Glen Canyon National Recreation Area boundary, offer short spur roads where you may car camp.

ACCESS AND SERVICES

Access to this remote region is by Utah Highway 95, a 121-mile highway linking Hanksville in the northwest with Blanding in the east, which is unquestionably the most scenic drive in the Colorado Plateau's canyon country. Cedar Mesa can also be reached via Utah Highway 261, which branches north from U.S. Highway 191, 4 miles north of Mexican Hat, and leads 33 miles to its junction with Utah 95.

Services are limited to the communities that lie far beyond Cedar Mesa. Groceries, gas, lodging, car repair and towing, and restaurants are available in Blanding, Bluff, and Hanksville. A medical clinic, Blanding Urgent Care, is located in Blanding, and the San Juan Hospital is located in nearby Monticello. Fry Canyon Lodge offers the only gas between Blanding and the gas station/convenience store at Hite Marina on Lake Powell. The lodge also offers a cafe, six guest rooms, ice, propane, and a telephone for emergency use only. Pay telephones are available at Natural Bridges National Monument and at Hite Marina. Hite also offers drinking water, garbage disposal, and a National Park Service ranger station.

For more information on the Cedar Mesa region, including the Dark Canyon Primitive Area, visit the Kane Gulch Ranger Station on Utah 261, 3.8 miles south of the junction with Utah 95, or call the BLM San Juan Resource Area office in Monticello at (435) 587-2141, or contact the office by mail at: P.O. Box 7, Monticello, UT 84535.

For more information about the Dark Canyon Wilderness, contact the Monticello Ranger District office of the Manti–La Sal National Forest at (435) 587-2041, or by mail at: P.O. Box 820, Monticello, UT 84535. In the event of an emergency, dial 911 or call the San Juan County Sheriff at (435) 587-2237. The phone number for Blanding Urgent Care is (435) 678-2254; and the number for the San Juan Hospital in Monticello is (435) 587-2116.

1 Mule Canyon

General description:	A half-day hike to an easily accessible canyon on Cedar Mesa, featuring several well-preserved Anasazi ruins.
Distance:	6 miles or more, round trip.
Difficulty:	Easy.
Trail conditions:	Boot-worn trails and wash route.
Trailhead access:	2WD.
Average hiking time:	3.5 to 4 hours round trip.
Trailhead elevation:	5,944 feet.
High point:	6,200 feet.
Elevation gain and loss:	250 feet.
Optimum seasons:	April through early June; September through October.
Water availability:	Seasonal intermittent flows in Mule Canyon; treat before drinking or bring your own.
Hazards:	Flash-flood danger.
Permits:	Not required.
Topo maps:	Hotel Rock and South Long Point USGS quads; Trails Illustrated Grand Gulch Plateau.

Key points:
3.0 Twin bays.

Finding the trailhead: From Blanding, follow Utah 191 south 3 miles to the junction of U.S. Highway 191 and Utah 95. Turn right (west) at the junction on Utah 95 and drive 19.3 miles (between mileposts 102 and 103) to the signed turnoff for San Juan County Road 263 (Arch Canyon). If you are coming from the west, the turnoff is 67 miles east of the Hite Marina turn-off on Utah 95, 9 miles east of UT 261 and .5 mile east of the signed turnoff to Mule Canyon Indian Ruins.

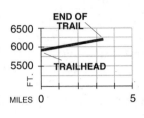

After turning northeast onto San Juan County 263, pass a parking area on the right (south) side of the road after 200 yards. Then descend a short but rough and rocky downgrade to the bridge spanning Mule Canyon, 0.3 mile from Utah 95. A turnout on the right (south) side of San Juan County 263 has room for two to three cars.

The hike: This pleasant, easy day hike follows the course of upper Mule Canyon, one of the most accessible canyons in the Cedar Mesa region. Great bulging cliffs of Cedar Mesa Sandstone embrace the canyon, which supports an interesting mixture of pinyon-juniper and montane forest environments.

The trail is sandy but well-worn and easy to follow, with few obstacles, making it passable even to novice hikers. You will see several well-preserved Anasazi ruins, most of them grain storage structures. The trail leads directly to some ruins—please respect these fragile ancient structures.

From the bridge spanning Mule Canyon wash, follow either of two obvious trails that descend abruptly to the floor of the shallow canyon. There the trails join and quickly lead to the trailhead register. Beyond the register, the well-defined trail follows the edge of the Mule Canyon arroyo, soon crossing the usually dry wash to the grassy bench on the opposite side.

The canyon is quite shallow at this point, flanked by low walls of Cedar Mesa Sandstone. Pinyon and juniper trees cover the north-facing slopes to your left. On south-facing slopes, the woodland is open and sparse.

After about 0.5 mile, where the wash begins a northwest trend, the canyon grows increasingly confined by bulging walls that rise 150 feet to the rims above. Soon, with slickrock under foot, you begin to follow the floor of the wash. Multiple trails are frequent in this part of the canyon, but the way is straightforward—you simply follow the wash.

The woodland vegetation in the sheltered confines of the canyon is rich and well-developed, more typical of a higher and wetter environment. The northwest trend of the canyon allows considerable shade to be cast by the canyon walls, reducing heat, sunlight, and evaporation.

After 1.7 miles, the first obvious draw opens up on the right (north). Beyond it, Mule Canyon grows deeper, flanked by red- and white-banded Cedar Mesa slickrock. Most of the ruins you will see are located above the draw.

Groves of Douglas-fir soon begin to appear on the southwest rim, while ponderosa pines grow tall and straight on the opposite rim, lending a sense of scale to the depth of the canyon. The trail ahead continues its criss-crossing

Mule Canyon • North Fork Mule Canyon

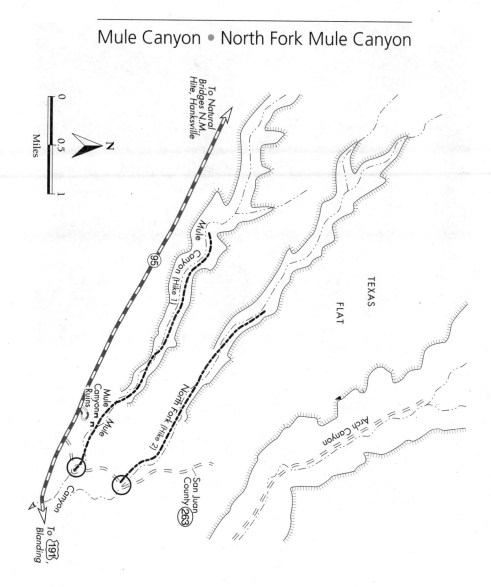

Ruins in Mule Canyon.

course across the wash, hugging the banks closely. This sheltered part of Mule Canyon supports an increasing number of tall conifers, which cast ample shade and add the flavor of a mountain environment to the canyon.

After 2.3 miles, the trail winds among the pines and skirts a deep plunge pool on the right side. At this point, the trail begins to deteriorate. A pair of bays (shallow amphitheaters) open up on the north wall of the canyon after 3 miles, where tall cottonwoods crowd the banks of the wash. The trail essentially disappears around the point just beyond the twin bays; the canyon becomes increasingly confined, and a forest of tall conifers is massed on the canyon floor.

Most hikers will be content to end the hike at the twin bays and relax in the shadow of pines and firs, or soak in the sunshine on the slickrock, before backtracking to the trailhead.

2 North Fork Mule Canyon

See Map on Page 43

General description:	A half-day hike to a scenic Cedar Mesa canyon rich in Anasazi ruins.
Distance:	5.2 miles or more, round trip.
Difficulty:	Easy.
Trail conditions:	Boot-worn trails and wash route.
Trailhead access:	2WD.
Average hiking time:	2 to 2.5 hours round trip.
Trailhead elevation:	6,000 feet.
High point:	6,200 feet.
Elevation gain and loss:	200 feet.
Optimum seasons:	April through early June; September through October.
Water availability:	Seasonal intermittent flows in the wash; treat before drinking or bring your own.
Hazards:	Flash-flood danger.
Permits:	Not required.
Topo maps:	Hotel Rock and South Long Point USGS quads; Trails Illustrated Grand Gulch Plateau.

Key points:
2.6   Reach the end of the trail.

Finding the trailhead: Follow driving directions for Hike 1 to Mule Canyon, then continue northwest on San Juan County 263. The road is rough and rocky in places, yet is easily passable to low-clearance vehicles.

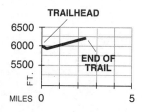

After one switchback, you pass a parking/camping area. At 0.7 mile from Utah 95, you pass a corral and undeveloped campsite. The road descends from the corral to the bridge spanning North Fork Mule Canyon, 1 mile from Utah 95. Park in the wide spot immediately west of the bridge. Hikers searching for a campsite will find numerous undeveloped sites in the pinyon-juniper woodland along the road, beyond North Fork.

The hike: Much like the main fork of Mule Canyon, the North Fork blends conifer forest and pinyon-juniper woodland with bold slickrock cliffs providing easy access to a number of fine Anasazi ruins. This fork of the canyon is more confined, and many of its ruins—including dwellings, kivas, and granaries—are better hidden than in the main fork of the canyon, making their discovery more rewarding. Walking in the North Fork is easy and trouble-free. Segments of sandy, boot-worn trail guide you up-canyon, and in between you simply follow the wash.

From the southwest abutment of the bridge spanning the North Fork, a well-worn trail gradually descends northwest to the trailhead register. Although the North Fork is more confined than the main fork, the canyon is shallow: only 30 to 40 feet deep for the first 0.5 mile.

The way ahead follows the small wash, where in spring there will likely be flowing water. You will follow segments of trail, but most often you will be walking along the floor of the wash, with slickrock under foot, and occasionally skirting boulders and plunging through willow thickets, forging your own way. Overall, the wash provides a clear avenue to follow up-canyon.

A cooler, sheltered microclimate prevails in the confines of the North Fork, contrasting with the dry woodlands fringing the rims above. Gambel oak, pinyon, and juniper trees stud the slickrock walls above, while on the canyon floor you'll find cottonwoods, ponderosa pines, and Douglas-firs.

The bulging, often overhanging red- and gray-banded Cedar Mesa Sandstone cliffs gradually rise higher as you push deeper into the canyon, flanking the North Fork with convoluted 200-foot walls. After 1.9 miles, a prominent wooded draw opens up on the right (north). Just beyond the mouth of the draw is a deep alcove, crowned on its rim by a rust red sandstone knob. A line of seepage in the alcove supports a ribbon of hanging garden vegetation, including the brilliant blue flowers of primrose.

The way up-canyon beyond the alcove follows the increasingly confined wash. The forested 8,000-foot plateau of South Long Point with its distinctive brick-red slopes rises boldly at the head of the canyon. Look for well-hidden ruins on the ledges and in the alcoves. The trail essentially disappears after 2.6 miles. Most people turn around here and retrace their steps to the trailhead, perhaps finding ruins they missed along the way.

3   Owl Creek to Nevills Arch

General description:	A demanding yet very rewarding all-day hike to the largest natural arch in the Cedar Mesa region, recommended for experienced hikers only.
Distance:	8.6 miles round-trip.
Difficulty:	Strenuous, occasional Class 2 and 3 scrambling.
Trail conditions:	Boot-worn trails, steep slickrock friction pitches; occasional route-finding required.
Trailhead access:	Impassable when wet. 4WD may be required if roads are flood damaged.
Average hiking time:	5 to 6 hours round trip.
Trailhead elevation:	6,160 feet.
Low point:	5,000 feet.
Elevation gain and loss:	1,160 feet.
Optimum seasons:	April through early June; September through October.
Water availability:	Seasonal intermittent flow in Owl Creek; pe-rennial pools at 2.2 and 2.5 miles; treat before drinking, or bring your own.

Hazards: Exposure to steep dropoffs; flash-flood danger.
Permits: Not required for day hikes.
Topo maps: Snow Flat Spring Cave USGS quad; Trails Illustrated Grand Gulch Plateau.

Key points:

0.25 Rim of Owl Creek canyon.
2.0   First pouroff.
2.7   Second pouroff.
3.3   Third pouroff.
4.3   Nevills Arch.

Finding the trailhead: Drive to the junction of Utah 95 and Utah 261, which is 56 miles east of the Hite Marina turnoff on Utah 95 and 28.3 miles west of the junction of U.S. Highway 191 and Utah 95, 3 miles south of Blanding. At the junction of Utah 95 and Utah 261, drive south on Utah 261. Pass the Kane Gulch Ranger Station after 3.8 miles and continue south up the grade for 1 mile, turning left (east) on San Juan County 253 (Long Spike), also signed for Owl Creek-5. If you are coming from the south, this turnoff is located between mile posts 28 and 29, 28.2 miles north of the junction of Utah 261 and U.S. Highway 163/191 between Mexican Hat and Bluff.

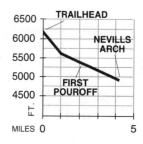

Sculpted hoodoos in the Cedar Mesa Sandstone are among the scenic highlights of Owl Creek canyon.

47

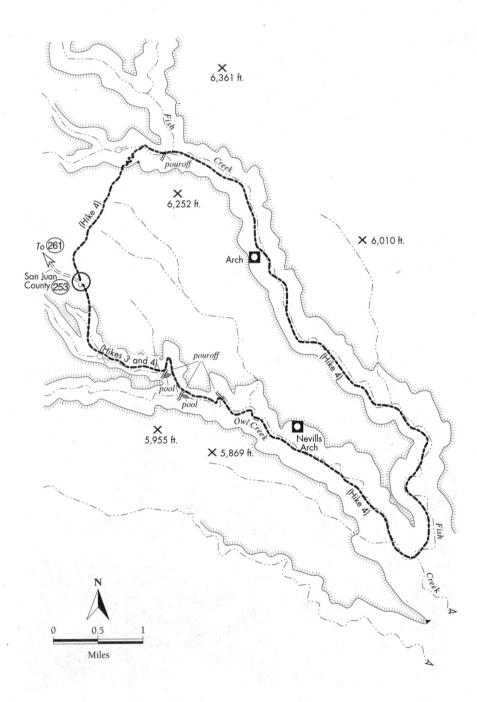

X 6,361 ft.

Fish

pouroff

Creek

X 6,252 ft.

X 6,010 ft.

(Hike 4)

To (261)

Arch 🔲

San Juan
County (253)

(Hikes 3 and 4)

pouroff

(Hike 4)

pool

pool

Owl Creek

🔲
Nevills
Arch

X 5,955 ft.

X 5,869 ft.

(Hike 4)

N

0   0.5   1

Miles

Fish

Creek

(Hike 4)

A

A

48

The graded eastbound road, which is impassable when wet, is often rocky and rutted in places, but should be passable to cars in dry weather, barring flood damage. The road winds over the mesa for 5.3 miles to the large parking area and signed trailhead at the road end. Hikers searching for a campsite will find a few undeveloped sites along the trailhead access road and at the trailhead.

The hike: Nevills Arch is the highlight of this premier day hike, an abridged version of the longer, multi-day Owl Creek to Fish Creek loop (see Hike 4). This is one of the few hikes in the Cedar Mesa region not aimed at visiting Anasazi ruins, though you are still likely to see ancient granaries and dwellings. A perennial stream, riparian foliage, deep pools, several pouroffs, and exciting stretches of slickrock walking make this an attractive day hike. Although the hike to Nevills Arch is much easier without the burden of a backpack, the route is not suitable for novice canyon country hikers. Routefinding, scrambling, and steep slickrock friction pitches en route down Owl Creek canyon demand that hikers have previous canyoneering experience.

At the Owl Creek Trailhead, a sign points to Owl Creek, and you turn right onto a short segment of trail that leads into the canyon's headwaters draw, which you then follow south with slickrock under foot. After 0.25 mile, Owl Creek canyon suddenly opens up far below, a cavernous gorge flanked by bold, bulging walls of Cedar Mesa Sandstone. Here, on the rim of the canyon, the cairned route begins its abrupt descent into the gorge.

This is a steep, plunging descent, often crossing high-angle slopes of slickrock. Careful scouting is necessary at times to locate cairns and stay on the right course. There is more than one possible route into the labyrinth, but hikers are advised to follow the route marked by cairns. En route you will be exposed to steep dropoffs and forced to engage in boulder-hopping, though backpackers will not find it necessary to rope down packs.

After about 1 hour and 1 mile from the trailhead, you reach the canyon floor where a prominent side canyon joins on the right (west). The way down the wash ahead follows a well-beaten path that criss-crosses the intermittent stream. After another 0.8 mile of avoiding obstacles and crossing the wash from one side to another, you reach a resistant red layer in the Cedar Mesa Sandstone and a major pouroff. A cairned slickrock route follows a ledge above and to the left of that barrier, then the route traverses several hundred yards to the north into a prominent side canyon.

You leave the ledge for a brief descent into that drainage, then follow its descending course south, rock-hopping and tracing segments of trail back into Owl Creek. There you will find several excellent campsites, also attractive to day hikers taking a break, located in the shade of large cottonwoods. Between the campsites and the pouroff just above, there lies a large, deep pool that holds water year-round.

The trail ahead crosses to the left (east) side of the wash, traverses above a very deep, green pool, and shortly thereafter reaches the confluence with another west-trending side canyon. At the confluence lies another, lower pouroff, yet one that still must be bypassed. Traverse a slickrock ledge to the left to skirt this obstacle and the deep plunge pool that lies just below it. Beyond the ledge a trail of sorts leads several hundred yards to the descent route. Some scrambling and a 6-foot downclimb are necessary here, and some backpackers may wish to rope down their packs.

About 0.5 mile below the second pouroff (and 3.1 miles from the trailhead), the canyon describes a prominent bend to the left (north), where you pass a fine campsite situated on a bench above the wash. Soon the trail leads across the wash and you then skirt the third and smallest pouroff on the right. The canyon ahead grows increasingly confined, and you follow its serpentine course past a striking array of intricately sculpted hoodoos colored in shades of red and white.

After following several bends in the canyon, a conspicuous fin, capped by a row of slender hoodoos, projects into the canyon from the south wall. Shortly thereafter Nevills Arch comes into view high on the northeast canyon wall. Good campsites dot the benches that flank the wash at this popular spot, set in the partial shade of junipers and Gambel oak groves. Social trails lead toward the base of the canyon wall beneath the arch, but the span itself is difficult to reach. Allow plenty of time to retrace your steps to the trailhead, since it will likely take much longer on the hike out than it did to get here.

4 Owl Creek–Fish Creek Loop

See Map on Page 48

General description:	An excellent short backpack, looping through two dramatic Cedar Mesa canyons.
Distance:	16.3 miles, loop trip.
Difficulty:	Moderately strenuous, with occasional Class 2 and 3 scrambling, including one 15-foot Class 3 pitch.
Trail conditions:	Boot-worn trails, steep slickrock friction pitches, slickrock scrambling; occasional route-finding required.
Trailhead access:	Impassable when wet. 4WD may be required if floods have damaged road.
Average hiking time:	2 to 3 days.
Trailhead elevation:	6,160 feet.
High point:	6,284 feet.
Low point:	4,840 feet.
Elevation gain and loss:	1,450 feet.
Optimum seasons:	April through early June; September through October.
Water availability:	Seasonal intermittent flows in Owl and Fish creeks; perennial pools in Owl Creek at 2.2 and 2.5 miles; perennial spring in upper west fork of Fish Creek at 13.6 miles.
Hazards:	Exposure to steep dropoffs, flash-flood danger.

Permits: Required after spring 1999; contact the Monticello
BLM office for details.

Topo maps: Snow Flat Spring Cave and Bluff NW USGS quads;
Trails Illustrated Grand Gulch Plateau.

Key points:

0.25 Rim of Owl Creek canyon.
2.0 First pouroff.
2.7 Second pouroff.
3.3 Third pouroff.
4.3 Nevills Arch.
6.3 Confluence with Fish Creek canyon; bear left.
13.4 Confluence with west fork of Fish Creek; turn left.
14.1 Begin ascent out of Fish Creek canyon.
14.6 Rim of Fish Creek canyon.
16.3 Owl Creek Trailhead.

Finding the trailhead: Follow driving directions for Hike 3.

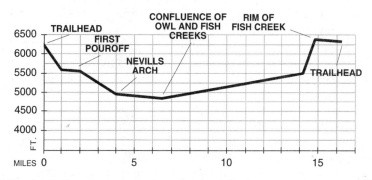

The hike: Fish Creek canyon, the principal drainage on the eastern flanks
of Cedar Mesa, winds southeast from its headwaters draw below South
Long Point, on Elk Ridge, for nearly 20 miles to where the drainage empties
into broad Comb Wash, a major southeast Utah tributary to the San Juan
River. This memorable circuit follows rugged Owl Creek canyon, a Fish
Creek tributary, down to its confluence with Fish Creek, then loops back to
the trailhead via the latter canyon and the mesa top.

Both canyons are among the most spectacular drainages in the Cedar
Mesa region, and this rewarding trip is an excellent alternative to the more
popular Grand Gulch. Although this trip is gaining in popularity, only experienced canyon country hikers should attempt it. Scrambling, friction pitches,
rudimentary rock climbing, and boulder-hopping is routine on this trip, and
it is far more demanding and time consuming than it appears on maps.

Spring is the preferred season for this circuit, when springs and streams
usually offer a reliable source of water. During dry times, hikers may have to
pack a day-and-a-half supply of water from the deep pools in Owl Creek to
the springs in upper Fish Creek. A 20-foot length of rope or nylon cord should
be standard equipment for this trip (or for any other canyon country expedition); you'll likely need to lower or raise backpacks at least once en route.

Although strong hikers can easily complete the trip in two days, plan on spending at least three days to get the most out of the trip, perhaps laying over at camp and taking a day out for exploring. There are many Anasazi ruins in these canyons, though they are seldom obvious.

From the Owl Creek Trailhead, follow the Owl Creek route (see Hike 3) for 4.3 miles to Nevills Arch, and continue down-canyon. The canyon begins a transition below the arch, growing increasingly wide, with longer stretches of bench walking between wash crossings ahead. Even during wet seasons, the creek seldom flows below Nevills Arch. Bold knobs and hoodoos persist in capping the northeast walls of the canyon, and rims on either side rest 700 feet above the wash. Red and gray ledges and slopes, composed of the siltstones, sandstones, and limestones of the Halgaito Formation, soon emerge on the canyon bottom, forming the foundation for great cliffs of Cedar Mesa Sandstone.

As you continue, the canyon floor grows even wider, its walls less imposing. The trail becomes a well-defined path, often with a tread of soft sand, traversing broad benches masked with cheatgrass and studded with prickly pear, big sagebrush, sand sagebrush, and four-wing saltbush, all denizens of the desert shrub community.

At length you reach a fork in the trail immediately before the confluence with Fish Creek canyon at 4,840 feet, 6.3 miles from the trailhead. One trail branches right to an excellent campsite among the cottonwoods just below the confluence. Since many ruins are located farther down Fish Creek canyon, that camp makes an excellent base for a day or so of exploration.

The other trail branches left, very soon crossing the wash of Fish Creek which, during wet seasons, may carry a flow of water, with more reliable pools in its upper reaches. At once you will find Fish Creek to be more confined than Owl, though there are benches throughout its course up-canyon that offer places to camp.

The trail proceeds at a gentle grade up the relatively straight canyon, crossing the wash and small intermittent stream many times ahead. Bulging Cedar Mesa walls soar overhead, seemingly held upright by an array of buttresses that are crowned with sculpted hoodoos. Always there is an over-hanging cliff just below the rim.

As you proceed deeper into the canyon, you'll begin passing ample evidence of beaver activity. Dams impound the stream into long pools of quiet water. Since the trail closely follows the stream, high water in the ponds and flash floods can erase the tread. Simply follow the wash up-canyon when the trail grows obscure. You pass only an occasional established campsite, though there is much potential for camping. Try to use a previously used site to reduce the spread of impact in this fragile desert environment.

The "natural arch" shown on maps is located 4.8 miles above the confluence, though like the Anasazi ruins in the canyon, it is often passed unnoticed. After walking 7.1 miles and perhaps 3.5 hours from the confluence, you reach a prominent fork in the canyon at 5,400 feet. Fish Creek proper continues north, while an equally deep canyon opens up on the left (west). During spring, both drainages usually carry a flow of water.

Follow the left fork for a few hundred yards to where a pool and a pouroff block the way. A good campsite is located here, and you pass through it to reach the bypass route on the right wall. This detour involves an 8-foot climb, accomplished with the aid of a pinyon root. Hikers may find it necessary to haul up bulky backpacks with a rope. The route ahead involves scrambling, traversing slickrock ledges, and occasional bushwhacking through the willows, but this segment passes quickly, and soon you reach the last campsite in the canyon, perched above the creek where it courses down a slickrock chute.

The trail crosses the creek beyond the campsite, then briefly ascends to traverse a ledge above an inviting pool. Many seeps in this damp stretch of the canyon support fine displays of the lavender blooms of primrose and gather to offer a reliable flow of water in the wash below. The ledge ends about 100 yards from the camp at 5,560 feet, where a BLM sign shows the beginning of the ascent to the rim, 0.6 mile from the Fish Creek forks.

The ascent is a steep, winding route, switching back and forth over ledges and crossing stretches of steep slickrock. Ample cairns and well-defined trail segments lead the way. Occasional hand and foot scrambling is necessary, but overall the route is simply a steep grind. Dramatic canyon views expand with every step on the trail.

As you approach the alcoves just below the rim, there appears to be no way to breach the overhanging cliff. Then the trail unexpectedly turns west at the foot of the overhang and you ascend to a 15-foot high crack, which you must climb to gain the rim. It is a Class 3 scramble up this crack, and some hikers may wish to rope up packs behind them. There are often ropes left behind by well-intentioned hikers, and you would be wise to avoid using them since their integrity is uncertain. Rangers ask that hikers please remove ropes they may find here.

Once you mount the rim, well-earned vistas stretch across the broad, wooded expanse of Cedar Mesa, where slickrock-rimmed canyons cleave the tableland. Tall ponderosa pines thrive in the cool microclimate in the canyon below you. From west to northwest, rising far above Cedar Mesa is the rim of Elk Ridge, punctuated by the brick-red twin buttes of the Bears Ears.

From the rim the obvious trail ascends a moderate grade over slickrock, passing through the pinyon-juniper woodland to a higher point on the mesa at 6,284 feet, where views across broad Cedar Mesa are even more expansive. The well-worn trail then begins to thread its way generally southwestward across the mesa. At first you capture tree-framed vignettes of Comb Ridge, and distant mountains and plateaus in the Four Corners to the southeast, but soon the woodland of short, spreading trees envelops you.

The trail follows an undulating course into a dozen shallow gullies, and after walking 1.4 miles from the rim, you drop into a more pronounced drainage. Follow this draw over slickrock and segments of trail for 0.3 mile, where you close the circuit at the trailhead.

5 Road Canyon

General description:	A memorable half-day hike into a Cedar Mesa canyon rich in archeological resources.
Distance:	6.8 miles or more, round trip.
Difficulty:	Moderately easy.
Trail conditions:	Boot-worn trails and wash route; occasional rudimentary routefinding required.
Trailhead access:	4WD required when wet.
Average hiking time:	4 hours or more, round trip.
Trailhead elevation:	6,390 feet.
Low point:	5,600 feet.
Elevation gain and loss:	800 feet.
Optimum season:	April through mid-June; September through October.
Water availability:	Seasonal intermittent flows in Road Canyon; treat before drinking or bring your own.
Hazards:	Flash-flood danger.
Permits:	Not required for day hikes. Reservations and permits required for overnight use beginning spring 1999. Contact Monticello BLM office for information.
Topo maps:	Cedar Mesa North, Snow Flat Spring Cave USGS quads; Trails Illustrated Grand Gulch Plateau.

Key points:
   0.4   Enter Road Canyon.
   3.4   First pouroff.

Finding the trailhead: Follow driving directions for Hike 3 to the junction of Utah 95 and Utah 261, and proceed south on Utah 261 for 13.5 miles. Turn east onto the road signed for Cigarette Spring, 200 yards north of milepost 19. If you are coming from the south, the turnoff is 23.5 miles north of the junction of Utah 261 and U.S. Highway 191/163.

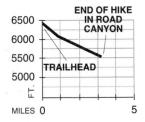

The Cigarette Spring road can be rough in places but should be passable to any vehicle in dry weather. The road leads 1 mile to a gate (leave it open or closed, as you find it), then becomes narrow and winding as it descends to an unsigned junction 3.4 miles from the highway. The right fork leads toward Lime Canyon.

Continue straight ahead (left) for about 100 yards, then turn left onto a northbound spur road. Follow the spur 150 yards to the road end and unsigned trailhead, 3.5 miles from Utah 261.

Hikers searching for campsites will find a few undeveloped sites near the junction with the road to Lime Canyon and also at the trailhead.

The hike: Road Canyon is one of a half-dozen major canyons carved into the eastern flanks of Cedar Mesa and draining into Comb Wash. The canyon ranges from 100 to 400 feet deep, embraced by bulging walls of red- and gray-banded Cedar Mesa Sandstone that are sculpted into ledges, alcoves, sheer cliffs, and strange hoodoos. A seasonal stream fringed by a ribbon of riparian foliage, inviting benches shaded by a pygmy forest of pinyon and juniper, its sculpted slickrock, and the quiet and solitude provided by its remote, off-the-beaten-track location offer ample incentives for visitors to seek out this canyon.

Road Canyon not only offers natural beauty but has many well-preserved Anasazi ruins and rock art. Allow plenty of time for the hike, perhaps an entire day, since you may spend more time here than you expect while scanning hidden recesses for ruins.

The ruins in Road Canyon (and those elsewhere on Cedar Mesa) are threatened by an increase in visitation. Simply walking around ruins can inadvertently cause irreparable damage to the site. Several exceptional kivas in Road Canyon have deteriorated significantly due to human impact since the 1980s. Before visiting any ancient ruins, please read the "Leave No Trace" chapter in this book. Walk softly when visiting ancient ruins and treat them with the respect they deserve.

Begin at the road end and follow the trail as it winds a way through the pinyon-juniper woodland, gradually descending across the mesa top. Please stay on the trail here to avoid crushing the well-developed microbiotic soil crust. After about 250 yards the trail begins a gentle descent above a wooded draw carving into the Cedar Mesa Sandstone. Here the woodland opens up to reveal the shallow upper reaches of Road Canyon below.

Soon you reach a steep, but brief, descent of 120 feet to the boulder-littered floor of Road Canyon. Look for the cairn indicating this exit trail upon returning. Turn right and head down-canyon, through the wash, over segments of boot-worn trail interspersed with slickrock.

Pinyon and juniper trees cloak the broken sandstone walls in the upper reaches of the canyon, sharing space with their typical companion shrubs: Utah serviceberry, alderleaf mountain mahogany, yucca, mormon tea, littleleaf mountain mahogany, and the silver foliage of roundleaf buffaloberry.

Boulders are massed on the canyon floor at 0.6 mile, and cottonwoods and willow thickets appear as you follow trail segments through this rocky stretch. You must forge your way through the willows at times, but the thickets present more of an inconvenience than a challenge.

After you skirt a deep pothole in the wash, the northwest fork of Road Canyon joins on the left at 0.8 mile. After a few more bends of the canyon, a bold red hoodoo, capped by a gray sandstone slab, projects into the canyon from the north wall. Observant hikers will likely spot several ruins high on the canyon walls along the following 3 miles. As you continue down-canyon, narrow benches studded with pinyon and juniper begin to flank the wash, inviting you to return another time with overnight gear to pass a night or two in the canyon.

Road Canyon

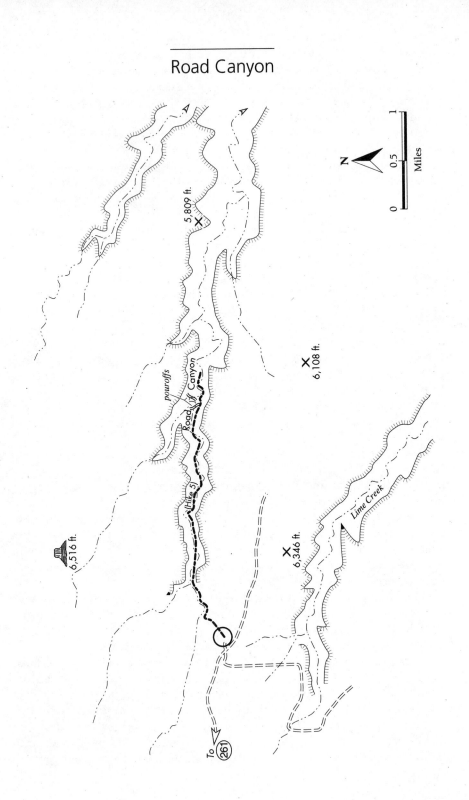

5,809 ft.

6,108 ft.

6,346 ft.

6,516 ft.

pouroffs

Road of Canyon

(Hike 5)

Lime Creek

To 261

N

Miles
1
0.5
0

Although the walking is generally easy, there are places where you may have to stop and backtrack a few yards to find the best route around an obstacle, typical of canyon hiking in southern Utah. The canyon grows increasingly deeper as you proceed, flanked by 200- to 300-foot cliffs of convoluted sandstone, streaked with desert varnish. Grassy banks often fringe the wash, and a ribbon of cottonwood, willow, and an occasional tamarisk follows you down-canyon.

After 2.5 miles, the serpentine canyon becomes much more confined, and you are eventually confronted by a typical Cedar Mesa pouroff, with a deep but ephemeral pool below it, at 3.4 miles. Some hikers may elect to backtrack at this point, but if you are determined to continue to more ruins farther down-canyon, bear right and follow a shelf beneath an overhang, following a course that takes you well above the wash.

The route ahead follows the shelf for about 0.5 mile, beyond which a steep slickrock friction pitch and a brief downclimb are necessary to regain the wash. The canyon below is much deeper, with colorful, banded sand-

Road Canyon drains the eastern flanks of Cedar Mesa.

stone walls reaching 400 to 500 feet to the rims above. After 5.6 miles, just down-canyon from a northwest-trending side canyon, are some of the last ruins in Road Canyon. Most day hikers who have persevered this far will turn around at this point and retrace the route through this scenic canyon to the trailhead.

6 Slickhorn Canyon, Access #1

General description: A challenging day hike or backpack into a remote Cedar Mesa canyon.

Distance: 8.8 miles round trip to Access #4 canyon.

Difficulty: Moderate, some Class 2 and 3 scrambling.

Trail conditions: Wash route and slickrock route, occasional routefinding required; segments of boot-worn trails in Slickhorn Canyon.

Trailhead access: 4WD required when wet or if floods have damaged the road.

Average hiking time: 5 hours round trip.

Trailhead elevation: 6,140 feet.

Low point: 5,420 feet.

Elevation gain and loss: 720 feet.

Optimum season: April through mid-June; September through October.

Water availability: Seasonal inermittent flows from Access #2 canyon, at 4 miles, downstream; day hikers should bring their own.

Hazards: Exposure to steep dropoffs, steep slickrock friction pitches, flash-flood danger.

Permits: Reservations and permits required for overnight use beginning spring 1999. Contact Monticello BLM office for more information.

Topo maps: Pollys Pasture, Slickhorn Canyon East USGS quads; Trails Illustrated Grand Gulch Plateau.

Key points:

1.7 Reach major pouroff; bypass via a slickrock route on the left (south).

2.2 Floor of Slickhorn Canyon.

4.0 Access #2 canyon joins on the left (east).

4.4 Access #4 canyon joins on the left (east).

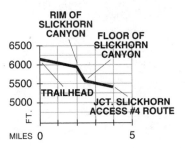

Finding the trailhead: Follow driving directions for Hike 5 and turn west onto a dirt road directly across Utah 261 from the

Cigarette Spring road, indicated by a BLM sign that advises "vehicle travel on existing roads only." After 0.4 mile you reach a gate (leave it open or closed, as you find it), a register, and an information signboard. The dirt road is usually graded but has a few rough and rocky stretches as you drive west to a prominent, though unsigned, junction 2.6 miles from Utah 261. (Hikers en route to the Government Trail, Hike 10, will turn right (west) here).

Bear left at the junction, and after 1.6 miles, turn right (southwest) onto an unsigned spur road. This narrow road, with a high center in places, requires that cars be driven carefully for the final 0.4 mile to the road end and unsigned trailhead.

Hikers searching for a campsite will find undeveloped sites at the trailhead, and along the road for about 1 mile east of the junction with the road leading to the Government Trail.

The hike: Slickhorn Canyon, a majestic gorge draining the western flanks of Cedar Mesa, is comparable to Grand Gulch in its landscape and attractions. An increasing number of hikers are discovering Slickhorn as an alternative destination to the more popular Grand Gulch. Yet access to Slickhorn Canyon is not easy, and since only experienced hikers can safely negotiate its many access routes, the canyon seldom seems overcrowded.

Some hikers push through Slickhorn Canyon to the San Juan River, while others combine Slickhorn and Grand Gulch to create an ambitious circuit, trekking along the river for 4.5 miles between the mouths of the two canyons. Most hikers, however, establish a base camp in the upper reaches of Slickhorn, where there are many fine campsites and more reliable water sources, and then pass several days exploring hidden Anasazi ruins and rock art sites, or simply soaking up the beauty of the canyon. Remember, regulations prohibit you from bringing dogs into Slickhorn Canyon.

Slickhorn Canyon's Access #1 traces the drainage from its headwaters draw into the canyon proper, where seasonal intermittent flows of water and wooded benches offer inviting sites for an overnight stay. Access #1 is definitely not a route for novice canyoneers, even though the route is deceptively gentle for the first 1.7 miles. Be prepared for routefinding, steep slickrock friction pitches, occasional exposure to sheer, sometimes overhanging cliffs, and boulder-hopping along this mostly trailless route.

From the trailhead at the road's end, begin the hike by following the wash southwest down the headwaters draw of Slickhorn Canyon. Thickets of tamarisk and rabbitbrush fringe the wash, but trails have been forged through the tangle by the cows that seasonally graze here on the mesa top. After several minutes of walking, the wash opens up, and stretches of slickrock and sand afford trouble-free travel.

The draw gradually develops into a more pronounced drainage as you proceed, and at times Cedar Mesa Sandstone bounds the wash with 20-foot walls. In other places the sandstone recedes, replaced by slopes mantled in pinyon-juniper woodland. After walking 0.7 mile, a 4-foot pouroff blocks the wash, with a left-side passage offering the easiest bypass. Just below

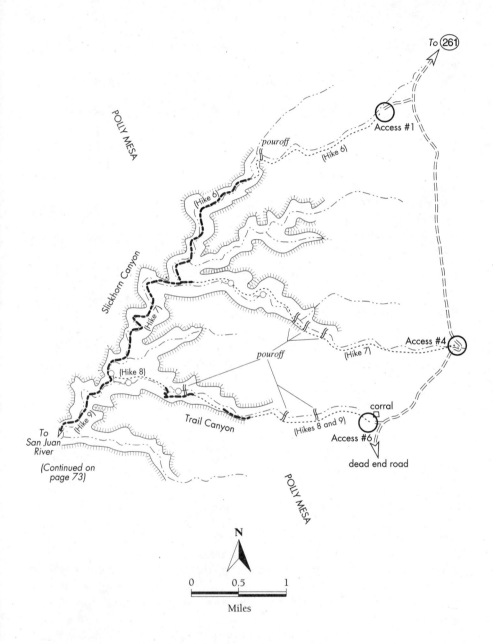

POLLY MESA

To (261)

Access #1

pouroff

(Hike 6)

(Hike 6)

Slickhorn Canyon

(Hike 7)

pouroff

Access #4

(Hike 7)

(Hike 8)

Trail Canyon

(Hikes 8 and 9)

corral

Access #6

(Hike 9)

To
San Juan
River

(Continued on
page 73)

dead end road

POLLY MESA

N

0   0.5   1

Miles

Slickhorn Canyon.

that obstacle a side canyon enters on the left and Slickhorn Canyon begins to deepen.

The following mile is a delightful hike down the gradually deeper canyon. Although along the way there are small ledges, pouroffs, and the occasional boulder, it is seldom necessary to break stride to avoid these minor obstacles.

The shallow canyon ends at 5,880 feet after 1.7 miles, at a major pouroff where a side canyon enters on the right (north). An angular arch can be seen at certain times of the day at the head of that side drainage. Far below you Slickhorn finally attains true canyon proportions, where bulging walls of Cedar Mesa slickrock reach 300 to 400 feet skyward from the depths of the gorge.

The route around the pouroff is not obvious, and it is evident that some hikers spend considerable time trying to find the way. The route begins as a path that rises to the left (south) of the wash several yards above the pouroff. This path quickly leads to a pair of 8- to 10-foot slickrock friction pitches, the second of which may require hauling packs up with a rope. A few cairns may show the way over the slickrock to a prominent ledge above.

After gaining the ledge, follow it south along the rim of an overhanging cliff band, now far above Slickhorn Canyon. The ledge soon bends into a minor bay, or amphitheater, where the domed crest of distant Navajo Mountain is in view. As you begin to curve southwest out of the bay, look closely for easy-to-miss cairns and segments of faint trail indicating the descent into Slickhorn, about 0.3 mile from the pouroff.

The descent route drops into the canyon abruptly, descending 250 feet via ledges and steep slickrock in 0.25 mile. Watch for cairns and trail segments between the bands of slickrock to stay on course, since the route often turns in unexpected directions. In some places, less experienced hikers may feel more comfortable roping down packs. After traversing the first two major ledges, the cairned route then contours south in search of a break in the next cliff band. The descent off this ledge is not readily apparent. Once again, misguided hikers have forged a path that continues along the ledge, which pinches out ahead upon very steep slopes.

Look for cairns to indicate the point of descent. Farther along, there are more cairns to guide you, though some routefinding may be necessary. The route switches back and forth, steeply descending a series of ledges, to finally reach the dry, boulder-strewn floor of Slickhorn Canyon. Turn left and proceed down-canyon via a rock- and boulder-hopping route along the wash. Soon traces of a path appear, and before long a well-beaten trail affords easy passage.

The wash is quite narrow, with pinyon and juniper trees fringing its banks. As you travel farther into the canyon, you find areas of riparian growth, including cottonwood and willow trees. You may find intermittent flows of water in wet seasons, particularly in spring. Soon the trail begins following wooded benches between wash crossings. The benches support a well-developed microbiotic soil crust, and hikers are urged to stick to the trail to avoid crushing this delicate, soil-stabilizing crust.

Great bulging walls of Cedar Mesa Sandstone, colored in shades of red, white, and buff, embrace the canyon. Deep alcoves and amphitheaters, which appear to have been scooped out of the cliffs, as well as sculpted knobs and towers on the rims, add to the stark beauty of the canyon landscape.

After following several bends of the sinuous canyon, a huge balanced rock appears high on the west wall, 3.75 miles from the trailhead. Opposite that landmark, a major side canyon opens up on the left (east). That canyon is the route of Slickhorn Access #2. This route is not described in this guide, but the BLM office in Monticello provides an information sheet on the access routes into Slickhorn canyon—see Appendix A.

At the mouth of that canyon are two well-used campsites. The first is a pleasant site set in a stand of pinyon and juniper trees, while the other, a sandy site located beneath an overhang, is unfortunately littered with charcoal from past campfires.

Below that confluence, intermittent water flows seasonally in the wash. Follow the willow-bordered wash ahead, crossing abundant slickrock for another 0.4 mile around the next bend in the canyon. Where the wash turns sharply to the right (west), another side canyon enters on the left (east) at 5,430 feet. That canyon is the route of Slickhorn Access #4 (see Hike 7), and a well-worn trail leads into its drainage. A good but small campsite is located several yards inside that canyon's mouth. To continue farther down Slickhorn Canyon, see Hikes 7-9.

*(According to a BLM handout available at the Monticello office, there are six accesses in Slickhorn Canyon. Access numbers 1, 4, and 6 are

covered in this guide. Here, the term "access" can mean both a trailhead and a canyon route.)

7 Slickhorn Canyon, Access #4

See Map on Page 60

General description:	A challenging day hike or backpack into a remote Cedar Mesa canyon.
Distance:	11.8 miles round trip.
Difficulty:	Moderately strenuous, occasional Class 2 and 3 scrambling.
Trail conditions:	Wash route and slickrock route, cairned only on pouroff bypasses; considerable routefinding required.
Trailhead access:	4WD required when wet or if floods have damaged the road.
Average hiking time:	7 to 8 hours round trip.
Trailhead elevation:	6,200 feet.
Low point:	5,230 feet.
Elevation gain and loss:	970 feet.
Optimum season:	April through mid-June; September through October.
Water availability:	Seasonal springs at 2.6 and 3.1 miles; seasonal intermittent flows in Slickhorn Canyon.
Hazards:	Exposure to steep dropoffs, steep slickrock friction pitches, flash-flood danger.
Permits:	Reservations and permits required for overnight use beginning spring 1999. Contact Monticello BLM office for information.
Topo maps:	Cedar Mesa South, Slickhorn Canyon East USGS quads; Trails Illustrated Grand Gulch Plateau.

Key points:
1.6   First major pouroff.
3.8   Confluence with Slickhorn Canyon; turn left, down-canyon.
5.5   Access #5 canyon joins on the left (east).
5.9   Access #6 canyon (Trail Canyon) joins on the left (east).

Finding the trailhead: Follow driving directions for Hike 6 to the junction with the spur road leading to Access #1, 4.2 miles from Utah 261. Drive south along the main road for another 2.75 miles. There, near the bottom of a rocky downgrade into a draw, a spur road branches right, leading several yards to a parking area and undeveloped campsite. Either park there or in a turnout on the left side of the road, 0.1 mile beyond the spur.

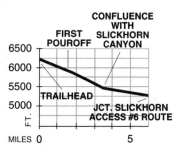

63

The hike: Slickhorn Canyon, Access #4 is the most challenging route into the canyon outlined in this book. Seasoned canyoneers will find the route to be fun and interesting, while inexperienced canyon country hikers will find it arduous and very difficult. Don't attempt this route without prior off-trail canyon hiking experience. Expect slow going and considerable routefinding and scrambling to be necessary along the way.

The route follows a major Slickhorn Canyon tributary into the upper reaches of the canyon, where backpackers will find ample campsites, seasonal flowing water, and numerous Anasazi ruins and rock art sites to explore. Remember, regulations prohibit you from bringing dogs into Slickhorn Canyon.

From the trailhead, drop down to the slickrock on the floor of Access #4 canyon and proceed west, almost immediately passing an old steel water trough adjacent to a seeping piped spring. The floor of the wash is dominated by slickrock, and you descend gradually westward via a natural stairway of low ledges and sandstone ramps. Pinyon and juniper fringe the wash and cloak the slopes above, while white Cedar Mesa slickrock rims the drainage. The draw gradually grows deeper but remains quite shallow for some distance ahead, and at first the walking is easy and trouble free.

The canyon then begins a sinuous course, bending first left, followed by a more pronounced bend to the right. A boot-worn trail across the wooded benches helps to shortcut the meanders. After shortcutting the second bend via a bench trail, you reach the first of several pouroffs in the canyon at 1.6 miles and 5,920 feet. Below, the much deeper, boulder-choked canyon comes into view.

Although hikers have created multiple trails here while searching for a bypass route, you will find the correct route by staying left and following the rim of the pouroff for several yards to a break in the cliff. Don't expect to find cairns here to show the way. A brief rock-hop and a short trail segment get you down through the break and back into the wash below the pouroff.

The canyon ahead, now about 250 feet deep, drops steeply away, and the route, which will be of your own choosing, will likely involve descending around and climbing over large boulders and dropping down steep ramps of slickrock. Travel through this part of the canyon is challenging, so expect your progress to be slow. The way requires constant routefinding, and you will encounter several minor pouroffs to bypass en route.

Eventually, after 2 miles, a major side canyon enters on the right (northeast) at 5,680 feet. Navigation ahead becomes a little less demanding and your focus can now turn from routefinding to absorbing the stark beauty of the 350-foot-deep canyon. Bulging walls of red- and tan-banded Cedar Mesa Sandstone occasionally loom overhead, interrupted by narrow ledges and decorated with a brown patina and streaks of black desert varnish. Balanced rocks, alcoves, and prominent overhangs abound.

A short distance below the confluence you encounter one final pouroff, with a cliff-hanging bypass route on the left side. The boulder-strewn sections of the wash provide the occassional routefinding challenge. After 2.6 miles, two prominent bays, or shallow amphitheaters, open up on the north wall of the canyon. There are good campsites at the mouth of the second bay, a few yards north of the trail. The boot-worn trail ahead follows benches beyond the bays, but you soon bushwhack your way back into the wash, where you will find a seasonal spring issuing from the sandy wash beneath a grove of Fremont cottonwoods.

At 3.2 miles a precipitous draw joins on the right, bounded by a broad amphitheater at its head. Just beyond that draw the trail follows a damp bench supporting a rich growth of horsetail and common reed grass. A dense ribbon of willow and cottonwood in the wash below suggests a reliable water supply. Soon you emerge from the riparian tangle, slickrock once again cropping out on the floor of the wash, and the trail becomes more distinct as you follow minor ledges for the final 0.5 mile to the confluence with Slickhorn Canyon.

Slickhorn comes as a surprise, opening up on the right, yet the canyon ahead seems a continuation of the access canyon, heading in the same direction. A good campsite can be found beneath a large, spreading juniper a few yards short of the confluence.

Sculpted Cedar Mesa Sandstone adds to the beauty of Slickhorn Canyon.

From the confluence, a scenic stretch of Slickhorn Canyon leads 2.1 miles down-canyon to Trail Canyon. A well-worn trail begins in Slickhorn opposite the mouth of Access #4 canyon, leading to the bench above and west of the confluence. The trail ahead crosses the wash many times, following benches between crossings that are dominated by exotic cheatgrass, a sure sign that past overgrazing has disturbed the habitat of native bunchgrasses.

The canyon-bottom benches support pinyon, juniper, Gambel oak, squawbush, four-wing saltbush, and rabbitbrush; the wash below hosts a riparian zone where willow and cottonwood thrive; and the banks are mantled with a dark green carpet of wiregrass. Yet only seasonal, intermittent water flows in the wash. Great alcoves, overhanging and undercut cliffs, mushroom-shaped hoodoos, all composed of Cedar Mesa Sandstone, characterize this sinuous portion of Slickhorn Canyon.

After following the course of Slickhorn for 1.7 miles, you reach the mouth of a major side canyon (the route of Access #5) entering on the left (east). Follow Slickhorn Canyon ahead around one more horseshoe bend, where large spreading cottonwoods appear, nurtured by a seep in the wash. A seasonal flow of water emerges a short distance beyond.

A ribbon of cottonwood and willow trees accompanies you down to the mouth of Trail Canyon (the route of Access #6—see Hike 8), which opens up on the left (east), 5.9 miles from the trailhead, at 5,230 feet. A sandy campsite is located beneath the cottonwoods at the mouth of Trail Canyon, and seepage up-canyon provides a seasonal water source.

An attractive, and shorter, alternative to retracing your route to the trailhead follows Trail Canyon (see Hike 8) for 3.4 miles to the Access #6 trailhead, then traces the dirt road 1.5 miles back to your trailhead, forming a rewarding loop of 11.8 miles.

8 Slickhorn Canyon, Access #6, Trail Canyon

See Map on Page 60

General description: A challenging day hike or backpack leading into a remote Cedar Mesa canyon.

Distance: 6.8 miles round trip.

Difficulty: Moderately strenuous, occasional Class 2 and 3 scrambling.

Trail conditions: Wash route and slickrock route, cairned only on pouroff bypasses; considerable routefinding required.

Trailhead access: 4WD required when wet or if floods have damaged the road; high-clearance vehicles recommended.

Average hiking time: 4 to 5 hours round trip.
Trailhead elevation: 6,190 feet.
Low point: 5,230 feet.
Elevation gain and loss: 960 feet.
Optimum season: April through mid-June; September through October.
Water availability: Perennial spring at 3.1 miles; seasonal springs at 3.4 miles and at confluence with Slickhorn Canyon. Day hikers should bring their own.
Hazards: Exposure to steep dropoffs, steep slickrock friction pitches, flash-flood danger.
Permits: Reservations for permits required for overnight use beginning spring 1999. Contact Monticello BLM office for information.
Topo maps: Slickhorn Canyon East USGS quad; Trails Illustrated Grand Gulch Plateau.

Key points:
  0.6   First pouroff.
  1.2   Second pouroff.
  1.8   Boulder-choked segment of the canyon; bypass on the left (south) side.
  2.4   Third pouroff above narrows; bypass on the left (south) side.
  3.4   Confluence with Slickhorn Canyon.

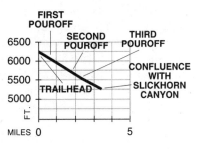

Finding the trailhead: Follow driving directions for Hikes 6 and 7 to Access #4 Trailhead, beyond which you follow the road as it bends sharply to the right, drops steeply to cross the bumpy slickrock of a wash, then ascends back into the pinyon-juniper woodland.

After driving 0.9 mile from Access #4, the road enters an area where the woodland has been "chained" and burned, and soon thereafter a corral comes into view. Turn right (southwest) after 1.3 miles (8.3 miles from Utah 261) onto the spur road leading to the corral. Park near the corral or at the end of the 0.2-mile-long spur. Hikers searching for a campsite have several undeveloped sites to choose from en route to the trailhead.

The hike: Slickhorn Canyon's Access #6 follows a prominent tributary locally known as Trail Canyon. Don't be deceived by the canyon's name, however, since only two short segments of constructed trail exist in the canyon. Much of the route involves following slickrock in the wash, boulder-hopping, and bypassing pouroffs and boulder jams while engaging in continuous routefinding. Slightly less challenging than Access #4, yet more demanding than Access #1, Trail Canyon is a scenic route that experienced canyon-country hikers will enjoy while en route to Slickhorn Canyon. Remember, regulations prohibit you from bringing dogs into Slickhorn Canyon.

From the corral at the trailhead, follow the doubletrack of the spur road west for 300 yards to its end, and continue west. Just beyond the road's end, an arroyo begins. If you stay on the mesa top above the arroyo, you will soon find cattle trails that traverse above the shallow, natural ditch of the arroyo. Other arroyos join on the right and left as you continue, and you must briefly dip into their drainages from time to time.

Fine views reach from the mesa past the Red House Cliffs to distant Navajo Mountain, framed by the trees of the pinyon-juniper woodland that flanks the gradually developing draw. After a ten-minute walk from the trailhead, Cedar Mesa Sandstone appears, paving the floor of the wash with slickrock. As the wash begins downcutting through the sandstone, you reach the first of a series of pouroffs blocking the wash. The cattle that graze on the mesa top can go no farther, but hikers can bypass the low pouroff on the left (south) side, descending via a series of small ledges into the slickrock wash below.

The canyon gradually deepens as you follow the occasionally rock-strewn wash ahead. After 1.2 miles you reach a second, higher pouroff at 5,920 feet. Bypass this obstacle on the left, following a boot-worn trail along the ledge. Although some hikers elect to drop back into the wash via a Class 3 to 4 downclimb of a 12-foot cliff band, there is an easier way. Instead of dropping off the cliff too soon, continue following the path along the ledge for about 200 yards beyond the pouroff, and you will reach a break in the cliff band that affords an easier rock-hopping descent into the wash below.

Around the next bend of the canyon, after 1.5 miles, you begin to skirt a chain of slickrock waterpockets scooped out of the wash. These natural tanks will likely be filled with water following a wet spring or active summer monsoon, and if so they will be brimming with the tadpoles of the red-spotted toad. In autumn, young emergent toads will be abundant, so step carefully.

Soon the canyon floor becomes choked with huge boulders and drops steeply away. Another pouroff in this precipitous gorge demands that hikers seek out a bypass route. There is a segment of constructed trail that avoids the rocky morass via the south slopes of the canyon, but its beginning is not obvious. At the head of the boulder jam, look for a severely eroded path resembling a runoff gully that ascends the slope on the left (south) side of the wash. This path ascends on the right-hand side of a large boulder resting on the slope. After climbing up the trail/gully for several yards the way becomes more obvious, traversing the canyon's south wall ahead. Views from the elevated position of the old trail stretch down the dramatic gorge of the 400-foot deep canyon, flanked by bulging walls of red- and white-banded Cedar Mesa Sandstone. The rims are crowned by intricately eroded hoodoos and balanced mushroom rocks.

After skirting the boulder jam the rocky trail descends steadily back to the wash, and soon thereafter the first large amphitheater opens up on the right (northeast), about 1.5 hours from the trailhead. About twenty minutes beyond the amphitheater, at 2.4 miles, another narrow side drainage enters on the right. At that confluence, begin looking for a path on the left (south) side of the wash, which you must locate to bypass the final large pouroff.

That path follows ledges above the pouroff and the narrow gorge below it. After skirting the rim of the gorge for several hundred yards, the trail descends to the wash via a series of four constructed switchbacks. Cottonwoods crowd the confines of the gorge up-canyon, nurtured by the waters of a perennial spring—your best source of water in dry seasons.

The walking ahead is slow and arduous as you pick your way among loose rocks and around boulders for another 0.8 mile to the confluence with Slickhorn Canyon. The fine sandy campsite at the confluence, in the shade of large, spreading cottonwoods, is a good choice for an overnight stay or as a base camp. A spring emerges in Trail Canyon a few hundred yards above the confluence, and a seasonal spring in Slickhorn Canyon can be found a short distance above. See Hikes 6 and 7 for details on upper Slickhorn Canyon. If you wish to explore down-canyon, see Hike 9.

Hikers may find Anasazi ruins en route to Slickhorn Canyon.

9 Slickhorn Canyon, Access #6 to the San Juan River

General description:	A challenging backpack in a remote Cedar Mesa canyon, recommended for experienced canyoneers only.
Distance:	19.2 miles round trip.
Difficulty:	Moderately strenuous, occasional Class 2 and 3 scrambling.
Trail conditions:	Slickrock route and wash route; considerable routefinding required.
Trailhead access:	4WD required when wet or if floods have damaged the road; high clearance vehicles recommended.
Average hiking time:	3 to 4 days.
Trailhead elevation:	6,190 feet.
Low point:	3,750 feet at the San Juan River.
Elevation gain and loss:	2,440 feet.
Optimum season:	April through early June; September through October.
Water availability:	Perennial springs at 3.1 and 7.6 miles; seasonal springs at 3.4 miles, and in lower Slickhorn Canyon; seasonal intermittent flows in Slickhorn Canyon.
Hazards:	Exposure to steep dropoffs, steep slickrock friction pitches, considerable boulder-hopping and scrambling.
Permits:	Reservations for permits required for overnight use beginning spring 1999. Contact Monticello BLM office for information.
Topo maps:	Slickhorn Canyon East, Slickhorn Canyon West USGS quads; Trails Illustrated Grand Gulch Plateau.

Key points:

1.6   Boulder-choked segment of the canyon; bypass on the left (south) side.

2.4   Third pouroff above narrows; bypass on the left (south) side.

3.4   Confluence with Slickhorn Canyon; bear left, down-canyon.

7.6   Last perennial spring.

9.6   San Juan River.

Finding the trailhead: Follow driving directions for Hike 8.

The hike: This demanding trip offers direct access to a wild stretch of the San Juan River at Slickhorn Rapids, not far above the river's impoundment in Lake Powell.

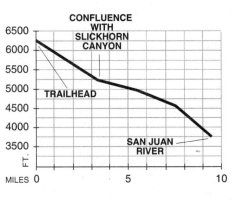

70

Slickhorn Canyon, below its confluence with Trail Canyon (see Hike 8), is a mostly trailless, boulder-choked gorge for 6.2 miles to the river. Yet the trip is far more demanding than its modest distance would suggest. Expect two days of arduous routefinding through boulder jams to reach the river. Unfortunately for backpackers, the mouth of Slickhorn Canyon (and Grand Gulch) are closed to camping within 1 mile of the river to reduce conflicts with river float parties. The rocky beach at Slickhorn Canyon is one of the few campsites available for float trips in the 1,000-foot-deep river gorge.

Allow at least three to four days to complete this trip, which is best suited to early spring or late autumn due to the low elevations and consequent high temperatures in the lower canyon. The spring months offer greater flexibility, since water sources at that time will likely be numerous. Remember, regulations prohibit you from bringing dogs into Slickhorn Canyon.

From the Access #6 Trailhead, follow Trail Canyon for 3.4 miles down to its confluence with Slickhorn Canyon (see Hike 8), then turn left and begin the slow, arduous journey down-canyon. The route ahead is of your own choosing, since there are few traces of boot-worn trails, mostly just the footprints of other hikers. You must forge a way through thickets of willow and tamarisk, and scramble over and around boulders and other obstacles. Lower Slickhorn Canyon features a steeper gradient than most other Cedar Mesa canyons; thus runoff and flash floods are more active in downcutting and rearranging the rocky canyon floor with each passing flood.

Although the going is slow and sometimes difficult, take time en route to appreciate the raw beauty of this rugged, wild canyon. Alternating red and white beds of Cedar Mesa Sandstone rise in a series of overhangs for 500 feet to the canyon rims, where hoodoos and mushroom rocks punctuate the skyline. Sheer cliffs streaked with desert varnish, numerous arch-shaped fractures, and deep alcoves at the bends of the serpentine canyon add to the attraction.

The first side canyon enters on the left (east) after 1.1 miles. Opposite that canyon's mouth, look for a trail that follows the western bench of Slickhorn Canyon, passing a small campsite set among a grove of junipers, one of few campsites in the lower canyon. Slickhorn opens up below that side canyon, and hikers have forged trails ahead that afford easier passage down-canyon. These pathways traverse benches above the wash, yet segments of wash walking persist, with frequent boulder-hopping necessary.

About 1.6 miles below Trail Canyon, you enter an area rich with the growth of common reed grass and other riparian foliage, watered by a seasonal spring. In contrast to the streamside greenery, the dry benches above host a woodland of pinyon pines, junipers, and groves of Gambel oak trees, yet there are no established campsites, or even potential places to camp.

At a point about 2.25 miles below Trail Canyon, huge boulders, some as large as a house, litter the slopes above and create a formidable boulder jam in the wash. When you first reach this major obstacle, stay to the right of the

Slickhorn Canyon is one of many dramatic gorges slicing into Cedar Mesa.

Bullet Canyon Trailhead to Collins Spring Trailhead

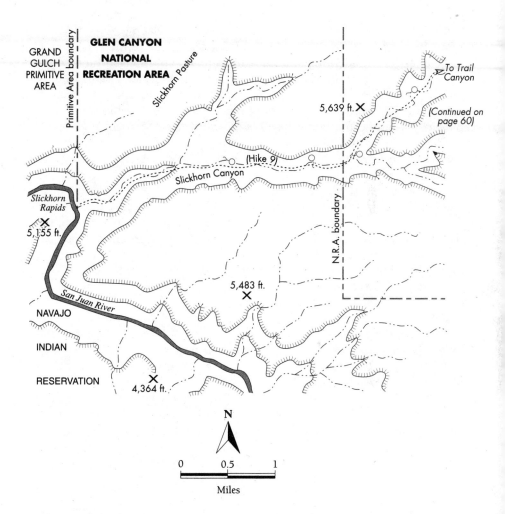

GRAND GULCH PRIMITIVE AREA

Primitive Area boundary

GLEN CANYON NATIONAL RECREATION AREA

Slickhorn Pasture

5,639 ft. ✕

To Trail Canyon

(Continued on page 60)

(Hike 9)

Slickhorn Canyon

N.R.A. boundary

Slickhorn Rapids

✕ 5,155 ft.

5,483 ft. ✕

San Juan River

NAVAJO

INDIAN

RESERVATION

✕ 4,364 ft.

N

0   0.5   1

Miles

wash, then pick your way through the rocky morass, hugging the right (northwest) side of the wash as you approach the second prominent east-trending side canyon.

Immediately north of the mouth of that side canyon, above the east side of the wash, you'll notice verdant growth surrounding a seasonal spring. After you reach the mouth of that canyon, 2.8 miles and perhaps 2.5 hours from Trail Canyon, Slickhorn describes a prominent bend to the west. Its walls open up and reveal a broad and increasingly deep gorge ahead.

At the bend, look for a path on the left (south) side of the wash, which leads a few hundred yards to a fair campsite, one of the last, then continues down-canyon. Soon, the reddish brown siltstones and sandstones of the Halgaito Formation surface in the canyon bottom, forming low pouroffs separated by numerous plunge pools. Boulders continue to block the wash, but the 0.5-mile trail segment avoids most of the canyon's obstacles.

The trail returns to the wash opposite a vigorous spring. Slickhorn Canyon, its wash now cutting through the softer Halgaito beds, drops steadily westward, and your route continues to be a combination of boulder-hopping and following short segments of boot-worn paths. The last reliable spring emerges in the wash 7.6 miles from the trailhead, providing a year-round flow that maintains an intermittent stream for the remaining 2 miles to the San Juan River. At 5.7 miles from Trail Canyon, a prominent side canyon opens up to the north, 1.4 miles from the river. A broad bench above (northeast) this confluence offers the last place to camp in the canyon, and from its platform fine views reach down between the 800- to 1,000-foot cliffs to the canyon of the San Juan River.

For the final 1.4 miles to the river, Slickhorn becomes an increasingly deep gorge, dropping 500 feet en route to the confluence. Thinly bedded limestones and sandstones of the Honaker Trail Formation flank the wash, forming slopes, cliff bands, and ledges, while the convoluted walls of Cedar Mesa Sandstone now rest far above.

At length you emerge from Slickhorn Canyon at the boulder-littered beach alongside the foaming waves of Slickhorn Rapids, deep in the canyon of the San Juan River, a narrow gorge ranging from 1,000 to 1,200 feet deep. Cedar Mesa slickrock caps the rims of this dramatic canyon, resting atop the ledgy red slopes the San Juan is famous for. You'll likely meet a river party here, as the beach is a popular stopover on San Juan River trips.

About 150 feet above the left (southeast) side of the mouth of Slickhorn are the scattered relics of an old oil drilling operation, including the remains of a wagon, pulleys, and cables. The old drill hole site also provides a fine view of the brown waters of the river below.

Allow about 2 days of hiking time to retrace your route to the trailhead.

10 Government Trail to Grand Gulch

General description:	An excellent, well-defined trail into lower Grand Gulch in the Grand Gulch Primitive Area, suitable as a day hike or as part of an extended backpack.
Distance:	3.2 miles one way.
Difficulty:	Moderately easy.
Trail conditions:	Closed road to the rim of Grand Gulch, constructed trail into the canyon bottom.
Trailhead access:	4WD required when wet.
Average hiking time:	1.5 hours one way.
Trailhead elevation:	5,650 feet.
Low point:	4,880 feet.
Elevation loss:	770 feet.
Optimum season:	April through early June; September through October.
Water availability:	Seasonal intermittent flows in Grand Gulch; seasonal Pollys Spring emerges from inside Pollys Canyon, 0.2 mile north (up-canyon) of the foot of the trail; bring your own water.
Hazards:	Flash-flood danger in Grand Gulch.
Permits:	Required for overnight trips; pay fee and obtain permit at the trailhead. Reservations for permits required beginning spring 1999. Contact Monticello BLM office for information.
Topo maps:	Pollys Pasture USGS quad; Trails Illustrated Grand Gulch Plateau.

Key points:

2.7   Rim of Grand Gulch, beginning of Government Trail.
3.2   Floor of Grand Gulch.

Finding the trailhead: Follow driving directions for Hike 6 to the prominent unsigned junction 2.6 miles west of Utah 261, then turn right (west). The good graded road leads west across the mesa, offering splendid views of the Red House Cliffs, Tables of the Sun, Navajo Mountain, and the distant Kaiparowits Plateau.

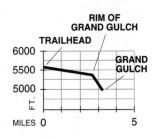

You reach a signed junction after 3 miles (5.6 miles from Utah 261), where you bear right onto graded San Juan County 245. Follow this road for 1.9 miles, then turn right (west) onto a narrow spur road signed for Government Trail. This poor road has high centers in places, but remains passable to cars for 0.5 to 0.6 mile. If you have a low-clearance, 2WD car, park in one of the wide spots on the slickrock at that point and walk the remaining distance to the trailhead. If you are in a high-clearance, 4WD vehicle, continue down the very rough and rocky road for the final 0.6 mile to the signed trailhead, 1.2 miles from San Juan County 245, next to a willow-fringed stock pond. Hikers searching for a campsite have innumerable undeveloped sites to choose from en route to the trailhead.

The hike: Constructed by the BLM in the 1970s, the Government Trail is the second shortest and easiest access into Grand Gulch. The way follows a long-closed road over the shrub-dotted expanse of Pollys Pasture, near the southwestern edge of the Cedar Mesa/Polly Mesa tableland, then descends 300 feet via a well-constructed trail into the middle reaches of Grand Gulch.

The hike is a rewarding day trip, but is most frequently used by backpackers as part of an extended trip in Grand Gulch. Although seasonal water sources are likely to be found in the gulch, day hikers and backpackers alike are advised to pack in an ample water supply.

At the end of the road, adjacent to the stock pond, you find an information signboard displaying maps, backcountry regulations, and abundant tips on leaving no trace. Overnight hikers must fill out a permit from the trailhead register and deposit the appropriate fee ($5 per person) into the fee collection tube. (Reservations for permits will be required beginning Spring 1999. Contact Monticello BLM office for information.)

Ample signs indicate the trail, which begins by crossing the dam of the willow-fringed pond. Just beyond, you curve left and skirt the bed of an abandoned Studebaker pickup. The first 2.7 miles of the way follows the doubletrack of a long-closed road, and signs at the trailhead ask hikers to walk in the left track only, but unfortunately few hikers do. As long as hikers keep walking in both tracks, the old road will remain a lasting, well-defined scar on the mesa.

Grand Gulch from the Government Trail.

Vistas from the open mesa are far-ranging and panoramic. The brick-red Bears Ears and Woodenshoe Buttes rise on the far northern horizon, defining the southern rim of lofty Elk Ridge. Moss Back Butte and the Tables of the Sun anchor the northern end of the Red House Cliffs to the northwest. The cliffs of Red Canyon, a prominent gap in the Red House Cliffs, frame a fine view of distant Mounts Holmes, Hillers, and Pennell in the Henry Mountains. And to the southwest, the sweeping ocher faces of the Red House Cliffs point to the dome of Navajo Mountain, over 50 miles distant.

The gently contoured platform of Pollys Pasture is covered in a veneer of red soil, with only widely scattered outcrops of Cedar Mesa Sandstone punctuating the mesa. A few pinyons and junipers dot the mesa, which is dominated by a groundcover of blackbrush.

Punctuating the mesa top in the distance are broad exposures of white Cedar Mesa Sandstone, yet there is little indication of a canyon lying across your path. Except for the slickrock ahead, the mesa seemingly stretches uninterrupted to the foot of the Red House Cliffs.

Midway to the rim of Grand Gulch, the road briefly disappears as you mount slickrock, where cairns point the way to the resumption of the doubletrack ahead. Soon, overhanging cliffs come into view at the rim of Grand Gulch in the southwest, and Pollys Canyon to the north. After 2.7 miles of road walking, you reach the slickrock rim of Grand Gulch at 5,370 feet, where a large BLM sign proclaims Government Trail, Grand Gulch Primitive Area.

Grand Gulch opens up before you, a 300-foot deep gorge embraced by sweeping walls of cross-bedded Cedar Mesa slickrock. Across the narrow gulf of the gulch rises the erosion-isolated butte of Pollys Island, cut off from the opposite rim by an abandoned meander of the Grand Gulch stream course.

The well-defined, constructed trail descends a moderate grade below the rim via switchbacks. In some places the trail is rocky, and in other places the trail has been carved into the bulging slickrock. Six switchbacks lead down to the brow of a pouroff, where the trail turns left (southwest) and begins a lengthy traverse. Soon, a series of short switchbacks lead steeply down to the floor of Grand Gulch. Once you reach the gulch you can roam at will (see Hike 15 for more information on middle Grand Gulch). There is a wealth of archaeological sites here, but the Anasazi sites notwithstanding, Grand Gulch is arguably one of the most beautiful desert canyons in the region.

After enjoying your visit to Grand Gulch, retrace your route to the trailhead.

Government Trail to Grand Gulch

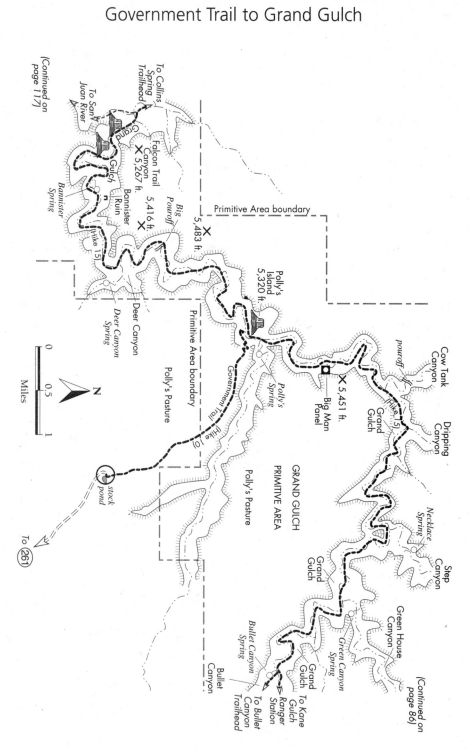

(Continued on page 117)

To Collins Spring Trailhead

To San Juan River

Grand Gulch

Falcon Trail
X 5,267 ft.

Canyon
5,416 ft.
X

Bannister Spring

Bannister Ruin

(Hike 15)

Big Pouroff

Primitive Area boundary

X
5,483 ft.

Deer Canyon Spring

Deer Canyon

Polly's Island
5,320 ft.

Primitive Area boundary

Polly's Pasture

Government Trail

(Hike 10)

Polly's Spring

To Collins
Spring
Trailhead

pouroff

Cow Tank Canyon

5,451 ft.
X
Big Man Panel

(Hike 5)

Grand Gulch

Dripping Canyon

Polly's Pasture

GRAND GULCH PRIMITIVE AREA

Grand Gulch

Necklace Spring

Step Canyon

0
0.5
1

Miles

N

stock pond

To 261

Green Canyon

Green House Canyon

(Continued on page 86)

Bullet Canyon Spring

Bullet Canyon

Grand Gulch

To Kane Gulch Ranger Station

To Bullet Canyon Trailhead

11 Todie Canyon to Grand Gulch

General description: A short but challenging route, recommended for experienced canyoneers only, that leads into the upper reaches of Grand Gulch. Suitable as a day hike, or part of an extended trip.

Distance: 2.1 miles one way.

Difficulty: Moderately strenuous, one short Class 3 downclimb below the canyon rim. Occasional Class 2 scrambling.

Trail conditions: Boot-worn trails, slickrock, and wash routes; occasional route-finding required.

Trailhead access: 4WD required when wet; may also be needed if floods have damaged the road.

Average hiking time: 1.5 to 2 hours one way; 3 hours round trip.

Trailhead elevation: 6,400 feet.

Low point: 5,740 feet.

Elevation gain and loss: 660 feet.

Optimum season: April through mid-June; September through October.

Water availability: Perennial spring at 1.8 miles; seasonal intermittent flows in Grand Gulch.

Hazards: Exposure to steep dropoffs, steep slickrock friction pitches, flash-flood danger.

Permits: Required for overnight use; obtain permit and pay appropriate fee ($5 per person) at trailhead register. Reservations required for overnight use beginning spring 1999. Contact Monticello BLM office for information.

Topo maps: Cedar Mesa North USGS quad; Trails Illustrated Grand Gulch Plateau.

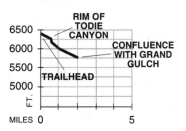

Key points:

0.6   Rim of Todie Canyon.
0.7   Floor of Todie Canyon.
1.8   Todie Spring.
2.1   Confluence with Grand Gulch.

Finding the trailhead: Turn south on Utah 261, 56 miles east of the Hite Marina turnoff on Utah 95 and 28.3 miles west of the junction of U.S. Highway 191 and Utah 95, 3 miles south of Blanding. Drive south on Utah 261 for 7.5 miles to an unsigned, westbound dirt road, located between mileposts 25 and 26. If you are driving from the south, the turnoff is 25.5 miles north of the junction of Utah 261 and U.S. Highway 163/191 between Mexican Hat and Bluff.

Follow this narrow dirt road through the tall sagebrush of Todie Flat for 1.2 miles to the road end at the signed Todie Canyon Trailhead. Hikers arriving late in the day will find undeveloped campsites along a southbound spur road immediately before reaching the trailhead.

The hike: Todie Canyon, a short, precipitous gorge, offers the shortest and most challenging route into upper Grand Gulch. Although most of the route is straightforward, a very steep scramble and slickrock friction descent off the rim adds excitement to the route. Backpackers are advised to carry a rope to lower packs off the rim.

The trail begins as a closed road behind the trailhead register and information signboard, leading west above the rim of Todie Canyon, narrowing to a single track after 175 yards. Views soon open up into the headwaters draw of Todie Canyon to the north, its gorge embraced by low walls of Cedar Mesa slickrock.

The nearly level trail passes through an open woodland of pinyon and juniper, with low mounds of sagebrush scattered across the trailside slopes between outcrops of sandstone. As in most areas of Cedar Mesa, the microbiotic soil crust is well developed, so hikers are advised to stick to the trail to preserve this delicate, soil-stabilizing crust.

Soon the trail ends and you mount slickrock, where ample cairns lead the way. Todie Canyon grows increasingly deep below you, and in the background your view stretches to the bold red tower of Moss Back Butte and the Tables of the Sun on the western skyline.

After 0.6 mile of strolling across the mesa, you reach the canyon rim at 6,340 feet, at the top of the 200-foot descent route into Todie Canyon. At first glance a descent here may not appear possible, yet there is a way down, albeit a route for experienced hikers only. Just below the rim you must negotiate a minor downclimb beneath the overhang of a boulder. Backpackers must rope down their packs through this tight passage.

The route below drops very steeply via a brushy, boulder-choked chute. Proceed with caution and always locate the next cairn before continuing. Several more minor downclimbs and some scrambling is necessary to reach the extremely steep trail in the Gambel oak grove below, which in turn leads you to *terra firma* on the floor of Todie Canyon, where you turn left, down-canyon. The usually dry wash ahead is a jumble of huge boulders, and the arduous route that follows is a matter of scrambling, occasional short downclimbs, and rock-hopping, involving considerable time and effort to find a passable way through the rocky maze.

Yet you will be compensated for your labors by the raw beauty of the canyon, a gorge enclosed by bold, desert-varnished sandstone walls looming 300 feet overhead. After passing the first side canyon on the right, at 6,020 feet and 0.9 mile from the trailhead, Todie Canyon becomes somewhat friendlier ahead, though occasional rock-hopping and routefinding is still necessary. As you continue down-canyon, the grass-fringed banks of the wash begin to host a scattering of small cottonwoods. Occasional willow thickets will further hamper steady progress.

When the first Anasazi ruins come into view high on the north canyon wall, begin looking for cairns that show a bypass route above the boulder-strewn

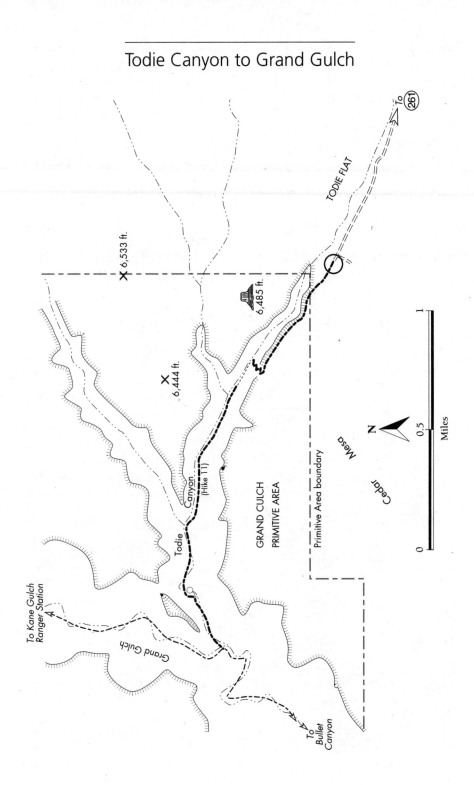

6,533 ft.

6,485 ft.

6,444 ft.

TODIE FLAT

To 261

Todie Canyon (Hike 11)

GRAND GULCH PRIMITIVE AREA

Primitive Area boundary

Cedar Mesa

N

Miles

0   0.5   1

To Kane Gulch Ranger Station

Grand Gulch

To Bullet Canyon

81

wash on the left (south) side. This bypass route ascends several yards above the wash, and soon returns. The going below that point is much gentler, and you will shortly begin following a well-worn trail that criss-crosses the wash. After 1.5 miles, a second, larger side canyon joins on the right, and beyond this confluence Todie Canyon opens up significantly. Bulging, cross-bedded cliffs of Cedar Mesa Sandstone now soar 500 feet to the rims above.

Vegetation is restricted to the canyon floor in this slickrock-dominated labyrinth. After 1.8 miles, more inaccessible ruins appear high on the north wall, and there the trail leads up to a broad bench on the left (south) side of the wash. Todie Spring emerges from the wash below the bench, supplying a reliable flow of water.

For the final 0.3 mile to the Grand Gulch confluence, you will pass numerous bench-top campsites, once shaded by stately, spreading cottonwoods that were, unfortunately, consumed during a May 1996 toilet paper fire. The hiker that started the blaze reported that it swept out of control almost immediately, and the fire charred the mouth of Todie Canyon, then spread nearly 1 mile up into Grand Gulch before it was contained by BLM fire crews. The lesson here is: burning toilet paper in a tinder-dry desert environment can, and often does, lead to disaster. Pack it out in a zipper-lock plastic bag instead.

The trail soon crosses the wash, skirts a slickrock shelf, and then emerges into the slightly deeper, and wider canyon of Grand Gulch. To continue up or down the gulch, see Hike 14.

Moss Back Butte looms above the western edge of Cedar Mesa in this view from the rim of Todie Canyon.

12 Bullet Canyon to Grand Gulch

General description:	A rewarding canyon route, recommended for experienced hikers only, that is suitable as an all-day hike or as one leg of an extended backpack trip.
Distance:	7.2 miles, one way.
Difficulty:	Moderately strenuous, steep Class 2 friction pitches.
Trail conditions:	Wash route, slickrock route, and occasional stretches of boot-worn trail.
Trailhead access:	4WD required when wet.
Average hiking time:	4.5 to 5 hours one way.
Trailhead elevation:	6,400 feet.
Low point:	5,160 feet.
Elevation gain and loss:	1,240 feet.
Optimum seasons:	April through mid-June; September throughOctober.
Water availability:	Perennial Jail House Spring at 5 miles; seasonal Bullet Canyon Spring at Grand Gulch confluence; seasonal intermittent flows in Grand Gulch.
Hazards:	Exposure to steep dropoffs, steep slickrock friction pitches, flash-flood danger.
Permits:	Required for overnight use; obtain permit and pay the appropriate fee ($5 per person) at the trailhead register. Reservations for overnight use will be required beginning spring 1999. Contact Monticello BLM office for information.
Topo maps:	Cedar Mesa North, Pollys Pasture USGS quads; Trails Illustrated Grand Gulch Plateau.

Key points:
- 0.2 Rim of Bullet Canyon.
- 1.4 Begin descending steep slickrock chutes.
- 4.5 Perfect Kiva Ruin.
- 4.8 Jail House Ruin.
- 5.0 Jail House Spring.
- 7.2 Confluence with Grand Gulch.

Finding the trailhead: Turn south on Utah 261, 56 miles east of the Hite Marina turnoff on Utah 95, and 28.3 miles west of the junction of U.S. Highway 191 and Utah 95, 3 miles south of Blanding. Drive south on Utah 261 for 7.1 miles to the signed Bullet Canyon Trailhead road, located between mileposts 21 and 22. On the way, you'll pass the Kane Gulch Ranger Station after 3.8 miles. If you are driving from the south, the Bullet Canyon turnoff is 21.6 miles north of the junction of Utah 261 and U.S. Highway 191/163 between Mexican Hat and Bluff.

Turn west onto the good, but winding and occasionally rocky dirt access road. You reach the signed trailhead and road end after 1.1 miles, where you may also camp.

The hike: Bullet Canyon is a popular access route into the heart of upper Grand Gulch, second only to the Kane Gulch route. This mostly trailless route follows Bullet Canyon, a major Grand Gulch tributary, for more than 7 miles as it evolves from a broad, shallow draw into a spectacular canyon, 500 to 600 feet deep. In

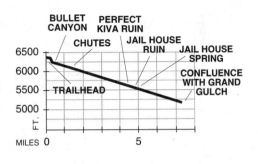

the canyon's lower reaches are several well-preserved Anasazi ruins, a large pictograph panel, a reliable spring, and many excellent campsites.

Although the canyon is most frequently used as an exit route from Grand Gulch by hikers beginning at Kane Gulch Ranger Station (see Hike 14), this trip also affords access to the middle reaches of the gulch (see Hike 15), and is suitable as a rewarding all-day hike. Some backpackers use the Bullet Canyon route to reach Grand Gulch and set up a base camp there, then spend several days searching out the innumerable Anasazi ruins and rock art sites. Keep in mind the regulations that restrict the use of campsites at Jail House Ruin and at the mouth of Bullet Canyon to two consecutive nights.

Bullet Canyon is a popular route, but it is not recommended for novices. Several steep slickrock descents in the upper reaches of the canyon are hazardous, even for experienced canyon country hikers.

The trail begins a westward course behind the trailhead register and information signboard at the road's end, following the rim of wide and shallow Bullet Canyon, its course cloaked in a woodland of pinyon and juniper. After 0.2 mile, cairns lead you on a short but steep zigzag descent over Cedar Mesa slickrock to the floor of the draw below. The route ahead follows the wash down-canyon, aided by segments of trail above the wash banks. The pinyon-juniper woodland in the upper reaches of the canyon casts small pockets of shade, offering some relief from the sun on a hot day.

Bullet Canyon gradually grows deeper for the first 1.4 miles, at which point the character of the canyon undergoes a rapid transformation. The trail skirts a low pouroff and a deep, seasonal pool, then cairns funnel you down a steep slickrock chute in the canyon bottom, which can be dangerously slippery when wet. Ledges in the chute aid the descent. Not far below the first chute lies another stretch of chutes and pouroffs. An exposed cairned route bypasses those barriers via the ledges on the right (north) side of the wash. When the ledges pinch out, you then negotiate a very steep slickrock friction descent to regain the wash. Here the canyon is much deeper, with bold Cedar Mesa Sandstone cliffs soaring 500 feet above.

The canyon is quite confined ahead, and the route is funneled along the rocky floor of the wash. Soon, boulder jams begin to form barricades across the wash, and a cairned route, with segments of boot-worn trail, bypasses the blockade via the north canyon wall, traversing slickrock ledges above the rock-strewn wash. This circuitous route eventually drops back into the wash beneath dramatic vaulting cliffs.

Soon after reentering the wash you pass a good, but small campsite alongside the usually dry wash, situated beneath a verdant canopy of willow and cottonwood. Several junipers and willows in the shady confines of the canyon here have attained unusually large proportions. The route ahead is typical of a southern Utah canyon, with considerable rock-hopping and routefinding among boulders, with few traces of actual trail.

This stretch persists for less than a mile, and then the canyon grows wider and wooded benches appear, flanking either side of the wash. After about 3 miles from the trailhead, you find a good trail leading back and forth across the wash between canyon-bottom benches. Great amphitheaters open up around every bend of the canyon beneath the scalloped outline of the rims, capped by intricately eroded hoodoos and mushroom rocks. This part of the canyon is delightful, offering premium scenery and numerous fine, but dry, campsites.

After 4.5 miles, the trail begins to shortcut a sharp bend in the wash, where a precipitous side canyon enters from the northeast. A deep alcove near the mouth of that drainage on the northwest wall harbors Perfect Kiva Ruin. Well worth the 0.3-mile round-trip detour up the rocky slope, Perfect Kiva deserves its name largely due to BLM stabilization efforts. Its roof has been replaced, and the ladder is obviously of recent origin, though most of the structure is original. Walk softly when you visit this ancient Anasazi ceremonial site.

After another bend in the canyon below Perfect Kiva Ruin, you pass beneath Jail House Ruin, a collection of interesting dwellings and three large, white, circular pictographs. A number of popular campsites lie nearby, where backpackers are restricted to staying no more than two consecutive nights. If you are day hiking, Jail House Ruin is the logical point to turn around and backtrack to the trailhead.

The canyon bends southwest beyond the ruin, and about 0.2 mile below, a reliable flow of water emerges at Jail House Spring, where tall cottonwoods form a shady canopy over the wash. The trail stays on the right-side bench below the ruin, dropping back into the wash after 0.25 mile. The ribbon of cottonwoods is soon supplanted by typical coarse, drought-tolerant desert shrubs after the wash dries up around the next bend.

The final 2 miles of hiking to Grand Gulch alternates between rocky stretches in the wash to bench-top trails, and avenues through abundant cheatgrass and spiny mounds of Russian thistle (tumbleweed). Dry stretches in the wash occasionally give way to riparian thickets and the inevitable bushwhacking that follows. Bullet Canyon attains its greatest depth here in its lower reaches, and the 700-foot canyon walls present a memorable scene of amphitheaters, towers, hoodoos, and bulging, desert-varnished cliffs.

Cottonwoods and willows begin to crowd the canyon bottom as you approach Grand Gulch, sharing space in the moist wash with box elder and tamarisk. This riparian ribbon becomes well-developed and jungle-like at the mouth of Bullet Canyon, where the trail passes a pair of excellent camp-

Bullet Canyon to Grand Gulch • Kane Gulch Ranger Station to Bullet Canyon Trailhead • Bullet Canyon Trailhead to Collins Spring Trailhead

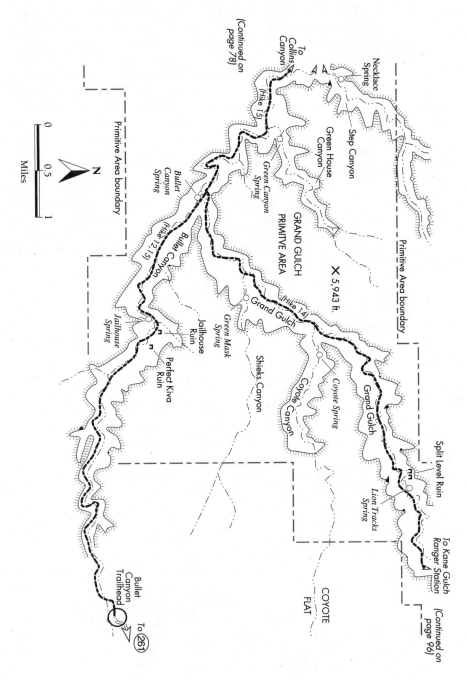

(Continued on page 78)

To Collins Canyon

(Hike 15)

Necklace Spring

Green House Canyon

Step Canyon

Primitive Area boundary

0

Miles

0.5

1

N

Primitive Area boundary

Bullet Canyon Spring

Bullet

Green Canyon Spring

GRAND GULCH PRIMITIVE AREA

✕ 5,943 ft.

Bullet Canyon (Hike 12.15)

Grand Gulch

(Hike 14)

Jailhouse Spring

Jailhouse Ruin

Green Mask Spring

Shieks Canyon

Coyote Spring

Coyote Canyon

Grand Gulch

Split Level Ruin

Perfect Kiva Ruin

Lion Tracks Spring

To Kane Gulch Ranger Station

(Continued on page 96)

COYOTE FLAT

Bullet Canyon Trailhead

To (261)

86

Bullet Canyon.

sites. The first lies in the sun-dappled shade of great cottonwoods, and the second is fringed by a thicket of tamarisk. BLM regulations also restrict the use of these sites to two consecutive nights.

A few yards beyond the last campsite the trail dips to a crossing of the grass-fringed wash of Grand Gulch, where you may find seasonal water. Seasonal Bullet Canyon Spring waters the gulch just down-canyon from the confluence.

To continue up or down Grand Gulch, see Hikes 14 and 15.

13 Kane Gulch Ranger Station to The Junction

General description:	A rewarding day hike or overnighter into one of the Colorado Plateau's most famous canyons, within the Grand Gulch Primitive Area.
Distance:	8 miles round trip.
Difficulty:	Easy to Moderate.
Trail conditions:	Constructed and boot-worn trails, generally well-defined and easy to follow.
Trailhead access:	2WD (paved access).
Average hiking time:	3.5 to 4.5 hours round trip.
Trailhead elevation:	6,427 feet.
Low point:	5,900 feet.
Elevation gain and loss:	530 feet.
Optimum seasons:	April through mid-June; September through October.
Water availability:	Perennial seep below pouroff at 2 miles; seasonal intermittent flows in Grand Gulch; seasonal Junction Spring a short distance below Kane Gulch/Grand Gulch confluence; bring your own water.
Hazards:	Flash-flood danger.
Permits:	Required for overnight trips; obtain your permit at the trailhead and deposit the appropriate fee ($5 per person) in the fee collection tube. Reservations for permits required for overnight trips beginning spring 1999. Contact Monticello BLM office for information.
Topo maps:	Kane Gulch USGS quad; Trails Illustrated Grand Gulch Plateau.

Key points:

2.0 Pouroff.

4.0 The Junction, confluence of Kane Gulch and Grand Gulch.

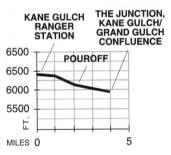

Finding the trailhead: Turn south on Utah 261, 56 miles east of the Hite Marina turn-off on Utah 95 and 28.3 miles west of the junction of U.S. Highway 191 and Utah 95, 3 miles south of Blanding. Drive south on Utah 261 for 3.8 miles and park at the trailhead next to the Kane Gulch Ranger Station on the east side of Utah 261. If you are driving from the south, the ranger station is 29.2 miles north of the junction of Utah 261 and U.S. Highway 163/191 between Mexican Hat and Bluff.

The hike: Beyond the confines of Utah's national parks there are hundreds of outstanding canyons that rival those within the parks in their drama and beauty. And among these many canyons, Grand Gulch is one of the finest.

Grand Gulch is not only one of the most beautiful canyons in the Glen Canyon region, with its well-developed riparian oases and sculpted sandstone walls; it also has one of the greatest concentrations of archaeological resources in a single canyon on the Colorado Plateau.

Kane Gulch Ranger Station is the jumping-off point for the majority of visitors to Grand Gulch, and the passage of so many hikers' boots keeps the trail well-defined and easy to follow. This short trip to the Kane Gulch/Grand Gulch confluence, called The Junction, not only offers a fine introduction to Grand Gulch, it also affords access to the large cliff dwellings of Junction Ruin and several excellent campsites at the confluence. The trip is suitable as a day hike, an overnighter, or as the first leg of an extended trip into the wild gorge of Grand Gulch.

Backpackers should note that overnight use of The Junction campsites is limited to two consecutive nights. During peak use periods, particularly during Easter week and the month of April, The Junction campsites may be continuously occupied.

From the Kane Gulch Ranger Station parking lot, find the trail on the opposite side of Utah 261, indicated by a BLM destination and mileage sign. The trail crosses a sagebrush-studded flat for about 250 yards, then drops to the willow- and clover-fringed banks of Kane Gulch wash. Soon you pass through a gate (leaving it as you find it), cross an expanse of slickrock, then plunge back into the willows, where the trail turns left to follow Kane Gulch down-canyon.

The gradually deepening draw soon becomes bordered by low walls of white Cedar Mesa Sandstone. Scattered cottonwoods and thickets of willow grow vigorously in the bottom of the gulch. Occasional bushwhacking through the willows here is more of a nuisance than it is a challenge.

After about 1 mile, you pass a rare sight in a high desert canyon. Groves of aspen are crowded in the shady recesses beneath the low, north-facing canyon walls, contrasting with the sparse woodland of pinyon and juniper trees that fringes the mesa just above. The nearest montane environment, where aspens typically thrive, is located atop Elk Ridge, 9 miles north and 2,000 feet above Kane Gulch.

After 2 miles, the trail bypasses a major pouroff on the right, then descends steadily over slickrock and a rocky tread back to the canyon floor. A line of seepage emerges from the slickrock beneath the pouroff, sometimes providing enough flow to dampen the wash below.

The trail, compared to canyoneering routes in nearby Cedar Mesa canyons, is pleasant and delightful. The nature of this trail allows you to simply hike and absorb the scenic landscape of this wild canyon.

The gulch has attained true canyon proportions below the pouroff, and the rims now rest 300 to 500 feet above the canyon floor. The only vague segment of the trail ensues just below the pouroff, where you follow the wash down-canyon, with slickrock under foot. Soon you mount another segment of constructed trail that stays high on the north wall of the canyon, following a ledge above a boulder jam and a series of minor pouroffs.

Kane Gulch Ranger Station to The Junction

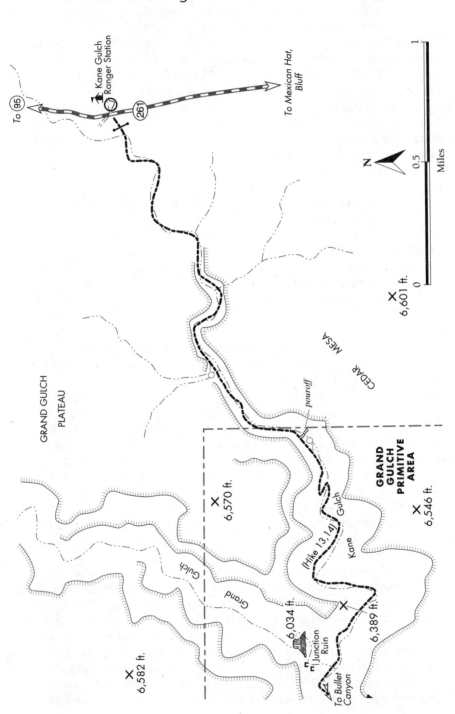

The only steep grade on the hike follows the traverse, where you descend the rocky tread back down to the slickrock wash below. Great alcoves and vaulting cliffs now flank the canyon, and the way ahead through this sandstone corridor alternates between stretches of well-worn trail with a tread of slickrock and sand, to brief trailless segments that follow the wash. There are few obstacles here to impede steady progress.

After 4 miles, Grand Gulch suddenly opens up ahead to the west at The Junction. Its upper reaches, slicing north back into the Grand Gulch Plateau, are quite similar in appearance to Kane Gulch. Straight ahead, Grand Gulch becomes a much wider canyon, flanked by benches studded with cottonwood, pinyon, and juniper. An excellent, though popular camping area lies on a bench at the confluence, while other sites are located just inside Grand Gulch to the north. The campsites, if unoccupied, afford shady resting places for day hikers as well.

Junction Ruin rests in an alcove high on the west wall of Grand Gulch just above The Junction. These well-preserved dwellings consist primarily of slab masonry construction, with one structure displaying wattle-and-daub architecture. To help preserve these ancient structures, hikers should be content to observe them from a distance, perhaps with the aid of binoculars.

After enjoying the peaceful beauty of The Junction, retrace your steps to the trailhead.

14 Kane Gulch Ranger Station to Bullet Canyon Trailhead

General description:	An extended backpack, requiring a shuttle, through incomparable Grand Gulch, within the Grand Gulch Primitive Area.
Distance:	22.8 miles, shuttle trip.
Difficulty:	Moderate.
Trail conditions:	Segments of constructed trail in Kane Gulch; boot-worn trails, generally well-defined, in Grand Gulch; and wash route, slickrock route, and occasional boot-worn trails in Bullet Canyon.
Trailhead access:	2WD paved access to Kane Gulch Ranger Station, unpaved to Bullet Canyon Trailhead.
Average hiking time:	3 to 4 days.
Trailhead elevations:	6,427 feet (Kane Gulch Ranger Station); 6,400 feet (Bullet Canyon Trailhead).
Low point:	5,160 feet.
Elevation gain and loss:	-1,270 feet, +1,240 feet.
Optimum seasons:	April through mid-June; September through October.

Water availability: Perennial springs at 2 miles, 7.4 miles (in Todie Canyon), Coyote Spring (in Coyote Canyon) at 13.2 miles, Green Mask Spring (in Sheiks Canyon) at 14.4 miles, and Jail House Spring (in Bullet Canyon) at 17.8 miles; seasonal intermittent flows in Grand Gulch.

Hazards: Flash-flood danger; exposure to steep dropoffs, and steep slickrock friction pitches in Bullet Canyon.

Permits: Required for overnight use; obtain your permit and pay appropriate fee ($5 per person) at the trailhead register. Beginning spring 1999, reservations for permits will be required for overnight use. Contact Monticello BLM office for information.

Topo maps: Kane Gulch, Cedar Mesa North, Pollys Pasture USGS quads; Trails Illustrated Grand Gulch Plateau.

Key points:

4.0   Confluence of Kane Gulch and Grand Gulch at The Junction.
4.7   Turkey Pen Ruin.
5.0   Stimper Arch.
5.6   Fortress Canyon.
7.2   Todie Canyon.
10.0   Split Level Ruin.
12.8   Coyote Canyon.
13.2   The Thumb Pouroff.
14.2   Sheiks Canyon.
15.6   Bullet Canyon; turn left (east).
17.8   Jail House Spring.
18.0   Jail House Ruin.
18.3   Perfect Kiva Ruin.
22.6   Rim of Bullet Canyon.
22.8   Bullet Canyon Trailhead.

Finding the trailheads: Follow driving directions for Hikes 12 and 13.

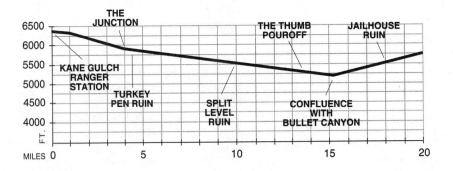

The hike: This premium 3- to 4-day trip surveys what is arguably the most attractive segment of 52-mile long Grand Gulch, one of the top backcountry destinations in the Glen Canyon region. Grand Gulch carves a serpentine course embraced by tremendous, bulging, and overhanging Cedar Mesa Sandstone walls, with alternating red and white beds of erosion-resistant slickrock. Great vaulted amphitheaters open up at every bend of the canyon, most separated by narrow fin-like ridges of sandstone. Bold towers and hoodoos cap the canyon rims. The riparian zone in the gulch will often envelop you with its verdant foliage. The riparian vegetation is so well-developed you may need to refer to a map to remind yourself that indeed this is a high desert canyon in southeast Utah.

The natural beauty of Grand Gulch makes it the jewel in the crown of Cedar Mesa canyons, yet there is even more to Grand Gulch that makes it such an outstanding backcountry destination. The gulch is an outdoor museum of the Anasazi culture that is unsurpassed on the Colorado Plateau in the number and variety of accessible sites. Cliff dwellings and granaries, representing the diversity of architectural techniques that evolved with the culture, abound in Grand Gulch. Six major ruins are labeled on the BLM Grand Gulch map, yet there are many times that number of ruins in the gulch. Rock art sites are also abundant, though much harder to find. Grand Gulch is so absorbing, and its archaeological sites are so numerous, many hikers return time and again, discovering something new with each visit.

Much of the route is straightforward, with a boot-worn trail leading the way. There are places that will require some bushwhacking and simple routefinding. The trail is particularly faint in the burned area near Todie Canyon for about 1 mile. The route out of Bullet Canyon requires a few steep slickrock ascents and should be avoided by novice canyon country hikers. If this is one of your first trips into Utah's canyon country, make it a round trip from Kane Gulch, and save the Bullet Canyon route until you gain more experience and confidence.

Campsites are widely scattered, and most are located near the ruins labeled on the BLM or Trails Illustrated maps. Camping is restricted to two consecutive nights at the following campsites: Junction, Turkey Pen Ruin, the mouth of Bullet Canyon, and Jail House Ruin. No camping is allowed at Split Level Ruin or on the juniper-clad bench adjacent to it.

The spring months offer the greatest probability of abundant water sources, though an active summer monsoon season can also help to recharge springs. During dry times, Todie Spring at 7.4 miles, Coyote Spring at 13.2 miles, Green Mask Spring at 14.4 miles, and Jail House Spring at 17.7 miles, may be your only sources of water. Always check water availability at the bulletin board at Kane Gulch Ranger Station before setting out, and top off your water containers at every opportunity.

This trip requires a car shuttle of 4.4 miles, though hikers most often hitchhike back to the ranger station from Bullet Canyon Trailhead. Although Utah 261 is not a particularly busy highway, it is frequented by other hikers who will likely be glad to give you a ride.

This memorable trek gets underway opposite the Kane Gulch Ranger Station, and you follow the good trail down the developing canyon of Kane Gulch for about 2 hours and 4 miles to The Junction (see Hike 13), where Kane Gulch and Grand Gulch converge. Below this confluence, follow the boot-worn trail westward down Grand Gulch, traversing benches between frequent wash crossings. Groves of stately cottonwoods mass their ranks on the canyon floor, with bulging walls of Cedar Mesa Sandstone rising above. Slickrock amphitheaters and shady alcoves appear around every bend.

Turkey Pen Ruin rests in a deep, sandy alcove on the north canyon wall, 0.7 mile below The Junction. You can ascend the sandy bench to reach the ruins, where you find granaries, the remains of a kiva, and numerous pictographs and petroglyphs. Small bones, perhaps of turkeys, litter the site. Turkeys were domesticated by the Anasazi for food, and their feathers were woven into blankets.

This ruin is a prime example of the inadvertent wear and tear sustained by frequently visited archaeological sites. Surrounding the ruin is the midden, or refuse dump, where potsherds and corncobs are scattered about the sandy ground and are disturbed with each hiker's passing.

There are campsites nearby, but hikers should avoid camping on the bench next to the ruins. Few campsites are available between here and Todie Canyon, 2.5 miles ahead.

After two more bends in the canyon, the aperture of Stimper Arch appears high on the fin that forms the north canyon wall. Fortress Canyon joins from the north 0.6 mile below the arch, 5.6 miles from the trailhead. Although that precipitous gorge becomes impassable a short distance above its mouth, the lower reaches are worth investigating.

About 0.5 mile below Fortress Canyon, you enter a mile-long burn, where graceful cottonwoods and Gambel oak groves were consumed in a May, 1996 toilet-paper fire that began inside the mouth of Todie Canyon. Tinder-dry conditions at that time caused the fire to race out of control almost immediately after it was ignited. This is a striking example of the tragic result of the unwise practice of burning toilet paper in arid regions. In Grand Gulch, and many other backcountry recreation areas in the desert Southwest, visitors are required to pack out used toilet paper.

The trail ahead traverses brushy benches, now vigorously overgrown with renewed growth following the fire. The way crosses the seasonal stream several times, where you may encounter long, deep pools during wet seasons. Typical of the route throughout Grand Gulch, occasional backtracking may be necessary to locate a better way and to avoid wading. More attention to the ill-defined trail is necessary in the burned area.

The charred mouth of Todie Canyon opens up to the east after 7.2 miles. A few campsites among blackened snags and a reliable spring can be found 0.25 mile inside of Todie Canyon. You emerge from the burn around the next bend below Todie Canyon, but the trail becomes even more vague than before. At times the only indication of a route is the footprints of other hikers. In the event you lose the path, there is only one direction to go, and that is down the wash.

Wide benches flank the wash below Todie Canyon, mantled in woodlands of pinyon and juniper trees, groves of Gambel oak, and stands of cottonwood trees. Yet these benches are so overgrown with brush they offer no opportunity for camping. Grand Gulch begins a southwest trend below Todie Canyon, and the canyon rims, rising 600 to 700 feet above, present a scalloped outline, while below the rims are a continuum of great amphitheaters separated by narrow, fin-like ridges. Fortunately for hikers, the wash and the trail follow a much less sinuous course. You may notice that many of the fins are crowned by bold towers that appear to be the abutments of great, long-vanished arches.

The first campsite is located 1.4 miles and about 45 minutes below Todie Canyon, on a bench north of the wash, just before the gulch describes a prominent bend past the confluence with a precipitous north-trending side canyon. After three more bends of the gulch and 0.5 mile, you'll reach another campsite perched on a bench west of the wash beneath the sheer walls of a 200-foot promontory.

At 10 miles, after passing through a 0.5-mile confined stretch of the gulch, you curve toward the deepest alcove in Grand Gulch, reminiscent of Coyote Gulch in the Escalante region, where vaulting walls rise 400 feet above the canyon floor. Within the shelter of the alcove lies Split Level Ruin, one of the finest sites in Grand Gulch. Two connected dwellings, very well preserved, set on different levels of the alcove, are the highlight of the site. Other dwellings, a kiva, and granaries combine to make this one of the more extensive ruin complexes in the gulch.

Although visitors are advised not to touch or rearrange cultural artifacts, some well-intentioned but misguided hikers have collected an array of artifacts from the midden and set them on boulders for display. Here you will see a variety of potsherds, strands of rope, bones, corncobs, stone hand tools, chippings, etc. Artifacts litter the ground at the site; visitors must think twice before investigating the ruins, and stick to established paths. Remember that the ruins, and the previously overused campsites on the juniper-clad bench below, are closed to camping.

Beyond Split Level Ruin, the gulch begins to open up once again as you cross the wash between benches. Keep an eye out for other ruins, as there are far more in the gulch than the BLM map would suggest. At mile 11.8, the canyon floor again becomes constricted; the trail grows brushy and travel becomes more challenging. Thickets of tamarisk cling to the banks of the wash, and groves of cottonwood, Gambel oak, and box elder trees crowd the narrow benches above.

Coyote Canyon, opening up to the east at 12.8 miles, comes as a surprise as you are walking through the brush-infested confines of the gulch. A bench at that canyon's mouth offers an excellent campsite in the shade of large, spreading cottonwoods, with room enough for three or four tents. Coyote Spring, 0.4 mile up the canyon, provides a reliable water supply.

Grand Gulch gradually begins to open up below Coyote Canyon, and after 0.4 mile (at mile 13.2) a large, deep pool, rimmed by slickrock, fills the wash bottom and often provides a source of water long after the gulch's

Kane Gulch Ranger Station to Bullet Canyon Trailhead

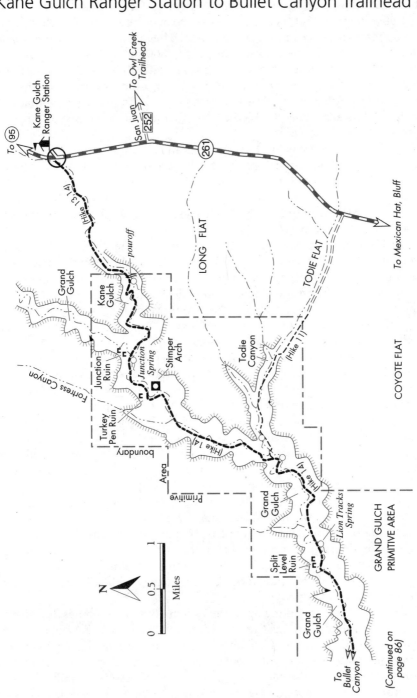

seasonal stream has dried up. The brushy trail follows the streambed more closely as you approach The Thumb Pouroff. The Thumb, a 40-foot sandstone spire, appears on your right just before the wash bends west, after which you reach the brow of the low pouroff at 13.7 miles. This minor obstacle can be bypassed on either side, though the left-side route is easiest.

The trail continues to be brushy beyond the pouroff, and soon you are funneled along the narrow canyon bottom by imposing slickrock cliffs and amphitheaters. Even during wet seasons, the small intermittent stream seldom flows below the pouroff, and often remains dry until you reach Bullet Canyon.

Sheiks Canyon joins on the left (east) at 14.2 miles, and you will find a small campsite just inside the canyon mouth on the south side of the wash, beneath the shade of box elder trees. Perennial Green Mask Spring is located 0.2 mile inside the left fork of Sheiks Canyon. Several good campsites are adjacent to the seeping spring. Spend some time scouting around here and you'll discover the origin of the spring's name. The campsites at Coyote Canyon or Sheiks Canyon are perhaps the best choices to pass your second night in the gulch on a four-day trip en route to Bullet Canyon Trailhead.

From Sheiks Canyon, continue down the narrow gulch beneath great towers and shadowed amphitheaters. After another 0.6 mile, the gulch abandons its southwest course and turns west. Another 0.6 mile of criss-crossing the usually dry wash leads to the mouth of Bullet Canyon, guarded on its north side by a bold slickrock promontory.

Cross the wash of Grand Gulch and enter Bullet Canyon via the well-worn trail. The Bullet Canyon Trailhead lies 7.2 miles and 1,240 feet above to the east. See Hike 12 for details on the Bullet Canyon route.

15 Bullet Canyon Trailhead to Collins Spring Trailhead

See Maps on Pages 78, 86, and 117

General description: A memorable extended trip through the incomparable gorge of Grand Gulch, an outdoor museum of the Anasazi culture, in the Grand Gulch Primitive Area.

Distance: 29.5 miles, shuttle trip.

Difficulty: Moderately strenuous, steep Class 2 friction pitches in Bullet Canyon.

Trail conditions: Wash route, slickrock route, and occasional boot-worn trails in Bullet Canyon; boot-worn trails and wash route in Grand Gulch, with considerable bushwhacking required at times; boot-worn and constructed segments of trail in Collins Canyon.

Trailhead access: 4WD advised when wet.

Average hiking time: 4 to 5 days.

Trailhead elevations: 6,400 feet (Bullet Canyon Trailhead); 5,080 feet (Collins Spring Trailhead).

Low point: 4,760 feet.

Elevation gain and loss: -1,500 feet, +320 feet.

Optimum seasons: April through early June; September through October.

Split Level Ruin, one of the finest cultural sites in Grand Gulch.

Water availability: Jail House Spring, at 5 miles; Green House Canyon Spring, at 9.9 miles; Big Pouroff Spring, at 21 miles; Bannister Spring, at 25 miles; seasonal springs and seasonal intermittent flows in Grand Gulch.

Hazards: Exposure to steep dropoffs, and steep slickrock friction pitches in Bullet Canyon; flash-flood danger.

Permits: Required; obtain permit and pay appropriate fee ($5 per person) at trailhead register. Reservations for permits required beginning spring 1999. Contact Monticello BLM office for information.

Topo maps: Cedar Mesa North, Pollys Pasture, Red House Spring USGS quads; Trails Illustrated Grand Gulch Plateau.

Key points:

0.2	Rim of Bullet Canyon.
1.4	Begin descending steep slickrock chutes.
4.5	Perfect Kiva Ruin.
4.8	Jail House Ruin.
5.0	Jail House Spring.
7.2	Confluence of Bullet Canyon and Grand Gulch; turn left, down-canyon.
9.7	Green House Canyon.
11.1	Step Canyon.
13.9	Dripping Canyon.
14.4	Cow Tank Canyon.
16.3	Big Man Panel.
17.8	Pollys Canyon.
18.0	Junction with Government Trail.
21.0	Big Pouroff.
22.7	Deer Canyon.
24.7	Bannister Ruin.
25.0	Bannister Spring.
27.5	False Trail Canyon.
27.7	Collins Canyon; turn right (west).
29.5	Collins Spring Trailhead.

Finding the trailheads: Follow driving directions for Hike 12 to reach Bullet Canyon Trailhead. To reach Collins Spring Trailhead, follow Utah 95 to the junction with southbound Utah 276, signed for "Lake Powell, Halls Crossing, and Bullfrog via ferry." This turnoff is located between mileposts 83 and 84, 83.8 miles southeast of Hanksville, 34.9 miles east of the Hite Marina turnoff on Utah 95, and 37.7 miles west of the US 191/Utah 95 junction, 3 miles south of Blanding.

Follow Utah 276 south through the rolling woodlands beneath the Red House Cliffs. Shortly after leaving the woodland, the road emerges onto a shrub-dotted terrace, and soon thereafter you pass milepost 85, 6.4 miles from Utah 95. At that point begin looking for a large, solitary juniper tree on the right (west) side of the highway. About 200 yards beyond the juniper, and 0.3 mile southwest of milepost 85, turn left (east) onto an unsigned dirt road. A BLM sign a short distance down this road points to Collins Canyon, and another sign designates the route as San Juan County 260 (Gulch Creek).

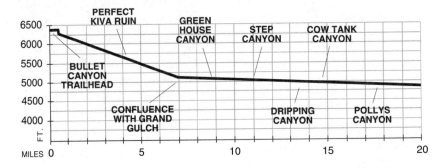

Vistas from this good graded dirt road reach to Navajo Mountain, Monument Valley, and into the slickrock labyrinth of Grand Gulch. After 2.4 miles, bear right at an unsigned junction. Slickrock appears in the roadbed after 4.4 miles, demanding careful driving by hikers in low-clearance vehicles.

The road ends at the signed trailhead, 6.5 miles from Utah 276. Hikers arriving late in the day will find two excellent undeveloped campsites en route to the trailhead.

The hike: This ambitious trip surveys the central portion of Grand Gulch, perhaps the most difficult part of the gulch to traverse. It is an arduous journey: the trail is often vague and overgrown, and much of the way follows the floor of the wash. The 3.9 miles between Bullet and Step canyons is a difficult segment, involving nearly continuous bushwhacking through a riparian jungle of willow and tamarisk. Water sources are widely separated, and there are long stretches in the gulch that offer no campsites.

Yet the rewards of persevering through this wild segment of Grand Gulch are many. Since far fewer hikers travel here than they do between Kane Gulch and Bullet Canyon, there are greater opportunities for solitude. An array of diverse cliff dwellings, granaries, and rock art sites await discovery, and numerous side canyons beckon to be explored. In few other canyons in the region will you find such a rich, well-developed riparian zone. And of course, convoluted slickrock walls, rising 300 to 500 feet above the canyon floor, follow you throughout the journey.

The difficulty of travel here dictates that hikers have previous canyon hiking experience and considerable determination. The trip requires about four hiking days, but on such a schedule, little extra time is available for exploration. From five to six days would be ideal for the trip, perhaps taking one or two layover days en route. Since not everyone can manage the 26.4-mile car shuttle, you may choose to make it a round trip, perhaps hiking down to the vicinity of Cow Tank Canyon or Bannister Ruin, and returning the same way. For those hikers, five to seven days, or more, would be appropriate for the trip.

Before setting out, stop at the Kane Gulch Ranger Station for updated information on water availability. Then carry enough containers to pack at least 1.5 gallons of water per person, and top off your containers at every opportunity.

100

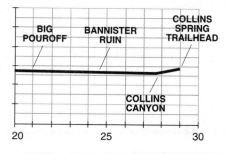

BIG POUROFF | BANNISTER RUIN | COLLINS SPRING TRAILHEAD

COLLINS CANYON

20   25   30

Begin this memorable journey at the Bullet Canyon Trailhead (see Hike 12). After descending 1,240 feet in 7.2 miles, you reach Grand Gulch. Two campsites are available at the mouth of Bullet Canyon, and Bullet Canyon Spring, which emerges in the wash of Grand Gulch, provides a seasonal water source. If reports indicate that spring is dry, tank up at Jail House Spring en route down Bullet Canyon. The next reliable source of water is Green House Canyon Spring, 2.7 miles ahead.

From the confluence of Bullet Canyon and Grand Gulch, jump across the streambed of the gulch and ascend the very steep but short trail to the bench above, where you will find a small, shadeless campsite providing a tremendous view of the gulch and the lower reaches of Bullet Canyon. The ascent to this bench is one of innumerable upgrades to streamside benches you must negotiate on this long trip.

The trail ahead is largely confined to the riparian zone in the canyon bottom. Travel is slow and arduous, so expect the 3.9-mile stretch to Step Canyon to last as long as three to four hours. There are no campsites en route, and few places in which to sit down and rest from your labors. After about half an hour, and little more than 0.5 mile from Bullet Canyon, you pass through an area of charred trees and shrubs, the result of another toilet paper fire that burned out of control.

Continuous bushwhacking leaves little time for appreciating your surroundings, as you are enveloped in a seemingly endless thicket of willow and tamarisk. You must pay close attention to the overgrown route of the trail, for travel through the thicket is nearly impossible if you lose the track. The Totem Pole, a tall and slender slickrock spire, guards the entrance to Green House Canyon, which opens up on the right 2.5 miles from Bullet Canyon at 9.7 miles. This tributary is well worth a side trip, and if you're running short on water, there is a year-round spring 0.2 mile up the canyon.

Other spires, hoodoos, and blocky towers cap the canyon rims 450 feet above, and punctuate the narrow fin-like ridges that separate a continuous procession of amphitheaters that are scooped out of the canyon walls. More bushwhacking ensues beyond Green House Canyon, and eventually you reach Step Canyon after 11.1 miles. To avoid possible pools in Grand Gulch, and the sluggish water and perhaps mud at the mouth of Step Canyon, expect to do some serious bushwhacking here. On the west side of Step Canyon's wash, you will find a fine cottonwood-shaded campsite. Step Canyon features many ruins, and your time will be well spent if you choose to explore it. Necklace Spring, reported to be the finest spring in Grand Gulch, is located 0.8 mile inside Step Canyon. During dry seasons, top off your water containers there. No reliable water is available until you reach Big Pouroff, 9.8 miles ahead.

Despite your location deep inside the canyon of Grand Gulch, the canyon rims have grown noticeably lower, about 400 feet high, than at its deepest point between Todie and Bullet canyons. There the gulch is 700 feet deep. The canyon will continue to grow increasingly shallow for the next 10 miles. Typically, canyons become deeper as you descend them.

Beyond the next bend from south to northwest, about 0.4 mile below Step Canyon, the gulch thankfully begins to open up, its floor no longer completely choked with a riparian jungle of Fremont cottonwoods, willows, and tamarisks. As you approach Dripping Canyon, deep alcoves begin to appear around every bend of the sinuous gulch. Although the canyon walls are lower in stature, they still display sheer, desert-varnished cliffs, bulging overhangs, and shady alcoves, making this an exceptionally scenic part of the gulch.

A good campsite lies opposite the mouth of the long gorge of Dripping Canyon at 13.9 miles. This is another worthwhile side canyon to explore, and it contains a seasonal spring 0.8 mile up-canyon from its mouth. Grand Gulch begins to trend southwest and tighten up beyond Dripping Canyon, and much of the 0.5-mile stretch ahead to Cow Tank Canyon is accomplished in the wash, with occasional detours around long pools in wet seasons. During dry times, expect easy walking along the sandy and gravelly wash.

You will find two Spartan campsites at the mouth of Cow Tank Canyon, one on a low bench on the right (west) side of the wash just below the canyon mouth, and the other on a sandy ledge opposite the mouth. Use the latter site in dry weather only, as it is susceptible to floodwaters. Cow Tank Canyon, like previous tributaries, is another recommended side trip, where you will find extensive rock art panels and several *metates*, rocks on which the ancient inhabitants ground corn into flour. Don't expect to find Cow Tank Spring, labeled as a perennial water source on the BLM map, since it lies above an impassable 10-foot pouroff.

Your route is largely confined to the wash below Cow Tank Canyon, where in wet seasons you may encounter quicksand and perhaps many long pools. The gulch describes a major bend to the south about 0.8 mile from Cow Tank Canyon at 15.2 miles. You will find a good campsite on the south-side bench at the bend. Looming above the site on the western canyon rim is a knobby slickrock tower. If you walk up-canyon a short distance you will see the aperture of the arch shown on topo maps. The tower is the arch's eastern abutment. By now you will notice that the canyon walls rise only 200 to 300 feet, hence the gorge is more deserving of the label *gulch* than *canyon*.

After 16.3 miles, hard-to-find Big Man Panel, high on the south wall beneath the overhanging brow of the rim, can be found opposite a good campsite set on a cottonwood-studded bench. A very steep path begins behind a screen of small cottonwoods on the south side of the wash and ascends 200 feet to the panel. This remarkable display of Anasazi rock art features both pictographs (painted images) and petroglyphs (images carved into stone). The highlights of the panel are three large anthropomorphic figures, two of which stand six feet high.

Beyond Big Man Panel, a stretch of pleasant walking in the smooth gravelly wash ensues, though quicksand can be a problem during wet seasons. An interesting angular arch, located just below a mushroom rock on the east rim signals your approach to Pollys Canyon. On the bench at the canyon mouth at 17.8 miles, you will find a good campsite shaded by large, stout cottonwoods. Pollys Spring, 0.1 mile up the cottonwood-fringed wash of Pollys Canyon, provides a seasonal source of water. A long rincon, or abandoned meander, of Grand Gulch, lies opposite the mouth of Pollys Canyon. Erosion along that meander and along the newer channel of the gulch has isolated the sandstone butte of Pollys Island, formerly part of the east rim.

Slickrock in the usually dry wash below Pollys Canyon affords easy walking as you skirt the base of Pollys Island, its bulging Cedar Mesa Sandstone walls looming overhead. The switchbacks of the Government Trail (Hike 10) soon come into view on the east canyon wall, and the large BLM sign for that trail appears on the rim 300 feet above. For the following 3 miles, much of the route passes in the gravelly wash, which when dry, affords delightful, trouble-free walking. Bench-top trails that shortcut the gulch's meanders require many brief ups and downs en route. The serpentine course of the canyon and its many overhanging cliffs provide welcome shade throughout the day.

You can't miss Big Pouroff, a 30-foot, two-tiered barrier in the wash at 21 miles. Bypass the pouroff on the right (north) side, descending slickrock past a small, shadeless campsite into the wash below. A seepline at the base of the pouroff helps sustain a deep plunge pool, which provides a reliable water source. Since the pool offers the only year-round water source in the gulch below Necklace Spring in Step Canyon, restrain the urge to soak in it. If it has been a dry season and reports indicate no reliable water ahead, tank up here for the final 8.7 miles to Collins Spring Trailhead.

Below Big Pouroff there are usually several mud-fringed pools in wet seasons, and after avoiding them you follow the brush-lined corridor of the gravelly wash down-canyon. After 0.3 mile, the wash is briefly confined by slickrock, where you find a chain of waterpockets that will briefly hold water following abundant rains or flooding. Two more bends in the gulch brings you to Deer Canyon, opening up through the eastern canyon walls. A fair campsite lies just inside the mouth of that canyon, and a reliable spring issues from its right (south) fork 0.5 mile above. The campsites at Deer Canyon and at Bannister Ruin, 2 miles ahead, are your only choices for passing your final night in the gulch.

About 2 miles of mostly trouble-free walking from Deer Canyon leads you to Bannister Ruin, located in a shallow alcove on the northwest canyon wall. Just before coming abreast of the ruin, you pass a small, bench-top campsite, and at the next bend ahead you find an excellent, spacious campsite. Seasonal Bannister Spring emerges from the wash here, often providing a vigorous, steady flow of water in the wash below. The gulch ahead begins describing a series of long, tight meanders, and the riparian growth

Big Man Panel is one of the finest rock art sites in Grand Gulch.

that has choked the canyon for so many miles begins to diminish. Benches, talus slopes, and the banks of the wash become dominated by pinyon and juniper trees, as well as coarse desert shrubs such as mormon tea, and single-leaf ash. Here the gulch assumes the appearance of a typical high desert canyon.

The route is confined to the wash once again, its course growing increasingly rocky. Bench-top trails are present through this serpentine section of the gulch, but they are not always apparent and some scouting may be necessary to locate them. When Bannister Spring is flowing enough to keep the wash damp, you may encounter occasional quicksand.

After the final long meander, you follow the wash through a recently (in geological time) carved narrows at 27 miles. Here Grand Gulch abandoned a former meander, which is now a brushy draw isolating a prominent slickrock monolith. Beyond the narrows the wash drops into a lovely ephemeral pool, then becomes wide, rocky, and usually dry. False Trail Canyon opens up to the north around the next bend, at 27.5 miles, where another seasonal spring emerges in the wash.

As you curve around the bend, the shadowed gorge of Collins Canyon opens up on your right (northwest) at 27.7 miles. If time allows, don't miss the short side trip down Grand Gulch to The Narrows, where the wash has abandoned another meander and carved an 8- to 10-foot channel through a sandstone fin.

At the mouth of Collins Canyon, ascend to the bench above and enter the canyon, where you will find the well-defined trail leading 1.8 miles to the

Collins Spring Trailhead (see Hike 18). En route, be sure to stay left after one-third mile, where a side canyon of similar depth and appearance to Collins Canyon opens up on the right (north).

16 Natural Bridges National Monument—Sipapu Bridge to Kachina Bridge

General description:	A memorable half-day hike to the spectacular natural bridges of Utah's first national monument.
Distance:	5 miles, loop trip.
Difficulty:	Moderately easy.
Trail conditions:	Constructed trail, well-defined and easy to follow.
Trailhead access:	2WD (paved access).
Average hiking time:	3 to 4 hours.
Trailhead elevation:	6,208 feet.
High point:	6,250 feet.
Low point:	5,640 feet.
Elevation gain and loss:	610 feet.
Optimum seasons:	April through mid-June; September through October.
Water availability:	Bring your own.
Hazards:	Flash-flood danger.
Permits:	Not required.
Topo maps:	Moss Back Butte USGS quad; Trails Illustrated Dark Canyon/Manti-La Sal National Forest.

Key points:
- 0.5 Sipapu Bridge.
- 1.2 Horse Collar Ruin.
- 2.6 Kachina Bridge.
- 2.9 Kachina Bridge Trail; turn left.
- 3.3 Kachina Bridge Trailhead; cross the road to find the mesa trail.
- 4.2 Junction with southbound trail leading to Owachomo Bridge Trailhead; bear left.
- 5.0 Sipapu Trailhead.

Finding the trailhead: Follow Utah 95 for 30.1 miles west from the US 191/Utah 95 junction (3 miles south of Blanding), or 42.5 miles east from the Hite Marina turnoff on Utah 95, to northbound Utah 275, prominently signed for Natural Bridges National Monument and Manti–La Sal National Forest—Elk Ridge Access.

This paved, two-lane road leads first north, then generally west, passing the turnoff to Elk Ridge after 0.6 mile, and the Deer Flat Road after 1 mile. You enter Natural Bridges National Monument at 3.8 miles, and reach the visitor center 4.5 miles from Utah 95. Pay the entrance fee inside the visitor center before proceeding.

Beyond the visitor center you pass the campground and reach the 8.5-mile, one-way loop road, Bridge View Drive (open from 7 A.M. to 9 P.M. daily) after 0.5 mile, and bear right. The signed Sipapu Trailhead parking area is located 2 miles from the beginning of the loop road.

SIPAPU TRAILHEAD   SIPAPU TRAILHEAD
KACHINA BRIDGE
6500
6000
5500
5000
SIPAPU BRIDGE   KACHINA TRAILHEAD
FT.
MILES 0   5

The hike: A visit to Natural Bridges National Monument is a must for anyone traveling on Utah 95 across Cedar Mesa. Located near the head of White Canyon, a 40-mile tributary to the Colorado River carving throughout its length through the resistant Cedar Mesa Sandstone, the bridges in the Monument are among the largest in the world.

Cass Hite, prospector and operator of the Hite Crossing ferry on the Colorado River, claimed to have seen the natural stone bridges of White Canyon in 1883. J. A. Scorup, who ranged cattle across one of the largest ranches in Utah, visited the bridges in 1895. A later trip to the bridges guided by Scorup resulted in magazine articles that focused the nation's interest on preserving the unique landscape. In 1908, President Theodore Roosevelt created Natural Bridges National Monument, the first national monument to be established in Utah.

The natural bridges of White Canyon were known by the Navajo and Paiute long before European settlers came to Utah. The Anasazi lived among the bridges in White Canyon, and hikers today visit the canyon not only to explore the unique natural spans of stone, but also to see Anasazi ruins and rock art.

This memorable half-day hike surveys the two largest of the natural bridges in the monument, separated by the dramatic bulging Cedar Mesa Sandstone cliffs of White Canyon. En route, the trail passes Horse Collar Ruin, an example of an unusual style of Anasazi architecture. The trail loops back to the trailhead via the mesa top, thus surveying the entire spectrum of monument landscapes.

From the Sipapu Trailhead, the trail begins as a rock-outlined slickrock route, descending over the White Canyon rim. The way quickly evolves into a constructed trail, carved into the slickrock, with steps in places that afford better footing. Once below the rim, the trail traverses beneath an overhang to the top of a steel stairway that affords passage over an otherwise impassable cliff band. Tall Douglas-firs, a montane tree common on southern Utah plateaus above 8,000 feet, thrive in the cool microclimates of shady niches on the north-facing canyon walls below.

Soon you reach a second stairway that offers an exciting passage over a 20-foot cliff. Just below the stairway, descend a tall, sturdy wooden ladder, then follow the trail as it curves out to a fine viewpoint on a sandstone ledge at 6,000 feet, overlooking Sipapu Bridge. The trail then descends steadily, via switchbacks among Cedar Mesa slabs, upon slopes studded with pinyon pines, junipers, Gambel oaks, and the spreading shrubs of Utah serviceberry.

106

You regain the slickrock below at the south abutment of Sipapu Bridge, which now towers above you. Descend two short but steep slickrock friction pitches, with the aid of handrails and two short ladders, then reach level ground beneath the bridge in White Canyon wash, about thirty minutes and 0.5 mile from the trailhead. A trail register is located in a Gambel oak grove beneath the bridge, alongside the cottonwood-fringed banks of the wash.

The bridge was formed as the waters of White Canyon abandoned a meander in the stream bed and carved a more direct course through a thin wall of sandstone. This mature bridge, the largest in the monument, is no longer being enlarged by stream erosion, since its abutments now rest high above the wash. In its dimensions, Sipapu is second only to Rainbow Bridge in Glen Canyon, and thus bears the distinction of being the second largest natural bridge in the world. The bridge's dimensions are listed on the trail register.

To continue, cross the seasonal stream beneath the towering span of Sipapu, and follow the well-worn trail down-canyon, crossing the wash three more times en route to Deer Canyon. The trail ahead is a delightful walk through spectacular White Canyon. The bulging, mostly white walls of Cedar Mesa Sandstone present an ever-changing scene of sheer cliffs, alcoves, ledges, and towers sculpted into fanciful forms by ages of weathering and erosion.

Deer Canyon opens up on the right (north) 1 mile from the trailhead. Don't miss the short side trip to Horse Collar Ruin about 5 minutes and 250 yards below the mouth of Deer Canyon. A steep slickrock scramble is necessary to reach the deep alcove that houses an unusual collection of small Anasazi dwellings and granaries.

Resuming your trek down-canyon on the well-defined trail, you will cross the wash five more times en route to Kachina Bridge. When you spy a small angular arch adjacent to blocky Ruin Rock on the southern skyline, only a few more bends of the canyon separate you from Kachina Bridge.

When you reach the bridge, notice the wooded draw branching left (northeast). That draw is an abandoned meander, the ancestral course of White Canyon, now resting several feet above today's stream course. Much like the formation of Sipapu Bridge, the stream abandoned its former course and carved a more direct course, creating the opening of Kachina Bridge in the thin wall of sandstone. Kachina is the youngest of the monument's bridges, and stream erosion is still at work enlarging the span.

There are multiple trails at Kachina Bridge, so to stay on course you should cross the wash twice beneath the bridge and head toward the trail register at the eastern abutment, where you will find a fine petroglyph panel.

After carving through Kachina Bridge, White Canyon begins a northwestward course toward its eventual confluence with Lake Powell. The trail, however, continues southbound, now ascending the White Canyon tributary of Armstrong Canyon. About 250 yards beyond Kachina Bridge, the trail to the rim, indicated by a small sign, begins ascending slickrock to the left, with the aid of carved steps and handrails. Avoid the path that contin-

Natural Bridges National Monument—Sipapu Bridge to Kachina Bridge

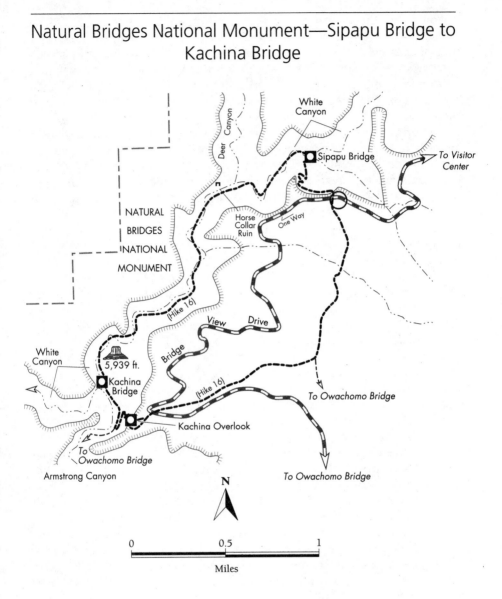

White Canyon

Deer Canyon

White Canyon

Sipapu Bridge

To Visitor Center

NATURAL

BRIDGES

NATIONAL

MONUMENT

Horse Collar Ruin

One Way

(Hike 16)

View

Drive

White Canyon

5,939 ft.

Bridge

Kachina Bridge

(Hike 16)

To Owachomo Bridge

Kachina Overlook

To Owachomo Bridge

Armstrong Canyon

To Owachomo Bridge

N

| 0 | 0.5 | 1 |

Miles

ues up Armstrong Canyon on the right side of the wash, since it soon dead-ends at a pouroff.

After the brief slickrock ascent ends, you traverse a short distance to a signed junction. The trail to the right continues ascending Armstrong Canyon, eventually leading to Owachomo Bridge (see Hike 17). But you should bear left toward the Kachina Parking Area, gaining 300 feet in the following 0.5 mile, the steepest part of the hike. This trail ascends steeply at times, via rock steps and a series of short, tight switchbacks. Views expand with every step, revealing the red, layered Organ Rock Shale that caps the wooded mesas above. Although Kachina Bridge remains in view for much of the ascent, its angle of repose and shadows often give it the appearance of a large alcove rather than a great span of stone.

At length the trail levels off as you curve around a bulging, mushroom-shaped knob just below the rim and mount slickrock, ascending several yards to the paved Kachina Overlook Trail. Bear right to reach the parking area and loop road after 100 yards, at 6,032 feet.

The trail resumes on the opposite (east) side of the road, winding over the corrugated mesa top with a gradual uphill trend. Pinyon and juniper form a widely scattered woodland here as a result of the competition for scant available moisture. Understory shrubs are widely separated, in sharp contrast to the rich vegetation in the canyon below.

Views from the mesa reach far down White Canyon to Mount Ellen in the Henry Mountains, to Deer Flat and the brick red Woodenshoe Buttes in the northwest and north, and southwest to the square-edged platform of Moss Back Butte.

After 0.9 mile, turn left (north) at the signed junction, heading toward Sipapu Trailhead. Much of White Canyon disappears from view as you proceed north through the woodland. Be sure to stick to the trail while hiking across the mesa; otherwise, the well-developed microbiotic soil crust will bear the marks of your passing for a generation.

Soon the northbound trail descends 120 feet into a prominent draw incised into the mesa. Enjoy the view to the twin buttes of the Bears Ears before dropping into the draw. Beyond the draw you briefly follow a steadily ascending cairned route over a broad expanse of slickrock, then resume your hike on good trail leading through the woodland.

At length White Canyon opens up below you to the north, and you descend the final few yards to the Sipapu Trailhead.

17 Natural Bridges National Monument—Owachomo Bridge to Kachina Bridge

General description: A rewarding half-day hike leading to two rare natural bridges in Utah's oldest national monument.

Distance: 5.9 miles loop trip.

Difficulty: Moderately easy.

Trail conditions: Constructed trail, well-worn and easy to follow.

Trailhead access: 2WD (paved access).

Average hiking time: 3 to 4 hours.

Trailhead elevation: 6,107 feet.

High point: 6,200 feet.

Low point: 5,640 feet.

Elevation gain and loss: 560 feet.

Optimum seasons: April through mid-June; September through October.

Water availability: Bring your own.

Hazards: Flash-flood danger.

Permits: Not required.

Topo maps: Moss Back Butte USGS quad; Trails Illustrated Dark Canyon/Manti–La Sal National Forest.

Key points:

0.2　Owachomo Bridge.

2.9　Junction with trails to Kachina Bridge (left), and Kachina Bridge Trailhead (right); bear left.

3.2　Kachina Bridge.

3.5　Return to junction, bear left to reach the rim.

3.9　Kachina Bridge Trailhead; cross the road to find the trail.

4.8　Bear right (south) at mesa-top junction.

5.1　Cross loop road.

5.5　Ladder.

5.7　Cross loop road again.

5.9　Owachomo Bridge Trailhead.

Finding the trailhead: Follow driving directions for Hike 16 to the Sipapu Trailhead and continue straight ahead on Bridge View Drive, passing the Kachina Bridge Trailhead after another 2.3 miles. You reach the Owachomo Bridge Trailhead 4.2 miles from Sipapu Trailhead and 6.7 miles from the visitor center.

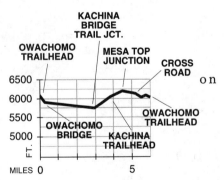

o n

Massive Sipapu Bridge spans White Canyon in Natural Bridges National Monument.

The hike: Natural Bridges National Monument is a justifiably popular destination, located on the edge of remote Cedar Mesa in southeast Utah. A scenic drive on Bridge View Drive leads past dramatic vista points and several trailheads that access the monument's excellent trail network.

Here hikers can follow short, paved paths out to overlooks on the rim, take longer walks into the canyon to visit one of the natural bridges, or utilize the trail network to take loop trips ranging from a half-day to all day in length.

This fine loop hike combines a trek down Armstrong Canyon, a White Canyon tributary, with a traverse of mesa top woodlands and a visit to both the oldest and most youthful bridges in the monument. This trip (and Hike 16) is an excellent alternative to the monument's 8-mile loop for hikers budgeting their time and energy, and offers a premium return for a minimum investment of time and effort.

This hike begins at the Owachomo Bridge parking area, where you follow the right hand, unpaved trail, descending slickrock slopes and ledges on a moderately steep grade. The graceful span of Owachomo Bridge soon comes into view in the canyon just below.

The trailside slopes are dominated by Cedar Mesa Sandstone and thus host only a scattering of gnarled pinyons and junipers, dark green mounds of littleleaf mountain mahogany, green clumps of mormon tea, and the spiny foliage of Fremont barberry.

Within 5 minutes most hikers will reach Owachomo Bridge, a delicate span with a thickness of only 9 feet, in the advanced stages of old age. The bridge no

111

longer spans an active watercourse, though a minor draw courses beneath it, just above the drainage of Armstrong Canyon. Surface erosion and weathering slowly enlarge the opening.

From the trail register beneath the bridge, head south down the slickrock draw for about 75 yards and turn right, heading down Armstrong Canyon. The route of the trail is obscure at first. Follow the ledge down-canyon, traversing above Armstrong Canyon's inner gorge. After about 250 yards, the trail appears and then becomes easy to follow.

After following the ledge for 0.25 mile from the bridge, drop into the canyon and follow the wash as it twists and turns ahead. The trail makes occasional detours around obstructions in the wash, but most often the way crosses the wash from one low bench to the next. Although the trail is not as well defined as it is between Sipapu and Kachina bridges, it is generally easy to follow, with cairns showing the way through ill-defined stretches.

Dramatic Cedar Mesa Sandstone cliffs flank the canyon, banded in shades of red and white and streaked with dark veils of desert varnish. Alternating resistant and softer layers of sandstone give the canyon walls a bulging profile.

After 1 mile, a detour leads up and around a boulder jam in the wash. Beyond that obstacle you follow a bend in the canyon around The Shoe, an aptly-named block of white Cedar Mesa Sandstone resting on a brittle red foundation, much of which has been removed by ages of erosion. Observant hikers may spot some of the small Anasazi ruins in the canyon, though they are well hidden on ledges beneath shady overhangs.

Armstrong Canyon, a tributary to White Canyon, Natural Bridges National Monument.

Natural Bridges National Monument—Owachomo Bridge to Kachina Bridge

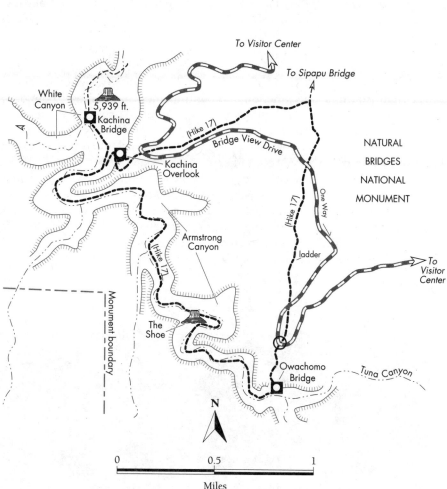

To Visitor Center

To Sipapu Bridge

White Canyon

5,939 ft.
Kachina Bridge

Kachina Overlook

(Hike 17)

Bridge View Drive

NATURAL

BRIDGES

NATIONAL

MONUMENT

One Way

(Hike 17)

(Hike 17)

Armstrong Canyon

ladder

To Visitor Center

Monument boundary

The Shoe

Owachomo Bridge

Tuna Canyon

N

0   0.5   1

Miles

After 2.7 miles, the trail mounts a slickrock ledge on the south side of the wash, which you follow around the next bend in the canyon, bypassing a pouroff. The traverse soon leads to a signed junction, where you have the choice of turning left toward Kachina Bridge or right to ascend to the rim.

Most hikers will want to turn left for the 0.6-mile round-trip detour to Kachina Bridge. The trail to the bridge briefly descends steep slickrock, where handrails and carved steps aid the descent. Once you reach the canyon floor, stroll down the wash to immense Kachina Bridge at the confluence of Armstrong and White canyons. Stream erosion is still at work enlarging this huge span, the most youthful of the three bridges in the monument.

After returning from the bridge to the signed junction, follow a series of short, tight switchbacks to gain 300 feet in 0.5 mile. Numerous rock steps en route help ease the grade. The grade abates beneath a mushroom rock just below the canyon rim. The Kachina Overlook is situated atop that rock. After curving around the overhang beneath the rock, you mount slickrock and ascend several yards to the paved overlook trail. Turn right there to reach the Kachina Parking Area and the loop road at 6,032 feet. The trail resumes on the opposite (east) side of the road, and you follow its gradually ascending course for 0.9 mile across the wooded mesa to a signed junction. Bear right (south) at the junction and continue across the mesa, now on a gentle downhill grade. Fine views open up from this stretch of the trail, reaching to the Red House Cliffs and the bold tower of Moss Back Butte in the southwest and far down White Canyon to the distant peaks of Hillers and Pennell in the Henry Mountains.

You cross Bridge View Drive for the first time 0.3 mile from the junction. Beyond it the trail crosses slickrock, soon descending a moderate grade into a west-trending draw. At the bottom of the grade, a 6-foot wooden ladder affords passage over a large boulder, beyond which the trail ascends steadily over slickrock to the second road crossing. A brief, generally downhill stroll of 0.2 mile closes the circuit at the Owachomo Parking Area.

The delicate span of Owachomo Bridge is the oldest in Natural Bridges National Monument.

18 Collins Spring Trailhead to The Narrows

General description:	A rewarding half-day hike or one leg of an extended backpack trip in the Grand Gulch Primitive Area, leading to The Narrows of lower Grand Gulch.
Distance:	4 miles round trip.
Difficulty:	Easy.
Trail conditions:	Constructed and boot-worn trails, well-defined.
Trailhead access:	4WD advised when road is wet.
Average hiking time:	2.5 to 3 hours round trip.
Trailhead elevation:	5,080 feet.
Low point:	4,750 feet.
Elevation gain and loss:	330 feet.
Optimum seasons:	April through early June; September through October.
Water availability:	Seasonal intermittent flows in Grand Gulch; bring your own.
Hazards:	Flash-flood danger.
Permits:	Required for overnight use only; obtain your permit from the trailhead register and deposit the fee ($5 per person) in the fee collection tube at the trailhead. Reservations for permits required for overnight use beginning spring 1999. Contact Monticello BLM office for information.
Topo maps:	Red House Spring USGS quad; Trails Illustrated Grand Gulch Plateau; BLM Grand Gulch Primitive Area.

Key points:

1.8   Confluence of Collins Canyon and Grand Gulch; turn right, down-canyon.
2.0   The Narrows.

Finding the trailhead: Follow driving directions for Hike 15.

The hike: Grand Gulch, a rich riparian oasis and outdoor museum of the ancient Anasazi culture, is one of Utah's classic canyons. Yet its remote setting is largely reserved for the backpacker willing to spend several days exploring its hidden depths.

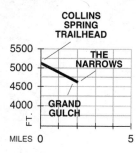

A notable exception is the easy walk down Collins Canyon to The Narrows, perhaps the best short hike in Grand Gulch. This fine trip traces the slickrock gorge of Collins Canyon, the only Grand Gulch access from the west, via a well-worn, and in places constructed, trail into the lower reaches of Grand Gulch. Unlike other Colorado Plateau slot canyons, The Narrows of Grand Gulch are very short, only stretching about 20 to 30 feet, but the canyon walls there are separated by only 8 to 10 feet. The confines of The Narrows often shade a shallow pool, making the slot an inviting destination. Remember, regulations prohibit dogs in Grand Gulch below the confluence with Collins Canyon, meaning you cannot bring your dog with you to The Narrows.

From the trailhead on the rim of the mesa above Collins Canyon, exciting views reach into the slickrock-embraced gorge, luring you onto the trail that begins behind the information signboard and trailhead register. At once the trail descends moderately via three short switchbacks over the first band of Cedar Mesa Sandstone and into the infant canyon below. There you gently descend over the corrugated slopes above the draw of Collins Canyon.

Soon you pass the mouth of a shallow northeast-trending draw and travel through a wooden gate that bars cattle from entering Collins Canyon and Grand Gulch. Be sure to keep the gate closed. A brief, moderately descending segment of constructed trail, the steepest grade on the hike, ensues beyond the gate, dropping down a dugway into the wash below.

Upon reaching the wash, the tread becomes obscure. Simply follow the wash ahead for about 150 yards to the lip of a major pouroff. Cairns should be in place to direct you around the pouroff to the right (south) and onto another dugway, where the trail has been carved into the canyon wall. Another short, moderately steep grade leads you back to the canyon floor. Here you'll notice that the drainage has evolved from a draw just above the pouroff into a true canyon, now 200 feet deep.

Collins Canyon.

Collins Spring Trailhead to The Narrows

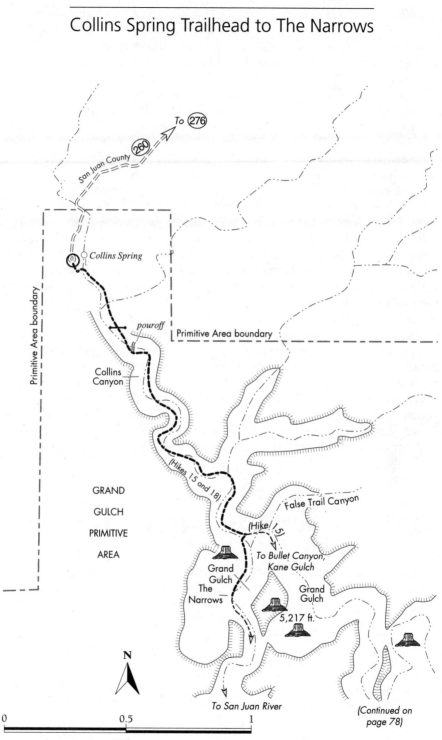

To ②⑦⑥

②⑥⓪

San Juan County

Primitive Area boundary

Collins Spring

pouroff

Primitive Area boundary

Collins
Canyon

(Hikes 15 and 18)

GRAND

GULCH

PRIMITIVE

AREA

False Trail Canyon

(Hike 15)

To Bullet Canyon,
Kane Gulch

Grand
Gulch

Grand
Gulch

The
Narrows

5,217 ft.

N

To San Juan River

(Continued on
page 78)

0   0.5   1

Miles

Collins Canyon is presently embraced by tall, bulging, red- and tan-banded walls of Cedar Mesa slickrock. Domes, towers, balanced rocks, and sculpted hoodoos cap the overhanging canyon rims. Pinyon pines, junipers, and Gambel oaks are scattered across the canyon floor, and the occasional cottonwood fringes the wash. Nearly every bend in the canyon presents a shady overhang, inviting a cool respite from the sun on the hike out.

After four bends of the canyon below the pouroff, the trail edges close to a small but distinctive arch. Be sure to take note of a north-trending side canyon that opens up on the left after 1.5 miles. On your way back to the trailhead, bear left at that confluence, making sure that you don't turn into that canyon, which is similar in depth and appearance to Collins Canyon.

After rounding the next bend ahead, Grand Gulch opens up below and soon you reach a shrub-studded bench at the mouth of Collins Canyon at 4,760 feet, 1.8 miles from the trailhead. There are two ways to reach The Narrows from this point. One route follows the rocky, sandy, and perhaps muddy wash of Grand Gulch down-canyon to the right (south) for 0.2 mile.

An easier way follows a boot-worn, occasionally brushy trail across the bench on the west side of the Grand Gulch wash. Find that trail from the mouth of Collins Canyon by heading south across the canyon's wash to the bench above. That trail dips into Grand Gulch just above The Narrows.

The Narrows appear suddenly and unexpectedly, where Grand Gulch's stream has carved a passage through a narrow, fin-like ridge, abandoning a long meander in the stream bed. The shade cast by the walls of The Narrows and its shallow, seasonal pool make this a fine and peaceful destination on the sandy banks of the wash beneath the fluttering foliage of small cottonwoods. Great bulging cliffs soar 300 feet overhead, amplifying the music of the small, seasonal stream.

After enjoying this tranquil locale, retrace your steps to the trailhead.

19 North Wash to Marinus Canyon

General description:	A half-day hike through a seldom-visited, straight-walled canyon alongside Utah 95 near Hite Marina and Lake Powell.
Distance:	7 miles round trip.
Difficulty:	Moderately easy.
Trail conditions:	Wash route.
Trailhead access:	2WD (paved access).
Average hiking time:	4 hours round trip.
Trailhead elevation:	4,180 feet.
High point:	4,560 feet.
Elevation gain and loss:	380 feet.
Optimum season:	Mid-March through mid-May; mid-September through mid-November.

Water availability: Bring your own.
Hazards: Flash-flood danger.
Permits: Not required.
Topo maps: Hite North USGS quad.

Key points:
2.2 Forks of Marinus Canyon;
   follow right fork.
3.5 Reach pouroff and alcove.

Finding the trailhead: Find the trailhead by driving 34.6 miles southeast from Hanksville on Utah 95, or northwest for 12.3 miles from the Hite Marina turnoff on Utah 95, and 1.7 miles north of the Glen Canyon National Recreation Area boundary. This unsigned, easy-to-miss canyon opens up on the east side of Utah 95 in North Wash canyon, 0.4 mile north of milepost 35, and 0.6 mile south of milepost 34.

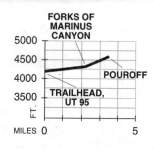

Avoid the very narrow track that leads about 100 feet across a small earth dam at the mouth of Marinus Canyon. Instead, park off the highway in one of the wide spots near the canyon mouth.

The hike: South of Hanksville and west of the Dirty Devil River, between the sandy mesas of Trachyte and Cedar points, Utah 95 follows the course of North Wash en route to Lake Powell and Hite. Utah 95 is one of the premier scenic drives in the Colorado Plateau region. It passes through nine distinctive layers of progressively older sedimentary formations, featuring colorful clay beds and massive sandstone formations carved into sheer and fluted cliffs, where great amphitheaters have been scooped out of the canyon walls.

Three major tributary canyons, Marinus, Butler, and Stair, join North Wash alongside Utah 95. All of them offer grand scenery comparable to North Wash, yet few hikers bother to explore these cliff-bound gorges.

Marinus Canyon is a classic, dry desert gorge, embraced by fluted 600-foot walls of Wingate Sandstone. The low elevations of the canyon make it a fine choice for an early spring or late autumn outing, when higher canyons, such as those on Cedar Mesa, are too snowy or cold. There are no trails here; you simply follow the dry wash up-canyon. Although the wash route is generally easy to follow, the wash is sandy and for much of the way you'll be rock-hopping and weaving a way among boulders. At the end of the canyon's right fork is a shady overhang supporting hanging gardens, offering a fine destination for a half-day hike.

Enter the mouth of Marinus Canyon via the small earth dam, then simply make your way up the rocky, boulder-strewn wash. A scattering

119

of Fremont cottonwoods, tamarisk, and rabbitbrush fringe the usually-dry wash, while the green foliage of single-leaf ash and apache plume, with its white spring blossoms and feathery summer fruits, dot the slopes above.

The wash begins amid the rocks of the Chinle Formation. Shortly after entering the canyon mouth you must briefly scramble up to the left of a resistant green ledge cutting across the wash, the only significant obstacle in the canyon.

Tall fluted cliffs of Wingate Sandstone, often coated with a metallic blue veneer of desert varnish, embrace the confined canyon, with the reddish brown ledges and cliff bands of Kayenta Formation rocks capping the rims. The lower slopes of the canyon are composed of the vari-colored Chinle Formation rocks, the colorful beds hidden behind a mask of coarse desert shrubs and great sandstone blocks fallen from the cliffs above.

After gradually ascending this quiet, majestic canyon for 2 miles, you can see the confluence of two branches of the canyon a short distance ahead. Just before reaching the confluence, the wash is choked with huge boulders for about 100 yards. It is not too difficult to pick a way through this obstacle, with only minor scrambling necessary.

When you reach the forks of the canyon after another 0.2 mile, at 4,275 feet, follow the right fork. In the left fork a boulder jam makes further travel difficult at best. The right fork ahead offers clear sailing, save for an occasional minor boulder jam and rock-strewn stretches.

As you proceed, the Wingate Sandstone walls steadily close in and further confine the gorge. After passing above the topmost layer of the Chinle Formation, the Wingate reaches down to the canyon floor, and the drainage grows increasingly narrow as it slices back into this resistant sandstone.

After hiking about 1 hour and 1.25 miles from the forks of the canyon, you reach a low pouroff blocking further progress. Beneath the pouroff is a shady overhang, supporting a seepline decorated with the delicate fronds of maidenhair fern. During wet seasons, you will find a deep pool below the pouroff.

The canyon slots up ahead, and determined hikers can bypass the pouroff on the left and continue up-canyon. Most hikers, however, will likely be content to turn around at the pouroff and retrace their steps through Marinus Canyon to the trailhead.

North Wash to Marinus Canyon

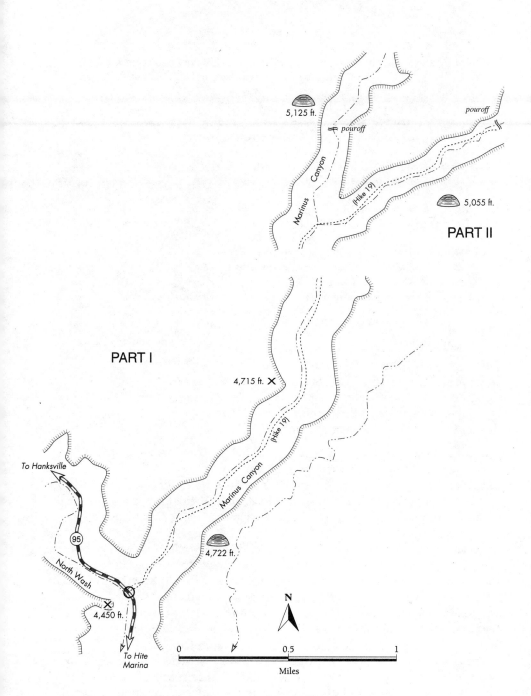

5,125 ft.

pouroff

pouroff

Marinus Canyon

(Hike 19)

5,055 ft.

PART II

PART I

4,715 ft. ✗

To Hanksville

(Hike 19)

Marinus Canyon

95

North Wash

4,722 ft.

✗
4,450 ft.

To Hite
Marina

N

0   0.5   1

Miles

20 Hog Springs Rest Area to Hog Canyon

General description:	A short, easy hike to a lovely pool and waterfall in scenic Hog Canyon, alongside Utah 95 near Hite Marina and Lake Powell.
Distance:	2 miles round trip.
Difficulty:	Easy.
Trail conditions:	Boot-worn trails and wash route.
Trail access:	2WD (paved access).
Average hiking time:	1.5 hours round trip.
Trailhead elevation:	4,080 feet.
High point:	4,230 feet.
Elevation gain and loss:	150 feet.
Optimum seasons:	Mid-March through mid-May; mid-September through mid-November.
Water availability:	Bring your own.
Hazards:	Flash-flood danger.
Permits:	Not required.
Topo maps:	Hite North, Black Table USGS quads.

Key points:

1.0   Pool and pouroff.

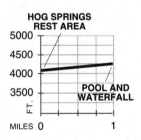

Finding the trailhead: The trailhead is located at the prominently-signed Hog Springs Rest Area alongside Utah 95 between mileposts 33 and 34, 14.6 miles northwest of the turnoff to Hite Marina and 33.3 miles southeast of Hanksville.

The hike: Hog Canyon is the principal drainage on the west side of North Wash along Utah 95. The small spring-fed stream, draining the eastern flanks of Trachyte Point, courses through a very scenic canyon embraced by the bold sandstone walls of the Glen Canyon Group of rocks: the Wingate, Kayenta, and Navajo formations.

Located at the canyon's mouth alongside Utah 95 is the Hog Springs Rest Area, a pleasant stopover featuring two picnic sites with awnings and tables and a restroom nearby. The short stroll up Hog Canyon from the rest area offers a more intimate association with a dramatic desert canyon than scenic Utah 95 can provide. One mile up the canyon, far beyond the noise of highway traffic, a deep pool and a small waterfall in the shade of a deep alcove offer an attractive destination for a short hike on a warm spring or autumn day.

From the large rest area parking lot, cross the bridge spanning North Wash and enter the picnic site. Immediately before reaching the second picnic table, follow the trail that descends to the banks of the small stream.

Hog Springs Rest Area to Hog Canyon

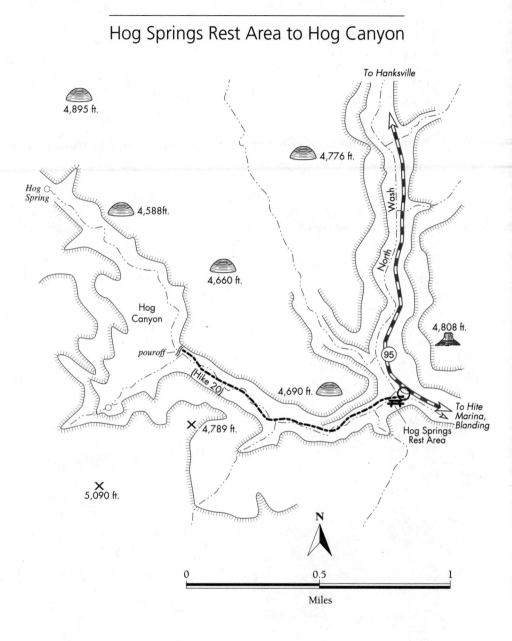

4,895 ft.

To Hanksville

4,776 ft.

Hog Spring

4,588ft.

4,660 ft.

Hog Canyon

4,808 ft.

North Wash

95

pouroff

(Hike 20)

4,690 ft.

To Hite Marina, Blanding

Hog Springs Rest Area

X 4,789 ft.

X
5,090 ft.

N

0   0.5   1

Miles

Cross the stream and proceed up-canyon via the slopes above the wash on the right. Bold slickrock walls of orange Wingate Sandstone, dimpled with solution cavities, bound the lower reaches of the narrow canyon.

The trail begins as an obvious boot-worn path, but recent flash-flood activity will determine how well-defined you find it. If the way is faint or occasionally nonexistent, simply follow above the banks of the wash, shortcutting its meanders via streamside benches. Avoid the rich growth of grasses and rushes where seepage creates a mire along the wash banks.

Great rounded cliffs of Navajo Sandstone soon appear at the head of the canyon on the rim of Trachyte Point. The sheer Wingate walls diminish in height as you work your way up the canyon; and the cliffs of Kayenta rocks replace the Wingate with their rubbly ledges mantled with coarse desert shrubs and low cliff bands. Navajo domes crown the canyon rims.

After 1 mile, listen for the music of running water. Pick your way through a short rock-strewn stretch of the wash to the source of that sound, hidden until the end behind a screen of tall willows. Then, suddenly, you will reach the wide pool lying beneath the overhang of a shady alcove. A 6-foot waterfall, draining the perennial springs issuing from the upper canyon, plunges into the pool over a resistant ledge of Kayenta Sandstone. Mosses and fronds of maidenhair fern decorate the moist walls of the alcove, where seeping water drips like rain into the pool and onto the sandy beach beside it.

After enjoying this cool, peaceful locale, retrace your route to the trailhead.

Hog Canyon.

21 North Wash to Stair Canyon

General description: A memorable day hike in a lonely, cliff-bound canyon, located near Hite Marina and Lake Powell.

Distance: 7.2 miles round trip.

Difficulty: Moderately easy.

Trail conditions: Wash route.

Trailhead access: 2WD (paved access).

Average hiking time: 4 to 4.5 hours round trip.

Trailhead elevation: 4,200 feet.

High point: 4,550 feet.

Elevation gain and loss: 350 feet.

Optimum seasons: Mid-March through mid-May; mid-September through mid-November.

Water availability: Bring your own.

Hazards: Flash-flood danger.

Permits: Not required.

Topo maps: Hite North and Stair Canyon USGS quads.

Key points:

0.1 Mouth of Stair Canyon.
1.2 First side canyon joining on the right; stay left.
1.7 Enter narrows; bypass route follows slickrock ledge on the right.
3.4 Forks of Stair Canyon; follow right fork.
3.6 Amphitheater and pouroff.

Finding the trailhead: Follow Utah 95 for 31.2 miles southeast from Hanksville, or travel 16.7 miles northwest from the Hite Marina turnoff on Utah 95 to an eastbound dirt spur road, 0.2 mile east of milepost 31 and 0.8 mile north of milepost 32. Follow the spur road as it descends about 150 yards to a rock-outlined, gravel parking area at Three Forks, where Butler, Stair, and North washes converge.

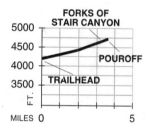

The hike: Of the trio of major North Wash tributaries (including Marinus and Butler canyons), Stair Canyon may be the most interesting to explore. This fine day hike surveys the lower 3.5 miles of this long canyon, and hikers have the option of scrambling out of the gorge for a memorable vista of the Henry Mountains or following the canyon into a shadowed, cathedral-like amphitheater.

This hike is more demanding than hikes in other North Wash tributaries, with occasional long sandy stretches in the wash and minor scrambling over and around boulders. There is no trail, and hikers follow a route along the avenue of the canyon's wash.

North Wash to Stair Canyon

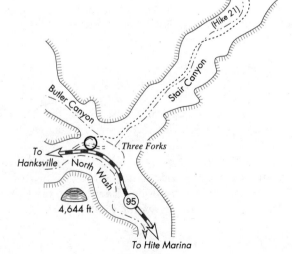

Butler Canyon

Stair Canyon

(Hike 21)

Three Forks

To
Hanksville   North Wash

4,644 ft.

95

To Hite Marina

North Wash to Stair Canyon

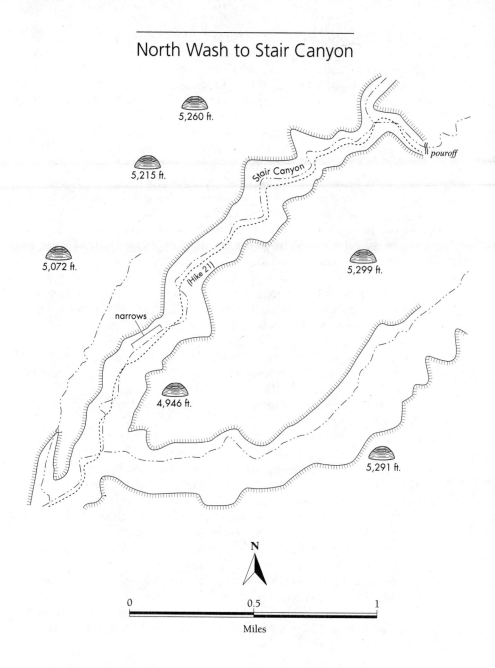

5,260 ft.

5,215 ft.

Stair Canyon

pouroff

5,072 ft.

5,299 ft.

(Hike 21)

narrows

4,946 ft.

5,291 ft.

N

0   0.5   1

Miles

Begin the hike at the road's end at Three Forks, where Butler, Stair, and North washes converge. Drop into Butler Canyon's wash a short distance east of the trailhead and follow the sandy corridor right toward the mouth of Stair Canyon. Avoid the tangle of willow and common reed at Stair Canyon's mouth by entering the canyon on the left, via a bench beneath the north canyon wall.

Much like its neighbor Butler Canyon, Stair Canyon is a dramatic cliff-bound gorge, flanked by bold orange Wingate Sandstone cliffs. The canyon rims are capped by the reddish brown ledges and cliff bands of Kayenta Formation sandstone. Stair Canyon is generally drier than Butler, and though the canyon is confined, its floor is wide enough to afford a clear route via benches around the riparian thickets near the canyon mouth.

Stretches of the wash are sandy, which makes walking slow and arduous. If recent rains have dampened the wash, its sandy course will afford a much firmer tread under foot. The wash banks support the scattered riparian growth of Fremont cottonwoods, willows, and tamarisk, yet most often only rabbitbrush and seep-willow fringe the banks. Every bend of this serpentine canyon reveals new views of the great red rock cliffs, alcoves, and sculpted sandstone knobs that embrace it.

After 1.2 miles, a side canyon joins on the right via a narrow slot, its walls framing a vignette of smooth Navajo Sandstone domes rising on the eastern skyline. The canyon ahead soon grows narrow, and a bushwhack through the willows becomes necessary. This part of the gorge ranges from only 4 to 20 feet wide, and spindly cottonwoods grow straight and tall, reaching for the sun above.

The narrows stretch about 0.2 mile up-canyon, then become blocked by a pouroff and chockstone. As you enter the narrows, look for the large trunk of a dead cottonwood perched against the right-hand wall. Exit the narrows here, on the south side, and scramble briefly up to the slickrock bench just above. Follow the bench up-canyon for 150 yards, then reenter the boulder-strewn wash. Soon, where a boulder-filled draw enters on the right (east), Stair Canyon describes a prominent right-angle bend to the north. About 200 yards up-canyon from the bend, a massive boulder fills the wash, but this obstacle is easily bypassed on the left side.

Two more prominent, north-trending, right-angle bends lie ahead. Upcanyon, there are occasional stretches of slickrock that provide a welcome change from slogging through the sand. Abrasive runoff has, over the ages, carved some interesting miniature narrows in the slickrock, illustrating the birth of a slot canyon.

After passing the third right-angle bend above the narrows, the canyon then bends to the east. Soon you reach the mouth of a minor draw and an adjacent talus slope on the south wall of the canyon. The draw and boulder-covered slope afford one of few routes out of the canyon onto the Kayenta ledges above. Experienced hikers can scramble a short distance up to the ledges for a memorable vista of the Henry Mountains and an array of Navajo Sandstone domes that crown the canyon rim.

Others will continue the trek up the wash, which leads east, then bends northeast, where you mount slickrock to avoid a series of plunge pools. After hiking 3.4 miles, you reach a major fork in the canyon, at 4,550 feet. At the forks, a broad sweep of bulging Wingate and Kayenta cliffs confines the wash in a shadowed gorge. The left fork, which is Stair Canyon proper, becomes even more confined by the sandstone walls up-canyon, and boulders choke its course below a pouroff, 0.2 mile from the forks.

Although the right fork appears equally inhospitable to travel, it does offer a route to a shady amphitheater at the terminus of the hike. To get there, scramble briefly up the left margin of the boulder jam that blocks the mouth of the canyon, then follow the wash for 0.25 mile to the amphitheater, a peaceful, shady locale embraced by vaulting Wingate cliffs. An impassable, two-tiered pouroff lies just above.

After enjoying the scenic delights of Stair Canyon, backtrack to the trailhead.

22 North Wash to Butler Canyon

General description: An excellent day hike into a seldom-visited canyon, featuring a short side-trip option leading to a dramatic vista point.

Distance: 7.2 miles round trip.

Difficulty: Moderate.

Trail conditions: Wash route.

Trailhead access: 2WD (paved access).

Average hiking time: 4 hours round trip.

Trailhead elevation: 4,200 feet.

High point: 4,960 feet.

Elevation gain and loss: 760 feet.

Optimum seasons: Mid-March through mid-May; mid-September through mid-November.

Water availability: Bring your own.

Hazards: Flash-flood danger.

Permits: Not required.

Topo maps: Hite North, Black Table, Turkey Knob, and Stair Canyon USGS quads.

Key points:
1.2   Pouroff; bypass on the right.
1.3   Major side canyon joins on the left; bear right.
2.25 Second major side canyon joins on the left; bear right again.
3.3   First major side canyon joins on the right; bear right.
3.6   Viewpoint.

Finding the trailhead: Follow driving directions for Hike 21.

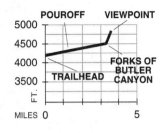

The hike: Combined with Marinus Canyon (Hike 19) and nearby Stair Canyon (Hike 21), Butler Canyon completes the trio of major North Wash tributary canyons that offer excellent day hiking opportunities along Utah 95 between Hanksville and Lake Powell. Of the three canyons, Butler is wettest, supporting occasional ribbons of rich riparian growth. The hiking here is occasionally challenging, though seldom difficult.

The highlight of the hike is an opportunity to scramble out of the gorge for a tremendous vista of the Henry Mountains, with a striking array of Navajo Sandstone domes rising in the foreground.

From the trailhead, follow the long-closed road north into the mouth of Butler Canyon and enter the wash after 200 yards, where the doubletrack ends. Turn left here and follow the sandy wash up-canyon. Scattered cottonwoods fringe the wash, and cliffs of orange Wingate Sandstone, dimpled with solution cavities, embrace the confined canyon.

The walking in the sandy and gravelly wash is easy, allowing you to make good time as you head up-canyon. After rounding a few bends in the canyon, a triad of Navajo Sandstone domes comes into view on the skyline ahead. Soon the damp banks of the wash become cloaked with the rich growth of wiregrass and cattails, with willow thickets occupying the wettest areas of the canyon floor. Your steady pace will be interrupted as you must plunge through the tall grasses and willow thickets, crossing the small seasonal stream that courses down the wash time and again.

After 1.2 miles, a pouroff and deep plunge pool block the wash ahead. Seeplines in the alcove beneath the pouroff are decorated with hanging gardens of maidenhair fern. You can easily bypass the pouroff by scaling ledges on the right side. Above that minor obstacle, the wash opens up and you stroll ahead, with slickrock under foot, to a prominent side canyon opening up on the left. The bold cliffs of that canyon frame a fine view of the broad Navajo Sandstone dome on the skyline.

Bear right at that confluence and continue weaving a course through the riparian tangle of wiregrass, common reed grass, willows, and cottonwoods. Usually by late May or early June, the 6- to 8-foot tall common reed has reached its maximum growth, forming nearly impenetrable thickets. Summer flash-floods flatten the tall grass, making autumn hikes more enjoyable than late spring outings.

The canyon begins to dry up about 250 yards beyond the last confluence, assuming a character more typical of a desert canyon, with only a scattering of coarse desert shrubs. The wash becomes sandy, with ledges of slickrock stair-stepping up the canyon floor. Single-leaf ash replaces the riparian ribbon, dotting the sandstone slopes with its green foliage. Yet riparian oases reappear intermittently as you continue up the canyon, requiring brief struggles to get through the jungle-like morass.

Domes and broad, sweeping expanses of Navajo Sandstone slickrock become a common sight on the canyon rims as you reach deeper into Butler Canyon. Several precipitous side canyons notch the canyon walls on the left, yet not one of them offers a route up to the rim.

After 3.2 miles and perhaps 1.5 to 2 hours of hiking, a prominent boulder-choked draw opens up on the right. This draw also affords access to the viewpoint on the ridge above to the southeast, but unstable slabs, steep slopes, and considerable route-finding make the route to the viewpoint outlined below preferable.

About 200 yards beyond that draw you reach a major fork in the canyon. Butler Canyon proper is the left fork. By following the right fork and walking up to a minor ridge, you will gain a memorable overview of the canyon and the surrounding landscape. The route to the ridge is neither difficult nor dangerous, and the vistas easily justify the extra effort required to enjoy them.

Proceed for 150 yards into the right fork of the canyon, which quickly becomes a narrow gorge. There you reach a willow thicket in an alcove, beneath a 15-foot pouroff, which blocks the main drainage. Here a lesser drainage enters the alcove at a 90-degree angle to the right, also via a water-carved pouroff. You will see the small aperture of an arch piercing a Kayenta Sandstone knob a short distance to the east.

Backtrack several yards from the second, smaller pouroff and ascend 50 feet up a broken, blocky slope to the right (south). This route leads to the draw above the pouroff, and from there you want to leave the draw on a southwest course and ascend a moderate grade up the ledgy slope to the low ridge ahead, gaining 200 feet en route. You top out on the ridge at 4,960 feet, among the iron-rich slabs of the lower layer of Navajo Sandstone.

The panorama that unfolds from the ridge is breathtaking. Bold Navajo domes and broad expanses of slickrock flank Butler Canyon on all sides. Ledges and low cliff bands of Kayenta Formation rocks bound the inner reaches of the canyon, creating a distinctive variation in the landscape. Rising on the western horizon, beyond a foreground of Navajo slickrock, are the towering peaks of the Henry Mountains: Ellsworth, Pennell, and Ellen. The contrast between the conifer forests and alpine summits of the Henrys and the vast slickrock landscape below is dramatic.

From the ridge, carefully retrace your route back into Butler Canyon, then backtrack to the trailhead.

North Wash to Butler Canyon

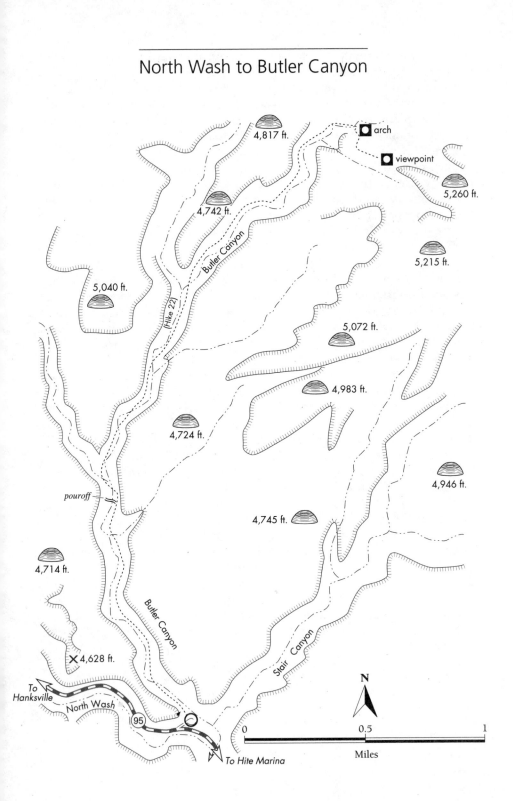

4,817 ft.

arch

viewpoint

5,260 ft.

4,742 ft.

Butler Canyon

5,215 ft.

(Hike 22)

5,040 ft.

5,072 ft.

4,983 ft.

4,724 ft.

4,946 ft.

pouroff

4,745 ft.

4,714 ft.

Butler Canyon

Stair Canyon

X 4,628 ft.

To Hanksville

North Wash

95

N

0   0.5   1

Miles

To Hite Marina

The lofty peaks of the Henry Mountains rise in the background beyond the slickrock domes on the rim of Butler Canyon.

23 Woodenshoe Trailhead to Dark Canyon

General description:	A round-trip backpack in the Dark Canyon Wilderness, traversing Woodenshoe Canyon, Dark Canyon's longest tributary.
Distance:	29.4 miles round trip.
Difficulty:	Moderate.
Trail conditions:	Well-worn trail, with one 3.7-mile segment of wash route.
Trailhead access:	4WD advised when road is wet.
Average hiking time:	3 to 4 days.
Trailhead elevation:	8,040 feet.
Low point:	5,800 feet.
Elevation gain and loss:	2,240 feet.
Optimum seasons:	Late May through June; September through October.
Water availability:	Perennial flows at 2 miles, and from a spring at 13.5 miles; seasonal intermittent flows above and below the confluence with Cherry Canyon, and below the limestone narrows between 12 and 13.5 miles.
Hazards:	Flash-flood danger.
Permits:	Not required.

Topo maps: Woodenshoe Buttes, Warren Canyon, and Black Steer Canyon USGS quads; Trails Illustrated Dark Canyon/Manti–La Sal National Forest.

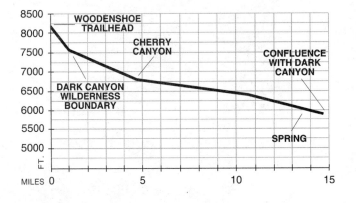

Key points:

1.2   Enter Dark Canyon Wilderness.
4.75   Confluence with Cherry Canyon.
13.5   Perennial spring.
14.7   Confluence of Woodenshoe and Dark canyons.

Finding the trailhead: Follow driving directions for Hike 16 to the junction of Utah 95 and Utah 275, then turn north onto Utah 275. After 0.6 mile, turn north (right) onto the graded dirt road signed for "Bears Ears-6, Kigalia Guard Station-10, and Elk Ridge Access."

This generally good road, usually passable to cars in dry weather, ascends to Maverick Point via two steep switchbacks. Once on the gentler terrace of the point, you enter the Manti–La Sal National Forest after 3.2 miles, where the road becomes Forest Road 088, then steadily ascend to 8,508-foot Bears Ears Pass, a prominent notch separating the brick-red Bears Ears buttes at 6.1 miles.

From the pass the road descends into the rich grasslands and cool conifer forests of South Elk Ridge for 1.8 miles to a signed junction. Turn left at the junction onto Forest Road 108/San Juan County 256, signed for "Woodenshoe-6." Follow Forest Road 108 west, passing the signed Peavine Trailhead after 1.9 miles. A short distance beyond is a large corral and cattle guard. After crossing the cattle guard, continue straight ahead on Forest Road 181 at the signed junction with northbound Forest Road 108.

After driving 3.7 miles from Forest Road 088, turn right onto a narrow dirt road signed for "Woodenshoe Canyon" and "Trail 165." This road, rough and rocky in places, gradually descends the headwaters drainage of Woodenshoe Canyon for 0.9 mile to a left-branching spur road that leads 100 yards to the signed trailhead.

Hikers arriving late in the day will find many undeveloped campsites on Maverick Point and South Elk Ridge.

The hike: Woodenshoe Canyon, Dark Canyon's longest tributary, stretches more than 15 miles from its headwaters draw high on South Elk Ridge to its mouth deep in the wild middle reaches of Dark Canyon. Throughout much of its length, Woodenshoe Canyon averages 1,200 feet in depth, carving a spectacular gorge through the thickest exposures of Cedar Mesa Sandstone on the Colorado Plateau.

Woodenshoe begins as a shallow draw mantled in forests of pine and fir, and groves of aspen. In its middle reaches the canyon floor is broad and the wash is fringed by a ribbon of riparian growth. The deepest part of the canyon, in its lower reaches, is a limestone-embraced inner gorge, a dry, narrow hallway that stretches to the pinyon- and juniper-clad benches at the canyon mouth.

This is the most popular backpack trip in the Dark Canyon Wilderness, yet use is still only light to moderate, and solitude is the rule rather than the exception. Most hikers make the hike a round trip, though Woodenshoe Canyon is occasionally used by long-distance hikers en route to the Sundance Trailhead (see Hike 29), and by those taking the rewarding loop via Peavine Canyon (Hike 24).

Ample campsites, an occasionally challenging route, intermittent flows of water and a perennial spring, Anasazi ruins, and a classic canyon country landscape combine to make a 4- to 5-day round-trip backpack in Woodenshoe Canyon a rewarding and memorable outing.

The trail begins behind the gate next to the trailhead register and sign-board. The well-defined trail descends gradually at first through an open forest of ponderosa pine, above the infant draw of Woodenshoe Canyon. As you proceed deeper into the drainage, you enter a shady forest of large pines, Douglas-firs, aspens, and Gambel oaks. Snowberry shrubs form thickets among the tall trees, and an array of wildflowers splash their colorful blooms across the trailside slopes.

At length the trail begins a moderate descent, with a rocky tread where it passes over outcrops of White Rim Sandstone. Soon you mount the red tread of the Organ Rock Shale, though few exposures of the brick red for-mation can be seen on the brush-clad slopes above. After entering the Dark Canyon Wilderness, you continue to traverse above the pine-shaded draw. Eventually the trail descends to the floor of the draw after 2 miles, at the emergence of the Cedar Mesa Sandstone. There is usually a good flow of water in the wash at this point.

After the Cedar Mesa Sandstone appears, Woodenshoe begins to assume the character of a canyon. The trail ahead repeatedly crosses the often dry wash, and you rise and descend on an undulating course between the cross-ings. The forest of ponderosa pine and fir persists, though as you proceed pinyon pines and junipers begin infiltrating their ranks. The canyon walls grow steadily higher, with bulging cliff bands and ledges of buff-toned sand-stone, displaying the sweeping lines of cross-bedding typical of wind-deposited sand.

The Upper reaches of Woodenshoe Canyon.

You pass the first campsite after 3.9 miles, located at the mouth of the first prominent side canyon entering on the right. A small seep that dampens the wash at the canyon's mouth provides an early season water source. From the campsite it is less than a mile to Cherry Canyon, and en route you will pass a few more good campsites. Just above the confluence with Cherry Canyon, you may find a seasonal flow of water, and even when water is not flowing, subsurface moisture supports willows and narrowleaf cottonwoods along the fringes of the wash.

Cherry Canyon, Woodenshoe's principal tributary, is indicated by a sign and opens up to the southeast after 4.75 miles. Boot-worn trails enter that canyon on both sides of the wash, forged by hikers in search of a purported seep that seldom flows. The floor of Woodenshoe Canyon opens up beyond Cherry Canyon, and a ribbon of narrowleaf cottonwood, willow, wiregrass, and horsetail fringe the wash, which usually carries a seasonal, intermittent flow of water. Pinyon pines and juniper trees steadily begin to supplant the conifer forest, though tall pines persist.

The 4.8-mile stretch below Cherry Canyon is perhaps the most beautiful part of Woodenshoe Canyon. Although much of the way passes on a trail of deep, soft sand, traversing benches between wash crossings, the surroundings offer ample compensation for your efforts. The tall pines and Douglas-firs on the canyon bottom offer plenty of shade and many excellent places to camp beneath their evergreen boughs. The most outstanding feature of the canyon is its bold slickrock cliffs.

Here the entire sequence of the Cedar Mesa Sandstone is exposed, forming great walls that rise 1,200 feet to lofty, conifer-fringed plateaus. These towering cliffs display the characteristics that make Cedar Mesa Sandstone a unique and justifiably famous scenery producer on the Colorado Plateau: bulging cliffs of red, white, and buff-toned slickrock, bold towers, slender hoodoos, veils of desert varnish, and deep alcoves and amphitheaters. Keep an eye out for Anasazi ruins, as there are a few that are readily visible from the trail, generally on the south-facing canyon walls.

After 9.6 miles, the gray ledges of the shales and limestones of the Elephant Canyon Formation emerge in the wash at a pouroff labeled "Falls" on the Warren Canyon USGS quad. The route of the trail ahead is inaccurately plotted on the Trails Illustrated map, but the USGS map shows its correct course.

Skirt the pouroff on the left side and drop into the wash below. As you follow this limestone inner gorge for the next 3 miles, views of Woodenshoe Canyon's great walls and conifer-fringed plateaus are obscured by the narrow hallway of the gorge. The trail through the gorge is well-worn and easy to follow as it crosses the dry wash from one bank to another. Few suitable camping areas will be found along this stretch, which is susceptible to flash-flooding.

The pines and firs at last give way to the pinyon-juniper woodland in the gorge. Other indicators of the more arid, desert-influenced environment are trailside shrubs such as mormon tea, yucca, mock orange, and prickly pear and hedgehog cacti.

Woodenshoe Trailhead to Dark Canyon, Woodenshoe-Peavine Loop

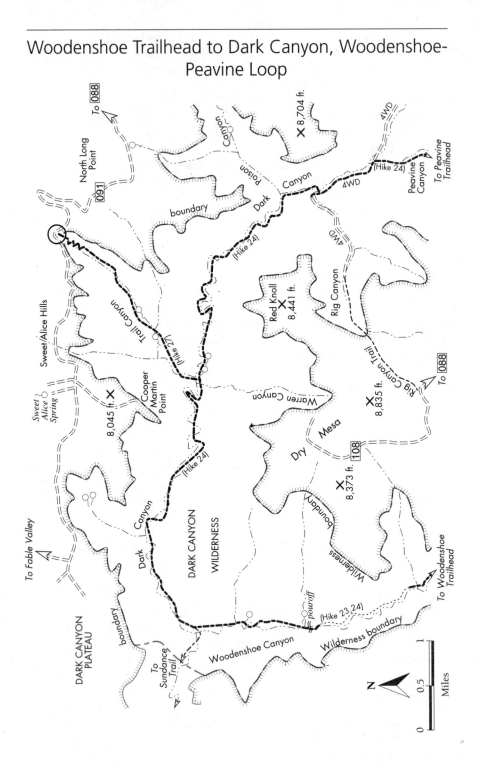

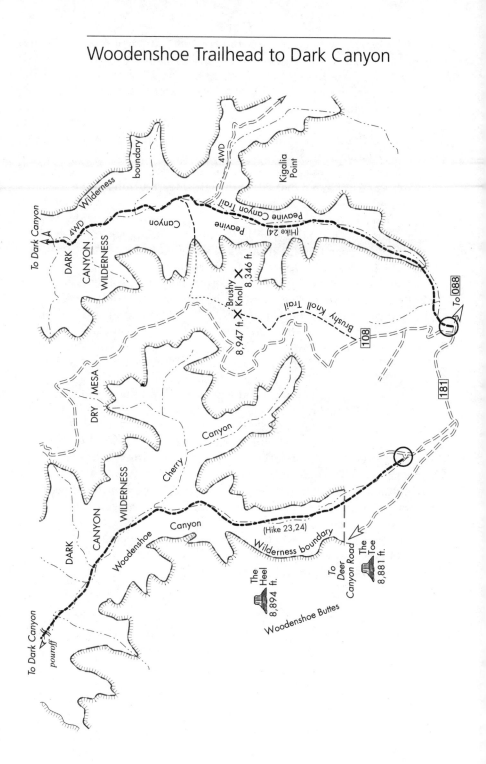

A narrow side canyon enters on the right at 6,260 feet after 11.4 miles, where you find an excellent campsite set in an isolated grove of Douglas-fir. Just ahead, two seeps in the wash provide a seasonal source of water, though their shallow, scummy pools, brimming with water boatmen, are appealing only in an emergency, and better water sources lie ahead. Quite soon thereafter you pass a good seasonal spring emerging from beneath another Douglas-fir grove. A large campsite is located opposite the spring on the left bench of the wash, in a woodland of pinyon and juniper.

As you approach a major side canyon that opens up on the right (east), you reach a pouroff and bypass it on the left side, returning to the wash just below the mouth of the side canyon (which carries a seasonal flow of water). Woodenshoe Canyon begins to open up ahead, with wide, wooded benches flanking the wash. The bold cliffs bounding square-edged Dark Canyon Plateau soar 1,800 feet skyward straight ahead.

After 13.5 miles, you pass between several good campsites among the gnarled woodland trees, opposite a vigorous perennial spring issuing from the limestone cliffs on the east flank of the canyon. This cold, reliable spring supports a rich hanging garden of maidenhair fern and alcove columbine. After 2 more bends of the canyon, another major side canyon opens up on the right (east), bounded on its north side by a dramatic knife-blade ridge. Much like the previous large side canyon, some hikers mistake the drainage for Dark Canyon, so be sure to continue straight ahead.

Woodenshoe Canyon continues to open up as you make your way along the final 0.9 mile to the confluence with Dark Canyon at 5,800 feet, and about 1 hour below the spring. Dark Canyon branches left (west) and right (northeast) at the confluence, with great cliffs jutting skyward to the north. There are several fair, mostly shadeless, campsites at the mouth of Woodenshoe Canyon, but no water.

Hikers bound up-canyon en route toward Peavine Canyon should bear right at the confluence onto a well-worn trail. Down-canyon, Dark Canyon wash is dry as it cuts through an increasingly deep limestone gorge for 8 miles to Youngs Canyon, where a perennial spring emerges. From Youngs Canyon to the Sundance Trail (6 miles), and on to Lake Powell, a good stream flows all year through the 1,400-foot deep gorge.

24 Woodenshoe-Peavine Loop

See Maps on Pages 138–139

General description:	An ambitious loop backpack in the Dark Canyon Wilderness, recommended for experienced canyon country hikers only, surveying scenery ranging from conifer and aspen forests to the arid, wooded depths of incomparable Dark Canyon.
Distance:	40.3 miles loop trip.
Difficulty:	Moderately strenuous.
Trail conditions:	Well-worn trail; a 3.7-mile segment of wash route; and a 6.2-mile segment of seldom-used 4WD road.
Trailhead access:	4WD advised when the road is wet.
Average hiking time:	4 to 5 days.
Trailhead elevation:	8,040 feet.
High point:	8,400 feet.
Low point:	5,800 feet.
Elevation gain and loss:	2,600 feet.
Optimum seasons:	Late May through June; September through October.
Water availability:	See Hike 23. Springs between 0.2 and 0.5 mile above confluence of Dark and Trail canyons; intermittent flows at confluence of Dark and Peavine canyons, in lower Peavine Canyon, and in the upper reaches of the Peavine Canyon Trail.
Hazards:	Flash-flood danger.
Permits:	Not required.
Topo maps:	Woodenshoe Buttes, Warren Canyon, Black Steer Canyon, Poison Canyon, and Kigalia Point (Peavine Canyon Trail not shown on quad) USGS quads; Trails Illustrated Dark Canyon/Manti–La Sal National Forest.

Key points:

1.2   Enter Dark Canyon Wilderness.
4.75 Confluence with Cherry Canyon.
13.5 Perennial spring.
14.7 Confluence of Woodenshoe and Dark canyons; turn right into Dark Canyon.
20.8 Trail Canyon joins from the left (northeast).
25.6 Poison Canyon joins on the left.
26.3 Mouth of Rig Canyon, junction with Peavine Corridor Road; bear left.
27.5 Peavine Canyon joins on the right (south); turn right.
32.5 Unsigned junction with Peavine Canyon Trail; turn right.
37.6 Peavine Trailhead; turn right onto Forest Road 108.
37.7 Continue straight ahead on FR 181.
39.4 Turn right onto spur road leading to Woodenshoe Trailhead.
40.3 Woodenshoe Trailhead.

Finding the trailhead: Follow driving directions for Hike 23.

The hike: This ambitious loop trip is perhaps the finest and most rewarding backpack in Dark Canyon. The trip surveys the spectrum of upper Dark Canyon landscapes, from cool, conifer-clad plateaus to deep and narrow canyons, and from riparian oases to long stretches of bone-dry wash. The potential for camping is almost unlimited throughout the trip, and you may choose sites ranging from those in the pinyon-juniper woodland to those in cool stands of ponderosa pine.

Although much of the trip follows a good (though very sandy) trail, the way between Rig Canyon and upper Peavine Canyon follows the Peavine Corridor Road for 6.2 miles. This corridor through the Dark Canyon Wilderness allows vehicular access into Peavine Canyon, Rig Canyon, and Scorup Cabin. Since vehicles, primarily OHVs, occasionally use this 4WD road, it is possible, but not very likely, for hikers to have the silence and solitude disrupted.

Water is the most important consideration on this long trip. Before setting out, check first with the Monticello Ranger District office or the Kane Gulch Ranger Station for the most recent reports on water availability. Since so few hikers enter Dark Canyon, and fewer still offer reports on water sources, the information you obtain may be outdated. Each hiker taking this trip must carry enough water containers to hold at least 2 gallons, and be prepared to top off those containers at every opportunity.

This trip is perhaps the most remote and seldom used of any trip covered in

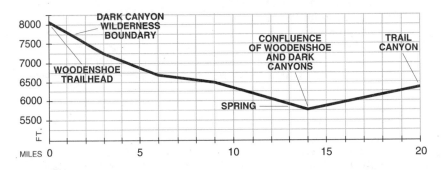

this book. In the event of an emergency, don't expect the help of other hikers; you'll likely have the canyon to yourself. Your party must be experienced, self-reliant, and prepared to deal with emergency situations, should they arise.

This demanding trip is recommended for experienced canyon country hikers only. The trail is sandy, there are long dry stretches, and after a few days on the trail the network of canyons begins to look much the same. A good feel for the layout of the landscape, the willingness to slog for miles through soft sand and carry 2 gallons of water are prerequisites for this trip.

Although the hike can be taken in either direction, most hikers taking this trip begin at the Woodenshoe Trailhead (see Hike 23) and follow beautiful Woodenshoe Canyon for 14.7 miles to its confluence with Dark Canyon at 5,800 feet. Plan on passing your first night in Woodenshoe Canyon, and on the second day, tank up at the spring at 13.5 miles, your last source of water for the next 6.3 miles.

At the confluence of Woodenshoe and Dark canyons, look for the dusty trail that turns right (northeast) and crosses the slopes above the rock-strewn floor of Dark Canyon wash. The 6.3 long, dry miles to Trail Canyon follow pinyon- and juniper-clad benches on either side of the wash. It can be a hot stretch with shade being a precious commodity. The gray limestone and red sandstone ledges and cliff bands of the Elephant Canyon Formation embrace the wash, while the red and white layer-cake cliffs of the Cedar Mesa Sandstone rise 1,400 feet above to the square-edged canyon rims. Bold towers and conifer-fringed points on the plateaus loom overhead throughout this section.

Trail Canyon is distinctive as the second major side canyon opening up on the left beyond the mouth of Woodenshoe Canyon, after 20.8 miles at 6,500 feet. You may also notice the northbound trail ascending along Trail Canyon's course (see Hike 27). A good campsite lies alongside the trail opposite Trail Canyon's mouth and offers the best place to pass your second night. About 0.2 mile up Dark Canyon wash, you may find a seep that provides a minor flow of water in the wash. A more vigorous seep 0.5 mile above Trail Canyon usually provides a reliable flow, though there are no campsites nearby. There is also a reliable spring located 1.8 miles up Trail Canyon.

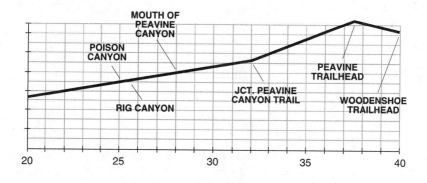

The last time I visited Dark Canyon, in mid-July, I day-hiked Trail Canyon and cached 1 gallon of water at the Dark Canyon confluence, where water was flowing in the wash. Four days later I retrieved the cache and found that Dark Canyon wash had dried up, though the spring mentioned above was still flowing vigorously. If you're taking the trip in an exceptionally dry year, you may want to consider caching water at Trail Canyon, and perhaps in Peavine Canyon.

The wash dries up beyond the spring, and you continue along the sandy trail, repeatedly crossing the wash. Progress through the stretch ahead seems to be made in slow motion as you follow the many tight meanders of the wash, yet gain little lateral distance, for the next 2.5 miles. The canyon floor opens up as you approach Poison Canyon. The wide benches that flank the wash are mantled in sagebrush and various other common shrubs, offering no potential for camping. North-facing canyon walls now begin to support a heavy forest of pine and Douglas-fir, though pinyon and juniper trees continue to dominate on the canyon bottom.

The limestone layers of the Elephant Canyon Formation persist on the lower canyon walls, but the convoluted Cedar Mesa Sandstone cliffs dominate the landscape. Domes, towers, buttes, deep alcoves, and cliffs draped with veils of desert varnish combine to make this a truly spectacular part of Dark Canyon.

Views of densely forested high plateaus open up as you reach the mouth of Poison Canyon at 6,840 feet, after 25.6 miles. The portal of that major side canyon is flanked by intricately sculpted slickrock walls. Here Dark Canyon bends south and the wash, though still dry, begins to support cottonwoods and willows along its banks. After another 0.7 mile of sandy trail walking, Rig Canyon opens up on the right (west). The trail then turns right to enter the mouth of Rig Canyon wash, skirts an old corral, then joins the Peavine Corridor 4WD road. This road was constructed by the Midwest Oil Company in 1927 for an unproductive oil drilling operation in Rig Canyon.

Bear left onto the road where the sign points to Dark Canyon, and follow the old, seldom used double track up the course of Dark Canyon. Although the road is sandy in places, it generally provides a firm tread, a pleasant improvement over the last 12 miles of slogging down the soft, sandy trail. Beyond Rig Canyon ponderosa pines begin to dominate the tree cover on the canyon floor, and the old road alternates between shady groves of pines and cottonwoods and brushy, sun-drenched openings for 1.2 miles. Horsetails, wiregrass, willow, and cottonwood fringe the wash, which may carry a flow of water during the cooler months of spring. During the road walk to Peavine Canyon, the left (northeast) canyon walls display a dramatic array of red and buff-toned domes and spires.

Peavine Canyon is the next major side canyon that opens up on the right (south) at 27.5 miles, and its broad drainage is flanked by pine forest and conifer-studded slickrock walls. You may find a sluggish flow of water just above Peavine's mouth in Dark Canyon wash. There is a large arch on the canyon wall opposite (northeast) Peavine Canyon's mouth, but its aperture is not readily visible.

Turn right at the unsigned road junction at 6,920 feet and proceed south into Peavine Canyon. The left branch of the poor road continues up Dark Canyon for 2.4 miles to its end at Scorup Cabin. Peavine is a beautiful canyon, and the first 1.5 miles along its course skirts lovely, verdant meadows fringed by conifer forest. The Cedar Mesa Sandstone cliffs flanking the eastern margins of the canyon rise 600 to 800 feet, sculpted by the ages into an array of dramatic erosional forms.

After about 2 miles, the limestone cliffs of the Elephant Canyon Formation dip underground, and the Cedar Mesa Sandstone dominates. The wash usually carries very little sluggish, intermittent water, possibly fouled by cattle, along the lower 3 miles of the canyon. A better, more reliable water source, lies 4 miles ahead in the upper reaches of the canyon. The narrow road dips to cross the wash several times, and alternates from shady stands of ponderosa pine, Douglas-fir, and narrowleaf cottonwood, to the sun-dappled shade of the pinyon-juniper woodland. It is a delightful walk up the forest-fringed canyon, and though the road undulates at times, little elevation is gained en route to Kigalia Canyon.

After 4.5 miles, where a prominent side canyon opens up to the west, a well-worn cow trail leaves the right side of the road and leads about 150 yards to a dry pine-shaded campsite, a fine place to pass your final night on a 4-day trip. Behind the campsite the abandoned Brushy Knoll Trail ascends steeply through heavy forest to Dry Mesa, then tops out on Brushy Knoll, and follows an old road to Forest Road 108 after 4.5 miles, 2 miles north of the Peavine Trailhead. Good routefinding skills are necessary to follow that overgrown trail.

Kigalia Canyon opens up on the left (southeast), 5 miles from Dark Canyon, at mile 32.5. Kigalia Point, recognizable by the landslide scars on its north slopes, separates the drainages of Kigalia and Peavine canyons. The unsigned but well-worn Peavine Canyon Trail branches right off the road shortly before you reach the mouth of Kigalia Canyon at 7,300 feet. If you miss the trail junction and reach an old corral, backtrack 125 yards to the wash crossing, and thence another 90 yards to the trail. There may be a cairn marking the junction.

The good trail proceeds into the broad upper valley of Peavine Canyon, its tread likely showing tracks of cows, deer, coyotes, mountain lions, or black bears, rather than the boot tracks of other hikers. Although outcrops of Cedar Mesa Sandstone project from the canyon's slopes, the overall appearance is that of a forested mountain drainage. The trail leads through open fields rich with tall needle-and-thread grass and lupine, and past thickets of chokecherry and snowberry. Tall narrowleaf cottonwoods hug the banks of the wash.

After about 1 mile, the canyon is dominated by a forest of ponderosa pines and Douglas-firs, offering a cool refuge on the hottest summer days. The dusty, sometimes sandy trail rises gently to moderately, crossing the dry wash on occasion.

After about 2 miles you reach a trailside water trough fed by a dripping piped spring. The following mile passes through the increasingly confined canyon through a shady spruce and aspen forest, reminiscent of most any high mountain canyon in the Rockies. After 3 miles you begin following a small, cold stream that often flows year-round. Soon the trail emerges in the headwaters bowl of Peavine Canyon, fringed by park-like stands of ponderosa pine. The red slopes and ledges of Organ Rock Shale above provide a strong contrast to the verdant growth in the bowl.

You exit the confines of Dark Canyon Wilderness after 3.7 miles, at mile 36.2, and then begin a moderate ascent of the southwest branch of the drainage. After rising 120 feet in the 0.6 mile from the wilderness boundary, the

Lower Peavine Canyon and the Peavine Corridor Road.

trail then inclines steeply through the forest of mixed conifers and aspens. Soon the tall aspens predominate, their white boles contrasting with the rich summer verdure that mantles the slopes. After gaining 400 feet of elevation in 0.6 mile, the grade moderates when you join a long-closed road, and a "Trail" sign points the way ahead. Soon thereafter you mount an 8,400-foot saddle, then stroll down the last few yards to the Peavine Trailhead. Bear right here and follow the road for 2.7 miles back to your car at the Woodenshoe Trailhead.

25 Big Notch to Scorup Cabin

General description: A rewarding day hike or overnighter to an historic cowboy cabin in upper Dark Canyon, within the Dark Canyon Wilderness.

Distance: 9.6 miles round trip.

Difficulty: Moderate.

Trail conditions: Well-worn trail for one mile, easy to follow cow trails thereafter.

Trailhead access: 4WD advised when road is wet.

Average hiking time: 5 hours round trip.

Trailhead elevation: 8,300 feet.

Low point: 7,180 feet.

Elevation gain and loss: 1,120 feet.

Optimum season: Late May through October.

Water availability: Intermittent in Dark Canyon beginning at 1.7 miles; a reliable spring lies several yards below the cabin in the wash. Bring your own if day hiking.

Hazards: Negligible.

Permits: Not required.

Topo maps: Kigalia Point and Poison Canyon USGS quads; Trails Illustrated Dark Canyon/Manti–La Sal National Forest.

Key points:
- 1.0   Floor of upper Dark Canyon.
- 3.7   Drift Trail Canyon joins from the northeast.
- 4.8   Scorup Cabin.

Finding the trailhead: Follow driving directions for Hike 23 to the junction of Forest Roads 088 and 108 (7.9 miles north of Utah 275), then turn right, staying on the smooth gravel of Forest Road 088. As you follow the road along South Elk Ridge through forests of pine, fir, and aspen, you first pass the turnoff to Kigalia Point 9.8 miles from Utah 275, then the spur to Kigalia Guard Station after 10.3 miles, and reach a confusing junction after 11.8 miles.

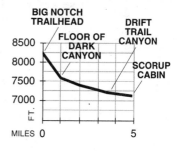

The road straight ahead is signed "Blanding-30," but you make a hard left turn, staying on Forest Road 088, which soon becomes rocky and rough in places. The road dips into Little Notch at 13.7 miles. After 16 miles, avoid the left fork to Steamboat Point. The road continues an undulating course over South Elk Ridge until you reach a long, steep downgrade that leads to Big Notch and the small, signed trailhead parking area, 19.3 miles from Utah 275.

The hike: This very scenic hike traces Dark Canyon from its Elk Ridge headwaters to historic Scorup Cabin, a well-preserved summer cowboy camp dating back to 1930. The trip blends montane forests and rich grasslands and wildflowers with a canyon country landscape of bold Cedar Mesa Sandstone walls. This trip is a fine choice for a day hike from late spring through autumn, and the intermittent stream and numerous potential camping areas make the trip inviting to overnighters as well.

Observant hikers may spot Anasazi ruins, though they are not abundant, or some of the diverse wildlife that dwell here. Mule deer, mountain lions, elk, coyotes, and black bears make their home on Elk Ridge and in upper Dark Canyon. Short-horned lizards, attaining the size of an adult's hand, are quite common. Watch where you step as these slow-moving reptiles frequently sun themselves on the sandy trail.

Upper Dark Canyon offers pleasant summer hiking, when temperatures are quite warm, but rarely uncomfortably hot. The only drawback to an early to mid-summer outing is the presence of no-see-ums and biting deer flies. Mid to late summer brings the possibility of strong thunderstorms and flash-flooding. Yet during this time you will likely have the canyon all to yourself, since most other hikers have retreated to the high country of the mountains.

The trail begins on the west side of Forest Road 088, 15 yards southwest of the signed trailhead. A small "Trail" sign shows the way. The trail is rocky at times as it descends gradually at first, then moderately, threading a way through an open forest of ponderosa pine.

The upper reaches of Dark Canyon soon come into view far below, flanked by convoluted cliffs of Cedar Mesa Sandstone and the cool forests and brush fields of the Elk Ridge plateaus. After 0.3 mile you reach an oak-clad bench, then descend a steep but short grade into a headwaters draw of Dark Canyon, soon thereafter entering the Dark Canyon Wilderness. Outcrops of Cedar Mesa Sandstone begin to appear as you descend the increasingly confined draw. Here Rocky Mountain maple joins the ranks of the conifer and aspen forest.

The draw opens up into Dark Canyon after 1 mile, 650 feet below Big Notch. Grass- and brush-clad benches, studded with groves of box elder and aspen, flank the wash, with forests of pine and fir mantling the slopes above. The trail, now descending an imperceptible grade on the canyon floor, proceeds through waist-high brome grass. This trail does not receive enough use through the tall grasslands to be very well defined and remains faint yet not difficult to follow. The tracks of cows and cowboys' horses generally define the way.

As you approach the first side canyon that opens up on the right (northeast), you reach a fenceline and pass through a gate (leave it open or closed, as you find it). You continue the pleasant stroll ahead over grassy, brush-dotted benches above the Dark Canyon arroyo. As you proceed, the canyon floor grows wider and the bulging cliffs of Cedar Mesa slickrock rise higher, studded with tall pines and firs.

When the second side canyon joins on the right after 1.7 miles, you dip into the arroyo and find a small stream that flows intermittently as far down-canyon as the confluence with Peavine Canyon, 5.7 miles ahead. After jumping across the small stream, follow the path that rises steeply

Big Notch to Scorup Cabin

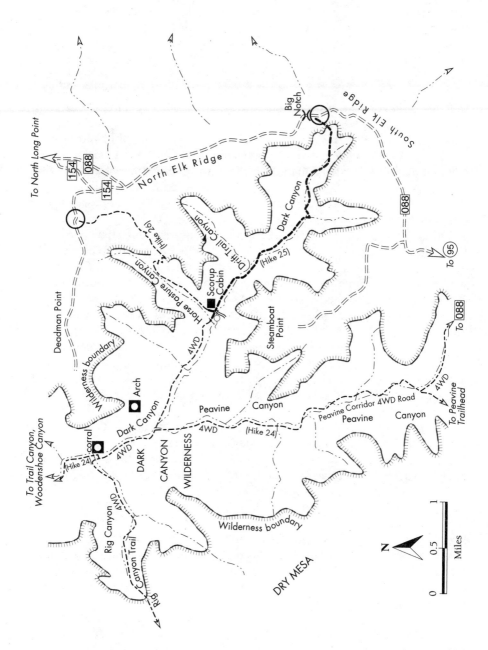

back up to the opposite bench. Soon you drop back into the arroyo where the first major side canyon enters on the left, at 2.2 miles. It is far easier at this point to simply follow the arroyo down-canyon than to continue following the up-and-down cow trails on the benches above. The small flow of water in the arroyo is fringed with willows and grasses, and the walking is easy over the damp, hard-packed sand. When the stream is flowing, you must step across it many times.

Although the arroyo averages about 50 feet in depth, it is wide enough to allow good views to the tree-studded canyon walls. As you reach deeper into Dark Canyon, the cliffs of Cedar Mesa Sandstone begin to assume their characteristic bulging profile, punctuated by hoodoos and towers and streaked with veils of desert varnish. Numerous broad slickrock amphitheaters open up on either side of the canyon. What is atypical about upper Dark Canyon is its montane, rather than high desert, environment. Hikers familiar with Grand Gulch, or the Needles District in Canyonlands National Park, will enjoy here a Cedar Mesa Sandstone canyon embraced by cool forests that offers pleasant summer hiking.

The arroyo grows more shallow after the intermittent steam draining Drift Trail Canyon joins on the right after 3.7 miles. The Scorup-Somerville outfit used that canyon for many years to drive their herds from Dark Canyon to Elk Ridge and on to the headquarters at Dugout Ranch, but time has reclaimed the abandoned trail there. As the arroyo opens up ahead, three prominent amphitheaters lend a scalloped outline to the north canyon walls. To avoid the willow thickets in the arroyo below, look for a cow trail that ascends out of the drainage on the right, leading to the terrace above.

A well-defined segment of trail leads past the triad of amphitheaters and around a slickrock point that juts into the wash. On a bench just around the point you find Scorup Cabin, immediately above the confluence with Horse Pasture Canyon.

The two-room plank cabin, set on a pine- and oak-dotted bench, still contains the relics dating from its heyday as a summer cow camp. The cabin was originally located in Rig Canyon, a Dark Canyon tributary, where, from 1927 to 1930, the Midwest Oil Company conducted an oil drilling operation. In 1930, the cabin was moved to its present location to serve as summer headquarters for Dugout Ranch cowboys, and it was used in that capacity until the 1970s, when it was turned over to the Forest Service. An old shed stands nearby, filled with the appurtenances necessary for a cowboy's job. The cabin is a well-preserved historical highlight to this fine hike and offers a shady retreat, but backpackers are not permitted to spend the night inside. Just the same as at ancient cultural sites, it is unlawful and unethical to remove historic cowboy artifacts.

Here at Scorup Cabin, Dark Canyon maintains the atmosphere of a mountain drainage. Stands of ponderosa pine and Douglas-fir punctuate the slickrock walls of the canyon that rise 600 feet above, and the conifers dominate the forest on the canyon floor. Flowing water can usually be found in Dark Canyon wash a short distance below the cabin and a pouroff labeled "Falls" on the topo map. Beyond the cabin, a very seldom-used

4WD road leads 2.4 miles down Dark Canyon to Peavine Canyon, and thence up to Little Notch and Forest Road 088. The primary users of the 4WD corridors through the Dark Canyon Wilderness are autumn hunters, but use is increasing on this road, so it is possible you may encounter OHVs before the late October hunting season.

26 Horse Pasture Trail to Scorup Cabin

General description:	A very scenic and diverse day hike or overnighter into upper Dark Canyon, within the Dark Canyon Wilderness.
Distance:	8 miles round trip.
Difficulty:	Moderate.
Trail conditions:	Well-worn trail into Horse Pasture Canyon, faint path thereafter.
Trailhead access:	4WD advised when the road is wet.
Average hiking time:	4 hours round trip.
Trailhead elevation:	8,600 feet.
Low point:	7,180 feet.
Elevation gain and loss:	1,420 feet.
Optimum season:	Late May through October.
Water availability:	Perennial spring in Dark Canyon wash a short distance below the cabin. Bring your own if day hiking.
Hazards:	Steep dropoffs near the bottom of the descent into Horse Pasture Canyon.
Permits:	Not required.
Topo maps:	Poison Canyon USGS quad (trail not shown on map); Trails Illustrated Dark Canyon/Manti–La Sal National Forest.

Key points:
- 1.8 Dark Canyon Wilderness boundary.
- 2.5 Floor of Horse Pasture Canyon.
- 4.0 Scorup Cabin.

Finding the trailhead: Follow driving directions for Hikes 23 and 25 to Big Notch, 19.3 miles from Utah 275, then continue north along Forest Road 088. The steep, narrow, and winding upgrade north of Big Notch passes through clay beds that can become slippery and dangerous to drive on when wet. At the top of the grade the road begins an undulating course over the broad expanse of North Elk Ridge. Forest Road 154 branches left 4 miles north of Big Notch. Although that road also leads to Horse Pasture Trailhead, it is easier to find the trailhead by continuing north on Forest Road 088 for another 1.3 miles (24.6 miles from Utah 275) to the westbound road signed for Horse Pasture Trail and Deadman Point, immediately south of the signed, shallow pond of Duck Lake.

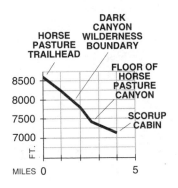

Turn left at the junction and follow the narrow, winding road, which is rough and rocky in places, for 1 mile to unsigned, southbound Forest Road 154, and bear right. (That road, mentioned above, leads 0.5 mile back to Forest Road 088.) After several yards, avoid a right-branching road ascending to the ridge above. The signed trailhead is located on the west side of the road, 1.6 miles from Forest Road 088, and 26.2 miles from Utah 275.

There are numerous undeveloped camping areas all along the course of Forest Road 088.

The hike: If you have only one day for a hike in the upper Dark Canyon area, the Horse Pasture Trail should be at the top of your list. This trail is the most scenic and popular of all the upper Dark Canyon trails, yet it is unlikely you will meet other hikers en route. Seldom steep, the trail maintains mostly moderate grades as it traverses rich conifer forests to the emergence of the Cedar Mesa Sandstone. From there the trail follows an exciting de-

Cedar Mesa slickrock embraces the rich meadows of Horse Pasture Canyon.

Horse Pasture Trail to Scorup Cabin

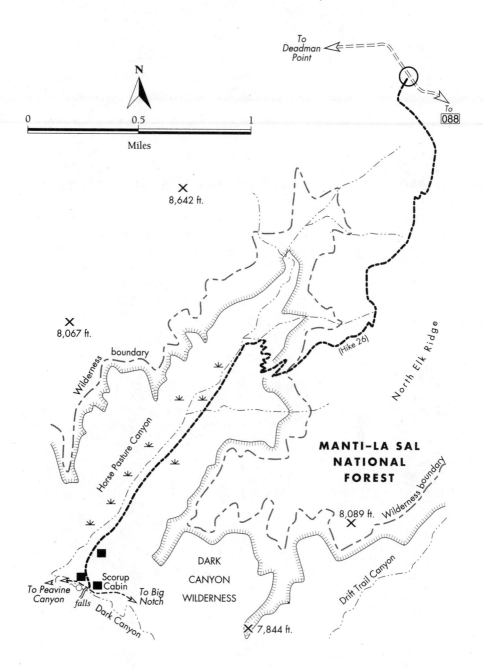

scent into the meadows of Horse Pasture Canyon, flanked by convoluted 500-foot walls, which stretch to the confluence with Dark Canyon.

Although the trip is typically taken as a day hike, it can be used as one leg of an extended shuttle trip to one of four other upper Dark Canyon trailheads. Backpackers should note that no water is available until they reach Dark Canyon, and sources are quite scarce beyond (see Hike 24).

The well-defined trail begins behind the trailhead register and signboard and leads among snowberry shrubs in the shade of the ponderosa pine forest for 200 yards to a "Trail" sign. There the trail curves left (southeast), staying a short distance back from the rim of Horse Pasture Canyon. A brief detour to the rim reveals tremendous views into the cliff-embraced meadows far below.

The trail ahead closely follows the rim through park-like pine forest and aspen groves for 0.5 mile, then begins its descent from North Elk Ridge. You drop steeply at first via four switchbacks, then the grade moderates, winding through dense aspen groves and beneath a shady canopy of ponderosa pines,Douglas-firs, and white firs. Some of the pines on these northwest-facing slopes are forest monarchs, exceeding 100 feet in height and 4 feet in diameter.

While on the southwest-bound, descending traverse you open up at times into sunny glades fringed with Gambel oaks and enlivened by the blooms of lupine and arrowleaf balsamroot. The rocky outcrops at the trailside are composed of White Rim Sandstone, a landmark formation on the rim of the inner gorges of the Green and Colorado rivers in Canyonlands National

Scorup Cabin in upper Dark Canyon.

Park. The elevated position of this and other nearby rock formations is due to uplift of the great bulge in the earth known as the Monument Upwarp, which reaches its highest elevations here on Elk Ridge.

After about 1 mile the trail begins to descend in earnest, emerging onto the brick red slopes of Organ Rock Shale. The red tread can become quite sticky and slippery when wet. Views from this stretch reach far below to the slickrock cliffs that form a box at the head of Horse Pasture Canyon, and to the red slopes of Deadman Point that rise above to the northwest.

At length groves of Gambel oak begin to supplant the conifer forest, and occasional pinyon pines and juniper trees appear as well. After 1.8 miles you enter the Dark Canyon Wilderness at 7,920 feet, atop a manzanita-clad bench. A pair of long switchbacks ensue, leading you down onto Cedar Mesa slickrock. The trail ahead crosses slickrock and sand as you follow switchbacks, descending steeply at times via a series of sandstone ledges. An open forest of mixed conifers persists as you wind down past a bold hoodoo to a wooden gate, beyond which the trail becomes very steep and quite sandy. The abrupt 550-foot descent ends 0.7 mile from the wilderness boundary on the floor of broad Horse Pasture Canyon among shady groves of box elders.

The trail leads southwest, down the gentle floor of the canyon, but soon grows increasingly ill-defined in the tall grasslands of the canyon's broad meadows. The 500-foot Cedar Mesa Sandstone walls that flank the canyon have been sculpted by ages of erosion into an especially dramatic facade. Great bulging cliffs, ledges studded with tall conifers, veils of desert varnish, shady alcoves, strange hoodoos, and bold towers make the scene a classic canyon country landscape seemingly out of place in a high elevation, mountain-like environment.

Another 1.2 miles of walking down the valley leads you to Scorup Cabin and the confluence with Dark Canyon. The trail, faint at times, follows the left margin of the valley as you approach Dark Canyon. Eventually you'll pass the remains of an old cabin, pass through a gate next to an old cow camp shed dating back to 1905, then curve around a slickrock point to a pine-shaded bench, where you find Scorup Cabin (see Hike 25 for more on Scorup Cabin).

27 Trail Canyon to Dark Canyon

See Maps on Pages 138–139

General description:	A rewarding day hike or overnighter, following a seldom-used trail into the remote depths of Dark Canyon, within the Dark Canyon Wilderness.
Distance:	8.2 miles round trip.
Difficulty:	Moderate.
Trail conditions:	Constructed trail, rocky in places but easy to follow.
Trailhead access:	4WD advised when the road is wet.
Average hiking time:	4 to 4.5 hours round trip.
Trailhead elevation:	7,846 feet.
Low point:	6,500 feet.
Elevation gain and loss:	1,346 feet.
Optimum season:	Late May through October.
Water availability:	Perennial springs at 2.3 miles, and between 0.2 and 0.5 mile above the mouth of Trail Canyon in Dark Canyon wash.
Hazards:	Exposure to steep dropoffs in upper Trail Canyon.
Permits:	Not required.
Topo maps:	Warren Canyon USGS quad; Trails Illustrated Dark Canyon/Manti–La Sal National Forest.

Key points:
0.1 Dark Canyon Wilderness boundary.
4.1 Confluence of Trail Canyon and Dark Canyon.

Finding the trailhead: Follow driving directions for Hikes 23, 25, and 26 to Duck Lake, 24.6 miles from Utah 275, then continue north along Forest Road 088. Avoid the spur road to Gooseberry Guard Station that branches right 1 mile from Duck Lake, and after another 1.2 miles (26.8 miles from Utah 275), you reach a prominent junction.

Forest Road 095 continues straight ahead, signed for "Causeway-12," but you will turn left, staying on Forest Road 088, signed for Beef Basin. You reach a second major junction 3.2 miles from the last (30 miles from Utah 275). Turn left (west) here onto Forest Road 91, signed for Sweet Alice Hills, Dark Canyon Plateau, and North Long Point.

The road straight ahead (north) is signed for Beef Basin, Dugout Ranch, and U.S. Highway 160 (now designated U.S. Highway 191). Drivers from the north can use this road to reach any of upper Dark Canyon's trailheads.

Find the north end of that road by following US 191 for 40 miles south from Moab, or 14 miles north from Monticello, then turn west onto Utah 211 toward the Needles District of Canyonlands National Park. Follow Utah

Trail Canyon, a remote tributary of the middle reaches of Dark Canyon.

Trail Canyon is a seldom-used access into Dark Canyon.

211 past Newspaper Rock Recreation Site to a southbound dirt road signed for Beef Basin and Elk Mountain. This turnoff is located 0.8 mile west of Dugout Ranch and 17.9 miles from US 191.

Turn left at the junction, and after 0.4 mile you reach a ford of Indian Creek, which may require a high-clearance vehicle at times. Follow the road generally south for 28.5 miles to the junction with westbound Forest Road 91.

As you drive west along dusty Forest Road 91 through the rich conifer forests of North Long Point, avoid the signed spur roads leading to Crystal Spring and Big Spring. Upon reaching the west end of North Long Point, the road begins a steady descent toward the saddle at the head of Trail Canyon, separating North Long Point from the Sweet Alice Hills. Superb canyon country vistas unfold en route, reaching west to the Henry Mountains, northwest to the Orange Cliffs, Beef Basin, and the Needles, and northeast to the La Sal Mountains.

When you reach the saddle at the bottom of the downgrade, 8.5 miles from Forest Road 088, look for the trailhead sign and register about 100 yards south of the road. Park in the turnouts on the north side of the road, 0.1 mile east of a corral and cattle guard.

Hikers arriving late in the day will find an almost unlimited selection of undeveloped campsites among the pines, aspens, and grassy parks of North Long Point.

The hike: The hike down open, southwest-trending Trail Canyon affords 2-hour access into the wild middle reaches of Dark Canyon via a scenic, seldom used, and rigorous trail. Due to its southern exposure, Trail Canyon is more typical of a high desert canyon than are other upper Dark Canyon tributaries. The trail traverses open pinyon-juniper woodlands beneath 800-foot cliffs, affording memorable vistas en route. The trail, which is often shadeless, can be hot, though usually not intolerable, during the summer months. This trip is a good choice for an early summer or autumn day hike, and can be used as part of an extended round-trip backpack or as one leg of a shuttle trip to the Woodenshoe, Peavine, Big Notch, or Horse Pasture trailheads (see Hikes 23–26).

The trail begins behind the trail register, and the way descends gradually through pinyon-juniper woodland to the boundary of Dark Canyon Wilderness. Immediately beyond the boundary, the trail becomes steep and rocky, descending among outcrops of Cedar Mesa Sandstone. Trailside trees frame a memorable vista deep into Dark Canyon, with bold sandstone cliffs and densely forested plateaus rising above its gaping trench.

The trail is alternately gentle and steep as it winds a way over a series of ledges and cliff bands, descending the precipitous headwaters draw of Trail Canyon. Since the tread is generally rocky, constant attention is required and progress will be slow. At times the trail turns in unexpected directions and crosses areas of slickrock. Keep an eye out for cairns to stay on course.

The sun-drenched slopes are dominated by a woodland of pinyon and juniper, with an occasional Douglas-fir mixing into their ranks. The rocky flanks of the canyon are mantled in a shrub cover of Utah serviceberry, littleleaf mountain mahogany, and manzanita. Green gentians adorn the trailside with their conspicuously tall, green flowering stalks.

At length you briefly touch the wash, then resume a steep and rocky descent above its banks on the left side. After about one hour of slow, careful walking from the trailhead, you regain the wash and follow it down-canyon. Tall ponderosa pines, Douglas-firs, and the trees of the pinyon-juniper woodland, combined with the confining canyon walls, now offer some relief from the sun. The trail ahead follows the rock-strewn, gravelly wash at times, but most often traverses either bank while avoiding pouroffs and boulder-choked stretches.

After 2.3 miles, just after passing the mouth of the first side canyon on the right (north), you find a seep and perhaps flowing water below it. There are many fine camping areas here on the trailside bench among tall pines, pinyons, and junipers. Beyond that side canyon, a gentle traverse through the woodland above the wash ensues. After another 0.5 mile (2.8 miles from the trailhead), you cross the wash, with slickrock under foot, and after 0.2 mile, you dip into the wash again. There you find another small spring, fringed with willow thickets, at 6,720 feet.

The limestone of the Elephant Canyon Formation emerges in the wash just below, and the profile of Trail Canyon grows markedly wider ahead. Trailside slopes host a well-developed woodland, and broken cliffs of red-

and white-banded Cedar Mesa Sandstone rise above in bold relief, reaching 1,200 feet up to the canyon rim. Fine views stretch southward across Dark Canyon into the precipitous gorge of Warren Canyon.

Eventually you emerge from the woodland onto a sagebrush-studded bench. Cross the broad, dry wash, then follow above its west bank for the remaining 0.25 mile to Dark Canyon, in a broad, wooded section of the gorge 1,500 feet below the canyon rims. Upon reaching Dark Canyon wash, cross to the opposite side and join the Dark Canyon Trail beneath the shade of a large, solitary plains cottonwood. A few yards south of the trail is an established campsite, one of few in this part of Dark Canyon, though potential camping places in the woodland are numerous.

A reliable series of seeps and springs emerge in Dark Canyon wash between 0.2 and 0.5 mile upstream from the Trail Canyon confluence. From there, Dark Canyon is dry for 6.7 miles to the mouth of Peavine Canyon, and the only water available down-canyon in the 14-mile stretch to Youngs Canyon is a perennial spring located 1.2 miles up the course of Woodenshoe Canyon.

28 Dark Canyon Plateau to Fable Valley

General description:	A memorable day hike or overnighter to a remote high desert valley within the Dark Canyon Primitive Area.
Distance:	9.6 miles or more, round trip.
Difficulty:	Moderate.
Trail conditions:	Rocky 4WD road and constructed trail into Fable Valley, cow trails thereafter, generally easy to follow.
Trail access:	4WD advised when the road is wet.
Average hiking time:	5 hours or more, round-trip.
Trailhead elevation:	7,600 feet.
Low point:	6,400 feet at Fable Spring.
Elevation gain and loss:	1,200 feet.
Optimum seasons:	Late May through June; September through October.
Water availability:	Seasonal intermittent flows in Fable Valley wash; Fable Spring, at 4.8 miles, offers perennial water.
Hazards:	Negligible.
Permits:	Not required.
Topo maps:	Warren Canyon and Fable Valley USGS quads; Trails Illustrated Dark Canyon/Manti–La Sal National Forest.

Key points:
2.0   End of 4WD road.
3.0   Floor of Fable Valley.
4.8   Fable Spring.

Finding the trailhead: Follow driving directions for Hikes 23 and 25 through 27 to the Trail Canyon Trailhead, 38.5 miles north of Utah 275 and 37 miles south of Utah 211, and continue west across the cattle guard and onto BLM-administered lands. The road ahead is graded, though there are occasional rocky stretches and areas of loose sand, where drivers must maintain momentum to avoid getting stuck.

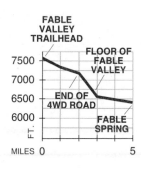

You pass a pair of northbound roads leading into the Sweet Alice Hills and to Sweet Alice Spring, respectively, 3.1 miles west of Trail Canyon Trailhead, and continue west through the pinyon-juniper woodlands of Dark Canyon Plateau for another 3.2 miles to a junction with a northbound 4WD road, signed for Fable Valley Trail. Park off the road at the junction, 14.8 miles west of the Forest Road 088/91 junction.

Hikers searching for a campsite will find ample undeveloped sites on North Long Point and several sites on Forest Road 91 up to 2 miles west of the Trail Canyon Trailhead.

The hike: Wedged between Dark Canyon Plateau and Wild Cow Point north of Dark Canyon is a very remote, high desert valley of exceptional beauty. Fable Valley, as its name suggests, is a special place, yet few hikers brave the 40 miles of dirt roads and rugged trails to get there.

The valley stretches 6 miles northwest to the rim of Gypsum Canyon, a precipitous gorge scaled by John Wesley Powell in 1869 from its mouth in Cataract Canyon on the Colorado River. The Fable Valley area, in addition to nearby Beef Basin, Butler Wash, Ruin Canyon, and northward into the Needles District of Canyonlands National Park, was a center of Anasazi culture more than 700 years ago, attested to by the great number of ruins in the area. While 4WD roads access Beef Basin, Butler Wash, and Ruin Canyon, only cow trails afford access into the wild interior of Fable Valley, where hikers have the opportunity to discover many ancient ruins and enjoy an unspoiled landscape in utter solitude.

The valley is best suited for a hike in to a base camp, with two or three days set aside for exploration. Hikers with limited time will still enjoy the all-day round-trip hike to Fable Spring. The spring offers a reliable, year-round water source, and the valley's wash usually offers an intermittent flow of water.

The valley is part of the BLM's Dark Canyon Primitive Area/Wilderness Study Area, and so is closed to motorized vehicles and bicycles. Cows, however, visit Fable Valley, though the trail is used primarily as a stock driveway linking Dark Canyon Plateau and Beef Basin. Fable Valley shows few signs of overuse from backcountry visitors. To maintain its pristine qualities, avoid camping within 0.25 mile of Fable Spring, and choose an established campsite rather than creating a new one.

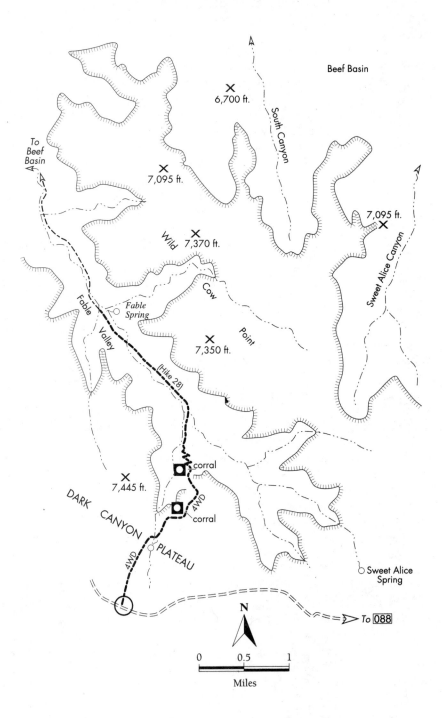

Beef Basin

To Beef Basin

South Canyon

× 6,700 ft.

× 7,095 ft.

× 7,095 ft.

Sweet Alice Canyon

Wild × 7,370 ft.

Cow

Fable Spring

Fable Valley

Point

× 7,350 ft.

[Hike 28]

corral

4WD

× 7,445 ft.

corral

DARK CANYON PLATEAU

4WD

Sweet Alice Spring

N

To 088

0   0.5   1

Miles

Begin the hike at the trailhead register and proceed north down the narrow track of the 4WD road. The rancher holding the grazing permit for this area uses this road, but the track is so poor it is barely passable to OHVs. You are not likely to encounter vehicles en route to the Fable Valley rim. Follow the avenue of the doubletrack through the woodland of stunted pinyon pines that mantle the surface of Dark Canyon Plateau. En route, fine views stretch northwest across the plateau to the bold barrier of the Orange Cliffs, visible beyond the barely perceptible canyon of the Colorado River.

After 0.5 mile, the road descends steeply over rocky ledges, dropping into a minor drainage supporting tall pinyon pines and junipers. After exiting the draw the roadbed becomes sandy as it skirts a broad sagebrush flat, then curves southeast into another minor drainage where you pass a water trough and piped spring. The road ahead winds past a large corral and eventually ends after 2 miles at 7,200 feet, on the rim of still invisible Fable Valley.

At the road end pass through a tight wire gate (keep closed) and enter the log corral. Cross to the northeast side of the corral (on your right) and you will find the wide, constructed stock trail descending off the rim. This steep, rocky trail descends via switchbacks, dropping 600 feet to the valley floor in 1 mile. En route you enjoy inspiring views into the remote high desert valley below, its broken Cedar Mesa Sandstone walls framing the Orange Cliffs in the distance.

As you approach the bottom of the descent, the trail skirts the base of a tall slickrock tower, and soon thereafter you emerge from the steep, wooded slopes onto the sagebrush-studded terraces of Fable Valley. The main trail, which can be confused with a network of cow trails, leads north through the sagebrush for 0.25 mile, then drops into the willow- and grass-fringed arroyo, where you may find a small stream. After regaining the bench on the opposite side of the arroyo, follow the sometimes faint, seldom-used trail northwest down the valley.

Sagebrush, native bunchgrasses, and exotic cheatgrass mantle the broad terraces, and fingers of the pinyon-juniper woodland reach out onto the valley floor from the foot of the cliffs. The red- and tan-banded, cross-bedded walls of Cedar Mesa Sandstone rise 400 to 600 feet above and feature a scalloped outline of prominent amphitheaters. Although rich grasses and willows fringe the wash in the arroyo and suggest the presence of water, there may be only intermittent flows, and in dry years, possibly no water above Fable Spring.

You will find the spring just inside the mouth of the first major side canyon that opens up on the right (east) after 4.8 miles, at 6,400 feet. The trail crests a low ridge opposite the spring, avoiding a narrow part of the wash, then drops back into the valley below the spring's side canyon. There are fine camping places along a mile-long stretch below the spring, upon benches clad in pinyon-juniper woodland.

The trail continues down the valley beyond Fable Spring for 3 miles to the rim of Gypsum Canyon, then proceeds generally east on a mildly undulating course for another 2.5 miles to the remote, difficult-to-reach Beef Basin Trailhead.

29 Sundance Trail to Dark Canyon

General description:	A backpack recommended only for experienced hikers, leading to a backcountry base camp deep in the lower reaches of Dark Canyon, within Glen Canyon National Recreation Area and the Dark Canyon Primitive Area.
Distance:	6.8 miles or more, round trip.
Difficulty:	Strenuous, one 20-foot Class 3 downclimb and friction pitch, and two Class 2 scrambles en route to canyon rim. Class 2 scrambling on descent into Dark Canyon.
Trail conditions:	Boot-worn trails and cairned route.
Trailhead access:	4WD required when wet, and may be required if floods have damaged the road.
Average hiking time:	3 to 4 days (5 hours round trip).
Trailhead elevation:	5,490 feet.
Low point:	4,000 feet in Dark Canyon; 3,700 feet at Lake Powell.
Elevation gain and loss:	+150 feet; -1,550 feet (-1,850 feet to Lake Powell).
Optimum seasons:	April through May; September through October.
Water availability:	Perennial intermittent flows in lower Dark Canyon; and Lake Powell.
Hazards:	Exposure to steep dropoffs; flash-flood danger in Dark Canyon.

Fable Valley, a remote high desert valley in the Dark Canyon Primitive Area.

Permits: Not required.

Topo maps: Indian Head Pass, Bowdie Canyon West, and Black Steer Canyon USGS quads; Trails Illustrated Dark Canyon/Manti–La Sal National Forest.

Key points:

0.6 Descend chute and slickrock friction pitch.
0.9 Cross 4WD road and enter Glen Canyon National Recreation Area.
2.2 Rim of Dark Canyon.
3.4 Floor of Dark Canyon.

Finding the trailhead: There are two ways to reach this remote trailhead, and both are via different segments of San Juan County 208A (Horse Tanks) that branch off of Utah 95. Drivers approaching from the east will find the signed junction with San Juan County 208A, branching right (northeast) from Utah 95 (opposite San Juan County 224A, signed for White Canyon), 68.8 miles west of the US 191/Utah 95 junction (3 miles south of Blanding); 40.5 miles west of the Utah

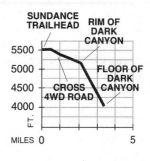

95/261 junction; 1.5 miles west of the Glen Canyon National Recreation Area boundary; 0.7 mile west of milepost 54; and 0.6 mile west of the White Canyon bridge.

This graded dirt road, usually passable to cars in dry weather, leads generally northeast for 4.6 miles to a Y junction, where you bear right, reaching a major junction with the westbound leg of San Juan County 208A after another 0.2 mile. Turn right (east) at the junction, and follow the driving directions below.

If you are approaching from the west, the west end of San Juan County 208A branches left (east) from Utah 95 at mile post 49, 0.2 mile east of the turnoff to Hite Marina, and 49 miles southeast of Hanksville. This branch of the road leads generally east beneath the buttes and spires of Browns Rim for 3.1 miles to a four-way junction. Continue straight ahead for 1 mile, avoiding the right-branching road leading to the Y junction mentioned above. After another 0.3 mile, the southbound segment of San Juan County 208A joins on the right at the major junction, 4.4 miles from Utah 95.

From either direction, continue following San Juan County 208A east. Avoid a southbound road that forks right 2.2 miles from the junction, and continue straight ahead to a signed junction with the western end of San Juan County 209A (Squaw Rock) after 2.9 miles. Turn right here, where a BLM sign points to "Trail," still on San Juan County 208A. The road ahead crosses a wash. Soon thereafter, at 3.3 miles, ignore a right-branching graded road.

You meet another signed junction after 4.2 miles. Turn left there onto San Juan County 209A, then after another 0.6 mile, bear right where signed San Juan County 209A forks left (west). The road ahead gradually ascends toward Browns Rim, where a spire of Organ Rock Shale, descriptively named Squaw and Papoose Rock, comes into view.

The road bends east after cresting Browns Rim, and after driving 6.5 miles from the major junction, look for an easy-to-miss northbound spur road, marked by a steel post and a large cairn. Turn left (north) onto this narrow, rocky road, and proceed 0.2 mile to the signed trailhead adjacent to a stock pond.

There are undeveloped camping areas at the trailhead, and in many locations along all access roads en route to the trailhead.

The hike: Although the Sundance Trail into lower Dark Canyon is short, the significant elevation loss and difficult nature of the trail make it the most strenuous hike in this book. Yet it is also one of the most spectacular hikes, affording far-ranging vistas en route to the Grand Canyon–like gorge of Dark Canyon.

Some hikers, particularly Sierra Club groups, use the trail as an exit route on a long distance traverse of Dark Canyon. Most hikers, however, hike in to a base camp and spend two or three days exploring, perhaps hiking down to Lake Powell, following bighorn sheep trails into Lean-To Canyon, investigating the deep gorge of Lost Canyon, or wandering up the limestone hallway of Dark Canyon toward Youngs Canyon.

A year-round stream flows in lower Dark Canyon from Youngs Canyon to Lake Powell. Numerous campsites, most of them shadeless, are between Lean-To and Lost canyons. The lower elevations of this trip offer access earlier and later in the season than trails in upper Dark Canyon.

The trail, signed "Dark Canyon, Sundance Trail," begins behind the trailhead register and information signboard, crosses the dam of the stock pond, dips into a shallow draw, and mounts bumpy slickrock, where cairns show the way. Soon the tread reappears, and you thread your way through an open woodland of gnarled and stunted pinyons and junipers. Snakeweed, cliffrose, and blackbrush form scattered low mounds of coarse shrubs across the mesa. Since multiple trails have been forged between the trailhead and the canyon rim, hikers should make an effort to follow the most-used trail, and avoid cutting across the well-developed microbiotic soil crust between the various paths.

Vistas from the mesa top are dramatic and far-reaching. The five peaks of the Henry Mountains rise on the western skyline, seemingly out of place in the sandstone-dominated canyon country desert. Your view also stretches far down the cliff-bound labyrinth of Glen Canyon, though the lake cannot be seen, to the distant Kaiparowits Plateau, and northwest to the tall Orange Cliffs, and to the Navajo Sandstone domes and Wingate Sandstone cliffs embracing Hite and the lower Dirty Devil River.

After 0.5 mile the trail tops out on a high point of the mesa, where an even more inspiring vista unfolds. The square-edged profile of the Orange Cliffs stand in bold relief to the northwest, and seemingly endless miles of tree-studded Cedar Mesa Sandstone slickrock reach to the horizon in the north and northeast. The cavernous depths of Dark Canyon come into focus far below.

Watch for cairns as you descend north off the mesa. Soon you reach a slickrock dropoff, and the cairns lead you around the dropoff to a chute. The initial descent involves jumping down over a 3-foot ledge, followed by a short but steep friction pitch. Rope down your backpack if you find the descent too unnerving.

The trail ahead proceeds generally northeast across a lower level of the mesa, and is crossed by several cow trails leading east and west. After 0.9 mile you reach an old 4WD road, then turn left onto the double track and follow it for 30 yards, then turn right where cairns indicate the resumption of the trail. Here you enter Glen Canyon National Recreation Area, though no signs mark the boundary. Memorable views into Dark and Lean-To canyons open up to better advantage as you proceed.

The trail circumnavigates the rim of a Dark Canyon tributary, and shortly after curving east, you drop off the rim via an interesting 30-foot descent of narrow stair-step ledges. You then bend into a minor draw, reach another projecting point, then descend to the next lower terrace via a minor scramble. The route ahead varies from cairned stretches over slickrock to an array of boot-worn trails. Trying to stay on the most-used trail is not always easy.

At length, you reach the head of the descent into Dark Canyon at 5,300 feet and enjoy your first look at the canyon floor, 1,300 feet below. The trail drops down to a point that juts into the canyon's void, below which the

Lower Dark Canyon from the Sundance Trail.

Sundance Trail to Dark Canyon

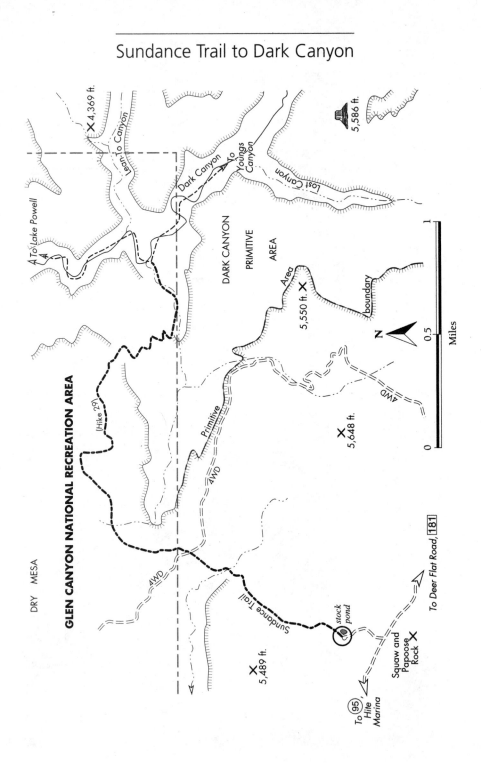

X 4,369 ft.

Lean-To Canyon

5,586 ft.

Dark Canyon

To Youngs Canyon

Lost Canyon

To Lake Powell

DARK CANYON

PRIMITIVE

AREA

Area

5,550 ft. X

boundary

N

0.5

1

Miles

(Hike 29)

GLEN CANYON NATIONAL RECREATION AREA

Primitive

4WD

5,648 ft. X

4WD

0

DRY MESA

4WD

Sundance Trail

X 5,489 ft.

stock pond

To 95 Hite Marina

Squaw and Papoose Rock X

To Deer Flat Road, 181

canyon walls seem to crumble away at your feet. Great slabs of Cedar Mesa Sandstone litter the high-angle slopes below. This point makes a fine destination for a half-day hike.

The scene that unfolds from the rim is breathtaking, and vaguely reminiscent of the Grand Canyon, and indeed, save for the canyon of the Colorado River, Dark Canyon is the greatest gorge in southeast Utah. In its lower reaches, Dark Canyon averages 1,400 feet deep, and slightly more than 0.5 mile of space separates its rims. The Cedar Mesa Sandstone comprises the upper 600 feet of the canyon's walls, resting on a foundation of the red and gray beds of the Elephant Canyon Formation. At the foot of those limestone, shale, and sandstone beds, you see a narrow terrace not unlike the Grand Canyon's Tonto Platform. Below the terrace, the inner gorge of Dark Canyon is embraced by the limestone walls of the Honaker Trail Formation, the oldest rocks exposed in the Glen Canyon region.

At the rim, prepare for an abrupt, knee-pummeling descent. The trail is a cairned path over slippery gravel slopes, and among loose rocks and boulders. You descend 1,100 feet in 0.8 mile to the boulder-strewn floor of a Dark Canyon tributary. There you are flanked by the limestone beds of the Honaker Trail Formation in the blackbrush-dominated Lower Sonoran Zone.

The trail leads 0.4 mile down the wash to the bench above Dark Canyon's wash. Again, try to stay on one trail here. Past hikers have forged a network of interconnecting paths above the wash, resulting in serious erosion and destruction of the coarse, yet delicate desert vegetation.

Lost Canyon can be reached by following the trail 0.8 mile up the course of Dark Canyon's small stream, crossing it several times en route. The better campsites are located along that stretch, on low benches above the wash. Most sites are shadeless, though a few are set beneath the scant shade of scattered cottonwoods.

The gorge becomes narrow and confined by limestone cliffs above Lost Canyon, and in the 6 miles from there to Youngs Canyon, much of the route follows limestone ledges above the wash. Although campsites are scarce in that section, hikers can find ledges wide enough to spread a sleeping bag or pitch a free-standing tent above the high water mark of past flash floods.

Dark Canyon's gorge tightens up immediately below Lean-To Canyon, with rock-hopping, ledge walking, and numerous stream crossings en route to Lake Powell.

The Escalante Canyons

The Escalante Canyons are the premier hiking destination in the Glen Canyon region, and the reason can probably be summed up in one word: slickrock. The Escalante Canyons begin as modest draws draining the flanks of Boulder Mountain, a lofty volcanic tableland that bounds the river basin to the north and northwest. Boulder Mountain, exceeding 11,000 feet in elevation, is the name given to the easternmost segment of the much larger Aquarius Plateau. The other two parts of the plateau are known as Escalante Mountain, and the Table Cliffs Plateau, locally known as Griffin Top and Barney Top, respectively. To the northeast, broad washes begin near the top of the Waterpocket Fold and course through the wide Circle Cliffs basin. Finally, to the west are the Straight Cliffs, also known as Fiftymile Mountain, bounding the vast Kaiparowits Plateau. Drainages begin on the broad terrace traversed by the Hole-in-the-Rock Road, gradually making their way toward the Escalante River. Once these drainages carve into the resistant Navajo Sandstone, they quickly develop into a network of slickrock gorges that are the myriad veins feeding the main artery of the river. Particularly in the upper Escalante canyons, just below Boulder Mountain, the slickrock gorges emerge so suddenly, and with such profound dimensions, that it is a scene of visual inspiration rivaled in few places on the Colorado Plateau.

Utah settlers first gazed out across this wonderland in 1866, and adjutant F. B. Wooley, a member of a command of the Utah Territorial Militia, described the view:

> Below...to the southeast is the Colorado Plateau, stretching away as far as the eye can see, a naked barren plain of red and white sandstone crossed in all directions by innumerable gorges.... The sun shining down on this vast red plain almost dazzled our eyes by the reflection as it was thrown back from the fiery furnace....

In 1880, Clarence Dutton, geologist for the Powell Survey, surveyed the Escalante River basin from the rim of the Aquarius Plateau and saw:

> ...a sublime panorama.... It is a maze of cliffs and terraces lined off with stratification, of rambling buttes, red and white domes, rock platforms gashed with profound canyons, burning plains barren even of sage—all glowing with bright colors and flooded with sunlight.

Navajo Sandstone is the predominant rock formation in the Escalante Canyons, and erosion has exhumed these ancient sand dunes and sculpted the resistant cross-bedded slickrock into a vast landscape of domes incised with innumerable serpentine canyons. Nowhere else in the canyon country of the Colorado Plateau is there such an immense expanse of slickrock. The unique landscape, reliable water in many canyons, and hiking routes that traverse the spectrum of difficulty combine to make the Escalante region an increasingly popular alternative destination to the national parks of Utah.

The unique beauty of the Escalante region was recognized as early as 1866, yet the region somehow escaped achieving national park status in the ensuing years. After the floodgates closed on Glen Canyon Dam in 1963, the lower Escalante canyons were lost beneath the waters of Lake Powell. In 1972, the lower Escalante canyons were included within the boundaries of Glen Canyon National Recreation Area, which includes nearly 1 million acres of deserts and canyons, much of which are roadless and managed by the National Park Service. With the establishment of the 1.7-million-acre Grand Staircase–Escalante National Monument in 1996, and the modicum of protection that that designation provides, all of the Escalante canyons are at last held in trust for the benefit and enjoyment of future generations.

Although the Escalante River courses some 80 miles through a wilderness canyon of incomparable beauty, travel down its gorge is often brutal, a test of endurance for even the most experienced canyoneer. The tributary canyons of the Escalante are equally attractive, and they are the primary destinations of most hikers visiting the region. Typical of the canyon country of southern Utah, there are few established trails in the Escalante Canyons. Most hikes follow the corridors of washes, or cross open expanses of slickrock. The exception is the trail to Lower Calf Creek Falls, one of the few constructed and maintained trails in the Glen Canyon region.

There are few easy hikes in the Escalante region, yet easy or difficult, they are all outstanding, providing some of the finest backcountry hiking in southern Utah. Active waterfalls, arches, narrow canyons, riparian oases, and sculpted slickrock are among the attractions of the Escalante's backcountry.

Typical of southern Utah's canyon country, the best times to hike here are in the spring, from mid-March through May, and again during autumn, from September through October. Cooler weather brought on by monsoon activity in summer, and warm, dry weather during winter can also be enjoyed.

BACKCOUNTRY REGULATIONS

Nearly all of the backcountry covered in this chapter lies within wilderness study areas, both in Glen Canyon National Recreation Area and Grand Staircase–Escalante National Monument. Only one federally designated wilderness, Box-Death Hollow, is located here, and it abuts the roadless canyons along the northern edge of the monument. Backcountry regulations for the new monument have not yet been finalized, thus hikers anywhere in the region are advised to follow the regulations listed below that apply to the Glen Canyon backcountry, and always employ no trace practices.

1. Backcountry permits are required for overnight use. Obtain permits at trailhead registers, or at the Escalante Interagency visitor center.

2. Maximum group size is limited to twelve people. Larger groups must split into two or more smaller groups and hike and camp at least 0.5 mile apart.

3. Campfires are prohibited.

4. Pack out all trash, garbage, food, and used toilet paper.

5. Pets must be leashed at all times.

6. Campsites must be established at least 100 feet from water sources.

HOLE-IN-THE-ROCK EXPEDITION

The Escalante region has a colorful history, but the highlight of that history is undoubtedly the Hole-in-the-Rock Expedition of 1879 and 1880. The Mormon frontier expanded like a blooming flower across Utah and neighboring territories, beginning in the 1840s. Hostilities between Mormons and Utes and Navajos prevented expansion into the canyon country until the 1870s, followed by a new threat to Mormon supremacy. This threat was the non-Mormons, the gentiles, who came to Utah in search of gold and to graze their cattle.

The Church of Jesus Christ of Latter-day Saints organized a mission to establish a settlement along the San Juan River in the southeast corner of the territory. In April 1879, a scouting party followed a route that took them across the Colorado River at Lees Ferry to the San Juan by way of the Navajo Reservation, a 500-mile journey from their starting point near Cedar City. The mission opted to shortcut the distance for the colonizing expedition by following a route that would take them through Escalante, rather than following the long circuitous route through the Navajo country.

Today, the scenic Hole-in-the-Rock Road follows much the same route as the one taken by the Mormon pioneers, and small posts bearing a picture of a covered wagon mark the trail, still visible in places, where the modern road deviates from the pioneer route.

CAMPING

The only two public campgrounds in Grand Staircase–Escalante National Monument (as of 1998) are located in the Escalante region. In the near future, other primitive campgrounds are expected to be established within the monument. The five-unit Deer Creek Campground, located on the Burr Trail Road, 6.2 miles southeast of Utah 12 and Boulder, is open year-round. Sites are available for a fee on a first-come, first-served basis. Set among willows and cottonwoods in the canyon of perennial Deer Creek, the site includes tables, fire grills, and pit toilets, but no drinking water.

The thirteen-unit Calf Creek Campground is located just off Utah 12 at the Lower Calf Creek Falls Trailhead (see Hike 34). This fee campground is open year-round, and features the same facilities as the Deer Creek site, though drinking water is available from spring through autumn.

Elsewhere in the monument or national recreation area, you may camp at large, wherever you wish, unless otherwise posted. Roads en route to most trailheads offer spur roads or pullouts where you can park and set up a tent. Always use established sites, and never drive off-road to create new sites. Avoid building campfires in the Escalante region, and remember that no campfires are allowed within Glen Canyon National Recreation Area. If you must build a fire outside of Glen Canyon NRA, you are urged to use a firepan.

ACCESS AND SERVICES

The only highway providing access to the region is Utah 12. This highway offers an exceptional scenic drive for 118 miles between Utah 24 at Torrey, and U.S. Highway 89 south of Panguitch, Utah.

The historic Hole-in-the-Rock Road, branching southeast from Utah 12, 5 miles east of Escalante, affords access to the west side of the lower Escalante canyons. This is an often rough, remote desert road, but it is surprisingly busy with both hikers driving to and from trailheads, and scenic drivers.

Travel down this road is slow, so expect a drive of several hours en route to some trailheads. The road is subject to washouts, and can become impassable during and shortly after heavy rains. I have seen cars stranded on this road for several days following a single afternoon of heavy rain. A 4WD vehicle is usually not required, but is recommended to safely navigate the road during changing weather conditions, though visitors drive the road in vehicles ranging from compact cars to motor homes. The Burr Trail Road offers access from Boulder into the Circle Cliffs, and continues on for 75 miles to Bullfrog Marina on Lake Powell. This scenic road is paved as far as the boundary with Capitol Reef National Park.

Obtain up-to-date road information from the Escalante Interagency visitor center in Escalante (see **For more information**, below) before driving any unpaved road, and be sure you top off your gas tank, and have several gallons of water, extra food, and other supplies in the event you become temporarily stranded.

Services in the region are limited to the small towns of Boulder and Escalante. Escalante offers gas, groceries, several motels, restaurants, hiking and camping supplies, auto repair and towing, and a medical clinic. In Boulder there are two gas/convenience stores, restaurants, motels, auto repair, limited groceries, and the Anasazi State Park and Museum.

FOR MORE INFORMATION

For updated information on road and hiking route conditions, contact the Escalante Interagency visitor center at 435-826-5499, or visit the office at the west end of Escalante on Utah 12. The visitor center is open seven days a week, from 7:30 A.M. to 5:30 P.M., from March 15 through October 31. Winter hours are in effect between November 1 and March 14: 8 A.M. to 4:30 P.M. Monday through Friday.

If an emergency arises, dial 911, or call the Garfield County Sheriff at 435-676-2411. Or call the National Park Service at 435-826-4315, or 24-hour Dispatch at 520-645-8300.

30 The Gulch to Lamanite Arch

General description:	A rewarding backpack into the headwaters canyon of an Escalante River tributary within Grand Staircase–Escalante National Monument.
Distance:	19 miles round trip.
Difficulty:	Moderate.
Trail conditions:	Wash route, with occasional segments of boot-worn trails and cow trails.
Trailhead access:	2WD (paved access).
Average hiking time:	2 to 3 days.
Trailhead elevation:	5,560 feet.
High point:	6,400 feet.
Elevation gain and loss:	840 feet.
Optimum seasons:	April through early June; September through October.
Water availability:	Perennial flows in Water Canyon at 4.4 miles; seasonal intermittent flows in The Gulch, Steep Creek, and in the canyon of Lamanite Arch.
Hazards:	Flash-flood danger.
Permits:	Required for overnight trips; obtain at trailhead register or at the Escalante Interagency visitor center.
Topo maps:	King Bench and Steep Creek Bench USGS quads; Trails Illustrated Canyons of the Escalante.

Key points:

0.0	The Gulch Trailhead; follow the Burr Trail Road first east, then north.
0.5	Bridge spanning The Gulch; turn left (north) into The Gulch.
1.0	Steep Creek joins on the left (west).
4.4	Water Canyon enters on the left (northwest).
6.2	First major side canyon joins on the right (northeast).
7.3	Egg Canyon opens up on the right (northeast).
8.4	First major side canyon beyond Egg Canyon opens up on the left (west); turn left into the canyon.
9.5	Lamanite Arch.

Finding the trailhead: From the Utah 12/Burr Trail Road junction in Boulder, 36.7 miles south of the Utah 12/24 junction, and 26 miles northeast of Escalante, turn east onto the paved Burr Trail Road (the Boulder/Bullfrog Scenic Backway), also signed for Circle Cliffs. Other signs warn drivers that the road is not recommended for trailers and has extreme grades and steep curves, and that no services are available for 75 miles.

For the first several miles outside of Boulder, the road passes through a dramatic landscape of Navajo Sandstone

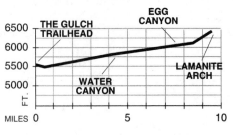

174

domes studded with tall ponderosa pines. Enter Grand Staircase–Escalante National Monument after 1.5 miles, and pass the Deer Creek Campground after 6.3 miles, located on a spur road alongside Deer Creek, north of the Burr Trail Road.

Beyond Deer Creek, the road ascends to the wooded mesa of Steep Creek Bench, then begins a very steep downgrade into The Gulch. At a sharp left curve near the bottom of the grade, a spur road branches right, signed for "The Gulch Trailhead" and "Trailhead Parking," 10.1 miles from Boulder. This rough spur leads 0.1 mile to the parking area and trailhead register. Overnight hikers should park here. Day hikers can continue along the Burr Trail Road for 0.5 mile to the concrete bridge spanning The Gulch, and park in the turnouts on either side of the road.

The hike: One of many long tributaries to the Escalante River, The Gulch is born on the flanks of Boulder Mountain and cuts a dramatic sandstone gorge for 25 miles. Carving through the western margins of the Circle Cliffs uplift, the upper reaches of The Gulch assume a different character than most other Escalante River tributaries, which are cut almost exclusively in the Navajo Sandstone. The sequence of rock formations in The Gulch is the opposite of what you might expect when traveling through a canyon carved through sedimentary layers. As you hike up-canyon, you are also hiking down-strata through progressively older rocks, thanks to the uplifted landscape of the Circle Cliffs.

This fine trip traverses the upper Gulch from the Burr Trail Road to the unique span of Lamanite Arch, following an open canyon embraced by fluted orange cliffs of Wingate Sandstone and the multi-hued clay beds of the Chinle Formation. Good campsites are situated in cottonwood groves and in the pinyon-juniper woodland throughout the course of The Gulch. A reliable year-round water source is found midway to the arch at Water Canyon, and during wet seasons, intermittent water often flows in The Gulch and in the canyon of Lamanite Arch.

Since Lamanite Arch is beyond the reach of most day hikers, the trip is best suited for an overnighter. Three days in The Gulch would be ideal, allowing for a visit to the arch and some exploration of the many interesting side canyons. Although part of the hike follows boot-worn paths and cow trails, much of the route involves walking in the streambed and following benches above the wash. The way is relatively easy, straightforward, and very scenic, yet few hikers visit the canyon and solitude is almost assured.

From The Gulch Trailhead parking area, follow the Burr Trail Road east then north for 0.5 mile to the concrete bridge spanning The Gulch. The trail begins on the east side of the bridge, and is indicated by wilderness study area and motor vehicle closure signs. It is an obvious sandy path that leads north among small cottonwoods, hugging the right (east) bank of the wash. Here The Gulch is shallow, with Wingate Sandstone cliffs rising 200 feet above to the reddish brown Kayenta Formation cliff bands that cap the canyon rims.

The Gulch to Lamanite Arch

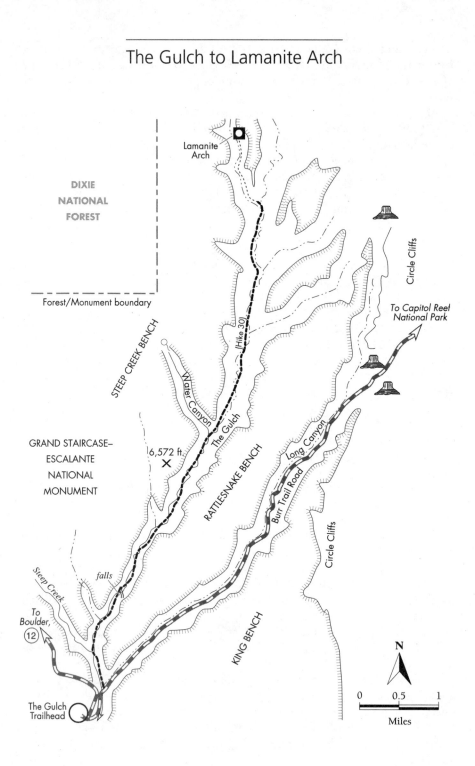

Lamanite Arch

DIXIE
NATIONAL
FOREST

Forest/Monument boundary

STEEP CREEK BENCH

Water Canyon

(Hike 30)

The Gulch

GRAND STAIRCASE–
ESCALANTE
NATIONAL
MONUMENT

6,572 ft.

RATTLESNAKE BENCH

Long Canyon

Burr Trail Road

Circle Cliffs

To Capitol Reef
National Park

Circle Cliffs

Steep Creek

falls

To
Boulder,
12

The Gulch
Trailhead

KING BENCH

N

0   0.5   1

Miles

Steep Creek enters on the left after 0.6 mile, and just before reaching it the trail is forced across the wash and into the cattail-bordered mouth of Steep Creek. Jump across the creek and continue up The Gulch, reaching a second drainage joining on the left at 0.9 mile. Just beyond that side canyon you will find a good spring issuing from a crack on the west wall of the wash. The walking ahead is pleasant and trouble free, with occasional jumps across the small stream during wet seasons when it is flowing. The stream cuts through deep alluvial deposits in places, with sagebrush-clad benches above. Soon, though, the canyon grows increasingly confined, and the Wingate cliffs, honeycombed with solution cavities, rise higher as The Gulch reaches deeper into the folded rocks of the Circle Cliffs.

After 1.4 miles, the resistant purple and green upper beds of the Chinle Formation emerge in the wash, and the stream begins flowing over a series of minor ledges. Shortly thereafter, you are faced with a pair of impassable pouroffs. Bypass this barrier on the left either by following a slippery path past an area of seepage, or by ascending an arroyo at the base of the pouroffs. Either route leads to the brushy bench just above. An old barb wire fence spans the canyon above the pouroffs, and you will find it easier to crawl under the fence rather than ascending the steep sandy slope to the gate above.

The character of the canyon transforms above the pouroffs, and is suddenly wider, with tall spreading cottonwoods arching their stout branches over the wash, while pinyon and juniper dot the rocky slopes beneath the fluted facade of the orange sandstone cliffs. Volcanic boulders, smooth and round, litter the canyon bottom, carried here by runoff from melting glaciers on Boulder Mountain more than ten thousand years ago. Flash floods help push these alien boulders toward the Escalante River, grinding and polishing them along the way.

As you continue deeper into The Gulch, you can begin to follow traces of cow trails that cross the wash from one bench to the next through groves of cottonwood and woodlands of pinyon and juniper.

The Wingate walls recede as the canyon widens, and the Chinle slopes below them are masked by a facade of boulders fallen from the cliffs above. The canyon rims are capped by the ledges and cliff bands of the Kayenta sandstones and fringed by picturesque, gnarled pinyons and junipers.

Although the trail appears only occasionally, the way up the gentle canyon floor is easy, and a trail really isn't necessary to maintain a steady pace. After 4.4 miles, at 5,830 feet, you reach Water Canyon, a major northwest-trending tributary that supplies the source of The Gulch's water. The stream quickly dries up in The Gulch above the confluence. Since the availability of water ahead is uncertain, backpackers are advised to fill their containers here. Water Canyon is also a likely place for a break, since it lies at roughly the half-way point of the hike. There are potential campsites on tree-studded benches fringed with cottonwoods a short distance above Water Canyon. These sites are a good choice for hikers wishing to establish a base camp with a reliable water supply nearby.

Not far above Water Canyon, a long range view up the straight-walled trench of The Gulch unfolds, flanked by bold orange cliffs and splintered buttes. During wet seasons, the wash may carry an intermittent flow of water for the next 4 miles. After 6.2 miles, a major side canyon opens up on the right (northeast), and near this confluence the lofty Navajo Sandstone dome of 7,767-foot Impossible Peak comes into focus far up the canyon.

After 7.3 miles, Egg Canyon opens up on the right (northeast), the colorful boulder-strewn Chinle slopes at its mouth contrasting with the fluted, white and orange cliffs that rise at its head. About 0.3 mile beyond Egg Canyon, a gaping amphitheater appears on the left, incised by a slot-like pouroff. The way ahead is less distinct. Either follow the rock-littered wash, or look for cow trails that wind through a forest of sagebrush 8 to 10 feet tall on the broad bench west of the wash.

A prominent side canyon joins on the left (west) after 8.4 miles. Tall cottonwoods and willows crowd together at the canyon's mouth, and during wet seasons, a steady but shallow stream flows through the canyon. Lamanite Arch, not shown on maps, is located inside this canyon. Hikers in search of campsites should ascend to the bench above and north of the mouth of the side canyon. There you will find several good sites in the pinyon-juniper woodland near the foot of the butte that rises to the north. The bench affords splendid views of the bold Wingate cliffs that embrace The Gulch.

The Gulch.

To reach Lamanite Arch from the bench, descend west into the shady confines of the side canyon and proceed upstream. There is no trail here, and you will be bushwhacking for much of the time through a rich growth of horsetails, willows, water birch, and box elder. A narrow, precipitous side canyon joins on the left after 0.6 mile, and beyond it, the riparian jungle is not quite so dense.

After 1.1 miles, you'll spy the large arch on the right (east) wall of the canyon, spanning a very steep slickrock drainage. This beautiful arch, composed of Wingate Sandstone, may have been formed with the aid of running water in addition to the weathering of the narrow sandstone fin. It's up to you to decide if Lamanite Arch is indeed an arch, or if it is a natural bridge.

31 Silver Falls Creek

General description:	A fine canyon backpack along a historic pioneer wagon route through the Circle Cliffs, within Grand Staircase–Escalante National Monument and Glen Canyon National Recreation Area.
Distance:	16.8 miles round trip.
Difficulty:	Moderate.
Trail conditions:	4WD road and wash route.
Trailhead access:	4WD advised when the road is wet or if floods have damaged it.
Average hiking time:	2 to 3 days.
Trailhead elevation:	5,440 feet.
Low point:	4,654 feet at the Escalante River.
Elevation loss and gain:	800 feet.
Optimum seasons:	April through early June; September through October.
Water availability:	Seasonal seep at Emigrant Spring, 4.9 miles; seasonal intermittent flows in the wash from 5.5 miles to the Escalante River; silty river water must be settled before treating.
Hazards:	Flash-flood danger.
Permits:	Required for overnight trips; obtain at Escalante Interagency visitor center, or at a trailhead register en route to the trailhead (such as Deer Creek or The Gulch trailheads).
Topo maps:	Horse Pasture Mesa and Silver Falls Bench USGS quads; Trails Illustrated Canyons of the Escalante (note: trailhead not accurately shown on this map).

Key points:
1.7   End of 4WD road at Glen Canyon National Recreation Area boundary.
3.1   North Fork Silver Falls Creek joins on the right (north).
4.9   Emigrant Spring draw opens up on the left (south).

6.1   Hobbs inscription.
8.4   Escalante River.

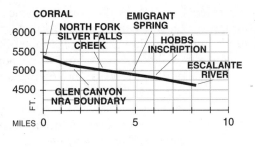

Finding the trailhead: Follow the Burr Trail Road for 10.6 miles east from Boulder to The Gulch (see driving directions for Hike 30), then continue northeast, ascending Long Canyon to the crest of the Circle Cliffs, 16.7 miles from Boulder. The road then descends into the wooded basin below and leads southeast.

After a winding uphill grade through the buttes of the Studhorse Peaks in the eastern reaches of the Circle Cliffs basin, the road descends to a junction with the east end of the signed Wolverine Loop Road, branching right (south), 27.9 miles from Boulder.

Turn right (south) onto this usually good, graded road and drive 8 miles to a signed junction. Bear left at the junction, where a BLM sign points to Silver Falls Creek. This graded road winds through pinyon- and juniper-studded hills for 2.7 miles to an unsigned junction with a west-bound dirt road at the southern margin of the Silver Falls Creek valley. Turn right here.

This road gradually descends the valley for 0.7 mile to the first of nine wash crossings en route to the corral. A high-clearance 4WD vehicle is recommended beyond this point. Although the road has been graded in the past as far as the Glen Canyon NRA boundary, recent flood damage will determine how far you can drive.

With a 4WD vehicle, most people should be able to drive as far as the corral, 2.2 miles west of the main road. Park off the road here, and be sure not to block access to the corral.

Numerous undeveloped campsites can be found between the Burr Trail Road and the trailhead.

The hike: In 1881 Charles Hall, operator of the ferry across the Colorado River at Hole-in-the-Rock Crossing, pioneered a better route to the river and established a new crossing 35 miles up-canyon, hoping to increase business on the wagon road between Escalante and the fledgling Mormon settlement at Bluff on the San Juan River. Although the new wagon road was a great improvement over the Hole-in-the-Rock Road, its route was far from easy. Yet the Halls Crossing Road remained the sole link to the southeast Utah settlements until 1884, when railroads and better wagon routes opened up east of the Colorado River canyon.

Silver Falls Creek, a deep and narrow tributary of the Escalante River, carving through the Circle Cliffs, was part of the Halls Crossing Road (as was Harris Wash to the west), and even today, a hike down its gorge is not easy. Not only is the hike down Silver Falls Creek an excellent, scenic three-day trip, it also offers insights into the struggles of Utah pioneers as they traversed one of the most difficult wagon roads in the West. Historical

180

inscriptions in the canyon walls date from the 1880s to the uranium boom of the 1950s, with the Hobbs inscription of 1883 being the highlight.

The lower reaches of the canyon and the Escalante River offer benches on which to camp, but finding a good water source can be a problem. Lower Silver Falls Creek usually carries a very small, intermittent stream, with the best flows occurring during spring and following extended wet periods. The Escalante River, always a turbid stream, turns to muddy gray soup that is impossible to settle following periods of substantial rainfall and during the spring snowmelt high on Boulder Mountain at the river's headwaters. When the river is calm, its cloudy waters can be settled to the point where your filter will not immediately clog with sediment.

If you are driving from the direction of Escalante, obtain a report of water availability from the visitor center, then stop at the river bridge on Utah 12 and inspect the condition of the river to determine if you can use it as a water source.

In an attempt to establish claim to roads within the county following establishment of Grand Staircase–Escalante National Monument in 1996, Garfield County (and adjacent Kane County) graded many remote dirt roads, including the road into Silver Falls Creek as far as the Glen Canyon National Recreation Area boundary. Record-book amounts of rainfall and flooding during the 1997 monsoon season washed out most roads, and it is uncertain if these roads will ever again be graded to the extent they were in 1996. Drivers of high-clearance 4WD vehicles should still be able to reach the corral mentioned in the trailhead directions, and begin hiking there.

The Hobbs inscription in Silver Falls Creek is one of many historic highlights to the hike.

From the corral follow the road ahead as it crosses the wash twice, then traverse a bench, avoiding a stretch of convoluted narrows slicing through the resistant sandstone of the Shinarump. As you stroll down the road you may notice that the sedimentary rock layers are dipping downward toward the west. Thus, after about 1 mile you begin passing through the badlands of the Chinle Formation, colored in shades of gray, green, red, and purple, and virtually devoid of vegetation. Ahead you will pass through progressively younger rock formations as you trek down-canyon through the folded strata of the Circle Cliffs uplift.

Several old uranium prospectors roads, most of them now reclaimed by nature, are carved through the Chinle slopes, wherein lie the "hot" beds of uranium and vanadium the 1950s prospectors were seeking. You will also see large cairns that are old uranium claim markers, not indicators of the route.

The road crosses the wash eight times in the 1.7 miles between the corral and the Glen Canyon National Recreation Area boundary. The boundary is marked by an orange post declaring that the route ahead is closed to vehicles, including bicycles. A 4WD road once followed the wagon route that traversed both Harris Wash and Silver Falls Creek, yet few remnants of the track remain. Segments of old eroded road shortcut the meanders of the wash and can briefly be followed beyond the NRA boundary.

The wash soon grows confined between boulder-studded Chinle slopes, where you are funneled into the gravel wash where the walking is easy and trouble free. Pillars of Chinle shales, capped by Wingate slabs fallen from the cliffs above, form the interesting hoodoos common along this colorful part of the canyon. At length, you are squeezed into a boulder-strewn stretch of the wash, and soon thereafter cottonwoods appear as you approach the confluence with North Fork Silver Falls Creek. After 3.1 miles, at 5,050 feet you reach the North Fork, where you find a shady but dry campsite at the canyon mouth, set in an isolated grove of cottonwoods. The North Fork is a broad canyon flanked by bold sculpted cliffs of Wingate Sandstone.

Below the North Fork, segments of trail and old road lead you across open benches studded with rabbitbrush, four-wing saltbush, and Fremont barberry. The benches alternate with stretches of walking in the rocky and gravelly wash. The Wingate walls, those great orange cliffs that rested 400 feet above the trailhead, reach to the canyon floor after about 4 miles. They enclose the increasingly narrow canyon with undercut walls and deep alcoves, and sheer cliffs sweeping 300 to 400 feet skyward, stained with a dark brown and metallic blue patina of desert varnish.

Several long, tight meanders lead the way through the narrow Wingate gorge. After 4.9 miles, what appears to be an abandoned meander, but is actually a pair of similar appearing amphitheaters, opens up on the south wall of the canyon, separated by a 200-foot slickrock tower. At the foot of the tower you will find several historic inscriptions, one dating back to 1921. The second, western amphitheater contains the seasonal seep of Emigrant Spring, an unreliable water source issuing from the foot of the

Silver Falls Creek

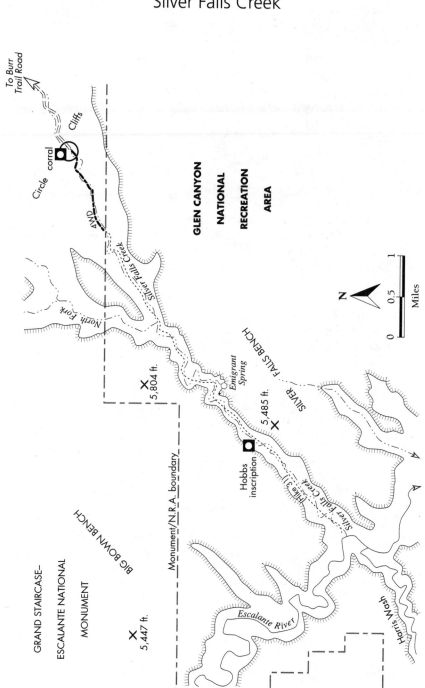

GRAND STAIRCASE-
ESCALANTE NATIONAL
MONUMENT

BIG BOWN BENCH

X
5,447 ft.

Monument/N.R.A. boundary

X
5,804 ft.

North Fork

Silver Falls Creek

4WD

Circle corral

Cliffs

To Burr
Trail Road

GLEN CANYON

NATIONAL

RECREATION

AREA

Emigrant
Spring

X
5,485 ft.

SILVER FALLS BENCH

Hobbs
inscription

Silver Falls Creek
(hike 3.1)

Escalante River

Harris Wash

N

0   0.5   1

Miles

cliffs above the screen of Gambel oak and single-leaf ash that crowds the draw.

Follow the canyon ahead through the most difficult section, where the gorge becomes quite narrow and is strewn with large boulders. Few traces of the old road remain here, and it is easy to imagine the toil of pioneers clearing a way through the gorge passable to horse-drawn wagons. After two bends of the canyon below Emigrant Spring the sinuous canyon straightens out, and cottonwoods appear, suggesting a reliable source of groundwater. Intermittent water often flows in the wash for the remaining 3 miles to the Escalante River.

Soon the wash cuts through the topmost green and purple layers of the Chinle Formation, where the stream, when flowing, cascades over a series of miniature waterfalls. Below the Chinle the canyon is littered with large boulders and remains narrow for about 1 mile, where the Wingate walls at last reach down to the canyon bottom. In places the canyon walls are separated by as little as 20 feet of space. Keep an eye out for inscriptions in the canyon walls, left behind by early travelers and uranium prospectors.

It is hard to miss the "G B Hobbs 83" inscription at 6.1 miles on the right (north) wall of the canyon. A plaque placed by the Hobbs family in 1957 tells the story of George Brigham Hobbs. Hobbs was trapped in the alcove here by a snowstorm in February 1883, while en route to the southeast Utah settlements to deliver supplies. Reasoning that his time was up, Hobbs chopped his name and the date in the canyon wall, apparently with an ax. But the storm broke, and Hobbs safely completed his journey.

Beyond the Hobbs inscription, the Wingate walls grow lower, and as the canyon begins to open up, streamside benches appear. Some benches are studded with pinyon and juniper, while others are fringed by cottonwoods. All of them offer good, safe places to camp above the high water mark of flash floods. Shelves of Kayenta Formation sandstone, supporting a scattering of gnarled woodland trees, soon come to dominate the lower canyon walls, and great desert-varnished cliffs and domes of Navajo Sandstone crown the skyline.

An old corral hidden on a bench north of the wash indicates that the river is just ahead, and at length you reach the cottonwood-fringed banks of the cloudy Escalante River, a wide, swift stream. Sandy benches here afford good but shadeless campsites. Great domes and towers of Navajo Sandstone flank the wide river canyon, and grassy slopes reach from the river banks to the foot of those cliffs above. Other campsites can be found on the wide bench opposite the mouth of Silver Falls Creek, but you'll have to ford the usually knee-deep river to get there.

32 Boulder Mail Trail to Death Hollow

General description:	A memorable 2- to 4-day backpack leading to a canyon base camp, and traversing the incomparable slickrock landscape of the upper Escalante region, within Grand Staircase–Escalante National Monument.
Distance:	11.4 miles round trip.
Difficulty:	Moderately strenuous.
Trail conditions:	Boot-worn trails and cairned route over slickrock.
Trailhead access:	2WD.
Average hiking time:	8 hours round trip.
Trailhead elevation:	6,780 feet.
Low point:	5,800 feet.
Elevation gain and loss:	+500 feet, -1,500 feet.
Optimum seasons:	April through early June; September through October.
Water availability:	Perennial flows in Sand Creek, 2.4 miles; and Death Hollow, 5.4 miles.
Hazards:	Exposure to steep dropoffs and steep slickrock friction pitches while descending into Death Hollow; flash-flood danger in Sand Creek and Death Hollow; abundant poison ivy in Death Hollow.
Permits:	Required for overnight trips; obtain at trailhead register.
Topo maps:	Boulder Town, Calf Creek, and Escalante USGS quads; Trails Illustrated Canyons of the Escalante.

Key points:

- 1.1 Junction of McGath Point Road and Boulder Mail Trail; turn right onto trail.
- 2.4 Sand Creek.
- 5.0 Rim of Death Hollow on Slickrock Saddle Bench.
- 5.4 Death Hollow.

Finding the trailhead: Follow Utah 12 to the prominently signed east end of the Hells Backbone Road at milepost 84, 3.2 miles southwest of the Utah 12/Burr Trail Road junction in Boulder, or 22.7 miles northeast of Escalante. Drive northwest on Hells Backbone Road for 0.1 mile, then turn left onto a narrow, rocky dirt road (McGath Point Road) at an unsigned, easy-to-miss junction.

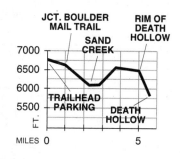

The road is quite rocky in places: drive your low-clearance vehicle carefully. After 0.5 mile, the road crosses the Boulder Airstrip, then gradually rises over its rocky bed for another 0.2 mile to the signed trailhead parking area. The many undeveloped camping areas along the dirt road beyond the trailhead have been closed by the BLM to protect the resources along the boundaries of a Wilderness Study Area; visitors should respect those closures and avoid the sites.

The hike: The Boulder Mail Trail, like several other trails in the Escalante region, has a colorful history. Established in 1902, the trail was a mail route traversed by packhorses, linking isolated Boulder Town with Escalante. By 1910, a patchwork telephone line, strung from tree to tree, provided Boulder with communication to the outside world, namely a switchboard in Escalante. When Utah 12 was finally completed in 1940, the Boulder Mail Trail fell into disuse.

Today the trail is a popular backcountry route, and it offers one of the finest slickrock rambles on the Colorado Plateau. Traces of the old phone line and segments of the trail are still visible, yet most of the way is a cairned route over vast stretches of Navajo Sandstone slickrock. This fine round trip follows part of the Boulder Mail Trail into Death Hollow, the most dramatic of all the upper Escalante canyons. Although the trail can be followed from Escalante through to the trailhead near Boulder, taking the trip as it is described eliminates the problems of a car shuttle or a hitchhike.

Alongside the perennial stream coursing between the sheer Navajo cliffs of Death Hollow you will find several fine campsites to use as a base for explorations of that intriguing gorge. Several waterfalls, deep pools, and interesting alcoves await discovery in Death Hollow, but beware of the abundant poison ivy there.

Begin the hike at the signed trailhead parking area, and follow the winding McGath Point Road southwest, descending at first, then undulating over the mesa through the pinyon-juniper woodland. Views extend southwest to the great barrier of the Straight Cliffs, west to the Pink Cliffs of the Table Cliff Plateau, and from the northwest to north rises the lofty tableland of Boulder Mountain. Emerging from the flanks of the mountain are many deep slickrock canyons cut into the sparkling white Navajo Sandstone.

After 1.1 miles of road walking, you reach a BLM sign that points right (west) to the Boulder Mail Trail (closed to mountain bikes). Turn right here and follow a closed road through the woodland for about 0.4 mile. As you approach the sandstone rim of a Sand Creek tributary, the route narrows to a single track marked with cairns, then gradually begins to descend. Broad, sweeping slopes of Navajo slickrock embrace the canyon of Sand Creek before you.

Once you reach the slickrock below, abundant cairns mark the route of travel through this Sand Creek tributary. In this side drainage you will pass several gnarled and stunted ponderosa pines, out of place in a slickrock canyon. At the trailside you find littleleaf mountain mahogany, a round shrub with thick, linear, dark green foliage that prefers its anchorage upon slickrock.

186

Yucca, manzanita, and Utah serviceberry plants are scattered across the sandy slopes adjacent to the sandstone.

Below the first expanse of slickrock, follow the trail across a sagebrush-dotted bench to the second band of slickrock, where cairns lead you down past an old log and board fence. The moderate descent then traverses pine-studded slickrock, then follows a shallow draw toward a prominent side canyon that opens up below on the right (north). You reach the mouth of that drainage at its confluence with Sand Creek at 6,100 feet, in a stand of Fremont cottonwood. Sand Creek flows clear and steady past a small cottonwood-shaded campsite at the confluence. Large volcanic boulders are heaped along the flanks of the creek, carried here with the help of glacial meltwater from the highlands of Boulder Mountain more than ten thousand years ago, and pushed farther down-canyon with the passage of each flash flood.

Follow the path downstream along the east bank of the willow-bordered creek, then rock-hop its twin channels via volcanic boulders to the opposite side. After about 150 yards, the obvious trail ascends to a low bench to avoid the willow-choked stream channel, and soon drops back to the creekside. You then work your way down-canyon via the west banks of Sand Creek, then skirt the base of a slickrock dome to enter a side draw joining on the right. Sand Creek canyon is shallow but scenic, with slickrock slopes flanking it on either side. Benches are littered with volcanic boulders, and sandy pockets support ponderosa pine, pinyon, juniper, and manzanita.

The Boulder Mail Trail crosses vast stretches of Navajo Sandstone slickrock.

Boulder Mail Trail to Death Hollow

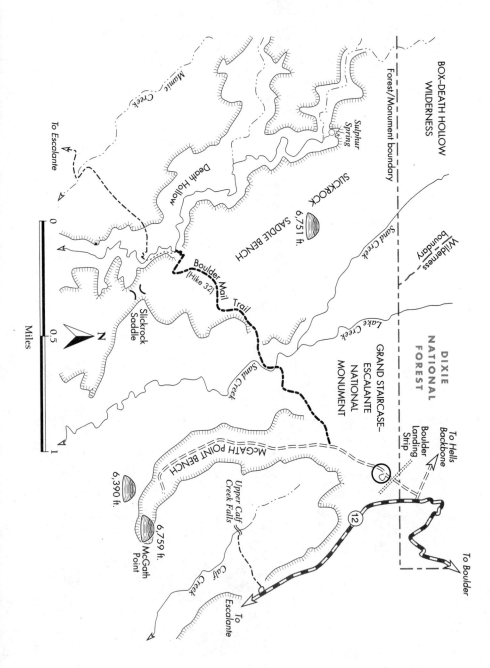

About 150 yards beyond the draw, cairns indicate the ascent out of the canyon. The route leads you steeply upward alongside a minor draw and onto the slickrock beyond, pointing you toward a skyline dome crowned by a triad of sandstone spires. Soon you regain sandy tread and ascend more moderately, traversing wooded benches. After passing northwest of the dome, the old telephone line appears as a single strand of wire strung between trees. The route ahead generally follows the path of the phone line. Before long you begin a steady ascent over slickrock, with breaks on wooded benches in between pitches. This climb leads you to the wooded expanse of Slickrock Saddle Bench after 4 miles, where the grade abates at 6,600 feet.

Views from the bench extend eastward to Mounts Ellen and Pennell in the Henry Mountains, southwest to distant Navajo Mountain, and south across wooded mesas and a labyrinth of slickrock canyons. After mounting the mesa, follow the sandy trail as it curves south, skirting the knob of Point 6617, then dip into a saddle at 6,520 feet, just below a hill fringed with ponderosa pines. The trail divides here; bear right onto the westbound branch and begin descending.

As you drop below the saddle an unforgettable view unfolds, reaching into the rugged gorge of Death Hollow, bordered by soaring cliffs and domes of white Navajo slickrock, and one of the more dramatic landscapes in Utah's canyon country, a land notable for its unparalleled scenery.

The trail quickly reaches a lower saddle on a narrow ridge, beyond which you follow the steep sandy trail down to slickrock, then descend the shallow draw from cairn to cairn. Near the cliff at the bottom of the draw, cairns lead you to the right (northwest) to the edge of the next, lower, cliff. The route ahead, not for the fainthearted, traverses the brink of a 600-foot cliff, where sections of the trail were carved into the slickrock to provide better footing for packhorses. The creek coursing through Death Hollow appears below as you negotiate a steep descent via switchbacks, passing the mouth of a gaping alcove en route.

At the foot of the plunging, 750-foot descent, you reach the canyon floor at a prominent bend where the creek curves around a bold sandstone fin. Gambel oak and box elder fringe the clear, vigorous stream, and creekside benches support tall pines in the microclimate of the narrow, shadowed gorge. Excellent campsites, set beneath a canopy of ponderosa pines, lie just downstream, around the next bend.

33 Upper Calf Creek Falls

General description:	A short but rewarding slickrock day hike in one of the upper Escalante canyons, within Grand Staircase–Escalante National Monument.
Distance:	2 miles round trip.
Difficulty:	Moderately easy, Class 2 friction pitches just below the rim.
Trail conditions:	Cairned slickrock route and boot-worn trails.
Trailhead access:	2WD.
Average hiking time:	1 to 1.5 hours round trip.
Trailhead elevation:	6,530 feet.
Low point:	5,920 feet.
Elevation loss and gain:	610 feet.
Optimum seasons:	April through early June; September through October.
Water availability:	Available at Calf Creek; treat before drinking or bring your own.
Hazards:	Flash-flood danger in Calf Creek canyon.
Permits:	Not required for day hikes.
Topo maps:	Calf Creek USGS quad; Trails Illustrated Canyons of the Escalante.

Key points:

1.0   Upper Calf Creek Falls.

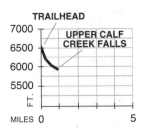

Finding the trailhead: The easy-to-miss spur road to the trailhead is located on the west side of Utah 12 between mileposts 81 and 82, 5.5 miles southwest of the Utah 12/Burr Trail Road junction in Boulder, and 22.4 miles northeast of Escalante. This spur road branches west 0.6 mile south of milepost 82, and 0.4 mile north of milepost 81. The very rough and rocky road leads 0.1 mile to the trailhead parking area on the rim of Calf Creek canyon. There are pullouts in which to park just off the highway if you are driving a low-clearance vehicle.

The hike: Few hikes in the Escalante region offer the rewards of this fine, short trip with such a minimal investment of time and effort. Vast expanses of Navajo Sandstone slickrock, far-ranging vistas, plus a tall waterfall, pools of cool water, and shady riparian oases await hikers following this well-worn trail.

Signs at the trailhead proclaim that no camping is permitted there, and that no camping or fires are allowed within 0.5 mile of the upper falls. The trail begins behind these signs and the trailhead register, leading immediately over the rim and to the top of a steep Navajo slickrock slope, littered with round gray volcanic rocks and boulders. The slopes of all the upper Escalante canyons are strewn with these Tertiary rocks, carried in glacial meltwater from their source high on the slopes of Boulder Mountain more than ten thousand years ago.

A swath has been cleared through the rocky veneer, and cairns show the way down the swath via a moderately steep slickrock friction pitch. The route is easier than it first appears, and hikers should be confident that the slickrock affords good purchase.

Vistas from the start are dramatic and far-reaching, stretching to the Pink Cliffs of the Table Cliff Plateau on the western horizon, and far southwest to the Straight Cliffs bounding the Kaiparowits Plateau. Below you the drainage of Calf Creek unfolds, exposing miles of sweeping, cross-bedded, white Navajo slickrock.

Below the first short band of slickrock, a few minor switchbacks ensue, leading through volcanic boulders on a moderately steep grade down to the next band of slickrock. Descend this sandstone slope, aiming for the obvious trail on the flats below. Once you reach this wide, well-worn sandy path, 300 feet below the rim, you begin a gradual descent over the sandy, gently sloping bench.

Seasonal wildflowers splash their colors across the trailside slopes. Look for the white blooms of cryptantha and evening primrose, the yellow blossoms of goldenweed, and the delicate purple, lily-like blooms of spiderwort.

As you approach the inner gorge of Calf Creek, the trail crosses slickrock once again, where ponderosa pines make an occasional appearance among the woodland trees. Soon the cottonwood and Gambel oak groves in the

The route to Upper Calf Creek Falls crosses slickrock and sandy benches.

Upper Calf Creek Falls

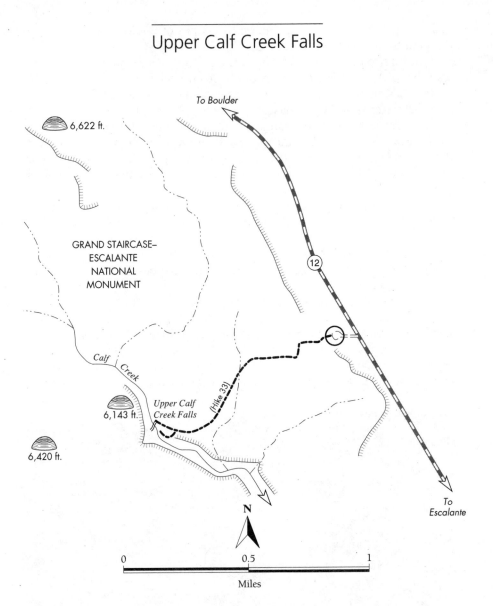

canyon bottom come into view, and as you reach the rim of the inner gorge, the trail turns right and leads up-canyon. By now you can hear the echo of the falls, but you cannot yet see it.

Shortly, the trail splits: the lower trail to the left descends over slickrock to the foot of the falls; and the upper trail to the right continues up-canyon to the head of the falls. Following the upper trail above the gorge, a lovely pool comes into view below, and behind it, a deep alcove rich with hanging-garden vegetation. Then another pool, deeper and larger, appears, and finally the falls are before you, an impressive veil of whitewater plunging about 50 feet over a sandstone precipice.

The trail leads to a small pool at the top of the falls, where Calf Creek's banks are fringed with a ribbon of willow, water birch, and silver buffaloberry. Scattered cottonwoods and ponderosa pines also occur in the canyon bottom, while slickrock slopes flank either side of the perennial stream. Just above the falls are a chain of small pools and deep waterpockets, irresistible on a hot day.

The lower trail descends slickrock, where there may be cairns to lead the way, for several hundred yards to a shady alcove at the foot of the falls. Beware of the abundant poison ivy here, which grows 3 to 4 feet tall and is recognizable by its woody stem and its large shiny green leaves, growing in sets of three. Here the music of the falls is enjoyed to its best advantage, and the large pool below is an added bonus on a hot day.

34 Lower Calf Creek Falls

General description:	A very scenic and popular day hike leading to a dramatic waterfall, within Grand Staircase–Escalante National Monument.
Distance:	6.2 miles round trip.
Difficulty:	Moderately easy.
Trail conditions:	Good constructed trail, moderately sandy in places.
Trailhead access:	2WD (paved access).
Average hiking time:	3.5 to 4 hours round trip.
Trailhead elevation:	5,320 feet.
High point:	5,500 feet at Lower Calf Creek Falls.
Elevation gain and loss:	250 feet.
Optimum seasons:	Mid-March through early June;September through October.
Water availability:	Available at the picnic site at the trailhead. Calf Creek supplies year-round water, but since it must be treated before drinking, bring your own.
Hazards:	Negligible.
Permits:	Not required.
Topo maps:	Calf Creek USGS quad (trail not shown on quad); Trails Illustrated Canyons of the Escalante.

Key points:
- 0.2 Trail begins on left (northwest) side of campground access road; bear left onto trail.
- 3.1 Lower Calf Creek Falls.

Finding the trailhead: The prominently signed BLM Calf Creek Recreation Area is located off of Utah 12, 11.4 miles south of

193

the Utah 12/Burr Trail Road junction in Boulder, 14.4 miles northeast of Escalante, and 1.1 miles north of the Escalante River bridge on Utah 12. Follow the paved spur road for about 250 yards below the highway to the day-use parking lot. A small day-use fee is collected by campground hosts at the entrance to the parking lot.

The hike: This trip is one of the premier day hikes in the Escalante region, and for good reasons. An excellent self-guiding nature trail easily accessible from scenic Utah 12, a pleasant campground located at the trailhead, a spectacular cliff-bound canyon, a perennial stream featuring beaver ponds and abundant trout, and a memorable veil of whitewater, one of very few active waterfalls in the southern Utah desert, plunging into a cold, deep pool, combine to make this trip a must for any hiker visiting the region. Bear in mind that lower Calf Creek is a day use area only—no overnight backpacking is allowed along the trail. Camp only in the Calf Creek Campground at the trailhead.

From the day-use parking area adjacent to the picnic site, follow the paved road north through the campground for 0.2 mile, following signs pointing to the trail. Just before the road dips down to ford Calf Creek, the prominently signed trail heads left up the west slopes of the canyon.

As you proceed, refer to the brochure provided by the campground hosts as you entered the recreation area. It is keyed to twenty-four numbered posts along the trail, pointing out the vegetation and geologic features at each and describing the area's history and prehistory. The brochure will greatly enhance your appreciation and enjoyment of the area. The actual distance to the falls is about 0.3 mile farther from the parking area than signs and the brochure indicate.

The wide, sometimes rocky, and often sandy trail winds up-canyon along the west slopes above Calf Creek, passing through fields of rabbitbrush, groves of Gambel oak, and woodlands of pinyon and juniper, which provide occasional shade. An active population of beaver have felled most of the cottonwoods along the grass-bordered creek, but they have ignored the abundant water birch fringing the streamside.

After about 2 miles, you reach the banks of Calf Creek for the first time, and the canyon floor ahead grows increasingly narrow. Box elders, water birches, and Gambel oaks mass their ranks on the canyon bottom and on the shady slopes just above. Now you can gaze into the clear waters of Calf Creek, brimming with fat brook trout reaching 12 inches in length, a rare sight in a desert canyon. The contrast here between the luxuriant riparian greenery and the stark profile of sandstone cliffs and domes is dramatic.

As you pass a chain of large beaver ponds you can hear the echoing crash of the falls long before you see it. Suddenly you round a bend and the falls appear. Soon thereafter you reach the trail's end in the confines of a slickrock amphitheater.

The memorable 126-foot waterfall plunges in one leap over the sandstone precipice above, then thunders onto a moss-draped slickrock wall and spreads a veil of whitewater into the deep green pool below. From the walls

Lower Calf Creek Falls

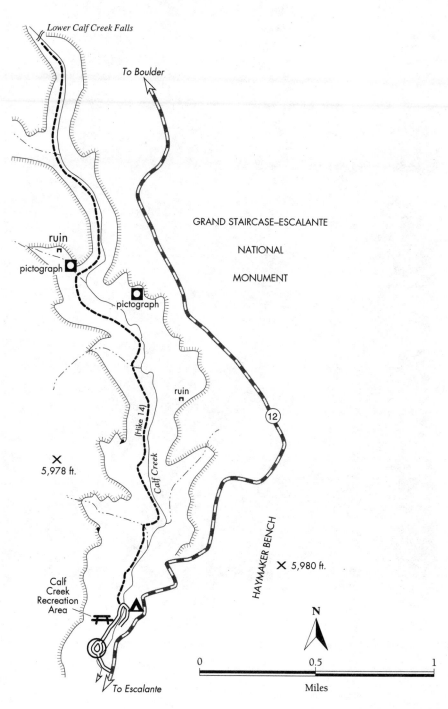

Lower Calf Creek Falls

To Boulder

GRAND STAIRCASE–ESCALANTE

NATIONAL

MONUMENT

ruin

pictograph

pictograph

ruin

(Hike 14)

12

Calf Creek

X
5,978 ft.

X 5,980 ft.

HAYMAKER BENCH

Calf
Creek
Recreation
Area

N

0   0.5   1

Miles

To Escalante

Lower Calf Creek Falls is one of the most popular destinations in the Escalante canyons.

of the amphitheater issue an array of dripping springs that nurture hanging gardens of maidenhair fern and alcove columbine. Here you can relax in a shady grove of water birch, or cool off in the deep pool in the spray of the falls.

35 Escalante River Trailhead to Maverick Bridge and Phipps Arch

General description:	A rewarding day hike along the Escalante River, visiting two interesting natural rock spans, in Grand Staircase–Escalante National Monument.
Distance:	6.6 miles round trip.
Difficulty:	Moderate; Class 2 and 3 friction pitches to reach Phipps Arch.
Trail conditions:	Good boot-worn trail along Escalante River; wash route in Phipps Wash; slickrock route to Phipps Arch.
Trailhead access:	2WD (paved access).
Average hiking time:	4 to 5 hours round trip.
Trailhead elevation:	5,200 feet.
High point:	5,560 feet at Phipps Arch.
Elevation gain and loss:	400 feet.
Optimum season:	Mid-April through early June; September through October.
Water availability:	Available from the Escalante River, but since this silty water must be settled and treated before drinking, bring your own.
Hazards:	Fording the Escalante River can be hazardous during high water flows; exposure to steep dropoffs and slickrock friction pitches en route to Phipps Arch.
Permits:	Not required for day hikes.
Topo maps:	Calf Creek USGS quad; Trails Illustrated Canyons of the Escalante.

Key points:
- 0.8 Ford Escalante River.
- 1.6 Reach the mouth of Phipps Wash; bear right into the wash.
- 2.2 Junction with first major side canyon on the right (west); turn right to reach Maverick Bridge.
- 2.4 Maverick Bridge.
- 2.6 Return to Phipps Wash; proceed up-canyon.
- 3.2 Junction with second major side canyon on the left (southeast); bear left.
- 3.5 Phipps Arch.

Finding the trailhead: The prominently signed Escalante River Trailhead is located west of Utah 12 immediately north of the Escalante River bridge, 14.6 miles south of the Utah 12/Burr Trail Road junction in Boulder, and 13.3 miles east of Escalante.

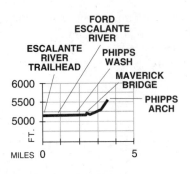

The hike: This rewarding day hike combines a walk along the Escalante River, including at least one ford, with an ascent of dry Phipps Wash and a visit to two distinctive natural spans, Phipps Arch and Maverick Bridge. To reach Phipps Arch requires good routefinding skills and ascending steep slickrock. Maverick Bridge can be reached by any hiker willing to ford the murky, shin-deep waters of the Escalante River.

From the Escalante River Trailhead, find the trail next to the trailhead register and information signboard and stroll several yards down the dusty path to the signed junction. Bear left where the sign points to "Lake Powell 70," pass beneath the highway bridge, then cross the log bridge spanning Calf Creek. A sign here warns that the trail ahead crosses private land for the next 2 miles (actually 1.2 miles), and no camping on the private land is allowed.

The trail ahead follows the bench on the left side of the river, passing through shady groves of cottonwood and other rich riparian growth. Red ledges of Kayenta Formation sandstone embrace the shallow river canyon. After about 0.2 mile the bench pinches out and you scale a juniper-log ladder to the Kayenta ledge above, but then quickly drop back to the riverside among thickets of willows. The trail ahead follows the turbid waters of the river more closely, alternating from beneath shady Kayenta overhangs to the rich riparian growth at the water's edge. After 0.5 mile, you cross a private dirt road where ample signs advise you to stay on the trail.

At the first major bend in the river, at 0.8 mile, you reach a humorous sign that announces "Yup, You Gotta Get Wet." Here you must ford the refreshingly cool river, which is about calf-deep in normal flow and has a modest current. Your trail walk resumes on a shady bench opposite the ford, but this bench soon pinches out where steep Kayenta slickrock reaches into the river. Depending upon the water level, you can either friction walk above the river, or wade in the shallow water at the river's edge for about 30 yards.

The canyon opens up ahead, with bluffs of Navajo Sandstone punctuating the skyline above the red Kayenta ledges and cliff bands that embrace the canyon. Shortly after passing through a stand of tall sagebrush, cross a fenceline via the V-shaped passage of a hiker's maze. The trail ahead hugs the right (south) wall of the canyon, and soon you enter Grand Staircase–Escalante National Monument at the signed boundary of the Escalante Canyons Outstanding Natural Area.

Shortly thereafter, return to the river and prepare to get your feet wet one last time. To proceed you must wade through the shallow water for about 50 yards, then mount a bench studded with unusually tall sagebrush. The trail weaves a way through the brushfields to the cottonwood-bordered mouth of Phipps Wash, opening up on the right (southwest). Leave the trail here at 5,180 feet, and follow dry and sandy Phipps Wash up-canyon. The soft sand in the wash results in a slow, labored pace, which allows time to soak in the beauty of the canyon.

The red Kayenta Formation and its characteristic ledges and cliff bands flank the wash, the terraces studded with pinyon and juniper and their typically associated woodland shrubs. Cliffs of desert-varnished Navajo Sandstone cap the canyon rims.

After about 0.25 mile, the wash becomes rocky, providing firmer footing and an improved pace. The Calf Creek USGS quad shows Maverick Bridge in a north-trending draw about 0.5 mile up the wash from the river. The map is in error, and to find the bridge look for a prominent Navajo tower that juts skyward up ahead. At the foot of that tower a major side canyon opens up on the right, 0.6 miles from the river and 2.2 miles from the trailhead.

Ascend into this canyon via its sandy wash. After 0.1 mile, a sandy path leads up the left slope for another 0.1 mile to the small bridge, a delicate span no more than 2 feet thick, stretching 15 feet across the wash. Runoff from this side canyon carved an opening in the ceiling of a small but deep

Phipps Wash.

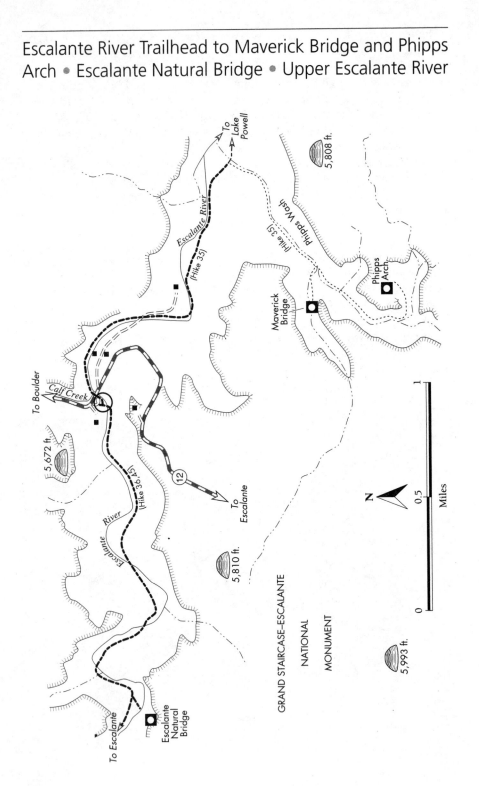

To Lake Powell

5,808 ft.

Escalante River

Phipps Wash

[Hike 35]

[Hike 35]

Phipps Arch

Maverick Bridge

To Boulder

Calf Creek

5,672 ft.

[Hike 36.45]

River

Escalante

12

To Escalante

5,810 ft.

N

0.5

Miles

1

0

GRAND STAIRCASE–ESCALANTE

NATIONAL

MONUMENT

5,993 ft.

To Escalante

Escalante Natural Bridge

alcove, isolating this thin sliver of slickrock. The undercut cliff below the bridge offers a shady refuge on a hot day.

Beyond that worthwhile detour, continue up Phipps Wash, following boot-worn trails on either side of the sandy wash. A precipitous side canyon joins on the left (southeast) 0.2 mile beyond the Maverick Bridge side canyon. Phipps Wash becomes even more picturesque ahead. Embraced by red- and white-banded slickrock, the wash remains fringed by cottonwoods, with a scattering of pinyon and juniper dotting the benches above.

After hiking 1.2 miles up Phipps Wash from the river, a second prominent side canyon opens up on the left, and you'll see a path leading into its mouth. Follow that path while looking for cairns on the left after several yards. The cairns are your cue to leave the canyon and begin steadily ascending a series of slickrock benches toward the northeast. Don't expect to find cairns marking the route. Use your topo map and follow a northeast course up the slickrock toward the still unseen arch.

The final ascent of the upper layers of the Kayenta involves a steep slickrock friction pitch with moderate exposure. Above that pitch follow an obvious ledge to the right for several yards, then curve left into a shallow slickrock draw. This leads several more yards to the skyline aperture of Phipps Arch.

This large arch penetrates a Navajo Sandstone dome, with a span of about 100 feet by 30 feet high. Its shaded interior provides a welcome refuge from the sun, where you can comfortably enjoy inspiring vistas. An expanse of red and white Navajo slickrock dominates the landscape in the north and southwest, with a compliment of wooded benches and mesas in between. Slickrock domes surround the arch and rise just above eye level here on the rim of Phipps Wash.

After visiting Phipps Arch, carefully retrace your steps to the trailhead.

36 Escalante Natural Bridge

See Map on Page 200

General description:	A fine half-day hike in the upper Escalante River canyon leading to a rare natural bridge, within Grand Staircase–Escalante National Monument.
Distance:	3.2 miles round trip.
Difficulty:	Moderately easy.
Trail conditions:	Well-defined boot-worn trails, with numerous river fords necessary.
Trailhead access:	2WD (paved access).
Average hiking time:	2 hours round trip.
Trailhead elevation:	5,200 feet.
High point:	5,250 feet.
Elevation gain and loss:	50 feet.

Optimum seasons: Mid-April through early June; September through October.

Water availability: Escalante River, but since silty river water must be settled and treated before drinking, bring your own.

Hazards: Fording the Escalante River can be hazardous during high water flows.

Permits: Not required for day hikes.

Topo maps: Calf Creek USGS quad; Trails Illustrated Canyons of the Escalante.

Key points:

1.6 Escalante Natural Bridge.

Finding the trailhead: Follow driving directions for Hike 35.

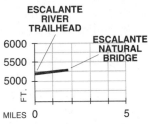

The hike: The upper Escalante River canyon, between the town of Escalante and the Utah 12 bridge, is not only one of the most beautiful parts of the 85-mile long canyon, it is also the easiest to reach, with friendly terrain unencumbered by dense brush thickets and boulder fields. One need not be a dedicated backpacker to enjoy hiking along the Escalante River, and this fine short hike to Escalante Natural Bridge is a trip accessible to any hiker willing to ford the shallow river.

The hike traverses the most open part of the river canyon, where broad benches flank the river and bold cliffs and domes define the canyon. Four refreshing fords of the shin-deep river are the only barrier to travel along the well-worn, sandy trail. During normal water flows, the fords are shallow and trouble free. An interesting skyline arch, 0.5 mile and two fords above the natural bridge, offers incentive to extend the hike.

From the Escalante River Trailhead off of Utah 12, find the trail next to the trailhead register and information signboard and follow the dusty path for several yards down to a signed junction. Turn right where the sign points to "Escalante 15." Follow the trail along the fence, skirting private property, pass through a hiker's maze, then reach the banks of the river where a sign declares "Yup, You Gotta Get Wet." Rangers sometimes place poles here to aid crossing at the swift, rocky ford. If poles are absent, ford the shin-deep waters just upstream from the trail. A walking staff proves quite useful not only to maintain balance while fording the river, but also for hiking the sandy trail ahead.

A well-defined trail greets you on the south bank of the river, and you follow the sandy tread up-canyon. This beautiful unconfined canyon is embraced by terraces alternately studded with head-high sagebrush and rabbitbrush, and open grasslands rich with the colorful desert blooms of Eastwood paintbrush, scarlet gilia, tansy-aster, penstemon, and globemallow. A ribbon of native cottonwoods and willows hug the river banks, joined by exotic tamarisk and Russian olive trees. Navajo sandstone cliffs, dimpled with alcoves, rise to a parade of slickrock domes capping the skyline.

As you follow the good trail, rising imperceptibly up the scenic canyon, you will ford the small river three more times. After the last (fourth) crossing, you reach the mouth of a north-trending side canyon. Careful attention to the route of the trail is necessary here to avoid becoming entangled in the thickets of riparian growth that fringe the wash.

Soon thereafter you mount an open bench, from where Escalante Natural Bridge comes into view on the south canyon wall. After 1.6 miles, a spur trail branches left from the main trail, leading 200 yards to the banks of the river opposite the bridge. Some hikers will ford the river for a closer look, though most are content to view the bridge from the river bank. Guarding the portal to a shadowed amphitheater, this massive 130-foot high, 100-foot wide bridge of sandstone spans a small slickrock drainage, standing away from the canyon wall. This is the fifth largest natural bridge in the Glen Canyon region. Only Rainbow Bridge and the spans in Natural Bridges National Monument are larger.

Two more river fords and 0.5 mile of hiking up-canyon leads you to a striking skyline arch, the opening of which was visible from far down the canyon. The sheer 300-foot wall beneath the arch, streaked with desert varnish, is a memorable sight.

From Escalante Natural Bridge, retrace your route to the trailhead.

37 Harris Wash

General description:	An extended round-trip backpack to the Escalante River, leading through a sinuous slickrock canyon, in Grand Staircase–Escalante National Monument and Glen Canyon National Recreation Area.
Distance:	21.4 miles round trip.
Difficulty:	Moderate.
Trail conditions:	Wash route with considerable wading necessary.
Trailhead access:	4WD advised when the road is wet.
Average hiking time:	2 to 4 days round trip.
Trailhead elevation:	4,980 feet.
Low point:	4,650 feet at the Escalante River.
Elevation loss and gain:	330 feet.
Optimum seasons:	April through early June; September through October.
Water availability:	Perennial flows in Harris Wash and at the Escalante River.
Hazards:	Flash-flood danger.
Permits:	Required for overnight trips; obtain at trailhead register or at the Escalante Interagency visitor center.
Topo maps:	Red Breaks and Silver Falls Bench USGS quads; Trails Illustrated Canyons of the Escalante.

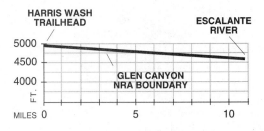

Key points:

0.1   4WD road leads north across wash; bear right and descend the wash.
1.0   Navajo Sandstone outcrops and canyon narrows.
3.3   Glen Canyon National Recreation Area boundary.
6.6   Third south-trending side canyon joins on the right (south).
7.2   Fourth south-trending side canyon joins on the right (south).
10.7 Escalante River.

Finding the trailhead: The Hole-in-the-Rock Road provides access to this hike and to Hikes 38–44. This generally good, graded dirt road branches southeast from Utah 12, 5.8 miles east of the Escalante Interagency visitor center and 23.8 miles southwest of the Utah 12/Burr Trail Road junction in Boulder.

Follow this good wide road southeast, passing a large destination and mileage sign a short distance from the highway. After driving 10.5 miles, turn left onto the signed eastbound road leading to Harris Wash. This seldom-graded but usually fair road leads 2.7 miles to a cattle guard, beyond which the road forks right to Buckaroo Flat and left to Harris Wash.

Bear left at the junction. Soon thereafter the road begins a steady descent, and the broad drainage of Harris Wash comes into view in the middle distance, with the slickrock landscape of the Escalante canyons, the Circle Cliffs, and the Henry Mountains rising in the distance.

After driving 4.7 miles from Hole-in-the-Rock Road, you reach the first of two wash crossings. Assess any flood damage to the road before proceeding. The road crosses another, larger wash 0.2 mile farther, then winds past a corral and becomes a poor track for the remaining distance to the signed trailhead parking area, located in a Russian olive thicket above the banks of Harris Wash, 6.4 miles from the Hole-in-the-Rock Road.

Hikers arriving late in the day will find a few undeveloped campsites en route to the trailhead.

The hike: The Escalante canyons are famous for their serpentine slickrock gorges, featuring deep alcoves, undercut cliffs, desert-varnished walls, and riparian oases, and Harris Wash is no exception. This beautiful canyon, part of the route of the Halls Crossing wagon road between 1881 and 1884, affords an excellent destination for a backpack of three to four days. Of all the canyon routes off of the Hole-in-the-Rock Road, Harris Wash is the most easily accessible, yet compared to some other canyons, most notably Coyote Gulch (see Hike 39), Harris receives only moderate use. Hikers here can expect a good degree of solitude.

Harris Wash

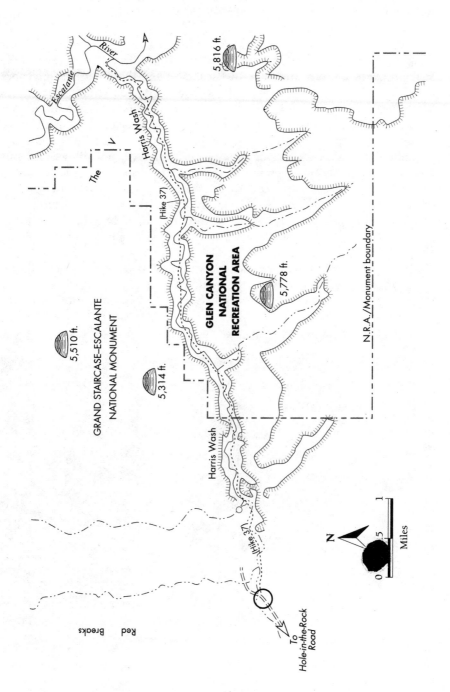

Harris Wash is comparable to Coyote Gulch in other ways. Although there are no arches or bridges here, the wash has carved a serpentine gorge through the resistant Navajo Sandstone, featuring a continuum of tremendous vaulting cliffs and alcoves around nearly every bend of the canyon. Indeed, Harris Wash is a canyon of alcoves, many of which afford excellent, shady places to camp.

The perennial stream in Harris Wash runs clear, except of course following periods of heavy rain and runoff. Harris Wash drains a vast area of the Straight Cliffs south of the town of Escalante, and the potential for severe flash floods is great. I have met hikers who have been stranded in Harris Wash for two days following only one afternoon of heavy rain and the subsequent flooding and quicksand. The entire canyon is a rich riparian oasis, contrasting sharply with the surrounding landscape of slickrock and sand. Depending upon recent beaver activity, occasional deep wading or serious bushwhacking may be necessary to negotiate this route. There is no trail in Harris Wash, save for short segments of boot-worn paths shortcutting some of the canyon's meanders. Hikers simply follow the wash downstream all the way to the Escalante River. Since you will be walking in the water at times, and crossing the small stream repeatedly, a pair of sturdy wading shoes or boots is recommended.

From the trailhead parking area, follow the 4WD track through the thicket of tamarisk and Russian olive to the banks of broad Harris Wash, then turn right (east) down its sandy and gravelly bed. Do not continue following the

Harris Wash.

4WD road north across the wash. That doubletrack, which has areas of deep sand that has trapped the vehicles of both recreationists and rangers alike, leads out onto The V, a wedge-shaped mesa separating Harris Wash and the Escalante River.

In its upper reaches Harris Wash is a broad flood plain, bordered by a scattering of cottonwoods, rabbitbrush, and exotic tamarisk and Russian olive trees. The Russian olive, with its gray foliage and thorny branches, is widely planted as a windbreak tree in arid parts of the West. It has escaped and become naturalized along many stream courses in Utah. Low hills composed of the red and gray beds of the Carmel Formation, studded with pinyon and juniper, flank the wide, shadeless valley.

After 1 mile, the Navajo Sandstone emerges, and low slickrock walls soon begin to embrace the increasingly confined wash, which follows a sinuous course through the resistant slickrock ahead. At times you may be following traces of an old 4WD road that once connected with Silver Falls Creek east of the river, though much of the route proceeds without the benefit of a trail.

The spring shown on the map at 1.7 miles is the source of the wash's stream during dry seasons. Much of the year the stream begins flowing well above the trailhead, and ahead you will either be wading or repeatedly crossing the small stream, choosing your own way from one bank to another. After 3 miles, you reach a fence where the doubletrack ends, and you pass through the fence via a hiker's maze, a V-shaped passage that allows people, but not cows, to proceed. At 3.3 miles, you enter Glen Canyon National Recreation Area, indicated by a large wooden sign on the right bank.

The wash ahead assumes the character of a classic slickrock gorge, with the canyon walls rising 200 to 300 feet to the rims above. The wash is confined by the bold sandstone walls, in places separated by only 15 feet of space. Nearly every bend, out of about three dozen bends the canyon describes, reveals deep alcoves or undercut, vaulting cliffs, where you will enjoy frequent shade. Small benches flank the wash ahead, offering a continuum of fine camping areas. The moist, shady confines of the canyon support a vigorous growth of riparian vegetation, making brief stretches of bushwhacking through the streamside jungle an occasional inconvenience.

On occasion boot-worn paths stay above the stream, but at 3.8 miles, a slickrock buttress on the left pushes you into the narrow streambed, where you pass the first major side canyon entering on the right (south). After another 2.8 miles of winding your way beneath shadowed alcoves, a second, more prominent canyon opens up on the right, draining the highland of Allen Dump to the south and offering a small flow of water to the stream in Harris Wash. There are good campsites near the mouth of the side canyon and on the bench north of the wash.

After passing a third side canyon at 7.4 miles, the gorge grows deeper and even more confined as you follow the meanders back and forth beneath dramatic desert-varnished cliffs. Wide wooded benches offer more fine camping areas for the next 2 miles. As the canyon reaches its greatest depth of about 400 feet at 9.6 miles, its course straightens, and you proceed northeast beneath a bold slickrock tower that thrusts 350 feet skyward above the east wall of the canyon. You wind a way around that imposing landmark for 0.5 mile to meet the green banks of the Escalante River.

The openness and dry landscape of the Escalante canyon is a stark contrast to the damp, shady confines of Harris Wash. Above the riparian tangle bordering the river are broad, sandy benches covered in fields of brush and grass, with a backdrop of bold Navajo cliffs rising 500 feet to the tree-fringed mesas above.

The better campsites are located on a wide, cottonwood-studded terrace 0.3 mile up-river, opposite the mouth of Silver Falls Creek. Few hikers forego the 5-mile round-trip hike up Silver Falls Creek to the Hobbs inscription (see Hike 31), a worthwhile foray on a layover day at the Escalante River.

The miniature slickrock wonderland of Devils Garden.

38 Devils Garden

General description: An easy stroll through the erosion-sculpted sandstone spires of the Devils Garden Outstanding Natural Area, within the Grand Staircase–Escalante National Monument.

Distance: Variable; up to 0.7 mile.

Difficulty: Easy.

Trail conditions: Boot-worn trails and slickrock routes.

Trailhead access: 4WD advised when the road is wet.

Average hiking time: Variable, up to 1 hour.

Trailhead elevation: 5,320 feet.

Elevation gain and loss: Minimal.

Optimum season: April through early June; September through October.

Water availability: None available, bring your own.

Hazards: Negligible.

Topo maps: Seep Flat USGS quad; Trails Illustrated Canyons of the Escalante.

Finding the trailhead: Follow driving directions for Hike 37 to the Harris Wash Road, then continue south on the Hole-in-the-Rock Road for another 1.6 miles (12.1 miles from Utah 12) to the signed spur road leading to Devils Garden, and turn right. Follow this often-rough gravel road for .25 mile to the spacious parking area adjacent to the picnic site.

The hike: The Devils Garden Outstanding Natural Area is an excellent place off the Hole-in-the-Rock Road for an afternoon picnic followed by an hour or so of rewarding exploration. The garden is small, covering only about 200 acres, but it is a miniature wonderland of Navajo Sandstone hoodoos, domes, narrow passages, and small arches, hidden from the view of drivers along the Hole-in-the-Rock Road.

Devils Garden provides a brief introduction to the kind of slickrock walking and routefinding over a trailless landscape typical of most backcountry routes in the Escalante region. Since the landscape features, such as pouroffs and cliffs, are in miniature here, obstacles are minor.

Devils Garden features a four-site picnic area with pit toilets, tables, fire pits, and elevated grills. No water is available. Bring your own firewood or charcoal, since firewood collecting is not allowed at the site. Dogs must be leashed at all times in Devils Garden. Although children will enjoy wandering with their parents here, remind your children to avoid trampling the coarse yet fragile desert vegetation.

There is no particular destination other than the garden itself, and there are numerous short, boot-worn paths to follow. Or you can strike out on your own over the slickrock. Since everything here is on a small scale, its easy to experience the entire area by wandering through it for an hour or so.

Miniature domes, tiny narrows carved by rivulets of infrequent runoff,

Devils Garden

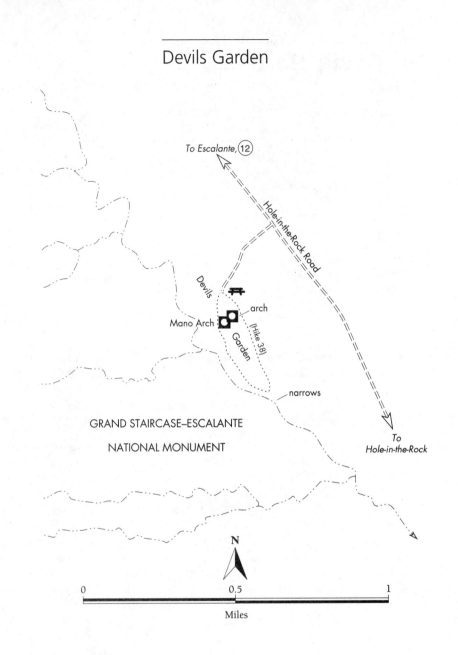

To Escalante, (12)

Hole-in-the-Rock Road

Devils

arch

Mano Arch

(Hike 38)

Garden

narrows

GRAND STAIRCASE–ESCALANTE

NATIONAL MONUMENT

To
Hole-in-the-Rock

N

| 0 | 0.5 | 1 |

Miles

and diminutive pouroffs are among the features you'll see during your wanderings. There is a small arch spanning a gully that can be found by following the upper, left-hand trail beginning at the picnic site. The lower trail skirts the base of Devils Garden's erosional formations, passing delicate Mano Arch and an array of red- and beige-toned sandstone hoodoos and mushroom rocks that rise from the pinyon- and juniper-studded bench. Other hiker-made trails criss-cross the area.

You can follow a short loop through the garden, covering about 0.7 mile along the way. The upper trail fades on the slickrock past the aforementioned arch, but you can continue over the sandstone slopes to a point above a bend in the wash, where it cuts through a 15-foot wide slot. Loop back to the picnic site via the bench above the wash, skirting the dramatic hoodoos along the garden's western margin. Midway back to the picnic site, you'll pick up a good trail to follow back to your car.

39 Hurricane Wash to Coyote Gulch

General description:	One of the finest, and most popular, backpacks in the Escalante canyons, leading through a memorable Navajo Sandstone canyon in Grand Staircase–Escalante National Monument and Glen Canyon National Recreation Area.
Distance:	26.6 miles round trip.
Difficulty:	Moderate.
Trail conditions:	Wash route with considerable wading necessary, and segments of boot-worn trails.
Trailhead access:	4WD advised when the road is wet.
Average hiking time:	3 to 4 days.
Trailhead elevation:	4,580 feet.
Low point:	3,700 feet at the Escalante River.
Elevation loss and gain:	870 feet.
Optimum season:	April through May; September through October.

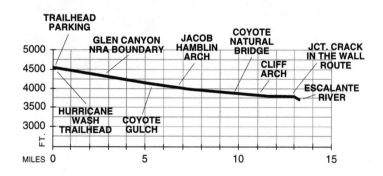

Jacob Hamblin Arch in Coyote Gulch.

Water availability: Coyote Gulch features a perennial creek; numerous good seeps and springs are found between Jacob Hamblin Arch and the river.
Hazards: Flash-flood danger, occasional poison ivy.
Permits: Required for overnight trips; obtain from the trailhead register or at the Escalante Interagency visitor center.
Topo maps: Big Hollow Wash, King Mesa, and Stevens Canyon South USGS quads; Trails Illustrated Canyons of the Escalante.

Key points:
0.3   Trailhead register at road end.
2.9   Enter Glen Canyon NRA.
5.4   Confluence of Hurricane Wash and Coyote Gulch; bear right, down-canyon.
6.9   Jacob Hamblin Arch.
8.9   Coyote Natural Bridge.
11.1   Cliff Arch.
12.9   Junction with southbound Crack in the Wall route (Hike 41).
13.3   Escalante River.

Finding the trailhead: Follow driving directions for Hike 37 to the Harris Wash Road junction, 10.5 miles from Utah 12, then continue southeast on the Hole-in-the-Rock Road. After passing the Kane/Garfield county line, the road is generally much rougher, with rocky stretches, and often many miles of washboards, though the road remains wide.

About 26 miles from Utah 12, the road descends below the rolling grasslands and pinyon-juniper woodlands onto a broad desert terrace dissected by numerous washes draining the Straight Cliffs. The trailhead parking area is located on the right (west) side of the road, immediately north of signed Hurricane Wash, 33.8 miles from Utah 12. Hikers can camp at the trailhead or in one of a few undeveloped campsites along the Hole-in-the-Rock Road.

The hike: Coyote Gulch is the most well-known, and well-used, canyon in the Escalante region, and for good reasons. Between the lower Escalante River and the Straight Cliffs, Coyote Gulch has carved a deep, serpentine gorge through the Navajo Sandstone, forming what is arguably one of the most spectacular slickrock canyons in the Glen Canyon region. Tremendous alcoves and vaulting cliffs soar 200 to 400 feet overhead around nearly every bend of the tortuously twisting gorge. Two memorable arches and a water-worn natural bridge add to the attraction. Campsites are numerous and scenic in Coyote Gulch, the stream flows year-round, and several good springs issue from the canyon walls among rich hanging gardens.

This memorable backpack follows Hurricane Wash, the standard entry route into Coyote Gulch, as it gradually evolves from a broad wash into a narrow gorge wedged between slickrock cliffs and domes. Much of the way down Hurricane Wash is trailless, and hikers simply follow the sandy wash down the canyon. Once you reach Coyote Gulch, boot-worn trails lead you down to the Escalante River.

The Escalante River at the mouth of Coyote Gulch.

Since you will be crossing the wide, ankle-deep stream in Coyote Gulch repeatedly, and sometimes walking in the stream itself, wading shoes are recommended. During spring and autumn, hikers flock to the Mecca of Coyote Gulch in a steady stream via four access routes. If you visit on Memorial Day Weekend, expect to share the gulch with 100 or more other hikers. Most overnight use is concentrated in the 6-mile stretch between Jacob Hamblin Arch and the Crack in the Wall route, with the arch being the focal point of the canyon. During peak use periods, particularly holiday weekends, good campsites may be hard to find. The meandering nature of the canyon, combined with many slickrock amphitheaters featuring exceptional acoustics, amplify every sound. Hikers seeking quiet and solitude are advised to avoid Coyote Gulch during Easter Week and Memorial Day Weekend.

One of the ways hikers can minimize their impact in Coyote Gulch is to hike in the streambed below the high water mark. This prevents the multiple trailing which is a major problem in Coyote Gulch and allows subsequent floods to wash away footprints. On many bends in the canyon there are often multiple shortcut trails, many ascending steep hills. Hikers will expend less energy and reduce their impact by simply following the stream around the canyon's bends.

From the trailhead parking area, cross the Hole-in-the-Rock Road and follow a sandy spur road (accessible to 4WD vehicles only) east along tamarisk-fringed Hurricane Wash for 0.3 mile to the road's end. There you find a trailhead register (obtain your permit there) and a parking area with room enough for about three vehicles. The route ahead follows the long-closed 4WD road down the wash, occasionally crossing its dry, rock-strewn bed. Soon you reach a fence and pass through a signed hiker's maze, a V-shaped passage that allows people, but not cows, to continue.

After 1.8 miles, a cairned trail branches right off the road, and you follow its single track into the rocky wash. After criss-crossing the wash for 0.3 mile, you pass the first major side drainage on the right. Here the trail dips into the sandy wash, and you follow this corridor ahead for another 2 miles. Broad slopes of colorful Navajo Sandstone slickrock soon appear, embracing the still shallow drainage on either hand. Vegetation on the slickrock slopes changes in response to this new substrate. Many gnarled, picturesque cliffrose shrubs, especially beautiful when massed with white blossoms in spring, have gained a foothold on the margins of the slickrock.

The wash is soon confined by slickrock, and very gradually grows deeper. The tread in the wash ranges from soft sand to stretches strewn with rocks and boulders, though the walking is straightforward, and for the most part, trouble free. At one point you are funneled into a narrow sandstone corridor, but soon emerge back into the open wash, reaching the signed Glen Canyon National Recreation Area boundary at 4,280 feet, next to the spreading canopy of a lone juniper, which offers the only significant shade for miles.

Echoing slickrock hallways and open rocky stretches define the route ahead. This is an arduous slog through soft sand, but the cliffs and domes of cross-bedded sandstone that surround you offer a distraction from your labors. After 3.7 miles, cottonwoods begin to fringe the wash. Soon thereafter, willow and common reed grass add their verdure to the canyon floor, and then a seep emerges, giving life to a small, trickling stream. Here you exchange the soft sandy wash for a firmer path of damp sand. The canyon rapidly grows deeper and increasingly narrow, and you follow a discernible path back and forth across the small stream.

As you continue, you begin to pass small campsites perched on the narrow terraces above the wash. One site is particularly inviting, situated on a sandy bench beneath cottonwoods and protected by an overhanging wall that blocks the sun for much of the day.

You follow the beautiful canyon of Hurricane Wash until it suddenly opens up at the confluence with Coyote Gulch at 4,050 feet, after 5.4 miles. Here you must cross the ankle-deep stream in the gulch to continue. Since you'll be spending considerable time in the water hereafter, the confluence is a likely place to don your wading shoes. Coyote Gulch is a deep, magnificent canyon, and it grows deeper and more dramatic as you proceed. Tremendous vaulting cliffs arch over the wash around nearly every bend of the gulch, offering a shady refuge on a hot day.

After 6.8 miles, you pass a sign pointing to a pit toilet on the bench just above the wash, a necessary "improvement" due to the increasing number of hikers visiting the gulch. Just beyond a great vaulted ceiling of sandstone arches overhead to form the most outstanding amphitheater in the gulch. Seeping water along the canyon walls supports rich hanging gardens of maidenhair fern, Eastwood monkeyflower, and alcove columbine. As you bend around the curving amphitheater, massive Jacob Hamblin Arch appears ahead, its tunnel-like opening piercing a thick slickrock buttress. The broad, domed ceiling of the arch frames a fine view of the convoluted canyon walls ahead.

The sandy bench opposite (west of) the arch is a popular campsite, and another site lies just ahead at the next bend. A tight meander beneath another great overhang leads around to the east side of the arch, where great boulders are heaped beneath the span. Just beyond the arch a series of vigorous dripping springs emerge from the canyon wall on the left side of the wash. These are the last good springs in the gulch for the next 3.5 miles. A small campsite lies on the narrow stream terrace opposite the springs, and several more sites can be found around the next bend.

As you follow the winding gorge ahead, you slowly gain lateral distance down-canyon. When drawing water from springs in the gulch, **beware of poison ivy**, a plant growing 3 to 4 feet tall from woody stems, unmistakable with its three large, shiny green leaflets.

After 8.6 miles, 1.7 miles from Jacob Hamblin Arch, the canyon floor becomes constricted and the stream tumbles and cascades over slickrock. Point 4121, a monolithic sandstone tower, rises ahead, and below it the stream is funneled through a narrow passage. A *rincon*, or abandoned meander, of Coyote Gulch's former stream course curves around behind the tower. Hikers have beaten a path that follows the rincon over a sandy bench carpeted with cheatgrass. Good campsites can be found there among groves of boxelder trees. Unless you are searching for a campsite or if floods have scoured deep holes that may require deep wading or a swim in this narrow

Hurricane Wash to Coyote Gulch

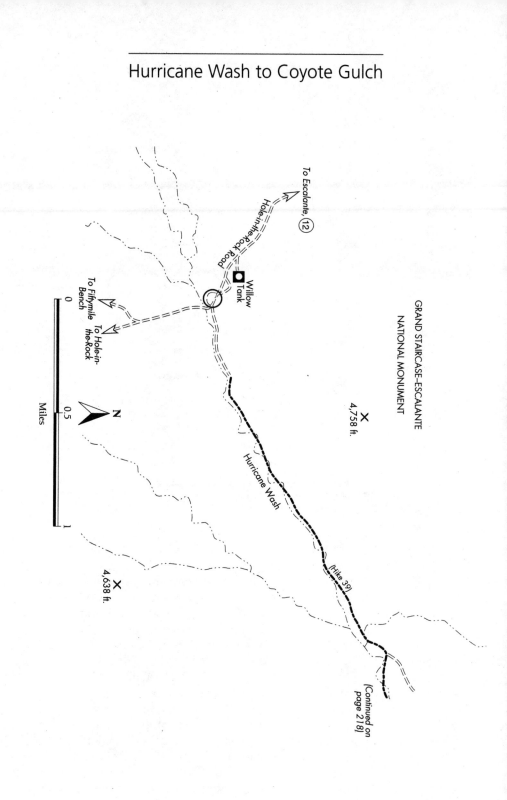

To Escalante, (12)

Hole-in-the-Rock Road

Willow
Tank

GRAND STAIRCASE–ESCALANTE
NATIONAL MONUMENT

To Fiftymile
Bench

To Hole-in-
the-Rock

X
4,758 ft.

N

0   0.5   1

Miles

Hurricane Wash

(Hike 39)

X
4,638 ft.

(Continued on
page 218)

Hurricane Wash to Coyote Gulch

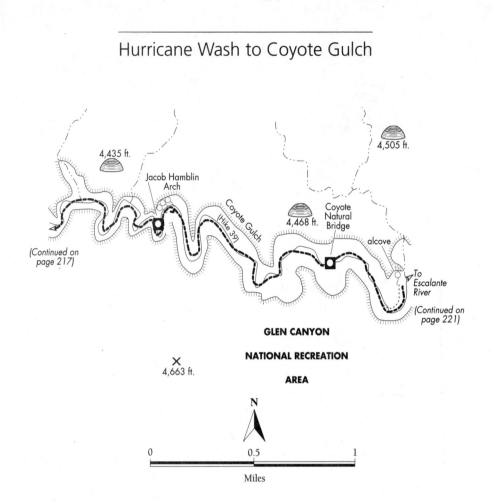

4,435 ft.

Jacob Hamblin Arch

4,505 ft.

Coyote Gulch (Hike 39)

Coyote Natural Bridge

4,468 ft.

alcove

(Continued on page 217)

To Escalante River

(Continued on page 221)

GLEN CANYON

NATIONAL RECREATION

AREA

X
4,663 ft.

N

0   0.5   1

Miles

passage, avoid the path and simply wade down the streambed, with slickrock under foot, through the narrows.

After following a few more bends in the canyon, you see a sandstone fin stretching across the wash from wall to wall. The stream curves north briefly, then turns east to flow through the fin beneath Coyote Natural Bridge. This fascinating aperture, carved by the abrasive waters draining Coyote Gulch, rises about 25 feet from the wash, with a span of about 100 feet between abutments.

After you pass underneath the bridge, the gulch gradually begins to open up ahead. Benches flanking the stream become common, supporting a thick growth of cottonwood and willow. After 10.8 miles, you round a bend and are confronted with a boulder jam blocking the canyon floor. Stay to the left of the stream and pick your way among the large, angular boulders, scrambling and rock-hopping at times. The red and lavender rocks of the Kayenta Formation emerge in the wash at the boulder jam, and the stream begins dropping in a series of small cascades, the water's music amplified by the canyon walls. Several yards below the boulder jam you reach the first of several waterfalls, and from the brink of the falls you will have a fine view of Cliff Arch, a jug-handle-type arch projecting from midway up the north canyon wall.

Bypass the waterfall via a short, steep path on the left, then continue down-canyon. Just around the next two bends, where the wash turns north, and about 0.5 mile from the waterfall, another prominent Navajo Sandstone tower punctuates the canyon. Behind it lies another abandoned meander of the Coyote Gulch stream course. A short distance beyond the tower you reach the lip of a 15-foot waterfall, which you bypass on the right via a steep, rocky path. Just below is yet another 15-foot waterfall, which you also bypass on the right. Part way down the bypass route, be sure to follow ledges and steep slickrock, switching back to the left and descending toward the falls. Do not contour straight ahead past a steep slickrock slope—it is a hazardous dead-end route.

About 100 yards below the third waterfall a vigorous spring emerges from a ledge above on the north wall, but it spreads out on the slickrock slope below. You can't fill a bottle there, but you can cool off under the spring's steady rain. Just ahead a small alcove opens up on the right, affording the last good campsite in the gulch. Soon thereafter you come to the fourth and final waterfall, this one neither as high as the last nor as great an obstacle. Stay to the right and descend the chute alongside the fall via Kayenta ledges. After another 200 yards, a small draw opens up on the left, where a reliable spring offers a good, easily accessible flow of water.

Waterfalls add to the beauty of Coyote Gulch.

Coyote Gulch grows increasingly narrow ahead as it slices deeper into the Kayenta Formation. Bold cliffs of Navajo Sandstone, decorated with dark brown patches of desert varnish, now rise far above, reaching 600 feet up to the canyon rims. Follow the meanders of the wash ahead for 0.4 mile, where the gulch then begins to straighten and you reach the last two springs.

Depending upon inflows and demands for electricity, the level of Lake Powell fluctuates from the normal pool elevation of 3,700 feet to its full capacity at 3,711 feet. Even when full, usually from late spring through early autumn, the mouth of Coyote Gulch is seldom flooded by the lake. Between 1987 and 1997, the canyon mouth has been flooded by the lake only twice. In the rare instance the canyon mouth is flooded, hikers en route to the Escalante River must then take the high route. This route, extending 1.2 miles to the Escalante River up-canyon from the mouth of Coyote Gulch, which may not be cairned, ascends the north wall of the gulch near the two springs, climbing via a series of Kayenta ledges. It then traverses a ledge to the east, leading to a prominent saddle on a point that projects into the river canyon. The well-worn trail continues the traverse to the northwest, staying 200 feet above the river. When you reach a minor draw, descend steeply to the river, 0.5 mile below the mouth of Stevens Canyon. Here in its lower reaches, you will find fords of the river to range from thigh- to waist-deep.

To reach the mouth of Coyote Gulch, continue down-canyon. Soon the Wingate Sandstone emerges on the canyon floor, a massive orange sandstone that, like the Navajo, displays the cross-bedding of its origin as wind-drifted sand. After one last bend to the north, the gulch turns east and becomes choked with a huge boulder jam. A well-worn bypass trail continues ahead on the right, and quite soon it is joined by the trail descending a sand slide between a pair of bold towers from the Crack in the Wall route (Hike 41).

Stay left on the sandy trail, emerging from the sand onto a very steep slope of Wingate ledges. Multiple trails are in evidence here, so stay on the lower trail, which offers the better and safer way. The slickrock traverse involves considerable exposure, with the boulder-littered canyon floor lying 50 feet below. Proceed with caution. Beyond the traverse the sandy path leads to a low slickrock overhang, just high enough to be impassable without the aid of the pole "ladder" hikers have placed here. Once beyond this final obstacle, the canyon walls close in and you must wade in the stream for the final 0.25 mile to the river.

The greenish waters of the Escalante appear suddenly, fringed by dense thickets of willow, tamarisk, and common reed grass. Domes and towers of Navajo slickrock soar more than 1,000 feet above the river. You must ford the river to continue up-canyon. Down-canyon lies Lake Powell. The river has a moderate current, a sandy bottom, and can be waist deep at the mouth of Coyote Gulch.

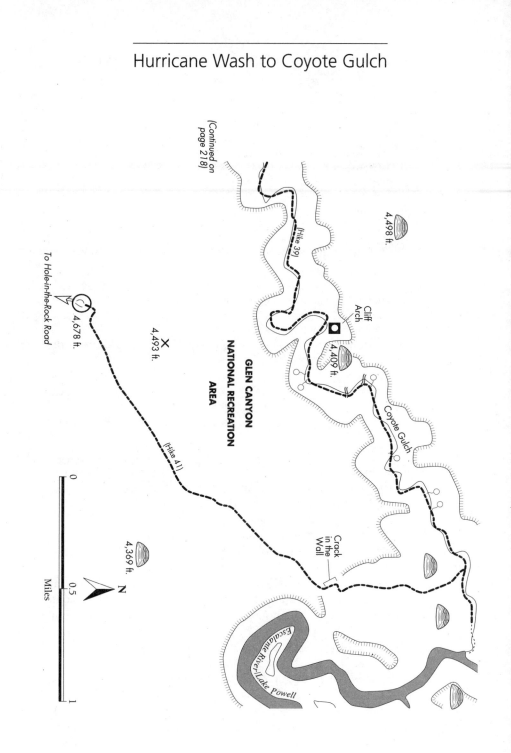

(Continued on page 218)

(Hike 39)

4,498 ft.

To Hole-in-the-Rock Road

4,678 ft.

X
4,493 ft.

GLEN CANYON
NATIONAL RECREATION
AREA

Cliff
Arch

4,409 ft.

Coyote Gulch

(Hike 41)

Crack
in the
Wall

4,369 ft.

N

0
0.5
1

Miles

Escalante River/Lake Powell

40 Fortymile Ridge to Sunset Arch

General description:	A short cross-country day hike to an unusual mesa-top arch high above the lower Escalante canyons, within Grand Staircase–Escalante National Monument.
Distance:	3 miles round trip.
Difficulty:	Easy.
Trail conditions:	Cross-country route, rudimentary route-finding required.
Trailhead access:	4WD advised when the road is wet.
Average hiking time:	1 to 1.5 hours, round trip.
Trailhead elevation:	4,805 feet.
Low point:	4,520 feet.
Elevation loss and gain:	285 feet.
Optimum seasons:	Mid-March through May; September through October.
Water availability:	None available, bring your own.
Hazards:	Negligible.
Permits:	Not required for day hiking.
Topo maps:	King Mesa USGS quad; Trails Illustrated Canyons of the Escalante.

Key points:

0.1   Return to Fortymile Ridge Road, turn left (northeast).

0.2   Leave road at right-angle curve, next to a small water tank and concrete cistern, and bear right (south).

1.5   Sunset Arch.

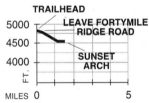

Finding the trailhead: Follow the Hole-in-the-Rock Road south from Utah 12 for 33.8 miles to Hurricane Wash (see driving directions for Hikes 37 and 39), and continue south for another 2.2 miles to the signed turnoff to Fortymile Ridge, then turn left (northeast).

This narrow, sandy road typically develops a severe washboard surface along its entire course. The road undulates over the shrub-dotted, sandy expanse of Fortymile Ridge. The openness of the terrain affords inspiring vistas into the slickrock labyrinths of Coyote Gulch and the lower Escalante canyons and to the more distant landmarks of the Aquarius Plateau, Straight Cliffs, Navajo Mountain, and the Henry Mountains.

After 4.3 miles, turn left (north) onto a short, but steep and rough, spur road, leading 0.1 mile to a large steel water tank and parking area atop the ridge.

There are a few pullouts used as camping areas along the Fortymile Ridge Road, and many more undeveloped campsites along the course of the Hole-in-the-Rock Road.

Fortymile Ridge to Sunset Arch

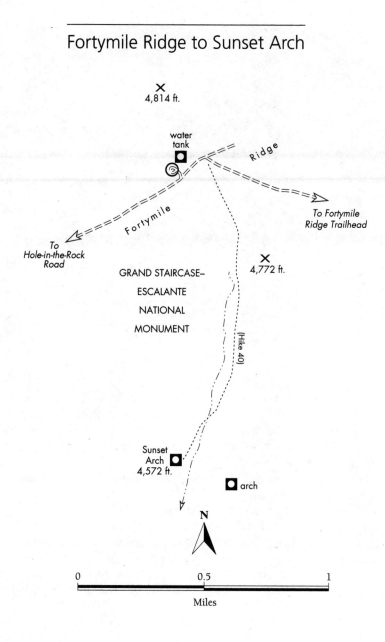

X
4,814 ft.

water
tank

Ridge

To Fortymile
Ridge Trailhead

Fortymile

To
Hole-in-the-Rock
Road

GRAND STAIRCASE–

ESCALANTE

NATIONAL

MONUMENT

X
4,772 ft.

(Hike 40)

Sunset
Arch
4,572 ft.

arch

N

0   0.5   1

Miles

Sunset Arch.

The hike: Few hikers bother to visit Sunset Arch, a delicate, graceful span on the south slopes of Fortymile Ridge, which is surprising considering the arch is accessible via such a short and easy route. Most hikers who come to Fortymile Ridge are en route to one of two access routes into famous Coyote Gulch, north of the ridge.

Vistas along the way to the arch are far-ranging, and the walking is easy, with no obstacles. There is no trail, but one isn't really necessary along this straightforward route across the open terrain.

From the hilltop trailhead at the water tank, drop down to the Fortymile Ridge Road and turn left (east), walking another 0.1 mile to a right-angle bend in the road. Leave the road here where you see a small steel water tank and concrete cistern, and follow a southeast course across the gentle, sandy expanse of Fortymile Ridge, heading toward prominent Point 4772 and its red slickrock slopes.

After about 10 minutes and 0.3 mile of weaving a course among blackbrush, sand sagebrush, mormon tea, and silvery sophora, you reach a minor drainage at the foot of Point 4772. Simply follow the drainage generally south and downhill. Broad vistas reach to the bold barrier of the Straight Cliffs and to the broad dome of 10,388-foot Navajo Mountain. Prominent features at the base of the Straight Cliffs include the isolated slickrock domes of the Sooner Rocks, and to the northwest of those domes you see an apron of Entrada Sandstone at the foot of Cave Point, where an array of deep alcoves create an intriguing contrast of light and shadow.

The better route ahead skirts the shallow arroyo of the drainage rather than following its winding course. The left (east) side of the arroyo is much less sandy than the right side. After about 1 mile the arroyo ends when you reach an expanse of Navajo Sandstone slickrock. Using the distant Sooner Rocks as your guide, continue on your southbound course. Traverse the rolling slickrock for about 5 minutes and suddenly Sunset Arch appears on the low rim just ahead.

Angle upward to the small arch, relax in its shade, and soak in the tremendous panorama. Sunset is a small arch, about 10 feet high and stretching perhaps 50 feet between abutments. But it is a thin, graceful span, created by the eroded remnants of a dome of iron-rich Navajo Sandstone. A few past visitors, some as early as 1924, have left inscriptions in the arch. Please restrain the urge to leave your own mark behind.

True to its name, the arch faces west and frames a memorable sunset over the Straight Cliffs. Views reach south across the vast terrace traversed by the Hole-in-the-Rock Road, a landscape little changed since the members of the epic Hole-in-the-Rock Expedition pioneered the route in 1879 and 1880.

About 0.25 mile away, across the draw below to the southeast, you can see another small arch piercing a low dome of Navajo Sandstone.

From Sunset Arch, retrace your route to the trailhead.

Graceful Sunset Arch frames a view of the Straight Cliffs and Navajo Mountain.

41 Fortymile Ridge to Coyote Gulch via Crack in the Wall

See Map on Page 221

General description:	A short, interesting, and rigorous route into lower Coyote Gulch, suitable as a day hike but most often used as a round-trip backpack, located within Glen Canyon National Recreation Area.
Distance:	2.6 miles one way.
Difficulty:	Moderate, with Class 2 scrambling at Crack in the Wall.
Trail conditions:	Closed 4WD road, boot-worn trails, and cairned slickrock route; much of the route crosses deep, soft sand.
Trailhead access:	4WD advised due to deep, soft sand, and especially when the road is wet.
Average hiking time:	1.5 to 2 hours one way.
Trailhead elevation:	4,678 feet.
Low point:	3,760 feet.
Elevation gain and loss:	+50 feet, -970 feet.
Optimum season:	Mid-March through May; September through October.
Water availability:	Springs in Coyote Gulch (see Hike 39).
Hazards:	Exposure to steep dropoffs.
Permits:	Required for overnight trips; obtain at the trailhead register or at the Escalante Interagency visitor center.
Topo maps:	King Mesa and Stevens Canyon South USGS quads; Trails Illustrated Canyons of the

Key points:
1.8   Crack in the Wall, rim of Coyote Gulch.
2.6   Coyote Gulch.

Finding the trailhead: Follow driving directions for Hike 40 to Fortymile Ridge, then continue beyond the turnoff to the water tank and around the prominent right-angle curve. You reach a junction 5.1 miles from the Hole-in-the-Rock Road, where a sign warns drivers of the deep sand ahead. Although low-clearance cars frequently negotiate this road, a 4WD vehicle is recommended. All drivers must maintain their momentum when driving through deep sand.

Turn left at the junction, and after another 1.3 miles enter Glen Canyon National Recreation Area. Soon thereafter you reach the trailhead at the road end, 6.9 miles from the Hole-in-the-Rock Road and 42.9 miles from Utah 12.

Undeveloped campsites are available in several spurs off of Fortymile Ridge Road, and some hikers camp at the trailhead.

The hike: This scenic, sometimes exciting route is second only to Hurricane Wash as the most popular access into incomparable Coyote Gulch. The trail not only provides short and quick access into lower Coyote Gulch, it also affords dramatic vistas across the vast domed slickrock landscape surrounding the lower Escalante canyons, and of the Escalante River drowned under the waters of Lake Powell.

The trail is shadeless throughout its length and passes over a tread of deep, soft sand. On the rim of Coyote Gulch is the Crack in the Wall, a tight and exciting passage. Although most hikers use the trail on a round-trip backpack into Coyote Gulch, ascending the steep and sandy trail, except during the cooler months or in the early morning hours, is not recommended. Not only is the exit on this trail a sandy, shadeless, uphill slog, the low elevations here translate to very hot temperatures from May through mid-September.

The Crack in the Wall route is not for novices. One segment across slickrock requires routefinding ability, and the narrow crack itself involves some exposure to plunging cliffs. In addition, the sandy trail makes the hike far more demanding than its modest distance would suggest.

The vista that unfolds at the trailhead is unforgettable, stretching across a vast landscape of varicolored Navajo Sandstone slickrock from the north to the southeast. Domes, sweeping slickrock slopes, bold cliffs, and shadowed amphitheaters stretch to the horizon and will remain in view until you reach the Crack in the Wall. The trail, the doubletrack of a long-closed 4WD road, begins behind the trailhead register. Follow this soft-sandy track as it descends northeast at a moderate grade into a broad, sandy, shrub-dotted flat flanked by gently contoured slopes of Navajo slickrock, vividly displaying the cross-bedding of ancient sand dunes.

After about 1 mile the trail begins a gradual rise, curving north to skirt the low domes bounding the eastern margin of the flat. Soon you reach solid ground as you mount slickrock and follow a northeast course, with the aid of cairns, across a hummocky landscape of small domes. Pockets have been scooped out of the slickrock by the processes of weathering and erosion, and some of them may contain water following recent rainfall. Other, old-age pockets are filled with sand and support a variety of bunchgrasses and shrubs such as snakeweed, yucca, prickly pear cactus, and an array of seasonal wildflowers.

You may need to spend a little extra time along this slickrock stretch sighting on the next cairn, since these markers tend to blend into their background. The cairns lead you straight ahead on a northeast course toward the rim of Coyote Gulch. This is slickrock walking at its finest, and your mesa top route affords excellent vistas. The bold barrier of the Straight Cliffs soars 3,000 feet to the rim of the Kaiparowits Plateau behind you, while ahead a domed landscape, with only occasional blackbrush flats or patches of pinyon and juniper to interrupt it, stretches to the horizon.

At length, you unexpectedly reach the rim, where plunging cliffs of Navajo Sandstone embrace the gaping amphitheater below. The memorable view that unfolds from the rim includes the lower reaches of Coyote Gulch, the Escalante River, fringed with impenetrable thickets of riparian greenery, and massive Stevens Arch located up the river canyon, the largest span in the Escalante region.

The Crack in the Wall lies just below, and it is a short but fascinating passage. Only about 50 yards long, the crack consists of a series of three sandstone slabs lying parallel to the cliff just below the rim, with a passage ranging from 1 to 2 feet wide. Drop off the rim and find the crack by turning left. It is a struggle at best to get through with a bulky backpack. You must either hold your pack overhead where the crack is wider or drag it behind you to proceed. The third crack is the narrowest, and some hikers elect to rope their packs down over the 20-foot cliff in the opening between the second and third cracks.

Once you get through the Crack in the Wall, it is a 600-foot descent into Coyote Gulch—a brutal sandy slog if you are returning the same way. Turn right and follow the base of the cliff for several yards, then follow one switchback on the well-worn trail down to the sandy slope below. The trail then assumes a moderate grade over salmon-tinted sand to a broad saddle separating a huge tower to the west and a monolithic dome to the east. From there the trail descends a very steep sand slide, quickly dropping 200 feet to join the trail in Coyote Gulch.

To reach Cliff Arch, Coyote Natural Bridge, and Jacob Hamblin Arch, turn left and follow the gulch up-canyon (see Hike 39).

An incomparable vista of the lower Escalante River canyon unfolds from the Crack in the Wall route.

42 Willow Gulch Trailhead to Broken Bow Arch

General description:	A half-day hike to a large natural arch in the lower Escalante canyons, located within Glen Canyon National Recreation Area.
Distance:	4 miles round trip.
Difficulty:	Moderately easy.
Trail conditions:	Wash route.
Trailhead access:	4WD advised when the road is wet.
Average hiking time:	2 to 3 hours round trip.
Trailhead elevation:	4,200 feet.
Low point:	3,800 feet.
Elevation loss and gain:	400 feet.
Optimum seasons:	Mid-March through May; September through October.
Water availability:	Intermittent flows below confluence with Willow Gulch after 1 mile, but since it must be treated before drinking, bring your own instead.
Hazards:	Flash-flood danger.
Permits:	Not required for day hikes.
Topo maps:	Sooner Bench and Davis Gulch USGS quads; Trails Illustrated Canyons of the Escalante.

Key points:
- 0.2 Enter wash.
- 0.9 Confluence with Willow Gulch.
- 2.0 Broken Bow Arch.

Finding the trailhead: Follow the Hole-in-the-Rock Road for 36 miles southeast from Utah 12 to the Fortymile Ridge Road (see driving directions for Hike 40), and continue straight ahead, soon passing historic Dance Hall Rock. The road ahead undulates through several shallow drainages and is often rocky, rough, and at times steep and winding.

You pass the signed left turn to Fortymile Spring (the site of one of the Hole-in-the-Rock expedition's camps during the winter of 1879–1880) at 37.5 miles, cross Carcass Wash at 39.4 miles, and finally, cross Sooner Wash at 40.5 miles. Several spur roads just beyond Sooner Wash lead to excellent undeveloped campsites among the Entrada Sandstone domes of the Sooner Rocks.

An unsigned road branches left (east) 1 mile beyond Sooner Wash, atop the desert terrace of Sooner Bench. Turn left here and follow the narrow track east. This road, which is occasionally rocky with washboards in places, is passable to carefully driven cars. You will enter Glen Canyon National Recreation Area after 0.6 mile and reach the trailhead at the road end after 1.4 miles, 42.9 miles from Utah 12.

Willow Gulch Trailhead to Broken Bow Arch

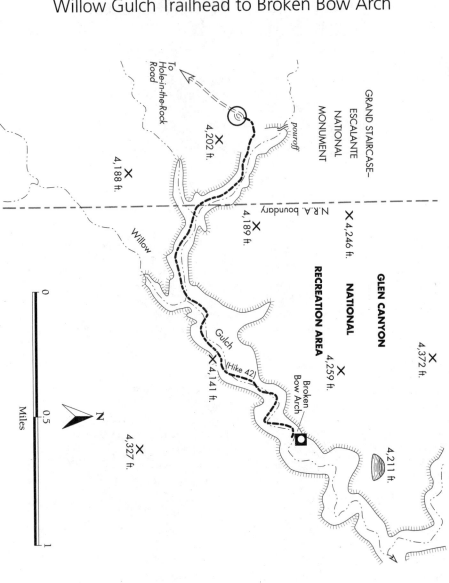

The hike: Willow Gulch offers one of the best short day hikes, also suitable as an overnight trip, in the lower Escalante canyons. The scenic route follows slickrock gorges sliced into a domed landscape of Navajo Sandstone. Interesting narrow passages, a ribbon of riparian foliage, beaver ponds in the small stream, and large Broken Bow Arch are major attractions.

A well-worn path begins behind the trailhead register, descending a moderate grade down the sandy slope. The beautiful canyon, embraced by desert-varnished walls of Navajo Sandstone, opens up 150 feet below. Within moments you pass an interesting slab-crowned hoodoo, then bend east and descend slickrock and sand into the broad wash below. An intriguing stretch of narrows lies a short distance up-canyon, where the wash boxes up in an alcove decorated with hanging gardens. Once you reach the canyon floor, follow the sandy wash down-canyon, shortly passing a line of seepage fringed with the delicate fronds of maidenhair fern.

Soon the wash slots up, and most hikers bypass this slot by following a path above, on the right (south) side of the drainage. The wash opens up again beyond that first constriction, but soon you are funneled into a passable stretch of narrows, beyond which the mouth of a prominent side canyon opens up on the right after 0.5 mile, while on the left, a smaller draw joins the wash.

Continue straight ahead down the narrow, sandy stone hallway. Seep-willow and rabbitbrush fringe the wash, and soon cottonwoods appear. As the wash grows damp ahead, a rich growth of cottonwood, willow,

The slickrock gorge of a Willow Gulch tributary.

231

and seep-willow crowd the canyon bottom. The contrast between the cross-bedded, salmon-tinted slickrock above and the verdant riparian foliage is dramatic.

Soon, a pair of paths begins following benches on either side of the wash as you approach the confluence with Willow Gulch, which joins on the right after 0.9 mile among tall Fremont cottonwoods. Turn left and now follow Willow Gulch down-canyon. Water soon begins to flow in the wash, and evidence of beaver activity attests to its reliability. Willow Gulch opens up below the confluence, with grassy, brush-studded benches flanking the wash and sheer desert-varnished cliffs and domes of Navajo Sandstone rising above. The canyon, however, remains fairly shallow. Rarely do the domes atop the rim rise more than 200 feet from the canyon floor.

After walking for several minutes below the confluence, a prominent trail forged by hikers trying to avoid wading in the stream leads you up onto the right-hand bench. At length the bench pinches out and you descend a minor gully back into the wash, where you jump across the stream and follow a trail on the north-side bench, skirting a beaver pond. Shortly you return to the wash where the canyon grows increasingly narrow, bounded by bold cliffs and domes. Follow the twists and turns of the wash ahead, repeatedly crossing the small stream and tracing bypass trails above it. The stream is small but maintains a steady flow, periodically widening into pools and scooped out waterpockets. Expect minor bushwhacking on occasion through thickets of limber willow and stiff tamarisk.

Broken Bow Arch in Willow Gulch.

After curving around a prominent bend in the canyon, large Broken Bow Arch suddenly appears ahead. Cross the stream and follow the obvious trail up to the bench opposite the arch. The creek flows beneath a low overhang just below the bench, but a screen of Gambel oaks hides most of the stream bed from view. From the bench, look for a steep sandy trail that drops into the oak grove below. Do not continue following the trail on the bench, as other hikers have, since it dead-ends at an overhang and you'll have to backtrack.

You regain the wash where an overhanging ledge, the top most layer of Kayenta Formation rocks, shades the stream and hanging gardens of maidenhair fern directly below the arch. From here you can turn left, upstream, and scramble up to the arch, or continue down-canyon and approach the arch from the opposite side. Follow the base of the overhang a short distance ahead to a bend in the canyon. A boot-worn path leaves the wash at the bend on the north side. Follow the path up to the bench, then head northwest the short distance up to the arch.

Piercing a thick fin of Navajo Sandstone that projects into the canyon from the north wall, the huge triangle-shaped aperture of Broken Bow Arch frames a memorable view of the convoluted canyon walls beyond. The base of the opening is heaped with great angular boulders, which fell from above as stress fractures inexorably enlarged the span. The arch is shaded with a rich brown patina of desert varnish. Tall, spreading cottonwoods in the wash below add a delicate contrast to the scene.

From Broken Bow Arch, retrace your steps to the trailhead.

43 Fiftymile Creek

General description: A day hike or overnighter into a seldom-visited lower Escalante canyon, located within Glen Canyon National Recreation Area.

Distance: 10.4 miles round trip.

Difficulty: Moderate, occasional Class 2 scrambling.

Trail conditions: Wash route.

Trailhead access: 4WD advised when the road is wet.

Average hiking time: 5 to 6 hours round trip.

Trailhead elevation: 4,230 feet.

Low point: 3,711 feet.

Elevation loss and gain: 520 feet.

Optimum seasons: Mid-March through May; September through October.

Water availability: Intermittent flows below 2.8 miles in Fiftymile Creek; if day hiking, bring your own.

Hazards: Flash-flood danger.

Permits: Required for overnight trips; obtain at Escalante Interagency visitor center, or at a trailhead register en route to this trailhead (such as Hurricane Wash or Willow Gulch trailheads).

Topo maps: Sooner Bench and Davis Gulch USGS quads; Trails Illustrated Canyons of the Escalante.

Key points:

0.7   Pouroff.

1.7   First side canyon joins on the right.

2.2   Confluence with Fiftymile Creek wash; bear left, down-canyon.

3.4   Arch.

5.2   High water mark of Lake Powell.

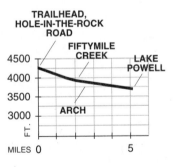

Finding the trailhead: Follow the Hole-in-the-Rock Road southeast from Utah 12 for 40.5 miles to Sooner Wash (see driving directions for Hike 42), and continue forward. You pass the unsigned spur road to the Willow Gulch Trailhead after 41.5 miles, pass the signed westbound 4WD road to Fiftymile Bench at 43.4 miles, then cross the unsigned wash of Willow Gulch after 44.2 miles.

The promontory of Cave Point soon looms ahead to the south; its prominent apron of Entrada Sandstone is honeycombed with deep alcoves. After 45.3 miles, you cross a cattle guard near the foot of Cave Point, then begin descending toward a wash. (About 0.1 mile beyond the cattle guard you pass a pullout on the left side of the road where you can park if no space is available ahead.) Immediately before crossing the wash below, turn right onto an unsigned spur road that leads to the foot of Cave Point. You will find parking spaces just off this road within 100 yards.

The hike: Fiftymile Creek is a remote slickrock canyon of exceptional beauty. Seldom visited, the canyon offers solitude and classic scenery. Narrow passages, 500-foot canyon walls, excellent campsites, a perennial stream, and an active population of beaver are among the attractions of this trip. This route is interesting enough to satisfy experienced canyon country hikers, yet easy enough for budding canyoneers to enjoy.

Like all of the lower Escalante canyons, your travels will terminate at Lake Powell. Fluctuating lake levels can further shorten the hike when waters rise to 3,711 feet. For a time after the lake is drawn down to 3,700 feet, its normal pool elevation, treacherous quicksand fills the lower end of the canyon for 0.7 mile.

The route begins beneath Cave Point, a lofty promontory of the Straight Cliffs. There is no trailhead register, no signs, nor is there any indication of a trail or route. Fiftymile Creek is relatively undiscovered and you are likely to have the canyon to yourself.

From the spur road, cross the Hole-in-the-Rock Road, locate the culvert that funnels the small wash downstream, and begin following the shallow sandy wash eastward. The wash describes two wide meanders; you can follow cow trails to shortcut the distance. The wash is open, fringed with rabbitbrush and tamarisk, and low brush-studded hills of the Carmel Formation rise above.

After 250 yards, another branch of the wash joins on the right, and ahead the way becomes rock-strewn. Rock-hopping is not necessary, but the soft sand in the wash will impede steady progress. Soon, Navajo Sandstone emerges along the flanks of the wash, its upper cross-bedded layers stained a salmon hue by the overlying red beds of the Carmel rocks. The tread ranges from sand to slickrock ahead, and the draw gradually deepens as it cuts farther into the Navajo.

After 0.7 mile, the draw begins to narrow into a slot. If you continue into the slot, you will reach a chockstone and a pouroff after about 60 yards. Backtrack to the beginning of the slot and ascend to the slickrock bench above the narrows on the left (north) side. Follow the bench east, staying just above the narrows, for 200 yards to a dilapidated fence. A low sandstone knob, capped by boulders, lies just ahead.

Vegetation on the sandy bench is far more diverse than within the confines of the wash. Blackbrush and mormon tea dot the bench with their gray and green mounds. Silvery sophora displays vivid blue pea-like blooms during spring, vying for your attention with the yellow blossoms of brittlebush and the delicate white flowers of evening primrose.

Stay to the right (south) of the knob, then descend a slickrock slope diagonally down toward the wash. Where the slickrock ends, a faint path leads you along the edge of the low cliff for several yards to a break, where you can scramble easily back into the wash. The stretch ahead is a delightful walk down the presently narrow gorge, with slickrock sweeping skyward on either side. Vegetation is sparse in the canyon, restricted to the banks of the wash and the slopes just above. Your sandy corridor through the canyon

Fiftymile Creek

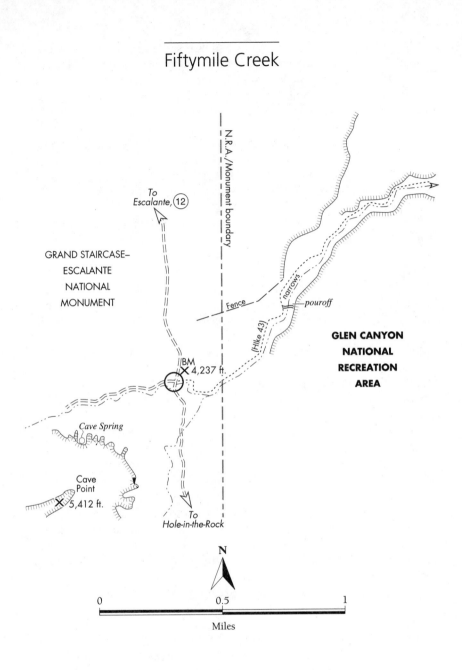

To
Escalante, (12)

GRAND STAIRCASE–
ESCALANTE
NATIONAL
MONUMENT

N.R.A./Monument boundary

narrows

Fence

pouroff

(Hike 43)

BM
X 4,237 ft.

**GLEN CANYON
NATIONAL
RECREATION
AREA**

Cave Spring

Cave
Point
X 5,412 ft.

To
Hole-in-the-Rock

N

0   0.5   1

Miles

Fiftymile Creek

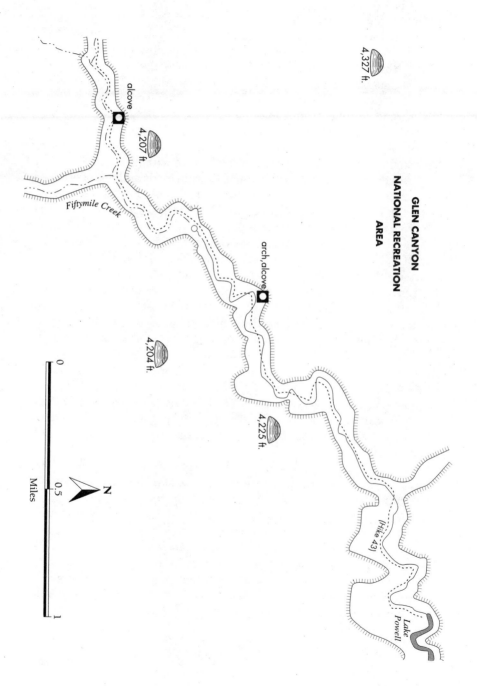

is fringed with the dark green foliage of seep-willow, and the gray mounds of rabbitbrush. Fremont barberry and single-leaf ash are common shrubs on the slopes above.

At length, the canyon walls grow lower, and the wash broadens and becomes littered with boulders, with sandy benches flanking either side. After 1.7 miles, a side canyon opens up on the right (southwest) to reveal a fine view of the Straight Cliffs. Beyond that confluence, the wash is flanked by low domes, and abundant boulders require considerable rock-hopping. Midway down to the next major side canyon you pass a deep alcove on the left wall, affording a refuge from sun or storm.

The next side canyon, at 2.2 miles, is actually Fiftymile Creek, a much wider, but still dry, wash. Down-canyon, the desert-varnished walls rise higher. After about 0.6 mile below the confluence with Fiftymile Creek, the character of the canyon begins to change. Cottonwoods and willows appear, and horsetails fringe an emerging stream. After another 0.6 mile, 3.4 miles from the trailhead, a gaping slickrock amphitheater, with vaulting cliffs rising 200 feet above, appears above a bench on the north wall. The narrow opening of an arch pierces the canyon wall above the amphitheater, reminiscent of Kolob Arch in Zion National Park. The sandy floor of the alcove offers a fine place to camp.

The canyon ahead assumes a more sinuous course, and the route entails rock-hopping and repeatedly crossing the small stream, and perhaps shortcutting the many meanders. Deep alcoves open up around nearly every bend, and the canyon walls rise 400 to 500 feet in sheer and overhanging cliffs, decorated with a patina of brown and black desert varnish. Evidence of beaver activity increases as you delve deeper into the canyon. You will find where cottonwoods of one foot or more in diameter have been felled by the industrious beaver. About 0.5 mile below the arch, you skirt a beaver dam with a mud and stick lodge near the pond's banks. A series of smaller beaver ponds lie ahead, and all are easily bypassed without getting your feet wet.

After 5.2 miles, a precipitous side canyon joins on the right (south). Here Fiftymile Creek bends left, then enters a narrow slot. Towering, often overhanging cliffs rise overhead, revealing only a narrow sliver of sky. When Lake Powell is filled to its maximum elevation of 3,711 feet, you can proceed no farther. At the normal pool elevation of 3,700 feet, usually during spring, you can continue down-canyon for as much as 0.7 mile to the lake. Backpackers will find no more campsites beyond the high water mark.

The final stretch of the canyon passes through a deep, narrow gorge, and involves wading in the shallow stream, where there may be deeper holes. Water stains on the canyon walls and cottonwood skeletons indicate your approach to the lake.

44 Davis Gulch

General description:	An excellent cross-country slickrock route, suitable as an all-day hike or a backpack for experienced hikers only, leading into a remote, seldom-visited lower Escalante canyon, located within Glen Canyon National Recreation Area.
Distance:	9.8 to 13.4 miles, or more (with side-trip options), round trip.
Difficulty:	Strenuous, occasional Class 2 scrambling.
Trail conditions:	Cross-country slickrock route; boot-worn trails in Davis Gulch; good route-finding skills required.
Trailhead access:	4WD advised when the road is wet.
Average hiking time:	6 to 7 hours, or more, round trip.
Trailhead elevation:	4,300 feet.
Low point:	3,711 feet.
Elevation gain and loss:	+350 feet, -800 feet (an additional 150 feet elevation gain required to reach Bement Arch).
Optimum seasons:	Mid-March through May; September through October.
Water availability:	Perennial in Davis Gulch and at Lake Powell; if day hiking, bring your own.
Hazards:	Exposure to steep dropoffs; risk to inexperienced hikers of becoming disoriented or lost.
Permits:	Required for overnight trips; obtain at Escalante Interagency visitor center, or from a trailhead register en route to the trailhead (such as Hurricane Wash or Willow Gulch trailheads).
Topo maps:	Davis Gulch USGS quad; Trails Illustrated Canyons of the Escalante.

Key points:

4.7 Top of stock trail descending into Davis Gulch.

4.9 Floor of Davis Gulch.

5.1-5.3 Lake Powell.

6.7 Bement Arch.

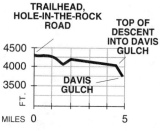

Finding the trailhead: Follow the Hole-in-the-Rock road southeast from Utah 12 for 45.5 miles to the Fiftymile Creek trailhead (see driving directions for Hike 43), then continue straight ahead. Enter Glen Canyon National Recreation Area at 46.2 miles, and at 49.9 miles begin a steady downgrade below Fiftymile Point. The road descends steadily over patches of Navajo Sandstone slickrock into the Davis Gulch basin, where the road becomes very rough.

Cross a cattle guard at 50.3 miles, and after 50.5 miles you cross a minor drainage where the roadbed is composed of slickrock at the bottom of the grade. This unsigned drainage is Davis Gulch. Park on the slickrock on either side of the drainage.

A 4WD vehicle is required to negotiate the final 5.6 miles over rough slickrock to the road's end at Hole-in-the-Rock. Hikers arriving late in the day will find several fine undeveloped campsites near Davis Gulch.

The hike: This memorable trip is recommended only for experienced slickrock wanderers, for once you leave the road, you enter a nebulous landscape of Navajo Sandstone domes, where a good feel for the lay of the land is necessary to stay on course. This hike offers slickrock rambling at its finest, with a wide choice of routes limited only by your imagination. The seldom-used route traverses an open landscape of slickrock for nearly 5 miles, where broad vistas and the unshaded sun are your sole companions.

Although the trip can be completed in one long day, it is better suited for an extended stay, and three to four days would be ideal. Narrow, cliff-bound Davis Gulch is passable for about 4 miles up-canyon from Lake Powell, where many bench-top campsites, beaver ponds, Anasazi rock art, shadowed narrows, and interesting Bement Arch await discovery and invite a leisurely pace.

No water is available until you reach the perennial stream in Davis Gulch, so be sure to pack an ample water supply, and avoid hiking the route during the heat of mid-day.

Davis Gulch begins as an inconspicuous draw, and you begin on its left (west) side after leaving the Hole-in-the-Rock Road, following a northeast course above its steadily deepening, narrow gorge. The roller-coaster route leads you up and over low domes, past deep waterpockets, and into small sandy basins where you find a concentration of blackbrush, silvery sophora, sand sagebrush, yucca, mormon tea, snakeweed, and wavy-leaf oak.

Vistas en route are far-ranging, encompassing much of the Escalante River basin. Behind you rises Fiftymile Point and the Straight Cliffs. Far to the north is the broad plateau of Boulder Mountain. On the northeast horizon are Mounts Pennell, Hillers, and Holmes of the Henry Mountains. And the broad dome of Navajo Mountain commands the southward view. In the middle distance are red, brush-clad Carmel Formation benches, and a seemingly endless expanse of domed Navajo Sandstone slickrock, stretching northeast to the Circle Cliffs.

As you proceed, you will notice Davis Gulch evolving into a deep slickrock gorge below you. You can stay high, traversing among low domes, or follow a route closer to the rim of the gulch. Whichever route you choose, maintain a northeast course parallel to Davis Gulch. The route will dip into numerous minor draws, but after about 0.75 mile, a larger side drainage cuts across your path. Stay high here, ascending nearly to the Carmel bench, and contour around the domes at the head of the draw. Beyond that draw you should descend to the gentler terrain among smaller domes and brushy basins closer to the rim of the gulch.

After about 1.5 miles, a much larger, broad side canyon opens up ahead to the north. To avoid narrow slots and impassable cliffs in this drainage,

Davis Gulch

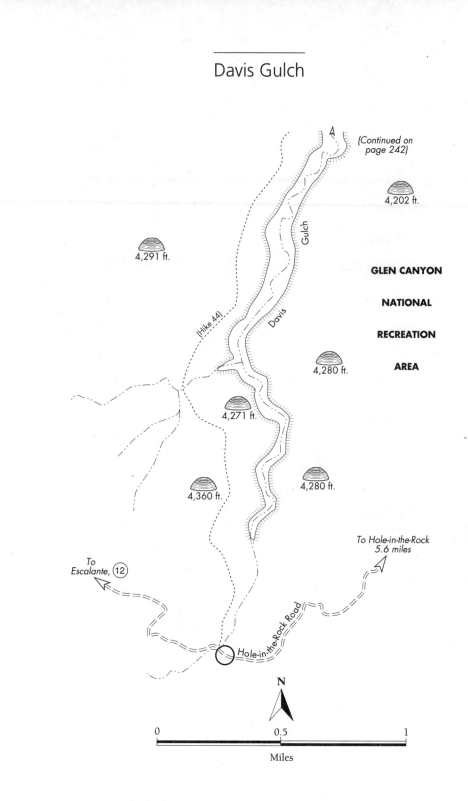

(Continued on page 242)

4,202 ft.

4,291 ft.

Gulch

GLEN CANYON

NATIONAL

RECREATION

AREA

(Hike 44)

Davis

4,280 ft.

4,271 ft.

4,360 ft.

4,280 ft.

To Hole-in-the-Rock
5.6 miles

To
Escalante, (12)

Hole-in-the-Rock Road

Hole-in-the-Rock

N

| 0 | | 0.5 | | 1 |

Miles

Davis Gulch

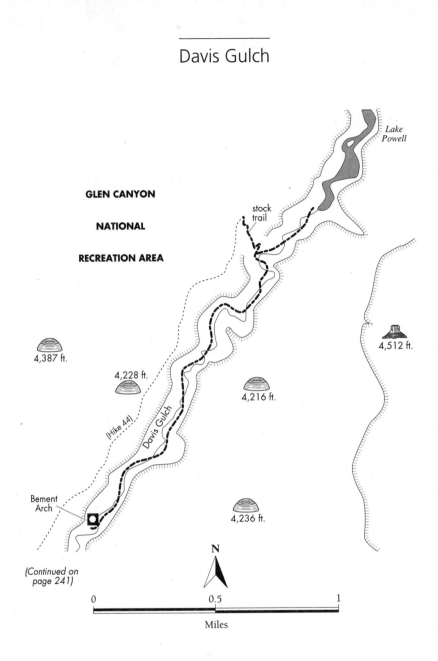

GLEN CANYON

NATIONAL

RECREATION AREA

Lake Powell

stock trail

4,512 ft.

4,387 ft.

4,228 ft.

4,216 ft.

(Hike 44)

Davis Gulch

4,236 ft.

Bement Arch

(Continued on page 241)

N

| 0 | 0.5 | 1 |

Miles

descend northwest into its upper reaches, then continue the up and down friction walk ahead. Once you leave that drainage behind, you can resume your route closer to the rim of Davis Gulch, where you are treated to dizzying views into its slickrock labyrinth, its walls cut with deep, large alcoves.

At length you begin to approach the descent route into Davis Gulch. The Carmel-capped butte across the canyon to the southeast provides clues to help you locate the descent. On the flanks of that butte, just below where the Navajo Sandstone begins, is a prominent slickrock chute. Below the chute is an obvious draw harboring a dense grove of Gambel oak and a few cottonwoods. When you reach a point opposite the chute, the descent begins where the cliff band below you is scored by a slickrock draw. Cairns may mark the route, which is an old abandoned stock trail into Davis Gulch.

Descend the main draw briefly, then curve right (west) into a lesser draw just below. Steep slickrock friction pitches lead to an eastbound traverse, where a discernible trail has been carved into the sandstone. The final descent follows a short segment of carved slickrock trail and steps that lead to part of an old fence on a terrace just above the arroyo of Davis Gulch.

Once you reach the canyon bottom, you intersect a well-worn trail leading both up and down the canyon. The high-water mark of Lake Powell lies 0.2 mile down-canyon, and at low water, you can continue another 0.2 mile to the lake. Don't be surprised to see boaters on the lake, they visit Davis Gulch frequently and are largely responsible for maintaining the trail here as a well-worn path.

The trail up-canyon is brushy at times, and requires crossing the stream repeatedly between a long chain of deep beaver ponds. Some crossings are precarious over the flimsy bridges of beaver dams. Depending upon stream conditions, wading may be necessary in places.

This remote canyon is truly beautiful. Terraces host groves of Gambel oak, and riparian growth is abundant along the perennial stream. Willow, seep-willow, tamarisk, cottonwood, box elder, and netleaf hackberry fringe the terraces above the arroyo. Deep alcoves are scooped out of the desert varnish-streaked canyon walls, which reach 200 feet to the rims above. There are many possible campsites in the canyon, with those on the sandy floors of the alcoves most attractive.

Bement Arch is found 1.8 miles above the stock trail. It is a large and unusually thick, tunnel-like arch that pierces the sandstone shoulder projecting from the north wall. Beyond the arch, the stream soon dries up, and the sandy wash eventually slots up and dead-ends at a pouroff.

45 Upper Escalante River

See Map on Page 200

General description:	A memorable point-to-point backpack traversing the dramatic sandstone gorge of the upper Escalante River, located within Grand Staircase–Escalante National Monument.
Distance:	13.8 miles, shuttle trip.
Difficulty:	Moderate.
Trail conditions:	Canyon route with much wading required, and segments of boot-worn trails.
Trailhead access:	2WD.
Average hiking time:	2 to 3 days.
Trailhead elevations:	Escalante Trailhead, 5,840 feet; Escalante River Trailhead, 5,200 feet.
Elevation loss:	640 feet.
Optimum seasons:	Mid-April through early June; September through October.
Water availability:	Escalante River; Death Hollow, 6.7 miles; and Sand Creek, 11.2 miles.
Hazards:	Flash-flood and high-water danger.
Permits:	Required for overnight trips; obtain at the trailhead register, or at the Escalante Interagency visitor center.
Topo maps:	Escalante and Calf Creek USGS quads; Trails Illustrated Canyons of the Escalante.

Key points:
- 0.5   Escalante River.
- 0.8   Pine Creek.
- 6.7   Death Hollow.
- 11.2   Sand Creek.
- 12.2   Escalante Natural Bridge.
- 13.8   Escalante River Trailhead.

Finding the trailheads: From Utah 12 on the eastern outskirts of Escalante, 0.25 mile east of the high school, turn north at the cemetery where a sign points toward the Escalante Trailhead junction. Drive past the cemetery to a cattle guard, then follow the dirt road east beneath the power lines. After

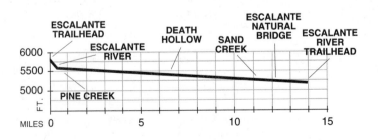

0.4 mile, turn left (northwest) at a junction, where a sign points to the trailhead. The unsigned trailhead parking area and trailhead register is located on the left side of the road, 0.25 mile from the junction. You can continue down the narrow, rocky road for another 0.25 mile to the road end, and also park there.

To shuttle a car to the Escalante River Trailhead, follow driving directions for Hike 35.

The hike: The upper Escalante River canyon between the town of Escalante and the Utah 12 bridge is perhaps the most scenic part of this major Colorado River tributary, and it is one of the premier canyons in the Glen Canyon region. It is certainly the most pleasant and accessible part of the canyon, and the route through the canyon is passable to any hiker willing to get their feet wet. The river itself is the only obstacle to travel here.

Usually only about ankle deep to shin deep, the river swells with snowmelt in early spring, and summer flash floods can make fording its waters impossible for a day or so following heavy rains. Also during high water flows, the river is far too turbid to settle for drinking. During low flows the river remains cloudy, and you will need a collapsible bucket or other container to settle the water before filtering. Excellent campsites abound in the canyon, though there are brief narrow constrictions with no campsites.

This hike, which requires a 14-mile car shuttle, or a hitchhike, can be completed in two days, though three days allows a more leisurely pace and a better chance to appreciate the dramatic canyon landscape. Side trips into Death Hollow and Sand Creek, both featuring cool, deep pools, can further extend the trip.

From the road's end, 0.25 mile below the trailhead register, negotiate a hiker's maze through the fence, then follow the descending trail over crunchy Carmel Formation gravel, passing through an open woodland of juniper, where trailside slopes are studded with low mounds of sagebrush. The portal of the Escalante River canyon lies just ahead, an opening through the steeply tilted beds of the Escalante Monocline. That Navajo Sandstone barrier rises in bold relief, contrasting with Escalante's flat green hayfields.

The trail at first follows a public-access easement through private property. Please respect the owners' property rights and stay on the trail. Soon you cross a wide, sandy wash, and then ascend beyond it, avoiding a dense tamarisk thicket. Shortly thereafter the trail leads you into the thicket of tamarisk and Russian olive trees, beyond which you meet the grassy banks of the Escalante River. During normal flows, the river here is only about ankle deep.

Wade across the shallow Escalante, more of a modest creek than a river, and after the second ford, you reach a gate (leave it closed) at the boundary of Grand Staircase–Escalante National Monument. Here the river carves through a portal in the Escalante Monocline, and you enter the realm of soaring sandstone cliffs, seemingly far removed from the civilization of Escalante that lies but 1 mile behind you.

A sandy bench trail through the sagebrush soon leads you to a ford of ankle-deep Pine Creek after 0.8 mile. This clear, sizable stream flows over a bed of mossy volcanic boulders, and these red and black, stream-rounded boulders litter the canyon floor ahead, resting far from their source on Boulder Mountain. The addition of Pine Creek's waters nearly doubles the volume of the river.

Just ahead stands a cylindrical steel structure that is a stream gauging station monitoring the flow of the river. By now the Navajo Sandstone cliffs have risen 400 feet overhead, and after a few more bends of the serpentine canyon, the walls rise 800 to 1,000 feet to the rims far above. The soaring walls are dramatic, often decorated with the brown shadings of desert varnish. The sweeping lines of the Navajo's cross-bedding are broken in many places by vertical cracks, giving the canyon walls a checkerboard appearance.

A path is well-worn on the sandy benches, and you only get your feet wet at each of the dozens of river crossings. Where the canyon narrows and the benches pinch out, you will be wading down the river channel, but these places are infrequent. Riverside benches are studded with the shrubs of four-wing saltbush, rabbitbrush, buckwheat, and single-leaf ash.

After 2.8 miles a huge alcove appears on the north canyon wall, and its sandy floor is sometimes used as a campsite. Although I do not usually lead you to Anasazi ruins or rock art, you should take a close look at the rock art in this alcove. The petroglyphs there have been thoughtlessly vandalized, and a link to the past has been destroyed, leaving visitors with a feeling of disgust and sadness.

In the lower reaches of the upper Escalante near the UT 12 bridge, the canyon becomes wider but no less spectacular.

Along the 5.9 miles from Pine Creek to Death Hollow, the canyon winds back and forth in a series of long meanders wedged between cliffs rising 600 to 1,000 feet. You will find occasional campsites along this stretch, some on open, shadeless benches, others in the partial shade of Gambel oaks or box elders. After 6.7 miles, the narrow gorge of Death Hollow and its vigorous stream, clearer than the river, enters on the left (northwest). After another mile, the canyon gradually begins to open up, the benches grow wider, and the canyon walls recede.

A vigorous growth of riparian vegetation begins to fill the canyon as you approach Sand Creek, and the cliffs now rise no more than 200 feet above. Sand Creek, joining from the north, contributes its sizable stream, again clearer than the river, at 11.2 miles. There are fair campsites on the sandy, rock-strewn bench at its mouth, but better sites are scattered along the main Escalante canyon. About 0.1 mile up the course of Sand Creek, a reliable dripping spring issues from the left (west) wall, next to a tall box elder tree, immediately before the first bend in the canyon. This spring provides the best water on the hike.

A short distance below the mouth of Sand Creek you begin following a good, but dusty trail, with long stretches of bench walking between fords. About 0.5 mile from Sand Creek, a dramatic desert-varnished cliff rises to a narrow skyline arch on the south wall of the canyon. Another 0.5 mile farther, Escalante Natural Bridge appears, standing away from the south canyon wall and spanning a precipitous slickrock drainage.

Just beyond the bridge, stick to the trail to avoid becoming entangled in the riparian ribbon that fringes a side canyon entering from the north. In the final 1.6 miles (see Hike 36), you ford the river four more times, in between following a good trail through the broad canyon, flanked by 200- to 400-foot cliffs and a skyline parade of slickrock domes.

At length, after avoiding a home on private property and one final ford, you reach the Escalante River Trailhead at the Utah 12 bridge, ending a memorable journey.

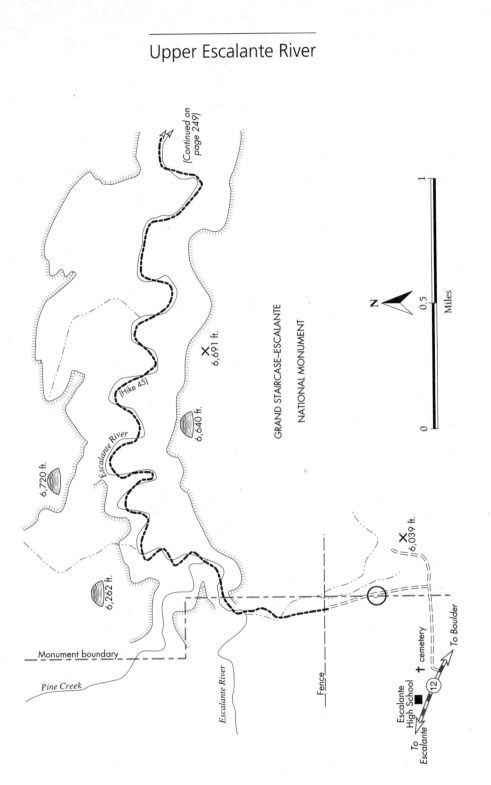

(Continued on page 249)

6,691 ft.

(Hike 45)

GRAND STAIRCASE-ESCALANTE
NATIONAL MONUMENT

Escalante River

6,640 ft.

6,720 ft.

6,262 ft.

Monument boundary

Pine Creek

Escalante River

Fence

6,039 ft.

N

0   0.5   1
Miles

cemetery

Escalante
High School

To
Escalante

12

To Boulder

Upper Escalante River

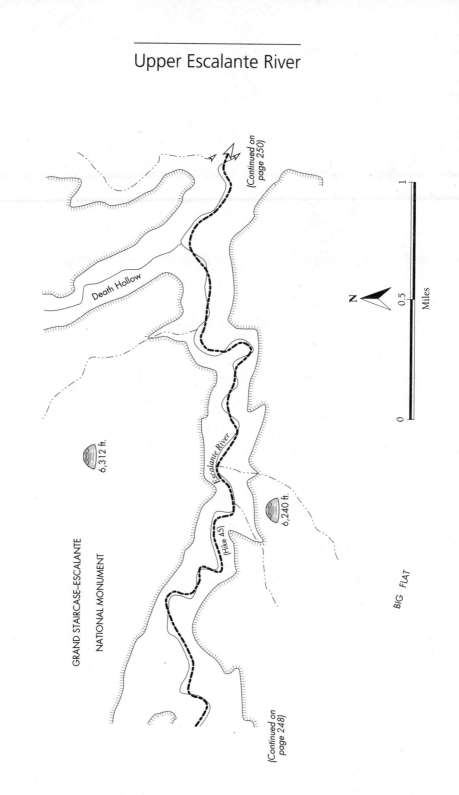

GRAND STAIRCASE–ESCALANTE
NATIONAL MONUMENT

6,312 ft.

Death Hollow

Escalante River

(Hike 45)

6,240 ft.

BIG FLAT

N

0   0.5   1

Miles

(Continued on page 250)

(Continued on page 248)

Upper Escalante River

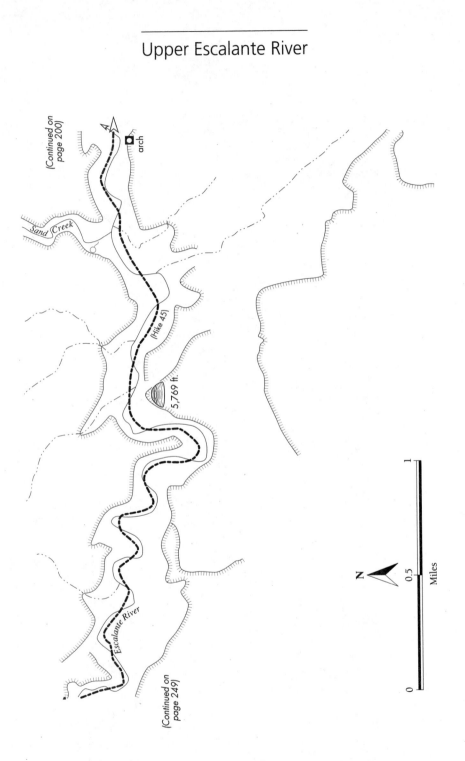

(Continued on page 200)

arch

Sand Creek

(Hike 45)

5,769 ft.

Escalante River

(Continued on page 249)

N

0   0.5   1

Miles

46 The Box

General description: A fine all-day hike or overnighter into the pine-shaded confines of an upper Escalante River tributary, located within the Box–Death Hollow Wilderness.

Distance: 8 miles, shuttle trip.

Difficulty: Moderate.

Trail conditions: Constructed trail, generally easy to follow.

Trailhead access: 2WD.

Average hiking time: 4 to 5 hours one way.

Trailhead elevations: Upper Box Trailhead, 7,750 feet; Lower Box Trailhead, 6,420 feet.

Elevation loss: 1,330 feet.

Optimum season: Mid-May through October.

Water availability: Plentiful along entire trail; if day hiking, bring your own.

Hazards: Flash-flood and high-water danger; 50 stream crossings en route.

Permits: Not required.

Topo maps: Wide Hollow Reservoir and Posy Lake USGS quads; Trails Illustrated Canyons of the Escalante.

Key points:

0.1 Trailhead register at the portal of The Box.
3.7 Deep Creek.
8.0 Lower Box Trailhead.

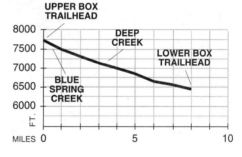

Finding the trailheads: From Utah 12 in the eastern part of Escalante, turn north onto "300 E" street where a sign points to "Scenic Backway, Posy Lake, and Hells Backbone." Drive north past the elementary school through the north end of town. After bridging the Escalante River you reach a Y junction after 0.8 mile, and bear right, driving past ranches and hayfields into Pine Creek canyon.

The pavement ends after 3.8 miles, after which you follow the good, wide gravel of Forest Road 153. A sign at 7.4 miles declares entry into Dixie National Forest, and 0.3 mile beyond, a gravel spur road branches right (east), signed for "Lower Box Access." That good road leads another 0.3 mile to the trailhead at the road end, 8 miles from Escalante.

To reach the upper trailhead, continue straight ahead on Forest Road 153 for another 6.2 miles (13.9 miles from Escalante) to the signed junction with left-branching Forest Road 154 leading to Posy Lake and Loa, Utah. Bear right, staying on Forest Road 153. The road ahead crosses Deep Creek at 15.3 miles, crests an 8,200-foot ridge at 16.8 miles, and crosses Blue Spring

Creek at 18.3 miles. Soon thereafter, you reach the trailhead, signed for "Upper Box Access," 18.6 miles from Escalante. Park in the turnout on the east side of the road.

Hikers searching for a campsite can stay in the Posy Lake Campground for a fee, 2 miles from the Forest Road 154/153 junction via Forest Road 154, or choose from several undeveloped sites en route to the trailhead.

The hike: The Box of Pine Creek, located in the Box–Death Hollow Wilderness of the Dixie National Forest, is one of the upper Escalante River's main tributaries. The creek emerges from springs high on the gentle, densely forested slopes of Boulder Mountain above 9,000 feet. As the waters gather they course through shallow draws in the cool shade of subalpine forests. Having gained sufficient volume, Pine Creek slices through the northern reaches of the Escalante Monocline and into the resistant Navajo Sandstone, where the waters have carved a tremendous straight-walled canyon ranging from 800 to 1,200 feet deep.

This canyon is called The Box, and it provides a backcountry landscape like no other in the Escalante region. Here you find a blend of slickrock canyon and cliffs, mountain forest, and a clear, cold creek. Although The Box is suitable as a backpack destination, most hikers take round-trip day hikes into The Box, beginning at either trailhead. With a car shuttle, the 8-mile hike through The Box from end to end is a rewarding trip.

Excellent camping areas are continuous throughout The Box, most located on streamside benches beneath tall ponderosa pines. This is a good weekend trip that is suitable for families with children and even novice hikers. The canyon invites a leisurely pace, so go as far as you wish, take a soak in the creek, fish for the abundant 10-inch brown and rainbow trout, or simply bask on the slickrock and drink in the dramatic canyon landscape.

The only obstacles on the trip are the frequent stream crossings, fifty in all, throughout The Box. Yet these crossings are not difficult during normal stream flows, and never dangerous. Most crossings of the modest creek are accomplished via a rock-hop from one sandstone or volcanic boulder to the next. You'll only get your feet wet if you slip into the water.

Since most hikers will follow The Box from either trailhead to roughly the midway point at Deep Creek, the following description is broken into two parts.

LOWER BOX TRAILHEAD TO DEEP CREEK

From the trailhead, walk past the vehicle barricade for several yards to the banks of Pine Creek, a clear stream 6 to 8 feet wide. Avoid the path that follows the left bank, and immediately cross the creek to the opposite side. Soon you will reach a wooden fence; climb over it with the help of a stile. Just ahead you will enter the Box–Death Hollow Wilderness, pass a signboard and trail register, and follow the creek ahead as it slices through the Escalante Monocline and becomes embraced by towering sandstone walls.

Tall conifers and broken cliffs of Navajo Sandstone in The Box.

Bold, broken Navajo Sandstone cliffs flank the canyon on the east, displaying the sweeping lines of cross-bedding. The cliffs are studded with juniper trees and pinyon and ponderosa pines, and are colored in shades of red, buff, pink, and even green.

After 2.2 miles, the creek describes a short but prominent bend to the west, and in the sheltered recess there large Douglas-firs join the ranks of the predominant pines. The canyon ahead resumes its relatively straight course, slickrock slopes reach down to the trailside, and you pass many inviting pools in the cool stream.

Between 3 and 4 miles, the trail is obscure in places, and some scouting may be necessary to stay on course. After 4 miles, a precipitous draw joins on the left (west), its confines supporting a heavy forest of tall pines. The buff-toned and rust red battlements of Point 7818, appearing to be a prominent butte, rise above the draw on the western skyline. The final 0.4 mile to Deep Creek crosses the creek several times in quick succession.

Deep Creek opens up to the west when you reach 7,020 feet after 4.4 miles. The creek is not deep at all, but instead is a shallow, 2-foot wide stream. Tall cottonwoods, Douglas-firs, and ponderosa pines frame the view up this cliff-bound side canyon. The Deep Creek environs offer a fine place to relax before backtracking to the Lower Box Trailhead.

UPPER BOX TRAILHEAD TO DEEP CREEK

This approach to The Box offers an entirely different experience than the lower access. The trailhead area provides no intimation that a deep canyon lies ahead. Here Pine Creek flows through a lovely high mountain valley.

Only a faint path, barely discernible, leads from the trailhead down the long grassy slope to the creek below, where Engelmann and blue spruce trees form groves among grassy openings alongside the chuckling waters of Pine Creek. When you reach the creek, follow the west bank downstream and soon you find the trail register. Just beyond it, the Navajo Sandstone emerges, and you rock-hop across the creek and pass through a hiker's maze where a fence spans the creek bottom.

By now the canyon walls have attained some height, and combined with the canopy of spruce boughs, ample shade is cast over the trail. Large volcanic boulders litter the canyon bottom, and the rocky trail winds among them and thickets of wild rose and currant. After the third stream crossing at 0.3 mile, Blue Spring Creek enters on the right (west) via a slot, with a lovely waterfall cascading just inside the canyon mouth. Red-osier dogwood is a common shrub at the creekside, and mountain bluebells hug the banks of the stream.

The trail is rocky and the going is slower and more arduous than in the lower reaches of The Box. Here you are continually undulating over obstructions: boulders, outcrops of sandstone, trees and roots; and you cross the stream repeatedly, usually via a rock-hop, occasionally via a log crossing. Spruce and Douglas-firs mass their ranks in the narrow confines of the canyon bottom. As you proceed, the cross-bedded walls of Navajo Sand-

The Box

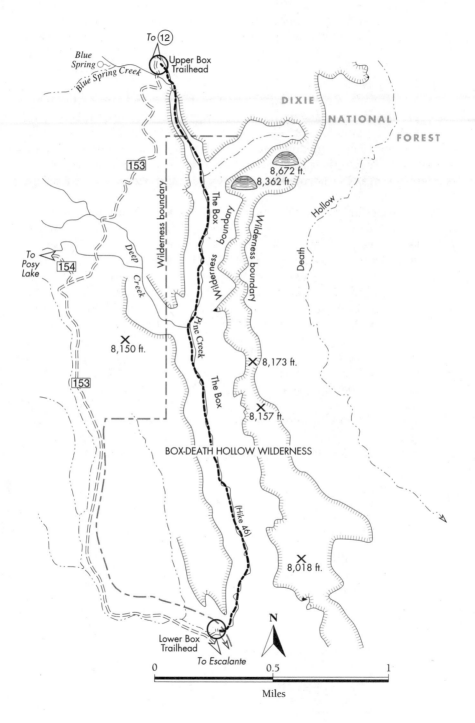

To ⑫

Blue Spring

Blue Spring Creek

Upper Box Trailhead

DIXIE

NATIONAL

FOREST

153

8,672 ft.

8,362 ft.

The Box

Wilderness boundary

Wilderness boundary

Death Hollow

To Posy Lake

154

Deep Creek

Wilderness boundary

Pine Creek

8,150 ft.

8,173 ft.

153

The Box

8,157 ft.

BOX-DEATH HOLLOW WILDERNESS

(Hike 46)

8,018 ft.

N

Lower Box Trailhead

To Escalante

0   0.5   1

Miles

stone grow increasingly higher. The Douglas-firs and ponderosa pines that have gained a foothold on the broken walls allow you to judge the scale of the cliffs.

Water birch and graceful boxelder trees appear as you reach deeper into The Box. Violets and geraniums decorate the moist earth at the trailside. After about 1.25 miles, the trail all but disappears on the grassy bench above the west banks of the creek, where you find excellent camping areas shaded by groves of box elder.

Soon the bench pinches out, the trail reappears, and you amble down past a prominent side canyon that opens up on the left (northeast) after 1.6 miles. Here at 7,400 feet, 800-foot cliffs embrace The Box, and ahead the canyon begins to open up and assume a different character. Although a few spruce trees persist, their groves have been supplanted by Douglas-firs and ponderosa pines. Tall narrowleaf cottonwoods, and occasional aspens, are the primary riparian trees.

Bold broken sandstone cliffs, studded with gnarled conifers, begin to dominate the landscape after the 2-mile point, and the canyon rims now rise 1,200 feet above. After 2.5 miles, at 7,200 feet, the canyon undergoes another transformation. Benches appear on either side of the creek, and the gradient of the canyon slackens. Park-like stands of ponderosa pines, along with scattered groves of Gambel oak and box elder, decorate the benches, which offer a continuum of fine camping areas throughout the remaining 5.5 miles of The Box.

At 2.5 miles, you cross the creek and mount the west-side bench and follow it, without crossing the stream, for 0.9 mile. This is perhaps the most inviting part of The Box. The canyon is wider and more open here than elsewhere, with soaring walls of corrugated Navajo Sandstone rising on either side.

Two final stream crossings, the first of which you may have to wade across, lead you to Deep Creek after 3.7 miles, a reasonable destination for a rewarding day hike through the upper Box.

Grand Staircase/ Paria Canyon

The Grand Staircase is the most remote and seldom-visited section of the Glen Canyon region covered in this book; it is spectacular and contains the most extensive network of slot canyons in Utah. By way of contrast, the Paria Canyon-Vermilion Cliffs Wilderness, at the southwest corner of the Glen Canyon region, is so popular that annual visitation there almost outnumbers all other hiking areas in the Glen Canyon Region combined.

The Grand Staircase marches northward from the North Rim of the Grand Canyon to the 9,000-foot edge of Utah's High Plateaus. The colorful succession of "risers" in the staircase include, from south to north, the Shinarump Cliffs, the Vermilion Cliffs, the White Cliffs, the Gray Cliffs, and the Pink Cliffs. Each cliff band is separated by progressively higher terraces. The Grand Staircase can be viewed to best advantage from a scenic overlook off of U.S. Highway 89A, between Fredonia and Jacob Lake, Arizona. From that vantage, the landscape to the north in Utah indeed resembles a staircase, and for people inclined toward hiking and scenic driving, it is an alluring view.

The Paria River is the principal drainage of the Grand Staircase within Grand Staircase–Escalante National Monument, coursing 80 miles from Utah's High Plateaus to its confluence with the Colorado River at Lees Ferry. Gathering its waters in the Bryce Valley between the Paunsaugunt and Table Cliffs plateaus, the river ignores the cliffs and terraces of the staircase and carves a deepening gorge through a succession of colorful, progressively older sedimentary rock formations. Once the river cuts the folded rocks of The Cockscomb on the eastern edge of the Grand Staircase, it meanders through broad valleys before plunging into the Paria Plateau. East of the monoclinal fold of The Cockscomb, younger rocks have returned to river level, and the river once again slices through much the same sequence of rock formations found in its upper reaches.

The Paria River carves the deepest canyon in the region through the Paria Plateau. It approaches 3,000 feet deep in places. Paria Canyon is also one of the region's longest backcountry journeys. Stretching nearly 40 miles from the White House Trailhead to the canyon's mouth at Lees Ferry on the Colorado River, the trail leads hikers through canyons renowned for their narrow slots. Paria Canyon straddles the Utah/Arizona border, and is the only hike covered in this book that extends into Arizona.

Most of the hikes in the Grand Staircase/Paria River region are off-trail, following dry, easily passable washes through some of the finest narrows in the region.

WILDERNESS AND ROADLESS AREAS

Most of Grand Staircase–Escalante National Monument encompasses the Grand Staircase and upper Paria drainage. This 1.7 million–acre preserve, designated a monument by presidential proclamation on September 18, 1996, includes all of the Grand Staircase from the Bryce Canyon National Park and Dixie National Forest boundaries south to U.S. Highway 89 and the boundary with the Paria Canyon-Vermilion Cliffs Wilderness. Eastward, the monument extends across The Cockscomb to the vast, 1,600-square-mile Kaiparowits Plateau, and through the upper Escalante canyons to Capitol Reef National Park. Six wilderness study areas (WSAs), currently managed by the Bureau of Land Management to retain their primeval character until Congress makes a final decision on their fate, encompass some 380,000 acres in the Grand Staircase alone, out of a total of 900,000 acres of WSAs in the monument. The 112,500-acre Paria Canyon–Vermilion Cliffs Wilderness was added to the Federal Wilderness Preservation System in August, 1984. With 92,500 acres in Arizona, and 20,000 acres in Utah, this wilderness, like the Grand Staircase–Escalante National Monument, is managed by the BLM.

All together, there is enough roadless terrain in the Grand Staircase/Paria region to keep hikers happy and busy for many seasons. The proclamation that established Grand Staircase–Escalante National Monument noted that "remoteness, limited travel corridors, and low visitation have all helped to preserve intact the monument's important ecological values." Unfortunately, in response to the national and international recognition the area has received, visitation to this once lonely landscape skyrocketed in 1997, and will likely continue to increase in coming years.

The new monument does not have the same level of resource protection a wilderness or national park has. Valid, existing rights, including rights-of-way, private inholdings, hunting and fishing, grazing and oil, gas, and mineral leases are not affected by the designation of the monument. No new Federal mineral leases will be issued within the monument. However, the BLM does not have jurisdiction over mineral leases on Utah state lands within the monument. Thousands of acres of the monument are held in mineral leases, and in 1997 the monument's first exploratory oil drilling operation (a dry hole) began on the Kaiparowits Plateau on state-owned lands. Other operations could follow. Address your concerns about the preservation and management direction for the new monument by writing to: Grand Staircase–Escalante National Monument, 337 South Main Street, Suite 010, Cedar City, UT 84720, or by calling (435) 865-5100.

WILDERNESS REGULATIONS

Regulations governing the use of the backcountry of Grand Staircase–Escalante National Monument have not yet been established. Trailheads are not signed, and there are no trailhead registers. The only regulation pertaining to WSAs (most hikes in this chapter are located in these areas) is that they are closed to all vehicles, including bicycles, except on existing roads, unless otherwise posted. All visitors to the Grand Staircase backcountry should employ no-trace practices (see the introductory chapter "Leave No Trace"), and review the regulations listed in other chapters in this book and use them as guidelines. Five hikes in this guide are in the Paria Canyon–Vermilion Cliffs Wilderness.

In this area, please follow these regulations:

Paria Canyon–Vermilion Cliffs Wilderness Regulations

1. Overnight hiking reservations/permits required.

2. Fees of $5 per day, per person are required.

3. No reservations or permits are required for day use.

4. For day use, children under 12 years of age are free.

5. Group size is limited to 10 people for day and overnight use.

6. Campfires are not allowed within Paria Canyon, Buckskin Gulch, or any tributary canyons or Special Management Areas (Coyote Buttes).

7. Pack out all trash, garbage, and used toilet paper.

8. Bury human waste in a cat hole no more than 6 inches deep, at least 200 feet from springs or as far away as terrain permits. Urinate on wet sand adjacent to the river, or in the river itself, but not on river terraces.

9. Dogs are allowed, with a $5 per day, per dog fee required, and they must be leashed and kept under control at all times. Remove your animal's feces from trails and camps and bury it. Private use of horses, while not recommended, is allowed. Horses must stay on shoreline terraces.

10. Do not camp within 200 feet of any spring.

11. Wrather Canyon is closed to camping.

12. Do not cut trees or limbs, or trample plants. Use existing trails onto river terraces and around campsites. Avoid making new trails or campsites.

13. The wilderness is closed to all motorized and mechanized vehicles, including bicycles and hang gliders.

14. Leave archaeological sites and artifacts undisturbed.

15. Visitors must register and day users must pay appropriate fees ($5 per person per day) at trailhead registers when entering the canyons.

Reservations for permits for overnight use are now required for the Paria Canyon–Vermilion Cliffs Wilderness. Since no more than twenty persons per day will be allowed to enter the wilderness via any trailhead, solitude in the canyons is greatly increased. But along with that solitude comes greater competition for permits, so hikers are advised to have several alternate trip dates to insure obtaining a permit to enter the wilderness. To apply for a permit, copy and fill out the application form shown below.

DATES OF TRIP REQUESTED (month/day/year)
CHOICE #1 ENTRY DATE_____
CHOICE #1 EXIT DATE_____
CHOICE #2 ENTRY DATE_____
CHOICE #2 EXIT DATE_____
(or) Any day between_____and_____

NUMBER OF DAYS_____

NUMBER IN GROUP_____
(maximum of 10 people)

NUMBER OF DOGS_____
($5 per dog per day)

NUMBER OF GOLDEN AGE/ACCESS CARDS IN GROUP_____
(Golden Eagle passes do not apply to use fees)

LIST GOLDEN AGE/ACCESS CARD NUMBERS:

_____

_____

_____

FEE AMOUNT DUE $_____
(calculated at $5 per person, per day)

ENTRY TRAILHEAD_____(select one)
1. White House
2. Wire Pass
3. Buckskin Gulch
4. Middle Route
5. Lees Ferry
6. Other_____

EXIT TRAILHEAD_____(select one)
1. White House
2. Wire Pass
3. Buckskin Gulch
4. Middle Route
5. Lees Ferry
6. Other_____

Along with your permit application, include your name, address, phone number, and the name(s) and phone number(s) of people to contact in the event of an emergency.

Hikers can mail their permit application (along with check, money order, or credit card fee payment) to:

Paria Permits
NAU Box 15018
Flagstaff, AZ 86011

Or fax your application and credit card payment to:

Paria Permits
(520) 523-0585

Make checks and money orders payable to "NAU Paria Project." For credit card payment, include the type of card, card number, and expiration date.

To determine if there are available hiking dates, or to submit an on-line application, consult the Paria Canyon Project calendar on the World Wide Web at: http://www.for.nau.edu/paria-permits/. If you do not have internet access or cannot get access at your local library, contact the Arizona Strip Interpretive Association at (435) 688-3230, and they will access the calendar for you.

If your hiking date is available, a hiking permit and map will be mailed to you. If your hiking date is NOT available, you will be notified through the mail and your fee payment will be returned. Be sure of your dates and group size before applying. Dates and group sizes are final. Once you receive your permit, there are no refunds.

CAMPING

There are only four public campgrounds in this region. The twenty-seven-unit campground in Kodachrome Basin State Park (see Hike 47) is located 2.2 miles north of Cottonwood Canyon Road, 9.4 miles from Utah 12 at Cannonville, Utah. This popular, scenic campground is open year-round and provides excellent facilities, for a fee, that include tables, water, fire grills, showers, a centrally located restroom, and a pay telephone. The sites are available on a first-come, first-served basis. Several sites can accommodate large trailers and RVs. A camper's store is located at Trailhead Station, next to the Panorama Trailhead, 0.5 mile from the campground.

The second campground is located at the White House Trailhead, the portal to Paria Canyon, 2 miles below the Paria Contact Station. Find this campground by following the trailhead directions for Hike 56. Pay the appropriate fees and register for your stay in the campground at the information kiosk just off the highway, immediately below the Paria Contact Station, then drive 2 miles down the bumpy dirt road to the campground and trailhead.

White House is a small, walk-in campground, used primarily by Paria

Canyon hikers. Its facilities include tables, fire grills, and pit toilets. You must pack out all your trash. No water is available, and there is a five-person limit at each site.

The third site is the Lees Ferry Campground below Glen Canyon Dam in Glen Canyon National Recreation Area, available for a fee. This campground, accessed via a paved road, is one of the most scenic sites in the region. The campground rests on a terrace that affords dramatic views of the emerald green waters of the Colorado River, the 3,000-foot facade of the Vermilion Cliffs, and the crags of the Echo Peaks. Facilities include awnings that shade tables, fire grills, water, toilets, and garbage collection.

At the Paria Movie Set, there is a small walk-in campground featuring three sites with tables, a barbecue grill and fire pit, and pit toilets. No water is available, and there is no fee.

Elsewhere in the region you are free to camp anywhere you wish on BLM-administered public lands, and there is ample opportunity to do so, particularly alongside the Cottonwood Canyon and Skutumpah roads. Please use established camping/parking spaces for car camping, and use extreme caution if building a campfire.

ACCESS AND SERVICES

Two scenic highways, Utah 12 and U. S. Highway 89, traverse this region from east to west. To the north, Utah 12 (the only access to Bryce Canyon National Park) provides a 59-mile scenic link between Escalante and US 89 south of Panguitch, Utah. To the south, US 89 deviates from its usual north to south route and leads east and west for 72 miles between Kanab, Utah, and Page, Arizona.

On the extreme southern fringes of the region, mostly in Arizona, US 89A, yet another scenic route, is a 91-mile highway linking Kanab, Utah, with US 89, 23 miles south of Page, Arizona, and 100 miles north of Flagstaff. This highway, the only way to reach the North Rim of the Grand Canyon, provides access to Lees Ferry at the mouth of the Paria River.

Linking Utah 12 in the north with US 89 in the south are two long, remote, and graded dirt roads: the Cottonwood Canyon Road, and the Skutumpah (pronounced SCOO-tum-paw) Road. Of these two routes, among the most scenic drives in Grand Staircase–Escalante National Monument, the Skutumpah Road receives more frequent maintenance and is the better road. The Cottonwood Canyon Road is subject to washouts and can be severely damaged by runoff from heavy rains. The road should be avoided in wet weather, when even minor rainfall renders its bentonite clay surface impassable. Before driving either road, obtain an updated road report from the Kanab BLM office, the Paria Contact Station on US 89 between Kanab, Utah, and Page, Arizona, or from the Escalante Interagency visitor center in Escalante.

Both roads begin in Cannonville, on Utah 12 in the Bryce Valley, 23 miles east of US 89 (10 miles south of Panguitch), and 36 miles west of Escalante. The Cottonwood Canyon Road (of which the first 7.2 miles are paved) stretches 46 miles from Utah 12 to US 89, 26 miles west of Page, Arizona. The Skutumpah Road leads 52 miles to US 89 8 miles east of Kanab, Utah.

Kanab, Utah, and Page, Arizona, are your best sources for whatever you may need while traveling through the region. Both towns offer a full range of services. To the north, the small town of Tropic, Utah in the Bryce Valley, is your only source of supplies between Panguitch and Escalante. Tropic offers five motels, gas, car repair and towing, restaurants, and groceries.

On US 89 between Page, Arizona, and the Paria Contact Station, are three small communities offering limited services. Church Wells, 7.4 miles east of the Paria Contact Station, offers a telephone. Big Water, 14.5 miles east of the Paria Contact Station, offers two motels, a general store, and a restaurant. Greene Haven, Arizona, 7.8 miles west of Page, and 21.4 miles east of the Paria Contact Station, offers a gas/convenience store.

On US 89A, Jacob Lake, Arizona, offers a service station and gas, diesel, and propane, and minor vehicle repair. Adjacent to the service station is Jacob Lake Lodge, offering a restaurant and rooms.

Marble Canyon Lodge, adjacent to the turnoff to Lees Ferry (see driving directions for Hike 59), provides a motel, restaurant, laundry, post office, gift shop, telephone, and fuel. Lees Ferry Lodge, 3.5 miles southwest of the Lees Ferry turnoff, offers a bar and grill, fly shop, motel, restaurant, and telephone. Cliff Dwellers Lodge, 8.75 miles southwest of the Lees Ferry turnoff, offers a motel, groceries, restaurant, and fuel.

For more information: The Kanab BLM office provides a phone menu of recorded information, primarily on the Paria Canyon-Vermilion Cliffs Wilderness, at (435) 644-2672. If you stay on the line, you can speak to a real person and obtain site-specific information. Or you can visit the office by following signs that point to the office in Kanab. The Paria Contact Station is another excellent source of information if you're traveling between Page, Arizona, and Kanab, Utah, on US 89.

In the event of an emergency, dial 911, or contact the Kane County Sheriff in Utah at (435) 644-2349. In Arizona, contact the Coconino County Sheriff in Flagstaff at (800) 338-7888, or the National Park Service in Page at (800) 582-4351.

47 Kodachrome Basin State Park—Panorama Trail

General description:	An exceptional day hike leading through the colorful Entrada Sandstone formations of Kodachrome Basin State Park.
Distance:	2.9 miles for the short loop; 5.4 miles for the longer loop.
Difficulty:	Moderately easy.
Trail conditions:	Stage coach road and constructed trail, well-defined.
Trailhead access:	2WD (paved access).
Average hiking times:	2 hours for the short loop; 3 to 3.5 hours for the longer loop.
Trailhead elevation:	5,780 feet.
High point:	5,960 feet.
Elevation gain and loss:	260 feet for the short loop; 360 feet for the longer loop.
Optimum seasons:	April through early June; September through October.
Water availability:	None available; bring your own.
Hazards:	Negligible.
Permits:	Not required.
Topo maps:	Henrieville and Cannonville USGS quads (trails and state park not shown on quads; a trail map is available at the trailhead).

Key points

0.3	Junction with return leg of loop trail; bear right.
0.6	Stage coach road branches left; bear right onto the foot trail.
1.0	Junction with Big Bear Geyser Trail; bear right for the longer loop, or left for the short loop.
1.6	Junction with Mammoth Geyser Trail; stay right.
1.7	Junction with loop trail; bear right.
2.3	Junction with trail to Cool Cave; turn right.
2.4	Cool Cave.
2.5	Return to loop trail; turn right.
2.8	End of loop trail; bear right.
3.5	Return to Panorama Trail; turn right (south).
3.7	Foot trail merges with coach road; continue straight ahead.
4.1	Junction with return leg of Panorama Loop Trail (left), and Panorama Point Trail; bear right to Panorama Point.
4.3	Panorama Point; backtrack to return trail and proceed east.
5.1	Loop Trail junction; bear right.
5.4	Panorama Trailhead.

Finding the trailhead: From Utah 12 in the Bryce Valley town of Cannonville, 33 miles east of Panguitch and U.S. Highway 89, and 36 miles west of Escalante, turn south onto the Cottonwood Canyon Road (the Cot-

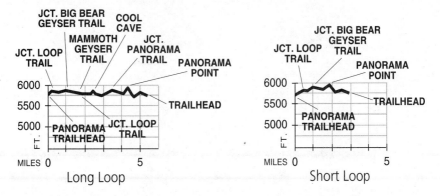

tonwood Canyon Scenic Backway), signed for "Kodachrome Basin-9." Follow this paved road south through Cannonville, then through the broad
valley of the upper Paria River. You pass the junction with southwest-bound
Skutumpah Road (see Hikes 50–52) after 2.9 miles, and after 7.2 miles reach
the end of pavement on the Cottonwood Canyon Road. Turn left here, staying on the paved road, to enter Kodachrome Basin State Park.

Stop at the self-service fee station (a modest day-use fee is required) after
0.5 mile, then continue north to a three-way junction after 1.1 miles, where
you turn onto the left-hand road, signed for the campground and scenic
loop.

The signed Panorama Trailhead is located on the left (west) side of the
road, 1.6 miles from the Cottonwood Canyon Road, and 8.8 miles from
Cannonville. The 26-unit campground is located 0.6 mile from the trailhead,
along the loop at the road end.

The hike: Kodachrome Basin State Park, a 2,240-acre preserve southeast of
Bryce Canyon National Park, is a place of vivid colors and dramatic landforms. Punctuated by the white chimneys of sand pipes, and the orange
cliffs, spires, and fin-like ridges of Entrada Sandstone that dominate the
basin make it one of the more spectacular areas in southern Utah, a land
renowned for its unique landscapes.

This state park is like a national park in miniature. Its concentration of
unusual landforms, good access, numerous short trails, and visitor services
that include a general store and campground, combine to make the park a
premier destination.

Six hiking trails traverse the park, most of them less than 1 mile in length.
The exception is the Panorama Trail, a nearly level 2.9-mile loop that surveys what is perhaps the finest scenery the park has to offer. Panorama
Point, an overlook just above the loop trail, affords an unparalleled vista
across the park's colorful landscape. The 2.5-mile Big Bear Geyser Trail can
be taken to extend the trip into a rewarding half-day hike.

One mile of the Panorama Trail is shared by hikers, mountain bikers, and
stage coach tours conducted by the park concessionaire at Trailhead Station
from Easter week through mid-October. The remaining singletrack is shared
by hikers and mountain bikers only. The Panorama and Big Bear Geyser
trails are the only trails open to mountain bikes in the park.

The sand pipes in the park add a unique dimension to a land dominated by unusual landforms. These white, chimney-like spires, averaging 30 to 50 feet in height, are composed of coarse sand that is far more resistant to erosion than the overlying orange Entrada Sandstone. Geologists believe that long ago the park was a geothermal area, with hot springs and geysers much like Yellowstone National Park is today. After the springs and geysers ceased to flow, they filled with sand, and they are the white spires you see today.

The wide trail, narrower than a typical dirt road, begins behind the trailhead display sign, and traverses a grassy flat studded with juniper, big sagebrush, rabbitbrush, and four-wing saltbush. From the start you are surrounded by an array of orange Entrada Sandstone spires. Other spires you will see along the trail are the white sand pipes, the resistant sediment-filled cores of ancient geysers and hot springs.

Many of the spires along the trail have been likened to familiar images and given fanciful names. Soon you reach the first, Fred Flintstone Spire, rising from bedrock, and just beyond it the trail forks after 0.3 mile, with the return leg of the loop branching left. Bear right and quite soon you reach the first of several short spur trails. It leads 100 yards to Old Indian Cave, a small, shady alcove. This trail describes a loop and shortly returns to the main trail.

The trail ahead traverses a gently contoured basin covered in grass and studded with the gnarled trees of the pinyon-juniper woodland. Fine views reach west to the Pink Cliffs of the Paunsaugunt Plateau in Bryce Canyon National Park. After 0.6 mile, the coach road branches left, and you follow

Panorama Trail in Kodachrome Basin State Park.

266

the singletrack ahead where the sign indicates Panorama Trail. A tall, slender sand pipe, Ballerina Spire, rises a short distance north of the trail. You curve around it and soon reach the 200-yard spur trail to Hat Shop, a concentration of orange Entrada spires capped by sandstone slabs.

Colorful badlands slopes rise 600 feet above the Hat Shop to the north rim of the basin. The spires here are composed of the orange Gunsight Member of the Entrada Formation, and above the red Cannonville Member and the white Escalante Member rise in barren, intricately eroded slopes to the rim of Henrieville Sandstone.

Beyond the Hat Shop, the trail traverses west across the open basin, bounded ahead to the west and southwest by a trio of large slickrock domes. The gentle trail passes through an open pinyon-juniper woodland where the flats are dotted with sagebrush and a variety of native bunchgrasses, including Indian ricegrass, needle-and-thread grass, and sand dropseed. As you approach the foot of the northernmost dome, you reach the Secret Passage Trail. That trail branches right, forming a 0.2-mile loop that includes the narrow slot of Secret Passage, and a view of White Buffalo, an unusual sand pipe formation perched atop the rim.

A short distance beyond the Secret Passage Trail, you come to the junction with the Big Bear Geyser Trail, branching right 1 mile from the trailhead. Hikers choosing to extend the hike will turn right onto that trail, following a brief steep descent off the ridge via badlands slopes. Below, you level off in a wooded basin, and skirt the base of intricately eroded 200-foot cliffs. Along this part of the trail you will capture glimpses into the canyon of the upper Paria River where it carves a gorge through the White Cliffs (Navajo Sandstone) of the Grand Staircase.

After hiking 0.6 mile from the Panorama Trail, you reach the signed spur trail that branches left, leading 0.1 mile to Mammoth Geyser, the largest sand pipe in the park. Another sand pipe, one of the Big Bear geysers, is visible on the rim of the cliffs north of the junction, and it can be viewed to better advantage ahead.

Bear right at that junction, and quite soon you reach another junction, where signs point right and left to Big Bear Geyser Trail. Taking the right fork, you soon curve into an amphitheater where a 100-yard spur trail leads to the base of the cliffs atop which Big Bear Geyser rests. The trail ahead briefly becomes indistinct as it follows a small wash to the mouth of a precipitous slot canyon sliced through the cliffs just above. There, atop the rim, is the second of the Big Bear geysers, called Mama Bear.

The trail ahead follows the wash draining the basin until the wash curves east. Avoid the path leading into that east-trending canyon unless you wish to explore it. The main trail bends west here, skirting the cliffs for another 0.2 mile to the Cool Cave spur trail. Hikers won't want to miss this side trip.

The spur trail leads north into a small wash, which you follow up into an increasingly narrow slot. When the slot bends to the right you reach Cool Cave, actually a deep alcove lying beneath a pouroff. Only a small patch of sky is visible overhead as the vaulting cliffs nearly envelop you.

Kodachrome Basin State Park—Panorama Trail

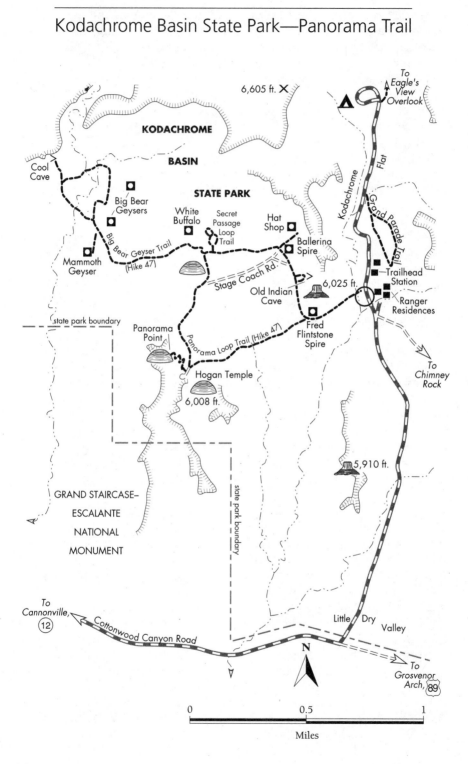

6,605 ft. X

To Eagle's View Overlook

KODACHROME

BASIN

Cool Cave

STATE PARK

Big Bear Geysers

White Buffalo

Secret Passage Loop Trail

Hat Shop

Ballerina Spire

Big Bear Geyser Trail (Hike 47)

Mammoth Geyser

Stage Coach Rd.

Old Indian Cave

6,025 ft.

Kodachrome Flat

Grand Parade Trail

Trailhead Station

Ranger Residences

state park boundary

Panorama Point

Panorama Loop Trail (Hike 47)

Fred Flintstone Spire

To Chimney Rock

Hogan Temple

6,008 ft.

5,910 ft.

GRAND STAIRCASE–

ESCALANTE

NATIONAL

MONUMENT

state park boundary

To Cannonville, (12)

Cottonwood Canyon Road

Little Dry Valley

N

To Grosvenor Arch, (89)

0   0.5   1

Miles

Back on the main trail, the final 0.25 mile of the loop follows a gently undulating course across the basin, affording a longer range perspective of the Big Bear geysers. After closing the loop, backtrack for 0.7 mile to the Panorama Trail and turn right.

The Panorama Trail skirts the eastern foot of the first dome, then curves west around it, where the coach road and the trail merge. Just beyond the southern foot of the dome, a short spur trail leads to a fine vista point, where views unfold across the western reaches of Kodachrome Basin, including Mammoth Geyser, with a backdrop of the glowing Pink Cliffs.

Follow the coach road generally south toward Hogan Temple, the bold, convoluted slickrock dome straight ahead. The road soon skirts the second of the three domes, where you reach a signed junction. The coach road continues ahead and quickly ends in a loop. The return leg of the Panorama Trail branches left. If you wish to reach Panorama Point, turn right and ascend 120 feet in 0.2 mile, via a series of steep switchbacks. The point is actually the apex of a debris cone that mantles the eastern flanks of the dome.

From there, Kodachrome Basin spreads out in all of its colorful splendor. The basin below the viewpoint, with its velvety grasslands and pinyon-juniper woodlands, adds a soft contrast to the raw, rockbound landscape that surrounds it.

From the junction below Panorama Point, the return trail undulates across the basin for 0.5 mile to the junction, where you turn right and backtrack around Fred Flintstone Spire for 0.3 mile to the trailhead.

Kodachrome Basin State Park.

48 Cottonwood Canyon Narrows

General description:	An exciting, short day hike through a narrow Navajo Sandstone canyon, located within Grand Staircase–Escalante National Monument.
Distance:	3 miles round trip.
Difficulty:	Easy.
Trail conditions:	Wash route.
Trailhead access:	Impassable when wet. 4WD advised if road is flood-damaged.
Average hiking time:	2 hours round trip.
Trailhead elevation:	5,660 feet.
Low point:	5,500 feet.
Elevation loss and gain:	160 feet.
Optimum seasons:	April through early June; September through October.
Water availability:	None available; bring your own.
Hazards:	Flash-flood danger.
Permits:	Not required.
Topo maps:	Butler Valley USGS quad; BLM Smoky Mountain.

Key points:

1.5   Mouth of narrows at Cottonwood Canyon Road.

Finding the trailhead: Follow driving directions for Hike 47 to the Kodachrome Basin State Park turnoff, then continue straight ahead on the graded dirt surface of the Cottonwood Canyon Road.

This road is infrequently maintained and subject to washouts. Throughout much of its course, this undulating, winding road traverses bentonite clay, which when wet can become impassable, and at best is very dangerous to drive. A high-clearance vehicle, preferably with 4WD, is recommended, though not required unless runoff has damaged the road.

After 1.5 miles, avoid a left-branching ranch road, and soon thereafter dip into the wash of Rock Springs Creek, fording its shallow stream. Enter Grand Staircase–Escalante National Monument, 4.9 miles from the pavement, then ascend a steep grade to a saddle at 5.8 miles. Avoid the left-branching graded road immediately beyond the cattle guard at the saddle, and continue straight ahead.

A very steep grade soon leads down to the crossing of Round Valley Draw at 7.6 miles. You reach the junction with the signed left fork to Grosvenor Arch after 8.5 miles (15.7 miles from Cannonville). Few travelers forego the 2-mile round-trip drive to that unique arch and picnic site.

Continuing south on the Cottonwood Canyon Road, you soon begin following The Cockscomb. The road crests a saddle 13 miles from the pave-

Cottonwood Canyon Narrows

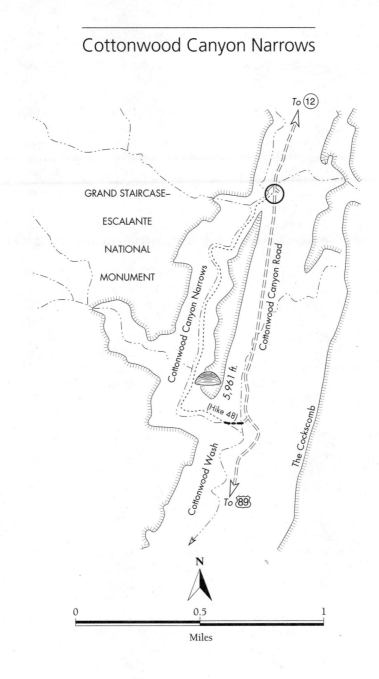

GRAND STAIRCASE–

ESCALANTE

NATIONAL

MONUMENT

To (12)

Cottonwood Canyon Narrows

Cottonwood Canyon Road

5,961 ft.

(Hike 48)

Cottonwood Wash

To (89)

The Cockscomb

N

0   0.5   1

Miles

ment, then begins an exceedingly steep downgrade into the drainage below. En route you can see the road cresting another prominent saddle 0.4 mile to the south. Between the two saddles at the bottom of the grade, the small portal of the Cottonwood Wash narrows opens up through The Cockscomb just west of the road. A small pullout on the left (east) side of the road affords the only available parking, 0.25 mile south of the north saddle, 250 yards north of the south saddle, and 20.5 miles from Cannonville. Another short spur road branches right 0.9 mile ahead, offering access into the mouth of the narrows.

The trailhead can also be reached from U.S. Highway 89 in the south. Find the southern end of the Cottonwood Canyon Road (between mileposts 17 and 18) 2.2 miles east of the Paria Contact Station, or 26.3 miles west of Page, Arizona. The turnoff is indicated by a large BLM destination and mileage sign pointing to Cottonwood Canyon, Grosvenor Arch, and Cannonville.

As the road leads north away from US 89, it is sandy at first as it ascends over The Rimrocks. The road passes the Grand Staircase–Escalante National Monument boundary after 1.4 miles, then skirts the dramatic gray shale badlands at the foot of the Kaiparowits Plateau. After curving northwest to the broad valley of the Paria River, the road then begins to ascend the course of Cottonwood Wash.

After 14.1 miles, a dirt road branches right (east) to ascend The Cockscomb, and hikers taking Hike 49 should park there. Continue north along Cottonwood Wash for another 11.4 miles to the aforementioned trailhead, 25.5 miles from US 89.

The hike: The Cottonwood Canyon Scenic Backway is perhaps the premier scenic drive in Grand Staircase–Escalante National Monument. Not only does the road afford access to well-known features such as Kodachrome Basin State Park and incomparable Grosvenor Arch, the road also follows The Cockscomb for many miles, one of the most unusual landforms in the monument.

Cottonwood Creek, an often dry stream course has, over the ages, carved a long, deep, and winding canyon through the steeply-tilted rock beds of The Cockscomb, ranging from the shadowed confines of narrow slots to a broad, open wash. This fine, short hike leads through the final narrow gorge of Cottonwood Creek before the canyon opens up and begins its long, straight journey to the confluence with the Paria River. The hike leads through the most easily accessible section of narrows along Cottonwood Creek, offering a rewarding, scenic diversion for anyone taking a drive down remote Cottonwood Canyon Road.

Opposite the small parking area, you will find a brown BLM post on the boundary of the 136,322-acre Paria-Hackberry Wilderness Study Area. From there, a path leads into the narrow wash just below, at the portal to the Cottonwood Canyon Narrows. There are three ways to enter: 1) follow the small wash for 50 yards down to an 8-foot pouroff, which requires one Class 4 move to get up or down; 2) just to the right (north) of the pouroff, a steep, rocky path descends briefly into the wash; or 3) a shallow draw, located about 100 yards north of the parking area, offers easy, trouble-free access into Cottonwood Creek.

Once you reach the wash of Cottonwood Creek, you may choose to turn right and explore the slot up-canyon. Chockstones and boulders make travel there challenging, and muddy pools persist in the gorge long after significant rainfall. Heading downcanyon, the walking is easy and passable to any hiker.

From the portal, the canyon bends west, briefly opening up. Soon thereafter, the canyon walls close in and you weave a way down the sandy, occasionally rock-strewn wash. Navajo Sandstone cliffs embrace the gorge, standing 10 to 20 feet apart, and rising 200 to 300 feet above. The canyon walls are often sheer, in places overhanging, but fractures and ledges support a scattering of shrubs, and gnarled pinyons and junipers fringe the rims above.

Two precipitous slot canyons join Cottonwood Creek on the right, one ending in a shadowed amphitheater at 0.5 mile, the other at 1 mile. About midway through the narrows, an array of spires looms above on the western rim, and the gorge has reached a depth of 400 to 500 feet. After about 0.8 mile, you reach a prominent keyhole-shaped alcove scooped out of the right-side wall. In the autumn of 1997, a small chockstone blocked the wash here. If the chockstone is still present when you visit, bypass it on the left via slickrock slopes, or simply jump over it to continue.

As you approach the lower reaches of the narrows, the canyon begins to open up and sandy benches appear. In response to increased sunlight and more available space, there is a marked increase in vegetation in this part of the canyon.

Near the end of the canyon the wash describes a prominent bend to the east, and a small arch becomes visible high on the flanks of Dome 5961 on your left, and soon several more skyline arches appear on the splintered canyon rim ahead to the southeast.

When the canyon bends east, it cuts through the steeply tilted Navajo Sandstone of The Cockscomb, and once again you enter a narrow stone hallway. A boulder jam soon blocks the wash ahead, but there is an easy rock-strewn bypass route on the left side. Beyond that obstacle you exit the gorge and enter an open wash flanked by low benches clad in pinyon-juniper woodland.

Don't be lured too far down the wash. When it bends south, you'll see a pair of cottonwood trees just ahead. Leave the wash there and angle up to the left, soon following a path that quickly leads you to the short spur off of the Cottonwood Canyon Road. That spur offers an alternative starting point for a hike into the narrows.

From the road you can return the way you came, or turn left and walk the road for 0.9 mile back to your car.

49 Yellow Rock/The Box of the Paria River

General description:	A demanding yet rewarding day hike, or overnighter if you pack water, for experienced hikers only, between Hackberry Canyon and the Paria River, located within Grand Staircase–Escalante National Monument.
Distance:	6.8 miles, loop trip.
Difficulty:	Moderately strenuous, Class 2 scrambling on the way to Yellow Rock.
Trail conditions:	Traces of old, eroded stock trails, cross-country slickrock routes, wash routes; good route-finding ability required.
Trailhead access:	Impassable when wet. 4WD advised if road is flood-damaged.
Average hiking time:	4 to 5 hours.
Trailhead elevation:	4,770 feet.
High point:	5,400 feet.
Low point:	4,640 feet.
Elevation gain and loss:	800 feet.
Optimum seasons:	April through early June; September through October.
Water availability:	Paria River; seasonal intermittent flows in Cottonwood Wash; since this water must be treated before drinking, bring your own.
Hazards:	Exposure to steep dropoffs; flash-flood danger in canyons; risk to inexperienced hikers of becoming disoriented or lost.
Permits:	Not required.
Topo maps:	Calico Peak and Fivemile Valley USGS quads; BLM Smoky Mountain.

Key points

0.3 First northwest-trending draw below Hackberry Canyon; turn right and enter draw.
1.4 Crest 5,400-foot ridge west of Yellow Rock.
1.8 Junction with trail to The Box of the Paria River; turn left (southeast).
3.7 Paria River.
4.5 Confluence of Paria River and Cottonwood Wash; turn left up Cottonwood Wash.
6.8 Return to trailhead.

Finding the trailhead: Drivers approaching from U.S. Highway 89 in the south will find driving directions to the trailhead in Hike 48.

If you are approaching from Utah 12 in the north, follow driving directions for Hike 48 to the Cottonwood Canyon Narrows via the Cottonwood Canyon Road, 20.5 miles from Cannonville, and continue straight ahead. As you proceed down the course of Cottonwood Wash, you pass seven spur roads branching right (west) to undeveloped camping areas beneath the spreading cottonwoods that fringe the wash. One such spur, signed for Pump Canyon Spring, is the former location of the campground shown on USGS and BLM maps, 24.9 miles from Cannonville.

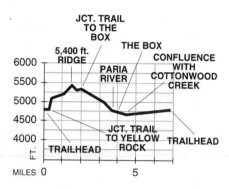

After another 6.7 miles (31.6 miles from Cannonville), the road crosses a west-trending wash opposite the well-hidden mouth of Hackberry Canyon, where flash-floods often wash out the road. Continue straight ahead for another 0.2 mile to the junction with an eastbound road that ascends The Cockscomb. Park in turnouts on either side of the road near this junction. Since there are no signs indicating a trailhead here, look for a prominent slickrock dome on the western skyline—Yellow Rock—to pinpoint your location.

The hike: Between the mouth of Cottonwood Creek wash, Hackberry Canyon, and The Box of the Paria River, rises a high, wedge-shaped mesa punctuated by an array of Navajo Sandstone domes and towers. On the far northern reaches of the mesa are the Death Valleys, upper and lower, and cattle have been grazed there for more than a century. Numerous trails have been

Yellow Rock, a landmark Navajo Sandstone dome between Hackberry Canyon and the Paria River.

Yellow Rock/The Box of the Paria River

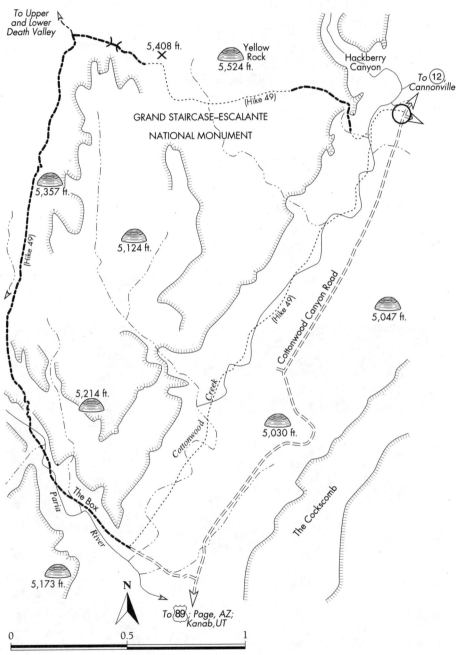

To Upper and Lower Death Valley

5,408 ft.
×

Yellow Rock
5,524 ft.

Hackberry Canyon

To (12) Cannonville

(Hike 49)

GRAND STAIRCASE–ESCALANTE

NATIONAL MONUMENT

5,357 ft.

(Hike 49)

5,124 ft.

(Hike 49)

Cottonwood Canyon Road

5,047 ft.

5,214 ft.

Cottonwood Creek

5,030 ft.

The Cockscomb

Paria River

The Box

5,173 ft.

N

To (89); Page, AZ; Kanab, UT

0   0.5   1

Miles

forged by ranchers between the rims of the mesa and the Paria River and Hackberry Canyon, affording access to water for their stock. Some of the trails are still used by cattle today, while others are no longer useful and have been abandoned.

This premier day hike follows two such long-abandoned stock trails and an interesting cross-country route across the mesa. This trip, recommended only for experienced hikers with good routefinding skills, offers a memorable blend of slickrock, mesa top, and canyon landscapes, including tremendous far-ranging vistas. While the trail from the mesa down to the Paria River is in fair condition and easy enough to follow in either direction, the old eroded trail from Cottonwood Creek up to Yellow Rock is extremely steep, rocky, and treacherous. It is far easier, and much safer, to ascend that trail, so begin your hike on the Cottonwood Canyon Road near the mouth of Hackberry Canyon.

Drop down into the wide, sandy bed of Cottonwood Creek wash, which often carries a flow of water below its confluence with Hackberry Canyon. Tamarisk, seep-willow, and Fremont cottonwood trees fringe the wash with a dense ribbon of riparian growth, so you'll want to stay in the wash, following it down-canyon to the south.

After about 0.3 mile, depending upon where you parked and began hiking, the first side canyon south of Hackberry Canyon opens up on the right (west). This short, precipitous drainage, cut into the steeply tilted beds of Navajo Sandstone on the west wall of The Cockscomb, appears to be a box canyon with no visible route to the rim above. Turn right into this drainage and follow the wash for about 50 yards, where you will find an old, seldom-used trail ascending the slope on the left. The faint path soon returns to the rocky wash just beyond the remains of a large fallen cottonwood. Follow the wash up-canyon for another 10 yards, then look for the steep trail ascending the prominent rocky chute on the right (northwest).

The "trail" ascends the soft red and gray rocks of the Carmel Formation via a break in the tilted Navajo cliffs. The path is exceedingly steep, rocky, and eroded, with poor, slippery footing, and a misstep could result in a tumble or uncontrollable slide. The ascent is accomplished by digging in your boot soles and grunting your way up the chute. It is short-lived, and in 200 yards you have gained 200 feet and top out in a notch on a rocky rib. Here the grade moderates and you ascend for several more yards above a plunging gorge to another notch on a ridge, carved into soft, red Carmel gravels.

At your feet, Hackberry Canyon carves a narrow gorge through The Cockscomb 300 feet below, and the vista stretches north up the trough of Cottonwood Creek wash, a wide valley eroded along the axis of The Cockscomb. Differential erosion of varying hard and soft rock layers have left scores of isolated pyramids and monoliths standing on the valley floor. In the south your view reaches down the Paria River to the vast Paria Plateau and the Vermilion Cliffs.

From the notch follow the knife-blade ridge west, ascending moderately over Navajo Sandstone. The trail here is obscure, so simply make your way up the ridge to a cluster of spires, at which point the immense dome of Yellow Rock fills your view ahead. Cross over the ridge immediately east of the spires, and head generally west on the faint trail into a broad bowl spreading out below Yellow Rock.

Between low mounds of Navajo slickrock, the sandy ground has been colonized by pinyon pines, junipers, manzanita, scrub live oaks, and a scattering of tall ponderosa pines. Soon you dip into a minor wash where the trail disappears, but you simply ascend the sandy slopes to the slickrock above, heading west. Once you mount the corrugated slickrock at the southern base of Yellow Rock, you'll see what appears to be a large orange cairn ahead to the west. Skirt the base of Yellow Rock, heading for that natural landmark.

Traversing the lower slopes of Yellow Rock is a delightful jaunt over Navajo slickrock. Parallel fractures run perpendicular to the cross-bedding of the sandstone, giving the entire dome a checkerboard surface, similar to the slopes of Checkerboard Mesa in Zion National Park. The coloration of Yellow Rock's dome is truly unique, featuring intricate swirls of orange, red, white, and yellow. A moderate friction scramble up the eastern flank of Yellow Rock to its crest for a commanding vista is highly recommended, either as a side trip or as a destination for a shorter hike.

After passing below or left of the orange "natural cairn," continue straight ahead (west), cross a shallow draw, then ascend slopes of slickrock and sand to the wooded ridge above. On the Calico Peak USGS quad, two dark brown

The Box of the Paria River.

oval lines represent the 5,400-foot contour on this ridge. Turn north after cresting the ridge and proceed about 300 to 350 yards to the southernmost 5,400-foot oval contour line. En route up and over the ridge, make an effort to walk on slickrock, sand, or in drainage gullies to avoid crushing the untracked microbiotic soil crust in this pristine area.

A small wooded basin spreads out about 0.3 mile below the ridge to the west, resting on the divide separating two north- and south-trending drainages. A spectacular array of Navajo domes embraces the basin. The Vermilion Cliffs form a colorful barrier that marches far into the southwestern distance. Far below you to the northwest lies the deep trench of Hackberry Canyon, flanked by Chinle Formation badlands, and the red cliff bands of Moenave and Kayenta formation rocks.

There are a trio of prominent Navajo towers 0.4 mile northwest of the basin below the ridge. Use these towers as your guide ahead. Descend the sand and slickrock slopes west off the ridge. Soon you skirt a 30-foot high conical pinnacle, with a round caprock, on the right. You should locate the faint sandy path on the north side of the pinnacle, and there may be cairns to show the way. You can follow the faint path down across the basin through an open woodland of pinyon and juniper trees.

After dipping into a minor saddle, the better-defined trail rises gradually over the crunchy brown rocks of the Kayenta Formation, where cairns begin to appear. You reach the indistinct junction with the trail coming from the Paria River at 5,320 feet, and about 1.8 miles from the trailhead, due south of the blocky Navajo towers seen from the 5,400-foot ridge. Fine views from the junction stretch north along the Navajo Sandstone crest of The Cockscomb, punctuated by Point 6070, a dramatic slickrock butte.

Cairns mark the junction with the trail, which leads northwest toward Lower Death Valley, and south to the Paria River. Make a sharp left turn onto the southbound trail, a faint single-track that soon becomes well-defined and easy to follow. This trail descends gradually between low Navajo domes, then levels out on a wooded flat. When the trail enters a shallow wash and disappears, follow the wash ahead for 150 yards, where you'll find the trail exiting the wash on the left side.

Now you head straight for Dome 5357, then bend right and skirt its western base, passing an array of interesting spires and domes. You descend gradually until you reach a small rocky draw, where the grade steepens. Dark red, tilted beds of the Kayenta Formation, forming cliffs on the western edge of The Cockscomb monocline, come into view ahead. The Vermilion Cliffs rise boldly to the west, and you can sense your approach to the rim of the Paria River canyon, but you cannot yet see it.

After leaving the draw on the left, you ascend briefly to a point near the canyon rim, then follow a minor ridge southeast, descending above a precipitous draw. Pause here, 1.7 miles from the junction, long enough to enjoy the fine view. Here the Paria River flows out of its broad valley wherein lies the ghost town of Old Pahreah, flanked by lavender, red, and gray Chinle Formation badlands, then carves a short but spectacular gorge through The Cockscomb. This gorge is known as The Box of the Paria River.

The trail becomes rocky and steep as it leaves the rim at 5,050 feet, descending a draw via switchbacks, and dropping 200 feet in 0.25 mile to the sandy banks of the Paria River. Don your wading shoes here and ford the wide and shallow waters of the turbid river to an old 4WD track on the opposite bench. You'll cross the river three more times as it cuts through the Navajo Sandstone narrows of The Box. Just before the third crossing, you pass a pair of deep cave-like alcoves scooped out of the south canyon wall.

Beyond the fourth and final ford, pick up the doubletrack leaving the wash via the north side bench, carving a swath ahead through the rabbitbrush. When you reach the mouth of Cottonwood Creek wash 0.9 mile from the rim, and 4.5 miles from the trailhead, turn left and follow the broad sandy wash north along the flanks of The Cockscomb for another 2.3 miles back to your car on the Cottonwood Canyon Road.

50 Willis Creek Narrows

General description:	An easy half-day hike through a dramatic narrow canyon in the White Cliffs of Grand Staircase–Escalante National Monument.
Distance:	4.8 miles round trip.
Difficulty:	Easy.
Trail conditions:	Wash route.
Trailhead access:	4WD advised when the road is wet.
Average hiking time:	2.5 hours round trip.
Trailhead elevation:	5,980 feet.
Low point:	5,700 feet.
Elevation loss and gain:	280 feet.
Optimum seasons:	April through mid-June; September through October.
Water availability:	Seasonal intermittent flows in Willis Creek and Sheep Creek; treat before drinking, or bring your own.
Hazards:	Flash-flood danger.
Permits:	Not required.
Topo maps:	Bull Valley Gorge USGS quad; BLM Kanab.

Key points

1.3   Averett Canyon joins on the left (north); narrows end.

2.4   Confluence with Sheep Creek.

Finding the trailhead: From Utah 12 in the Bryce Valley town of Cannonville, 33 miles east of Panguitch and U.S. Highway 89, and 36 miles west of Escalante, turn south onto the Cottonwood Can-

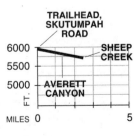

Willis Creek Narrows

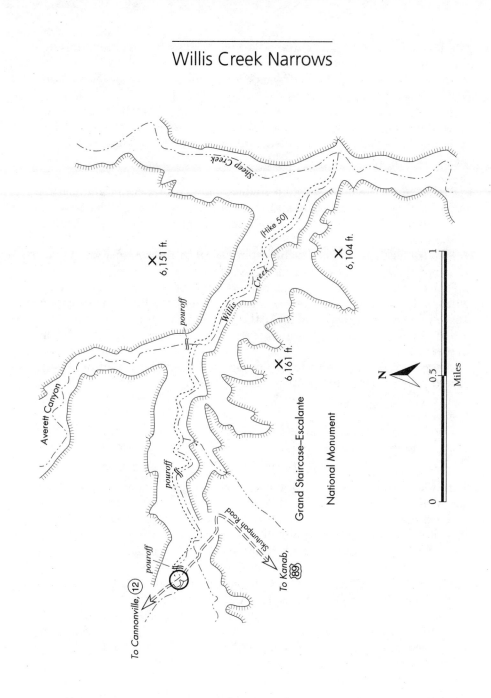

yon Road, signed for "Kodachrome Basin-9." Follow the pavement through Cannonville, then through the broad valley of the upper Paria River. After 2.9 miles, the Skutumpah Road branches right (southwest), signed for "Bull Valley Gorge-9," and "Kanab-61."

After turning right onto this road, the road immediately dips down to cross the Yellow Creek wash, then rises to the boundary of Grand Staircase–Escalante National Monument after 0.25 mile. After 3 miles, you cross runoff below the spillway of a dam spanning broad Sheep Creek wash, ascend to a ridge, then drop down to the dry wash of Averett Canyon after 4.7 miles. After 5.5 miles, avoid a graded road that branches right near the crest of a ridge. Bear left there and descend to the wash of Willis Creek, 6.3 miles from the Cottonwood Canyon Road. Parking is available on either side of the wash.

The trailhead is also accessible from US 89 in the south. From US 89, turn north where a sign indicates Johnson Canyon, immediately east of milepost 55, and 8 miles east of Kanab, Utah, or 64 miles west of Page, Arizona. Follow this paved road as it gradually ascends Johnson Canyon for 16.2 miles to a signed junction. At the junction, turn right onto the good gravel road (Skutumpah Road), signed for Deer Springs Ranch and Cannonville.

After driving 11.5 miles from the junction, avoid several prominently signed spur roads leading to the private property of Deer Springs Ranch. You reach Willis Creek wash 26.5 miles from the pavement and 42.7 miles from US 89.

Drivers approaching from either direction will find numerous undeveloped campsites in the pinyon-juniper woodland, many with fine views of the Pink Cliffs of Bryce Canyon National Park.

The hike: Some of the most dramatic slot canyons in the world have been carved into the White Cliffs of the Grand Staircase in southern Utah. Many of these slot canyons are accessible only to veteran canyoneers well-versed in a variety of rock climbing techniques.

Yet there are slot canyons that involve no more than a pleasant walk down their shadowed stone hallways. Willis Creek is such a canyon. Born on the flanks of the Pink Cliffs in Bryce Canyon National Park, the broad wash of Willis Creek carves a swath through densely wooded terraces until it reaches the Navajo Sandstone of the White Cliffs. There the wash seems to disappear, becoming entrenched between 200- to 300-foot slickrock walls. This gorge, with many narrow passages, stretches 2.5 miles down to its confluence with much larger Sheep Creek Canyon, another Pink Cliffs drainage.

On this fine short hike there is no particular destination other than the narrows of Willis Creek. Go as far as you wish; the best narrows are found along the first 1.3 miles.

Where the broad wash of Willis Creek crosses the Skutumpah Road there is little intimation of the narrow gorge below. Cross the road and follow the wash downstream. Quite soon the Navajo Sandstone emerges and the wash immediately slots up. Scramble down into the wash just below a low pouroff and proceed down-canyon.

At first the Navajo cliffs are low but confining. The occasional appearance of ponderosa pines allows you to judge the height of the canyon walls. After following a few bends of the developing canyon, the walls suddenly rise higher, and you are funneled into a slot where only 6 to 10 feet of space separate the slickrock walls. Although there may be a very small, shallow stream in the upper reaches of the gorge during early spring or following extended periods of rainfall, most of the hike passes over the dry gravel wash.

The canyon beyond the first narrows is variable, ranging from short, narrow slots to more open stretches where benches flank the wash, providing habitat for pinyon pine, juniper, Gambel oak, Rocky Mountain maple, Utah serviceberry, seep-willow, alderleaf mountain mahogany, single-leaf ash, and occasional ponderosa pine trees. Within the narrows, only a sliver of sky is visible overhead, where the vaulting walls seem to nearly coalesce. The convoluted slickrock walls, sculpted by ages of abrasive runoff, echo with your footsteps.

After 0.6 mile, you reach another pouroff, easily bypassed via the slickrock ledge on the left side. The drainage of Averett Canyon, entering on the left via a rugged gorge, opens up after 1.3 miles. That canyon was named in honor of Elijah Averett, a member of a party of Utah Territorial Militia in search of Indian raiders who killed settlers in Long Valley, near the town of Glendale, in the spring of 1866. Averett himself was killed by Indian rifles in August of 1866, while crossing the canyon that now bears his name.

There are no more slots below Averett Canyon, though Willis Creek remains a confined, spectacular canyon, and the walking is easy over the wide gravel wash. When you see a 200-foot cliff apparently blocking your way ahead, you are only minutes away from the confluence with Sheep Creek wash. From Sheep Creek at 2.4 miles, backtrack through the shadowed gorge to the trailhead.

51 Lick Wash

General description: An excellent day hike through a deep and narrow canyon in the Grand Staircase, located within Grand Staircase–Escalante National Monument.

Distance: 8 miles round trip.

Difficulty: Moderately easy.

Trail conditions: Wash route.

Trailhead access: 4WD advised when road is wet.

Average hiking time: 4 hours round trip.

Trailhead elevation: 6,330 feet.

Low point: 6,000 feet.

Elevation loss and gain: 330 feet.

Optimum seasons: April through mid-June; September through October.

Water availability: None available; bring your own.

Hazards: Flash-flood danger.

Permits: Not required.

Topo maps: Deer Spring Point USGS quad; BLM Kanab.

Key points
4.0 Park Wash.

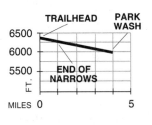

Finding the trailhead: Drivers coming from Utah 12 in the north should follow driving directions for Hike 50 to Willis Creek, 9.2 miles southwest of Cannonville via the Cottonwood Canyon and Skutumpah roads, and continue straight ahead on the Skutumpah Road. After 10.9 miles the road crosses the narrow bridge spanning cavernous Bull Valley Gorge. Enter signed Bullrush Hollow after 16.9 miles and enjoy the first good views of the towering White Cliffs in the southern distance. After emerging from the woodland at 18.6 miles, you enter the broad, brushy basin of Dry Valley, then gradually descend to an unsigned crossing of Lick Wash at 19.9 miles, where the road is subject to washouts. A short distance beyond the wash, immediately before reaching a cattle guard, turn left onto a faint spur road. Follow the spur for 0.1 mile to its end above the banks of Lick Wash and park there.

From U.S. Highway 89 in the south, you can find the trailhead by turning north where a sign indicates Johnson Canyon. This turnoff is located immediately east of milepost 55, and 8 miles east of Kanab, Utah, or 64 miles west of Page, Arizona. Follow the paved Johnson Canyon Road north for 16.2 miles to a signed junction, then turn right onto the good gravel Skutumpah Road, signed for Deer Springs Ranch and Cannonville.

Avoid several signed spur roads leading to the private property of the Deer Springs Ranch between 11.5 and 11.7 miles from the junction. After driving 14.8 miles from the junction at the end of the pavement (31 miles

Lick Wash

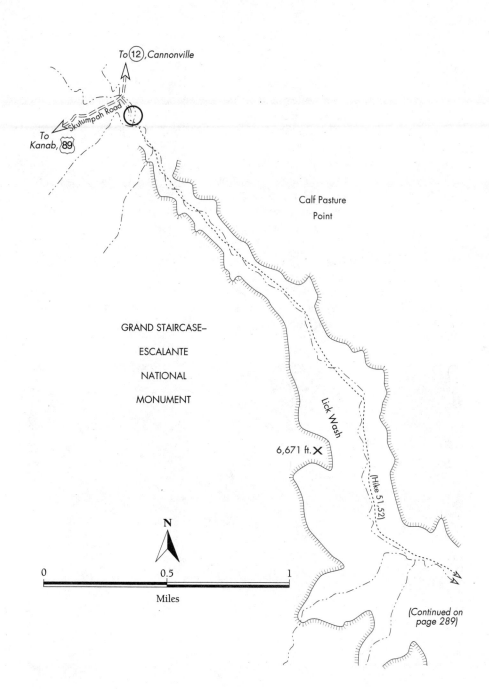

To (12), Cannonville

To
Kanab, (89)

Skutumpah Road

Calf Pasture
Point

GRAND STAIRCASE–

ESCALANTE

NATIONAL

MONUMENT

Lick Wash

6,671 ft. X

(Hike 51,52)

N

0   0.5   1

Miles

(Continued on
page 289)

from US 89), you reach the aforementioned spur road leading to the trailhead, just before the Skutumpah Road crosses Lick Wash.

The hike: Lick Wash is one of many largely unknown, uncelebrated canyons carved into the remote White Cliffs of the Grand Staircase in southern Utah. What Lick Wash lacks in notoriety is compensated for by its incomparable beauty. Indeed, it is perhaps the most scenic, and seldom-visited, canyon covered in this book. Exciting narrow passages in the upper reaches of the canyon give way to a wider canyon below, embraced by the bold White Cliffs of Navajo Sandstone studded with tall pines, rising 600 to 800 feet to the mesa rims above. The wash is dry, and travel down its sandy and gravelly bed is easy, passable to any hiker.

Begin the hike from the end of the spur road by walking down the rock-strewn wash. Bluffs of Navajo Sandstone, studded with ponderosa pines, rise ahead, and the wash seems to disappear between them. Soon you enter the sandstone-enveloped gorge, which quickly slots up, and you make your way ahead through the narrow slickrock corridor. Within minutes you reach a short fence that spans the gap between the canyon walls. Climb over or crawl through the fence, passing the only obstacle in the canyon.

After about 1 mile you leave the narrow passages behind, and the canyon begins to open up, cutting through deep alluvial deposits that form benches flanking the wash, hosting a variety of shrubs and gnarled woodland trees. The canyon walls grow higher as you proceed, with

The Pink Cliffs of Bryce Canyon National Park form the backdrop to remote Park Wash.

smooth convex slopes of slickrock sweeping upward for hundreds of feet to the square-edged mesas above. Curved lines of cross-bedding on the slickrock shoulders reach to the base of fluted cliffs, decorated with dark black streaks and a brown patina of desert varnish. Ponderosa pines grow tall and straight at the base of the great cliffs and fringe the rims of the mesas above.

During the lower 2 miles of Lick Wash, you'll find cow trails to follow, shortcutting the minor meanders of the wash via the benches above. After about 3 miles the hulking mass of No Mans Mesa fills your view ahead. By now the arroyo of Lick Wash has grown deeper. As you approach the mouth of the wash you'll spy a shallow but obvious alcove on the left (north) canyon wall, scooped out of a shoulder of slickrock that projects into the canyon. This is your indication that it is time to leave the arroyo, which you should do before you come abreast of the alcove.

Ascend out of the arroyo via cow trails to the north-side bench, where you will find an old 4WD track. Follow this faint doubletrack out into the valley of Park Wash, first east, then north, crossing a bench thick with the growth of big sagebrush and exotic Russian thistle (tumbleweed).

Calf Pasture Point and its sheer white cliffs loom 800 feet overhead on your left, while the equally impressive cliffs bounding No Mans Mesa define the eastern margin of the valley. These are the White Cliffs of the Grand Staircase, and they form the second tallest riser (only the Vermilion Cliffs are higher) in the series of cliffs and terraces that stair-step north out of the Arizona Strip into south-central Utah.

After enjoying the dramatic landscape of the White Cliffs, return the way you came.

52 Lick Wash to No Mans Mesa

See Map on Page 285

General description: A demanding all-day hike or overnighter, for experienced hikers only, to a remote, pristine mesa in the Grand Staircase, located within Grand Staircase–Escalante National Monument.

Distance: 12 miles round trip.

Difficulty: Strenuous, Class 2 and 3 scrambling on ascent of No Mans Mesa.

Trail conditions: Wash route; 4WD road; and a very steep and poor, abandoned goat trail.

Trailhead access: 4WD advised when the road is wet.

Average hiking time: 6 to 7 hours round trip.

Trailhead elevation: 6,330 feet.

High point: 6,800 feet, up to 7,200 feet.

Low point: 6,000 feet.

Elevation loss and gain: 330 feet, +800 feet.

Optimum seasons: April through early June; September through October.

Water availability: None available; bring your own.

Hazards: Flash-flood danger in Lick Wash; exposure to steep dropoffs en route to No Mans Mesa.

Permits: Not required.

Topo maps: Deer Spring Point and Deer Range Point USGS quads; BLM Kanab.

Key points

4.0   4WD road in Park Wash valley; proceed north up the valley.

4.6   Line cabin.

5.1   Road crosses Park Wash; follow wash to the left (up-canyon) if the road is washed out.

5.3   Turn right at junction with eastbound 4WD road.

5.5   Turn right (south) east of the low cone and ascend to the goat trail.

6.0   North point of No Mans Mesa.

Finding the trailhead: Follow driving directions for Hike 51.

The hike: No Mans Mesa, bounded by the White Cliffs of the Grand Staircase, halfway between U.S. Highway 89 and the Pink Cliffs of Bryce Canyon National Park, is the only large mesa in the Grand Staircase completely isolated from its surroundings. Bounded by 600- to 800-foot cliffs of Navajo Sandstone, the mesa rises up to 1,200 feet above the sagebrush-studded valleys that encircle it.

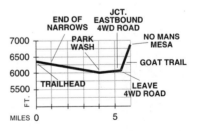

Ranging in elevation from 6,600 feet to 7,222 feet, the gently rolling surface of the mesa encompasses 1,788 acres of pristine, relict vegetation virtually untouched by the human hands. No annual grasses, such as cheatgrass,

Lick Wash to No Mans Mesa

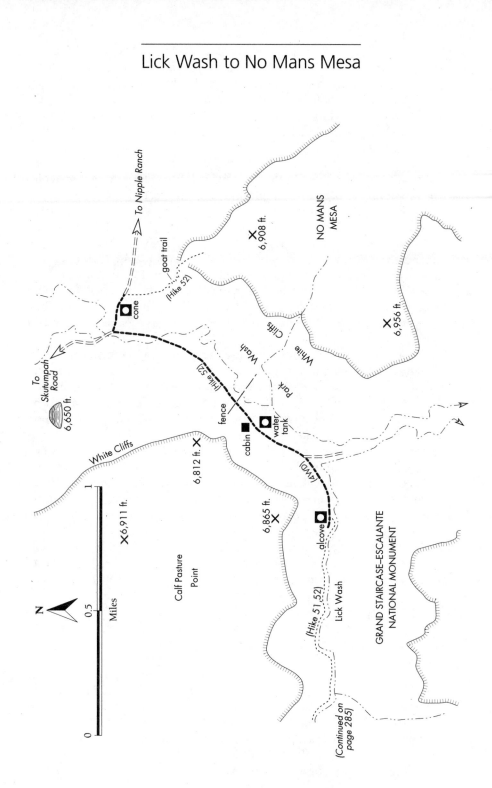

(Continued on page 285)

grow here, attesting to the mesa's undisturbed condition. The mesa harbors species of plants that are endangered elsewhere in southern Utah. Most notable and abundant of these rare plants is the buckwheat *Eriogonum zionis*. In response to its unaltered vegetation, the BLM has designated No Mans Mesa an Area of Critical Environmental Concern (ACEC). Its relict communities establish a baseline against which to measure changes in areas impacted by human activities.

The concentration of native grasses on the mesa is unmatched in other areas of southern Utah. Even to the amateur botanist, the contrast between the vegetation on No Mans Mesa and much of the rest of southern Utah, which has been utilized for grazing and other activities for more than 100 years, is remarkable. Few mammals and only one species of lizard have been observed on the mesa, though a variety of birds visit the woodlands and sagebrush parks.

There is only one break in the many miles of sheer cliffs that bound the mesa, and the native peoples of the region must have used that break to reach the mesa. Evidence of chipping sites, potsherds, and structural rocks on the mesa are of undetermined origin, believed to from early Paiute or Anasazi cultures.

The mesa was grazed only briefly in 1927 and again in the spring of 1928. A local rancher by the name of Jepson, attempting to avoid paying taxes on his goat herd, constructed a trail up through the break in the White Cliffs to the north point of the mesa. In 1927, his goats grazed the mesa for about 6 weeks. Domestic livestock have not since grazed No Mans Mesa, and no evidence remains of the goats' presence.

This rigorous hike follows the dramatic canyon of Lick Wash to the valley of Park Wash, then ascends what remains of the goat trail to No Mans Mesa. Time and erosion have reclaimed much of this "trail," and today it is a treacherous scramble over loose slabs precariously balanced on broken, high-angle cliffs which only experienced hikers should attempt. The hike can be completed in one day, but the broad mesa invites exploration and an extended stay. The long-range vistas from its rim, its isolation, high level of solitude, and an unlimited array of possible campsites make the mesa a rewarding destination for an overnight trip. Don't forget to carry an ample supply of water, as none is available en route or on the mesa top.

Whether you spend only a few hours or stay overnight on No Mans Mesa, its pristine landscape demands that you employ no-trace practices to the fullest extent. Avoid crushing fragile vegetation and the microbiotic soil crusts. Build no campfires, and keep the numbers of your group to a minimum. Very few people visit No Mans Mesa, and save for the old goat trail and a scattering of prehistoric artifacts, there is no evidence of human impact. Do your utmost to leave no trace of your passing.

From the Lick Wash Trailhead just off of the Skutumpah Road, follow the cavernous gorge of Lick Wash, passing through stretches of short but exciting narrows for 4 miles to the old 4WD road in Park Wash (see Hike 51). Then turn north, following the overgrown double track across the broad bench through fields of prickly Russian thistle (tumbleweed) and sagebrush. Calf Pasture Point, bounded by sweeping slickrock slopes and sheer cliffs of white Navajo Sandstone, looms 800 feet above on your left, and the fluted White Cliffs of No Mans Mesa define the eastern margin of the Park Wash valley.

Look to the northwest shoulder of No Mans Mesa, where you see an obvious tree-studded debris fan spreading out from the mesa rim to the valley floor. The goat trail ascends that rocky slope. The old doubletrack leads you up the spectacular cliff-bound valley, past a stock water tank, an old cabin used by the rancher who holds the grazing permit for the area, and then to a gate in a fenceline. Leave the gate open or closed, as you find it, then proceed ahead through a "forest" of tall sagebrush. The road is the only corridor through the brush until you reach the arroyo of Park Wash.

You can leave the road here, cross the wash, and ascend the broken bank of the arroyo to the bench above, then weave a way northeast through the sagebrush to the foot of the debris fan on No Mans Mesa, and ascend it until you find the goat trail.

The better route continues straight ahead. The road is likely to be washed out on the opposite side of the arroyo. Either scale the bank as mentioned above, then bushwhack for several yards to the northbound continuation of the road, or follow the sandy wash ahead for 0.2 mile, where the road crosses again. There you meet an eastbound 4WD track and turn right, following that doubletrack for 250 yards and skirting the northern base of a prominent gray cone studded with pinyons and junipers. Continue 100 yards east of the cone, then turn south-southeast, leaving the road, and ascend the north slopes of the debris fan on the flanks of No Mans Mesa. You ascend 100 feet in 0.2 mile via slopes of slickrock and sand to the center of the rocky slope, where you should locate the old goat trail.

The trail rises steeply via switchbacks that traverse loose rocks perched on the sandy slopes. You rise past large sandstone blocks during the final ascent to the apex of the debris fan at the foot of broken cliffs. There the trail begins to ascend very steeply over ledges of Navajo slickrock via a series of chutes and sandstone ribs. Care and attention are necessary to stay on course and to avoid a dangerous fall. Rocks are loose, and at times it is a hand-and-foot scramble, with precipitous chutes falling away at your feet. Don't expect to find cairns here to guide you. The route switches back and forth in unexpected directions, and as you proceed little evidence of a trail remains. Skilled routefinding, and a little luck, will keep you on course.

The route tops out immediately south of the north point of the mesa, where you pass through an old wire gate that held the goats on the mesa top. Suddenly the gentle terrain of No Mans Mesa unfolds before you, and at once you'll know the trip was well worth the effort. From the north point of the mesa the panoramic view stretches far across the wooded terraces of the Grand Staircase to the Pink Cliffs of the Paunsaugunt and Aquarius plateaus, defining the horizon with vivid, glowing color. Hikers familiar

The White Cliffs of the Grand Staircase.

with Bryce Canyon National Park will recognize Rainbow and Yovimpa points on the southern edge of the Paunsaugunt Plateau in the northwest.

Walk to the east rim of the mesa for an unobstructed view across miles of Navajo slickrock bounding the upper Paria River canyon, to the distant square-edged profile of the Kaiparowits Plateau, and on to the broad dome of Navajo Mountain. From the west rim, views open up into Park Wash and Calf Pasture Point, flanked by the dramatic White Cliffs.

Ponderosa pines dot the north point of the mesa and other places along the rim, yet most of the sandy mesa top, capped by the rocks of the Carmel Formation, is mantled in a pinyon-juniper woodland.

The mesa invites exploration, so allow plenty of extra time before carefully backtracking to the trailhead.

53 Mollies Nipple

General description:	A demanding all-day hike, for experienced hikers only, to the summit of the most outstanding landmark of the Grand Staircase, located within Grand Staircase–Escalante National Monument.
Distance:	10 miles round trip.
Difficulty:	Strenuous, Class 2 and 3 scrambling on ascent of Mollies Nipple, **including one 50-foot Class 4 pitch.**
Trail conditions:	Sandy 4WD road and cross-country scramble.
Trailhead access:	4WD advised due to soft sand.
Average hiking time:	6 to 7 hours round trip.
Trailhead elevation:	5,890 feet.
High point:	7,271 feet.
Elevation gain and loss:	+1,650 feet, -350 feet.
Optimum seasons:	April through May; September through October.
Water availability:	None available; bring your own.
Hazards:	Exposure to steep dropoffs.
Permits:	Not required.
Topo maps:	Deer Range Point USGS quad; BLM Kanab.

Key points

0.9 Junction with right-branching doubletrack; bear left.
4.0 Junction with northbound doubletrack on Pilot Ridge; turn left (north).
4.6 End of doubletrack at base of Mollies Nipple.
5.0 Summit of Mollies Nipple.

Finding the trailhead: Follow U.S. Highway 89 to milepost 37 and the junction with an unsigned, northbound graded road, 46 miles northwest of Page, Arizona, and 26.5 miles east of Kanab, Utah, and follow the road north.

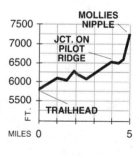

This usually good graded road leads north up the valley of Kitchen Corral Wash toward the Vermilion Cliffs. Ignore less-used spur roads en route and stay on the obvious main road. After 5.6 miles, you pass a cow camp and corrals, beyond which the road becomes occasionally sandy. The road crosses a wash after 8.4 miles (which is subject to washouts), and at 9.1 miles you pass through a gate (leave it open or closed, as you find it).

You reach a signed junction 10 miles from US 89, and bear right onto the road signed for Nipple Ranch, Mollies Nipple, and Starlight Ridge. Immediately beyond the junction you reach another gate (leave it open or closed, as you find it). Beyond the gate the road becomes quite sandy as it ascends a shallow draw. Drivers of low-clearance 2WD vehicles

Mollies Nipple

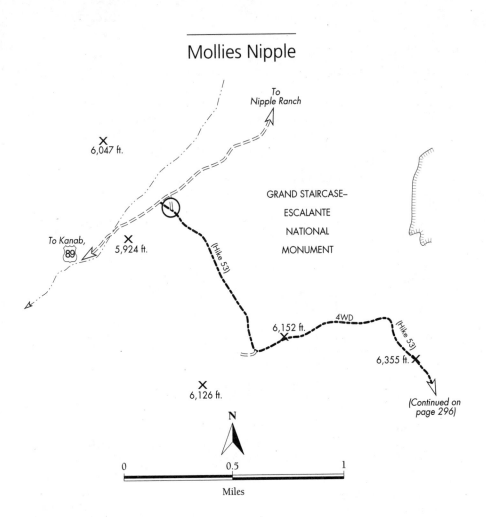

(Continued on page 296)

must maintain momentum through the areas of sand to avoid becoming stuck.

After driving 1.3 miles from the junction (11.3 miles from US 89), a sandy spur branches right (east). Turn right onto this double track and park after 100 yards, between a pair of obvious Kayenta Sandstone knobs. (Another road branches right off the main road a short distance ahead, but offers no parking places along its sandy course.)

Hikers arriving late in the day can camp in the undeveloped sites at the trailhead.

The hike: The Grand Staircase province of the Colorado Plateau displays a classic cliff and terrace landscape that is remarkably uniform, rising from the Arizona Strip to southern Utah's Pink Cliffs in a series of risers (cliffs) and steps (terraces).

Punctuating this uniform landscape, the landmark cone of Mollies Nipple is an anomaly, a mountain-like peak standing alone in a land of mesas, cliffs, and canyons. Composed of very resistant beds of Navajo Sandstone, Mollies Nipple has been eroded into a great cone that is one of the Colorado Plateau's most distinctive landmarks. This cone stands out in views from overlooks in Bryce Canyon National Park, and from US 89 between Kanab, Utah, and Page, Arizona.

From a distance Mollies Nipple may appear impossible to climb, but in fact there are routes to its summit that entail little more than hand-and-foot scrambling. There are several ways to approach this peak, and this hike follows the shortest, most straightforward route, via a sandy doubletrack that is passable only to motorcycles, 4WD OHVs, and hikers. Motorized recreationists seldom use the road, and you'll likely be undisturbed during your outing. The BLM considers this road a "way," and if the Paria–Hackberry Wilderness Study Area is designated wilderness, the way will be closed to motorized vehicles. The sandy track leads to the base of Mollies Nipple via Pilot Ridge, where experienced hikers will find an exhilarating 700-foot scramble to the top. The far-ranging vistas that unfold from the summit are unmatched from any viewpoint in the region.

Beginning on the sandy spur road between the pair of sandstone knobs, follow the doubletrack across open sagebrush flats, then steadily ascend into the pinyon-juniper woodland above, heading southeast. You crest a ridge after 0.9 mile, just west of Point 6152. Here the road describes a right angle bend, where you should avoid another road that branches right. The road ahead, often sandy, undulates over broad ridges, passing through picturesque woodlands of pinyon and juniper trees. The shrub cover of sagebrush, mormon tea, bitterbrush, horsebrush, and yucca is well developed on the gentle landscape. Along with the native bunchgrasses, Indian ricegrass and blue grama, the woodland vegetation helps stabilize the sandy slopes.

Occasional tree-framed views stretch over mesas to the White Cliffs in the west and north, where you will see the bold mass of No Mans Mesa and the domes of Deer Range Point. On the far horizon the Pink Cliffs glow with vivid color, and to the south, the gentle uplands of the Kaibab Plateau stretch to the horizon.

After 1.8 miles, shortly after topping out on Point 6355, a broad panorama unfolds from the ridge to the north and northeast, surpassed only by the vista from the summit of Mollies Nipple. South Swag is the flat brush-studded basin that spreads out below you. It stretches north to ephemeral Nipple Lake, often just a rich green meadow. John G. Kitchen established the Nipple Ranch adjacent to the lake in 1879, and the ranch is still in operation today. The peak was named after Kitchen's wife, Molly.

From Point 6355 the road descends to a broad saddle, where you begin a brief steep grade to the ridge overlooking Box Elder Canyon, a shallow drainage embraced by Navajo Sandstone cliffs. A steady ascent of this ridge ensues, leading northeast. The cone of Mollies Nipple looms boldly ahead, and it no longer appears to be the unattainable goal it seemed to be from a distance. You are close enough by now to begin visualizing possible routes to the summit.

Mollies Nipple

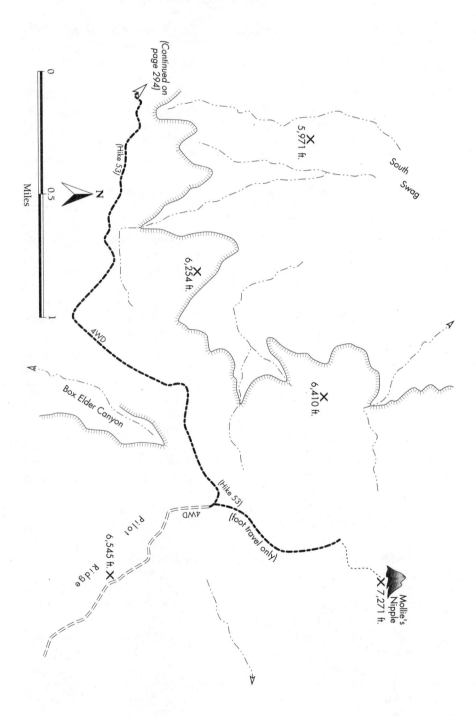

(Continued on page 294)

(Hike 53)

Miles

N

0

0.5

1

4WD

Box Elder Canyon

5,971 ft.

South Swag

6,254 ft.

6,410 ft.

(Hike 53)

4WD

(foot travel only)

Pilot Ridge

6,545 ft.

Mollie's Nipple
7,271 ft.

The landmark cone of Mollies Nipple punctuates the Grand Staircase.

Once you reach Pilot Ridge, the main road bends sharply south at a junction at 6,560 feet, 4 miles from the trailhead. Turn left onto the poor doubletrack, open to foot traffic only, at the junction and follow it north, first dropping into a saddle, then ascending a steep sandy grade to the road end on a sandy hill studded with ponderosa pines. Pause here and carefully scan the peak, searching out the best route. One possible way is outlined below.

From the road's end you can see two patches of white slickrock on the southwest slope of the peak. Stay on the right side of this slickrock and ascend the steep, manzanita-clad talus slope, sandy and littered with rusty sandstone slabs. After you reach a point above the two patches of slickrock, aim for a chute in the white sandstone (most of the cone and the summit are composed of an unusual, rusty red, iron rich Navajo Sandstone). You ascend the chute of lighter colored rock from the apex of the talus slope. Then you scramble over ledges, staying to the left of the chute until reaching the blocky summit ridge. There is a short Class 3 to Class 4 pitch of about 50 feet, with abundant ledges offering hand and foot holds. You should crest the summit ridge at its middle point. To stand on the true summit block, rising at the east end of the crest, requires advanced rock climbing skills.

From the summit ridge, the vistas that unfold are breathtaking, commensurate with the effort required to enjoy them. The Grand Staircase is revealed in profile, including its major features: the Vermilion Cliffs, White Cliffs, and the distant Pink Cliffs. All of the upper Paria River drainage is visible to the north and east, a landscape dominated by miles upon miles of Navajo slickrock. The Kaiparowits Plateau and Navajo Mountain are distinctive landmarks on the far eastern horizon. The Paria Plateau, the Kaibab Plateau, and lower Glen Canyon are notable features in the southward view.

After soaking in the tremendous vistas from Mollies Nipple, carefully retrace your route to the trailhead.

54 Paria Movie Set to Starlight Arch

General description:	This hike begins at the Paria Movie Set, where five plank buildings have provided the backdrop for films such as "The Outlaw Josie Wales," as well as episodes of the TV show "Gunsmoke" in the 1960s. This is a demanding day hike for experienced hikers only since it involves an ascent of the Verm ilion Cliffs to Starlight Arch.
Distance:	8.4 miles round trip.
Difficulty:	Strenuous, Class 2 and 3 scrambling while ascending the Vermilion Cliffs.
Trail conditions:	Wash route and cross-country scramble; good route-finding skills required.
Trailhead access:	Impassable when road is wet. 2WD access only when road is dry.
Average hiking time:	5 to 6 hours round trip.
Trailhead elevation:	4,760 feet.
High point:	6,216 feet.
Elevation gain and loss:	1,450 feet.
Optimum seasons:	April through May; September through October.
Water availability:	None available; bring your own.
Hazards:	Flash-flood danger; exposure to steep dropoffs; inexperienced hikers risk becoming disoriented or lost.
Permits:	Not required.
Topo maps:	Fivemile Valley and Calico Peak USGS quads; BLM Kanab.

Key points
0.9   Second drainage entering on the right; turn right into the wash.
3.0   Large cairn beneath Chinle dome; turn right (east) toward ridge.
3.9   Surmount the Vermilion Cliffs.
4.2   Starlight Arch.

Finding the trailhead: Follow U.S. Highway 89 to a northeast-bound dirt road prominently signed for "Historical Marker" and "Paria Movie Set-5." Find this turnoff 37.2 miles east of Kanab, Utah, and 0.2 mile east of milepost 31, or 39.3 miles northwest of Page, Arizona, and 0.8 mile west of milepost 30.

Immediately north of the highway is a large parking area and an historical marker offering a brief history of the settlement of the Pahreah townsite, now a ghost town with few signs of habitation remaining.

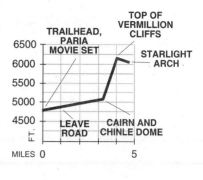

Drive northeast over the cattle guard and onto the good graded road, which is not recommended for RVs or trailers. The road is graveled in places, and invariably has a washboard surface. Do not attempt to drive this road when wet, at which time its slippery clay surface can become dangerous if not impassable.

Enter Grand Staircase–Escalante National Monument after 0.9 mile, and as you continue, Starlight Arch becomes visible on the northern skyline, and you can begin to visualize a route through the Vermilion Cliffs to the arch.

One of the greatest exposures on the Colorado Plateau of the colorful Chinle Formation comes into view as the road begins a steady descent toward the badlands surrounding the movie set. After 4.7 miles, as you enter the movie set, avoid an often-washed out road that branches left and descends to a wash crossing. Continue straight ahead among the plank buildings of the movie set for another 0.1 mile to the center of "town," where you meet a westbound road leading into a side canyon.

Barring severe flood damage, cars can usually make the drive to the movie set. Unless you are driving a high-clearance 4WD vehicle, park in one of several spots about 0.1 mile down the spur road west of the movie set. BLM rangers ask that hikers avoid parking at the movie set, since parked cars ruin the mood for other visitors. The extent of flood damage will determine how far west of the movie set 4WD vehicles can proceed. West of the movie set, the road crosses the wash four times in 0.7 mile to the first north-trending arroyo, where the road is often washed out.

There is a small, no-fee walk-in campground adjacent to the movie set, with tables, fire grills, and pit toilets, but no water.

The hike: The route begins on a usually washed-out dirt road, then follows a narrow, sinuous drainage to the foot of the Vermilion Cliffs. There hikers ascend steep talus slopes, surmounting the cliffs on the rim of a wooded mesa, which is followed to the foot of the skyline arch.

The aperture of Starlight Arch is visible from US 89 and briefly en route to the movie set as a pinpoint of light near the top of a cluster of Navajo Sandstone domes atop the Vermilion Cliffs. It seems a far away, nigh unreachable goal, and those who complete this demanding hike gain a well-earned sense of accomplishment. Only hikers with determination, experience, and good route-finding skills should attempt this trip.

Since the spur road leading west from the movie set receives minimal maintenance and is usually washed out, park in the pullouts about 0.1 to 0.2 mile down that side road and begin hiking there. The unnamed wash

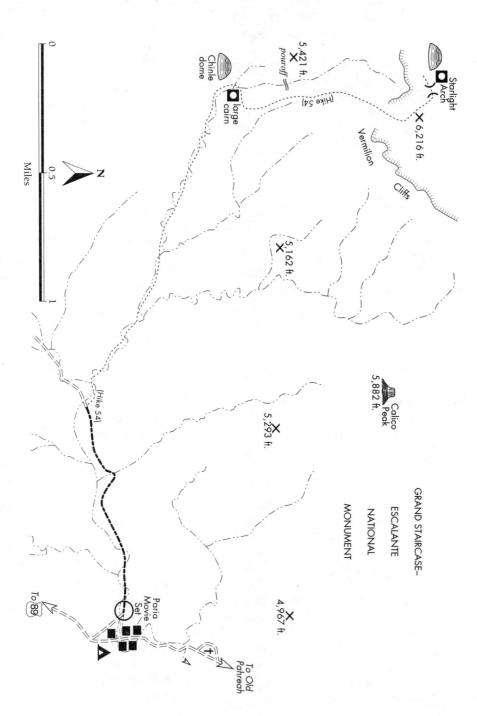

that the spur road follows is very scenic, flanked by low, thinly layered cliffs and slopes composed of the red rocks of the Moenkopi Formation. The road crosses the wash five times ahead, and at the fourth crossing you pass through a gate (leave it as you find it), then curve into a northwest-trending side drainage where the road is likely to be severed by a deep arroyo.

At the fifth crossing of the main wash 1 mile from the movie set, tamarisk fringes the wash and you'll see a pair of BLM Wilderness Study Area signs on either side of the wash. Leave the road here at 4,820 feet and turn right, dropping into the wash. Follow it ahead for 0.1 mile around the first bend, where a shallow side drainage joins on the right. Turn west into this drainage and follow the narrow, usually dry wash up-canyon between low, reddish brown and green walls of sculpted Moenkopi rocks.

After hiking about 0.3 mile up this side canyon, your way is blocked by a rock jam, which can be easily bypassed on the left side. Notice the thin white layers of gypsum and the sparkling veneer of mica exposed on the slabs in the rock jam. Immediately beyond the slide, the first of many side drainages enters on the right (north). Bear left here, staying in the larger wash.

In these intricately dissected hills there is a maze of small drainages, and staying in the correct wash is probably the most challenging part of the hike. You want to stay in the deepest drainage; the wash itself is quite small and narrow. Your route follows the southernmost drainage on the Calico Peak USGS quad, leading northwest through the lower half of Sections 14 and 15.

Starlight Arch.

The most confusing confluence of drainages is found 0.7 mile from the road. Here a Moenkopi fin projects into the drainage, separating two washes of equal size and similar appearance. Stay left at that juncture and curve around the fin beneath overhanging walls. After avoiding several more lesser drainages branching right and left, you begin approaching the upper layers of the Moenkopi Formation, eroded into badlands hills nearly devoid of vegetation. The wash, in contrast, supports a variety of shrubs because run-off is concentrated in the sheltered drainage.

The drainage begins to open up when the colorful red, gray, and lavender beds of the Chinle Formation appear just above, with a backdrop of the soaring Vermilion Cliffs. The wash bends to the north and you skirt the eastern base of a colorful, barren Chinle dome, rising 150 feet above on your left. Here you have your first good look at the Vermilion Cliffs. Straight ahead to the north you see a prominent cluster of Navajo Sandstone domes crowning the cliffs. Just to the right (east) of those domes is a break in the Vermilion Cliffs—a long, steep talus slope studded with pinyon and juniper. Your route ahead ascends that slope to the top of the cliffs.

Just beyond the Chinle dome, at 5,100 feet and 3.1 miles from the movie set, the wash forks again. A large cairn just east of the fork is an old uranium claim marker dating back to the 1950s. Do not continue up the right fork of the wash, since it is soon blocked by a pouroff. The cairn is your signal to leave the wash and carefully pick your way east up a 150-foot talus slope to the crest of a minor ridge. Then turn north and follow the ridge gradually uphill, aiming for the break in the Vermilion Cliffs a short distance ahead.

A dramatic, colorful panorama unfolds from the ridge, stretching east across the vast Chinle and Moenkopi badlands to The Cockscomb and the west rim of the Kaiparowits Plateau. Starlight Arch can be seen piercing the Navajo domes atop the Vermilion Cliffs to the north.

En route up the ridge, you will pass another large cairn, and just behind it you find a 1916 U.S. General Land Office survey marker. The ridge soon becomes less distinct as it is dissected by numerous minor drainages. The route ahead is up to the individual, and most hikers will probably aim for a prominent white Navajo Sandstone knob that appears to lie on the rim above to the northeast. There is a semblance of a hiker-developed path in places leading up the talus slope of the Vermilion Cliffs. However, you may not find it and you should not expect to be following a trail.

The slope is littered with unstable slabs, and you must exercise care as you pick your way up the steep slope, staying left of the aforementioned Navajo knob. En route the view of the Vermilion Cliffs is superb, exposed in profile and marching off toward the west. Once you reach the knob, scale the final ledges of slickrock to gain the mesa top, then follow its wooded, gently rolling surface, rising up and over Point 6216 to the northwest edge of the mesa. Excellent vistas from this lofty vantage reach into the upper Paria River's broad flood plain in the canyon far below, across miles of Navajo slickrock within the Paria–Hackberry Wilderness Study Area, to Deer Range Point, No Mans Mesa, and to the distant Pink Cliffs.

The slickrock domes seen from below now loom above to the west, separated from the mesa by a shallow wooded bowl. Descend about 50 feet from the mesa down to a minor saddle and enter the bowl, crossing to its west side. From there you must scale slickrock ledges to gain a view of the arch. Its opening is rather small, approximately 30 feet between abutments and 20 feet high, piercing the top of a thick Navajo dome.

After enjoying this remote, peaceful locale high atop the Vermilion Cliffs, carefully retrace your route to the trailhead.

55 Wire Pass to Buckskin Gulch

General description:	A short but exciting day hike through the very tight narrows of Wire Pass, located in the Paria Canyon–Vermilion Cliffs Wilderness.
Distance:	3.4 miles round trip.
Difficulty:	Easy.
Trail conditions:	Wash route.
Trailhead access:	4WD advised when the road is wet.
Average hiking time:	1.5 to 2 hours round trip.
Trailhead elevation:	4,880 feet.
Low point:	4,700 feet.
Elevation loss and gain:	180 feet.
Optimum season:	April through early June; September through October.
Water availability:	None available; bring your own.
Hazards:	Flash-flood danger.
Permits:	Reservations for permits for overnight use required; day hikers must pay the appropriate fee ($5 per person and dog per day) at the trailhead register/self-service fee station. No fees required for children 12 and under.
Topo maps:	Pine Hollow Canyon (Utah-Arizona) USGS quad; BLM: Paria Canyon–Vermilion Cliffs Wilderness map, Hiker's Guide to Paria Canyon, or Kanab.

Key points
1.2   Narrows begin.
1.7   Confluence with Buckskin Gulch.

Finding the trailhead: Follow U.S. Highway 89 to an unsigned, southbound dirt road that branches off the highway at the west end of a "50 mph" right-angle curve just west of The Cockscomb. Find the turnoff 0.8 mile west of milepost 25, and 34 miles northwest of Page, Arizona, or 0.2 mile south of milepost 26, and 37.5 miles east of Kanab, Utah.

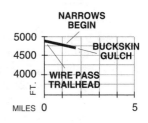

Wire Pass to Buckskin Gulch

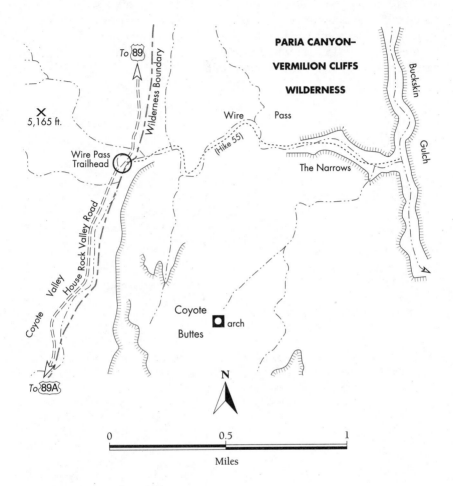

To 89

X
5,165 ft.

Wire Pass
Trailhead

Wilderness Boundary

PARIA CANYON–

VERMILION CLIFFS

WILDERNESS

Wire   Pass

(Hike 55)

The Narrows

Buckskin

Gulch

House Rock Valley Road

Coyote   Valley

Coyote

Buttes

arch

To 89A

N

0   0.5   1

Miles

This dirt road (known as the House Rock Valley Road) is passable to cars in dry weather barring severe runoff damage, and steadily ascends for 2.5 miles to a saddle separating The Cockscomb and Buckskin Mountain. Ignore the right fork to Fivemile Mountain at the saddle, then descend to a crossing of the Buckskin Gulch wash after 4.4 miles, where the road is subject to flood damage. The signed turnoff to Buckskin Gulch Trailhead (located 0.2 mile east of the road), which you avoid, is located a short distance south of the wash.

You reach the spacious Wire Pass Trailhead, located on the west side of the road, 8.4 miles south of US 89. Several undeveloped camping areas can be found en route to the trailhead. Pit toilets are in place at both the Buckskin Gulch and Wire Pass trailheads.

Wire Pass.

The hike: Buckskin Gulch is the ultimate in canyon country slot canyons. For 12.5 miles, the gulch is enveloped in a very narrow gorge 100 to 200 feet deep, flanked by vaulting, convoluted walls of Navajo Sandstone. Buckskin Gulch is renowned not only because of its continuous, challenging narrows, but also because there is no other canyon like it in the world.

Wire Pass, a gorge carved through The Cockscomb by Coyote Wash, is the most popular entry route into Buckskin Gulch. Wire Pass is short, but its narrows are even more confined than those in Buckskin. This is an excellent, easy hike through Wire Pass into the famous gorge of Buckskin Gulch. You can extend the day hike as far as you wish by exploring Buckskin's narrows either up-canyon or down.

As in any slot canyon, do not enter Wire Pass or Buckskin Gulch if there is the slightest chance of rainfall. In these canyons, as little as one-quarter inch of rain can run off the slickrock landscape and turn the slots into inescapable death traps. Save this memorable trip for fair weather only.

From the Wire Pass Trailhead, cross the road and follow the well-worn trail to the trailhead register and fee station. The trail ahead is well-signed and sandy as it leads to a hiker's maze in a fenceline. The maze is a V-shaped passage that allows people, but not cows, to enter Wire Pass. Here Coyote Wash carves the portal to Wire Pass through The Cockscomb, where tilted red-tinted beds of Navajo Sandstone flank the wash.

Beyond the hiker's maze, signs direct you into the wash, a wide, sandy, and cobble-strewn avenue where the walking is easy and there are few obstacles to slow you down. Be aware, however, that hiking conditions can change with the passage of each flash flood. Always check current hiking conditions at the Paria Contact Station on US 89 before entering the canyon.

As you proceed, you gain views of the serrated crest of the Coyote Buttes rising to the south, and ahead, the massive Navajo Sandstone cliffs of The Dive, where gaping alcoves have been scooped out of the walls, dominate the view. Benches flank the broad wash and support a scattering of junipers, sand sagebrush, mormon tea, and squawbush. Rabbitbrush fringes the wash banks, sharing space with apache plume, recognizable by its myriad white, rose-like blooms and feathery fruits.

Wire Pass remains wide and shallow for 1.2 miles, bounded by low slickrock bluffs and sandy slopes. The slopes north of the wash are mantled in a veneer of white rocks and cobbles of the Kaibab Limestone washed down over the ages from the slopes of broad Buckskin Mountain to the west.

Eventually, slickrock walls close in and the wash becomes rock-strewn. Soon thereafter, at 1.2 miles, you enter the first short stretch of narrows. Beyond the confines of this constriction, you are soon swallowed up in another, very narrow slot where only 4 feet separate the canyon walls. Logs wedged between the tight, convoluted cliffs overhead are mute reminders of the tremendous force of flash floods in narrow desert canyons.

The third narrows are the deepest and most confining of all, pinching down to merely 2 feet wide in places. After exiting this final slot, you skirt a deep and shadowed alcove, then emerge into the boulder-littered wash of Buckskin Gulch. Down-canyon the walls quickly close in and Buckskin slots up. Though not as tight as Wire Pass, the gulch is still very narrow and stays that way for many miles ahead. Interesting narrows are located up-canyon as well.

When you've had enough of being swallowed up deep within this confined gorge, backtrack to more open country and the trailhead.

56 Wire Pass Trailhead to White House Trailhead via Buckskin Gulch and the Paria River

General description:	A memorable and justifiably popular point-to-point backpack, recommended for experienced hikers only, that leads through the world-famous narrows of Buckskin Gulch and Paria Canyon, located within the Paria Canyon–Vermilion Cliffs Wilderness.
Distance:	20.3 miles, shuttle trip.
Difficulty:	Moderately strenuous, one 15- to 18-foot Class 4 downclimb at 11.5 miles. (A rope is necessary to lower packs.)
Trail conditions:	Narrow wash route.
Trailhead access:	4WD advised when the road is wet.
Average hiking time:	2 days.
Trailhead elevations:	4,880 feet (Wire Pass Trailhead); 4,280 feet (White House Trailhead).
Low point:	4,180 feet.
Elevation loss and gain:	-700 feet, + 100 feet.
Optimum seasons:	April through June; September through October.
Water availability:	In Buckskin Gulch beginning at 12.5 miles; and springs 3 miles below confluence with Paria River.
Hazards:	Flash-flood danger; possible wading and/or swimming of deep, stagnant pools in Buckskin Gulch; exposure to steep dropoffs at the boulder jam in lower Buckskin; considerable wading in Paria Canyon.
Permits:	Reservations for permits for overnight use required.
Topo maps:	Pine Hollow Canyon, West Clark Bench, and Bridger Point (all Utah-Arizona) USGS quads; BLM: Paria Canyon–Vermilion Cliffs Wilderness map, Hiker's Guide to Paria Canyon, or Kanab and Smoky Mountain.

Key points
- 1.7   Confluence with Buckskin Gulch.
- 8.0   Middle Route joins from the northwest.
- 11.5   Boulder jam.
- 13.0   Confluence with Paria River; turn left (up-canyon).
- 16.3   Upper end of narrows.
- 17.8   Pass beneath power lines.
- 20.3   White House Trailhead

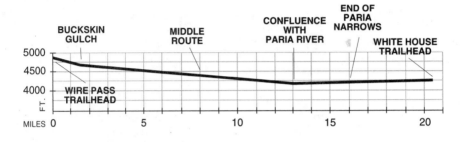

Finding the trailhead: Follow driving directions for Hike 55 to reach the Wire Pass Trailhead.

To reach the White House Trailhead, turn south off of U.S. Highway 89 between mileposts 20 and 21, where signs point to "Paria Canyon–Vermilion Cliffs Wilderness, Information and Trailhead." This turnoff is located 29.4 miles northwest of Page, Arizona, and 42.5 miles east of Kanab, Utah.

The kiosk and self-service fee station is located 0.1 mile south of the highway. Updated weather and hiking conditions are posted here; day hikers can pay backcountry fees, and overnight visitors can pay fees for the White House Campground. The Paria Contact Station is located 200 yards away atop the hill via the right-branching spur road.

To reach the White House Trailhead, bear left at the kiosk and follow the rocky, washboard road as it gradually descends for 2 miles to the trailhead parking area adjacent to the walk-in White House Campground.

The hike: Buckskin Gulch is the ultimate in slot canyons, being longer and more consistently narrow than any other canyon in the world. Nearly one thousand hikers from across the nation and around the globe visit Buckskin each year. A backpack, or even a day hike, in Buckskin Gulch is a truly memorable adventure, but the trip should not be taken lightly. Only experienced canyoneers who are well prepared and equipped for an extended trip through a slot canyon should attempt Buckskin. Tight narrows are uninterrupted for 15 miles on this hike, so if you don't like confined spaces, choose another trip instead.

There is no drinking water available until you reach the lower end of Buckskin Gulch near the confluence with the Paria River, making this a rigorous dry hike of 12.5 miles. There are also no safe places to camp until the 12.5 mile point, and flash flood danger is extreme, with few safe exits to higher ground. The dry wash is rocky and cobble-strewn, and there is a

308

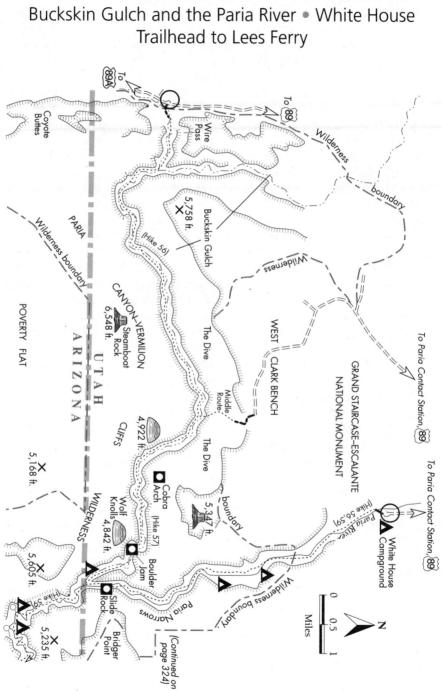

(Continued on page 324)

good possibility of encountering pools of stagnant water that at certain times may be deep enough to require a swim.

Unless you exit the gulch at the Middle Route (see Hike 58), 8.0 miles from the trailhead, and camp on the bench above the gulch (provided you packed in an ample water supply), plan on an all-day hike to the campsites near the confluence with the Paria River at 12.5 miles. There are also sites about 0.5 mile below the confluence in Paria Canyon. Yet these are popular sites, and there is a possibility they will be occupied when you arrive. Thus you will have to continue either up or down Paria Canyon in search of a campsite. That makes for a long, strenuous all-day hike, so an early start is essential. In fair weather only, when you are certain no rain will fall anywhere in the Buckskin Gulch drainage, you can find campsites along the wash in Buckskin, but in an unexpected flood event such sites can be deadly.

Don't ignore flash flood warnings or the serious danger floods represent. Anyone who has witnessed a cloudburst in this rockbound country will testify that as little as 0.25- to 0.5-inch of rain will quickly run off of the rocky landscape and gather in drainages, and hikers will have little warning or time to escape floodwaters in a canyon like Buckskin. Buckskin Gulch drains a large area, and to better understand the BLM's admonition that rainfall miles away can send a wall of water down the canyon, you must first grasp the enormous extent of this drainage. Buckskin Gulch gathers runoff from several tributaries that begin in the Pink Cliffs of Bryce Canyon National Park, some 30 miles from the Wire Pass Trailhead. Deer Range Canyon, Park Wash, Lower Podunk Creek, Lick Wash, and Deer Springs Wash all coalesce in Kitchen Corral Wash, near US 89 and Mollies Nipple. South of US 89, Kitchen Corral Wash becomes Buckskin Gulch, but is shown on old maps as Kaibab Gulch. These canyons drain a significant portion of the Grand Staircase, so indeed, heavy rainfall over the Pink Cliffs or any one of the tributary canyons can result in flooding, even when blue skies dominate over Buckskin Gulch.

Before leaving home for a hike in Buckskin Gulch (or Paria Canyon), telephone the BLM office in Kanab for a recorded menu of information. Frequently updated information on hiking conditions will enable you to plan and be prepared for whatever obstacles await. Conditions are never static in Buckskin Gulch and Paria Canyon. The sun rarely shines in the bottom of the gulch, and its upper half is well-known for its cold pools of stagnant water in some years, which don't readily evaporate. The size and location of pools can change with each passing flood; some may be filled in with sediment, others created, and still others scoured out and deepened. It is impossible to determine the depth of these muddy pools until you step in. A walking staff is recommended to probe the depth of pools and to maintain your balance amid the rocks and possible mud in the gulch. If reports indicate that swimming some pools will be necessary, a useful piece of equipment is a small, inflated inner tube to float your pack across. Since you will likely be wading for several miles from lower Buckskin Gulch to the White House Trailhead, also pack along a pair of sturdy wading shoes.

310

Buckskin Gulch.

A permanent obstacle in the gulch is a boulder jam at 11.5 miles, which requires a 15- to 18-foot Class 4 downclimb. A rope is essential for lowering packs there. A 15.3-mile car shuttle is necessary for this point-to-point trip. Don't plan on hitchhiking back to the Wire Pass Trailhead, since it is very unlikely you will catch a ride. And finally, undertake this hike only if you have a weather forecast predicting dry conditions for the duration of your trip.

From the Wire Pass Trailhead (see Hike 55), stroll across the road to the trailhead register and self-service fee station, and if day hiking pay the appropriate fee ($5 per person per day) before proceeding. After entering Coyote Wash just beyond a hiker's maze, follow the wash through Wire Pass for 1.7 miles through three sections of extremely tight narrows to the confluence with Buckskin Gulch. Here, seemingly deep within the bowels of the earth, you are swallowed by slickrock cliffs, and you will see little sky or sunshine for the following 15 miles.

Upon reaching an atypically wide portion of Buckskin Gulch at 1.7 miles, follow the wide, boulder-strewn wash to the right, down-canyon. Quite soon the canyon walls close in and Buckskin slots up. The wash is littered with rocks and boulders, and following a period of rainy weather you may quickly begin to encounter stagnant pools. There are no route-finding problems in the gulch. Simply follow the narrow stone hallway ahead. The sculpted walls of Navajo Sandstone, convoluted and often overhanging, seem to nearly touch overhead. The gulch is a seemingly endless stone corridor sliced into the crust of the earth, averaging only about 12 to 15 feet wide. In places barely 3 feet separate the canyon walls, while in other places the slot opens up to as much as 25 to 30 feet, still no place to be if you are claustrophobic.

One such wide place is where the Middle Route exits to the north at 8 miles, though if you're not looking for its sandy slickrock crack, you'll probably pass it by. Although the canyon walls average only 100 to 200 feet high, the narrow confines of the gulch make it feel much deeper. Much of the wash is barren of vegetation, though in more open stretches a scattering of shrubs dot the sandy banks of the wash and the broken cliffs above.

After 11.5 miles, a short distance below a prominent right-angle bend in the wash from south to east, you reach the boulder jam. There are at least two possible routes through this obstacle, and on one route hand and footholds have been carved into one of the boulders to aid the descent. Expect a 15- to 18-foot Class 4 downclimb here, and a rope is essential to lower packs. Sometimes well-intentioned hikers leave ropes behind at the boulder jam, but you are advised to avoid using them since their integrity is uncertain. The ranger routinely removes these ropes each time he passes.

The canyon walls grow higher below the boulder jam, and as you approach the confluence, great cliffs of Navajo Sandstone rise 300 to 500 feet overhead, elevating Buckskin from a "gulch" to true canyon status. After 12.5 miles, sandy benches appear above the wash, offering the first suitable campsites so far. These sites are popular, so expect to have company if you're too exhausted to continue. Seepage in the wash here gives life to a perennial stream that flows down to the river, 0.5 mile ahead. Whether you camp in Buckskin or not, fill your water bottles from this stream for the hike out to White House Trailhead. The Paria River, which is always turbid and carries a high mineral content, should only be used for drinking in an emergency and is the only source of water ahead. Above the confluence with Buckskin Gulch, the river might be dry during May and June when upstream irrigators divert much of the water onto their hay fields.

From the confluence at 13 miles, turn left (north) and follow the equally narrow Paria Canyon (see Hike 59) for 3 miles upstream through the Paria Narrows. After 0.6 mile, the river is sometimes funneled beneath Slide Rock, a huge slump block fallen from the canyon wall. You can pass through it or go around it. If the river is flowing, you'll be wading in ankle-deep to shin-deep water for much of the way through the Paria Narrows. After 3 miles the canyon begins to open up, with sandy benches flanking the wash on either side. At 3.5 miles camping is possible on the bench east of the wash, though there is no shade. Another campsite, located in the partial shade of a few cottonwoods, is found 4.3 miles from the confluence, on the right (northeast) side of the wash.

The remaining 3 miles to the White House Trailhead follow sandy benches between frequent river crossings. A pair of high-voltage power lines spanning the canyon announces your approach to civilization, and from there it is only 2.5 miles to the trailhead. Look for signs indicating the point where you leave the river bed, and then follow the sandy trail a short distance east to the trailhead parking area.

Cobra Arch lies on the rim above Buckskin Gulch.

57 Middle Route Trailhead to Cobra Arch

General description:	A cross-country day hike, recommended for experienced hikers only, leading to a unique arch high above Buckskin Gulch in the Paria Canyon-Vermilion Cliffs Wilderness.
Distance:	6.6 miles round trip.
Difficulty:	Moderate, occasional Class 2 scrambling.
Trail conditions:	Cross-country route; good route-finding ability required.
Trailhead access:	4WD required due to extensive areas of soft sand.
Average hiking time:	4 to 5 hours round trip.
Trailhead elevation:	4,960 feet.
Low point:	4,680 feet.
Elevation gain and loss:	+300 feet, -650 feet.
Optimum season:	Mid-March through May; September through October.
Water availability:	None available; bring your own.
Hazards:	Exposure to steep dropoffs; inexperienced hikers risk becoming disoriented or lost.
Permits:	Not required.
Topo maps:	West Clark Bench (Utah-Arizona) USGS quad; BLM: Paria Canyon–Vermilion Cliffs Wilderness map, or Smoky Mountain.

Key points

0.2 Reach the rim of The Dive.
1.9 Descend from rim of The Dive.
3.3 Cobra Arch.

Finding the trailhead: The unsigned Long Canyon Road leading to West Clark Bench, branching south from U.S. Highway 89, is the first southbound road you reach 0.2 mile west of the Paria River bridge, between mileposts 21 and 22. Find the turnoff 0.6 mile west of the turnoff to the Paria Contact Station, and 30 miles northwest of Page, Arizona, or 42 miles east of Kanab, Utah.

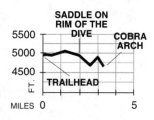

After finding the turnoff, proceed south on Long Canyon Road. Due to deep sand, minimal maintenance, and possible flood damage, a 4WD vehicle is recommended and may be required to reach the trailhead. Do not attempt to drive to the trailhead in a low-clearance car. This road is a public road through private property for 0.9 mile. Shortly after leaving the highway you pass the landmark teepees of the Paria River Guest Ranch, and reach the first of five cattle guards after 0.25 mile. After passing over the fourth cattle guard you enter public lands and soon thereafter reach the first sandy crossing of Long Canyon wash, which is subject to washouts, 1.1 miles from the highway.

The road ahead, which can be slippery if not impassable when wet, ascends the shallow drainage of Long Canyon. You pass over the fifth and final cattle guard after 2.5 miles, and cross the wash one last time at 3.1 miles. After the road tops out on the broad sandy plateau of West Clark Bench at 4.2 miles, you pass the first of several right-branching roads, and you bear left at all but one junction ahead. This point is generally the end of maintenance on this road, so expect challenging driving conditions ahead.

As you continue along the sandy track, bear right at 5.1 miles where a faint track branches left (north). After 7.8 miles you reach a green steel gate. Park next to the large solitary juniper just beyond the gate or in one of the pullouts, where you can also camp, about 0.1 mile west of the gate.

The hike: The hike to aptly-named Cobra Arch is a rewarding day trip for hikers with good route-finding ability. The route follows the rim of The Dive, high above the nearly invisible slot of Buckskin Gulch. Vistas en route are part of this trip's attraction, stretching across the vast, sandy surface of the Paria Plateau, punctuated by such slickrock landmarks as the Coyote Buttes, Steamboat Rock, and Wolf Knolls. True to its name, Cobra Arch is reminiscent of an ancient stone sculpture of a serpent's head.

Only hikers entering the canyons of the Paria Canyon–Vermilion Cliffs Wilderness are required to obtain a permit and pay a fee. Hikers en route to Cobra Arch not only enjoy a fee-free hike, they also enjoy the freedom of open spaces far above the shadowed confines of the narrow canyons.

Avoid this shadeless hike during the summer heat from about mid-May through mid-September, and be sure to carry plenty of water. The USGS West Clark Bench quad is highly recommended.

From the gate at the trailhead, follow a sandy old 4WD doubletrack south along the fenceline. You rise gradually at first, then descend past the posted wilderness boundary to the juniper-studded rim of The Dive, 0.2 mile from the trailhead. Buckskin Gulch lies far below, but its narrow gorge is hidden from view by its tight canyon walls. Prominent features on the sandy, tree-studded Paria Plateau to the south include the red slickrock butte of Steamboat Rock and the craggy Coyote Buttes to the southwest.

Now on a firm tread of slickrock at the rim, follow the rim east around the head of the first drainage, then south out to Point 5047. The walking is easier closer to the sandstone rim rather than along the sandy mesa top. As you proceed views open up to the northwest and north, reaching to the pyramid of Mollies Nipple and to the distant Pink Cliffs of the Aquarius Plateau.

When you reach Point 5047, you have a much better view of the gash of Buckskin Gulch. Your route ahead also comes into focus. The west-facing Navajo cliffs bounding Point 5119 are clearly visible about a mile away to the southeast. Your route will follow the sandy bench below, leading south along the base of those cliffs to the 4,800-foot flat beneath Point 5119. To get

Middle Route Trailhead to Cobra Arch • Middle Route
to Buckskin Gulch

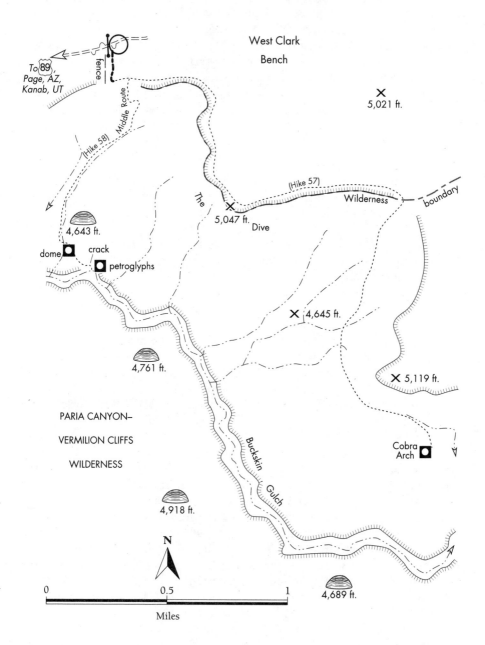

there, continue along the rim, heading east from Point 5047, enjoying expansive vistas along the way. Junipers dot the mesa of West Clark Bench, sharing space with wavy-leaf, or Harriman, oaks, a kind of scrub oak common in sandy locations, and mormon tea, snakeweed, and the silvery mounds of roundleaf buffaloberry.

Pay attention to where the rim begins to curve southeast, at the head of a drainage. About 100 yards beyond the bend from east to southeast, there is but one break in the Carmel sandstone on the rim. A solitary, twisted juniper lies just below the break. Descend off the rim here over the crumbly sandstone, then mount the red Page Sandstone, where you find a 3-foot ledge. Just below the ledge you reach the Navajo Sandstone in the headwaters draw of the drainage and descend a 30-foot slickrock friction pitch down a shallow chute. Pause along the way and memorize your descent route so you can easily find it upon returning.

The route ahead leads generally south across the sandy bench, and you work your way in and out of numerous small washes that dissect the bench. The route traverses deep, soft sand for 1 mile, but if you hug the base of the cliffs as best you can, you'll be walking on slickrock part of the time.

There is no avoiding the last, and steepest, sand hill, as you round the point and mount the aforementioned 4,800-foot flat beneath Point 5119. When you reach the flat, which would make an excellent place to camp for backpackers who don't mind carrying water, follow along the foot of the Navajo Sandstone cliff, its cross-bedded slickrock stained a salmon hue by the overlying red beds of the Page Sandstone. Head southeast along the

True to its name, Cobra Arch looks like an ancient stone sculpture of a cobra's head.

cliffs into a developing draw. About 0.2 mile down this draw you'll see a mass of low, red slickrock domes off to your right (south). When you reach a low pouroff in the draw turn south, descending several short slickrock friction pitches among the domes, heading for the presently visible arch at the southeast end of the dome complex.

The arch is small but unique, a graceful ribbon of stone that is wide and flat at the top of the span, resembling the hood of a cobra's head. Indentations on either side are the "eyes" of the serpent.

After enjoying this very remote and unusual arch, carefully retrace your route to the trailhead.

58 Middle Route to Buckskin Gulch

See Map on Page 316

General description:	A challenging route, recommended only for experienced hikers with no fear of heights and exposure, offering a shortcut for backpackers hiking into Buckskin Gulch, located within the Paria Canyon–Vermilion Cliffs Wilderness.
Distance:	1.4 miles one way.
Difficulty:	Strenuous, Class 3 and 4 downclimbing to enter Buckskin Gulch; ropes to lower packs are essential.
Trail conditions:	Cross-country and wash route; good route-finding ability required.
Trailhead access:	4WD required due to extensive areas of soft sand.
Average hiking time:	1.5 hours one way.
Trailhead elevation:	4,960 feet.
Low point:	4,320 feet.
Elevation loss:	650 feet.
Optimum season:	April through June; September through October.
Water availability:	None available; bring your own.
Hazards:	Exposure to steep dropoffs; very steep slickrock friction pitches, and loose sand on rock ledges; flash-flood danger in Buckskin Gulch.
Permits:	Reservations for permits for overnight use required; day hikers must pay the appropriate fee ($5 per person and dog per day) at kiosk/self-service fee station located below the Paria Contact Station (see driving directions for Hike 56). No fees are required for children 12 and under.
Topo maps:	West Clark Bench and Bridger Point (both Utah-Arizona) USGS quads; BLM: Paria Canyon–Vermilion Cliffs Wilderness map, or Smoky Mountain.

Key points
  0.2   Reach the rim of The Dive.
  1.25 Crack at the top of the final descent into Buckskin Gulch.
  1.4   Buckskin Gulch.

Finding the trailhead: Follow driving directions for Hike 57.

The hike: The Middle Route offers a short, no-nonsense approach to the lower reaches of Buckskin Gulch. For backpackers hiking through Paria Canyon to Lees Ferry, or out to the White House Trailhead, this route shaves about one hiking day off the trip, yet still leaves 5.5 miles of

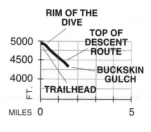

Buckskin's famous narrows to be traversed. This approach also avoids most, but probably not all, of Buckskin's stagnant pools (see Hike 56).

Like any other slot canyon hike, don't consider this trip if rain is even a remote possibility. Once you reach Buckskin Gulch, there is no safe high ground for many miles.

Experienced canyoneers will find the route to be simple and straightforward down to the rim of Buckskin Gulch. From there the route plunges down a sandy slickrock crack, where one misstep could be your last. A healthy respect for steep dropoffs and experience descending very steep slickrock with a backpack are necessary to negotiate the descent route safely. Be sure to pack along a 50-foot length of rope or nylon cord since you will be forced to lower packs en route. A rope will also be necessary to lower packs over the boulder jam in Buckskin 3.5 miles below the Middle Route.

Before taking this trip, hikers are advised to visit the Paria Contact Station off of US 89, where you can view a video of the Middle Route, giving you an idea of what you are getting into. You'll want to stop there anyway to obtain last minute information on weather and hiking conditions.

From the green steel gate at the trailhead, follow the sandy old 4WD double-track along the fenceline, at once passing a sign that warns of the hazardous route ahead, in this case hazardous being an understatement of the route's dangers and difficulty. You rise gradually at first, then descend past the posted wilderness boundary to the sandstone rim of The Dive at 4,960 feet. Turn left (east) and follow the rim for about 50 yards. There you find a break in the low Carmel Formation cliff, where you scramble down and friction walk over slickrock to the red bench just below.

Pause here and take note of the landmarks on the broad bench below to help you stay on track ahead. Two washes cut across the bench, winding among a scattering of slickrock domes to the rim of Buckskin Gulch's gorge. The left or easternmost wash is the one you must follow. Near the rim of the gulch in the lower reaches of that wash is a low dome that stands out among the others with its flat crown. Stay in visual contact with that dome as you proceed.

From the red rock bench briefly descend the loose rock of a gully southwest for several yards to the top of the Navajo Sandstone. There you will

319

find a narrow boot-worn path clinging to the edge of the Navajo cliffs as it curves first south, then east, below the point of the bench. Where the path ends you will find a break in the Navajo cliff, and a steep friction descent then leads onto the sandy bench below. The first part of the descent is simply steep and covered with marble-like gravel. The second part is extremely steep. Look for a minor crack running off to the left that will provide better footing.

Once on the bench, follow the soft sand in the bed of the wash southwest, soon reaching the same fenceline as that on the rim above. There is no gate, so you'll have to crawl under or through the fence to proceed. The lower reaches of the wash are not without minor obstacles. Low pouroffs and narrow chutes help relieve the boredom of slogging through the sand.

At length the aforementioned flat-topped dome appears on the left (east) side of the wash, though from this angle it appears to be capped by tilted slabs. A short distance beyond that landmark, another, much smaller flat-crowned dome appears ahead. Leave the wash on the east side when you see it, skirting the dome on its left side via a boot-worn path. The sandy path quickly leads to the rim of the gulch at the beginning of the descent route. From here you have your first look into the depths of Buckskin Gulch 120 feet below.

Look to the east wall of the gulch and you'll see an interesting, but inaccessible, bighorn sheep petroglyph. Keep that petroglyph in sight as you descend. This is where the route becomes very dangerous, and only well-prepared veteran canyoneers should attempt it. There may be a cairn indicating the point of descent at the top of a narrow crack. The crack is too confined to fit through with a backpack, so rope down your packs to the sandy ledge about 20 feet below, then squeeze through the crack and retrieve them.

Follow the sandy ledge to the left from the crack, then descend a wider slickrock ledge to the foot of the sheer wall, where you find a larger crack. Survey the route ahead and decide if you want to begin lowering packs with your rope once again. The descent is a very steep slickrock friction pitch and downclimb, with just enough hand and foot holds for experienced canyoneers to descend. The slickrock is made even more treacherous by a thin layer of sand.

Once you reach the floor of Buckskin Gulch the petroglyph is no longer visible. If you intend to exit via the same route (it seems much less intimidating ascending the route) take note of its location; things often look much the same from inside the gulch's narrows.

Most hikers are en route down Buckskin to the confluence with the Paria River (see Hike 56), though a possible alternative would be to follow Buckskin up-canyon and exit at Wire Pass, 8 miles ahead. It is not recommended that you try to find and ascend the Middle Route for the first time from Buckskin Gulch, unless you are confident and experienced enough to negotiate the route.

59 Paria Canyon—White House Trailhead to Lees Ferry

See Map on Page 309

General description:	A premier multi-day backpack, with several trip options, leading through the Glen Canyon region's most dramatic canyon, located in the Paria Canyon–Vermilion Cliffs Wilderness.
Distance:	38.2 miles, shuttle trip.
Difficulty:	Moderately strenuous.
Trail conditions:	Wash route; segments of boot-worn trails.
Trailhead access:	2WD.
Average hiking time:	4 to 6 days.
Trailhead elevations:	4,280 feet (White House Trailhead), 3,150 feet (Lees Ferry).
Elevation loss:	1,130 feet.
Optimum seasons:	April through early June; September through October.
Water availability:	The Paria River flows year-round below the mouth of Buckskin Gulch. Silty and mineral-laden river water must be settled before drinking, and hikers should use it usually only as a last resort. There are numerous seasonal springs in Paria Canyon: Perennial springs are located at 10.2 miles, Big Spring at 12.2 miles, Shower Spring at 22 miles, and nameless springs at 25.2 miles, and 0.4 mile up Bush Head Canyon at 26.4 miles.
Hazards:	Flash-flood danger.
Permits:	Reservations for permits for overnight use required; day hikers must obtain permit and pay appropriate fee ($5 per person and dog per day) at the kiosk/self-service fee station below the Paria Contact Station (see driving directions for Hike 57 for location).
Topo maps:	West Clark Bench and Bridger Point (Utah-Arizona); and Wrather Arch, Water Pockets, Ferry Swale, and Lees Ferry (Arizona) USGS quads; BLM: Paria Canyon–Vermilion Cliffs Wilderness map, Hiker's Guide to Paria Canyon, or Smoky Mountain and Glen Canyon Dam.

Key points

4.0	Narrows begin.
6.7	Slide Rock.
7.2	Confluence of Paria Canyon and Buckskin Gulch.
10.2	First spring.
12.3	Big Spring.
17.4	Judd Hollow Pump.
19.1	The Hole.

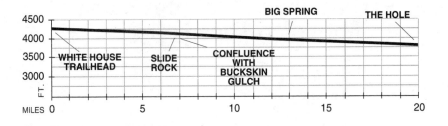

								BIG SPRING				THE HOLE	

4500
4000
3500 WHITE HOUSE   SLIDE   CONFLUENCE
       TRAILHEAD   ROCK   WITH
3000   BUCKSKIN
FT.   GULCH

MILES   0   5   10   15   20

20.4   Wrather Canyon.
22.0   Shower Spring.
25.2   Last reliable spring.
26.4   Bush Head Canyon.
28.0   High Water Route begins.
30.2   High Water Route ends.
31.5   Petroglyphs.
33.4   Wilson Ranch.
35.9   Glen Canyon National Recreation Area boundary.
37.6   Lonely Dell cemetery; turn left onto dirt road.
37.8   End of dirt road; ford river and turn right, downstream.
38.2   Reach north end of long-term parking lot at Lees Ferry.

Finding the trailheads: Follow driving directions for Hike 56 to reach the White House Trailhead.

To reach Lees Ferry from Kanab, Utah, follow U.S. Highway 89A south through Fredonia to Jacob Lake, Arizona, then east across the House Rock Valley and the Marble Platform to Marble Canyon Lodge and the prominently signed turnoff to Lees Ferry, 77 miles from Kanab.

Drivers approaching from the east should follow US 89 to the junction with northbound US 89A, 23.1 miles south of the south end of Page, Arizona, and 101 miles north of Flagstaff, Arizona. From that junction, follow US 89A first north, then west, for 14.3 miles to the Lees Ferry turnoff.

The paved road to Lees Ferry leads north, through a dramatic landscape of nearly barren red Moenkopi Formation badlands, with the Vermilion Cliffs towering above, for 4.4 miles to Lees Ferry Campground and a signed junction. Continue straight ahead where the signs point to the launch ramp. Pass the ranger station (where a pay phone is available) after 4.7 miles, and continue straight ahead (left) at the next junction. Pass the turnoff to Lonely Dell Ranch after 5.1 miles. (Day hikers can turn left onto that road and drive 250 yards to the small parking area.) Backpackers must continue ahead for another 0.4 mile and park in the spacious long-term parking lot, signed for Fish Cleaning Station, 5.5 miles from the highway.

The Lees Ferry Campground offers the only available camping in the area.

The hike: This ambitious trip is one of the classic canyon backpacks on the Colorado Plateau. Hiking in Paria Canyon is challenging, but unlike Buckskin

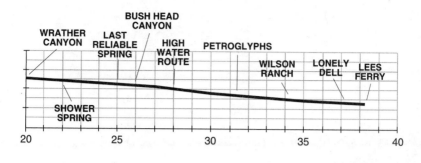

Gulch, the trip is passable to most hikers willing to get their feet wet. Deep and shadowed narrows, rich hanging gardens and numerous good springs, great vaulted amphitheaters and alcoves, and many fine campsites combine to make a hike in Paria Canyon a memorable backcountry vacation.

Paria Canyon is becoming an increasingly popular backcountry destination. Fewer hikers are taking the long trip through the canyon to Lees Ferry. Most hikers take round-trip hikes from White House Trailhead into the upper half of the canyon, which is perhaps its most spectacular section. An alternative that provides greater solitude follows the canyon upstream from Lees Ferry. With no water available for 13 miles, few hikers follow the canyon in that direction. Yet the landscape in the lower reaches of Paria Canyon is grand. The canyon is broad, warm in the early spring and late autumn, and the Vermilion Cliffs provide a dramatic backdrop of 2,000-foot canyon walls.

Nearly 10,000 hikers visited the Paria Canyon–Vermilion Cliffs Wilderness in 1996, but you shouldn't allow the canyon's popularity to deceive you. Once you leave either trailhead, you are entering a rugged wilderness canyon in the desert, where travel is demanding and help is very far away. Hikers must be prepared and equipped for a long hike under difficult conditions.

Before setting out, telephone the BLM office in Kanab, Utah, for updated hiking and weather conditions, and come prepared for whatever awaits you in the canyon. The bulletin board at the kiosk below the Paria Contact Station will provide a last minute check of conditions while you are en route to the trailhead. The BLM's hiking guide is a good resource that shows reliable springs and many campsites on a series of strip maps.

Flash floods can be life-threatening in the Paria Narrows, where there are few escape routes to higher ground. Although benches begin to appear above the wash at about 7.5 miles, ready access to higher ground remains infrequent until about mile 15. Be sure to hike this stretch only if there is no possibility of rainfall anywhere in the Paria River drainage. Keep in mind that the river begins to gather its waters from the Bryce Valley, east of Bryce Canyon National Park, some 40 miles from the White House Trailhead. Always carry extra supplies in the event a flash flood strands you in the canyon. Although the river will generally subside from flooding in 12 to 24 hours, the mud and quicksand left in a flood's wake will really slow you down.

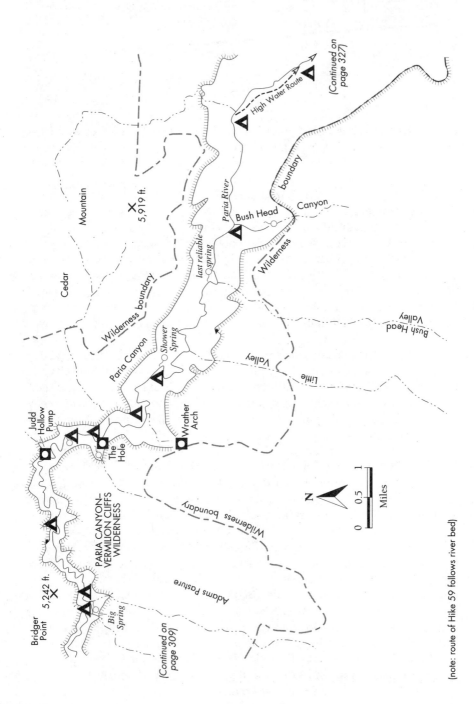

(Continued on page 327)

High Water Route

boundary

Paria River

Bush Head Canyon

Mountain

X
5,919 ft.

last reliable
spring

Wilderness

Cedar

Wilderness boundary

Paria Canyon

Shower
Spring

Little Valley

Bush Head
Valley

Judd
Hollow
Pump

Wrather
Arch

The
Hole

N

0   0.5   1
Miles

PARIA CANYON–
VERMILION CLIFFS
WILDERNESS

Wilderness boundary

Adams Pasture

Bridger
Point

5,242 ft.
X

Big
Spring

(Continued on page 309)

(note: route of Hike 59 follows river bed)

Paria Canyon is a broad desert gorge in its lower reaches.

Bring enough water containers to carry 1.5 gallons of water per person, and top off your containers at every opportunity. The Paria River generally flows year-round from the confluence with Buckskin Gulch down-canyon to Lees Ferry. But water quality is poor, with high levels of salinity and sediment. Drink river water in an emergency only, and then only after settling and filtering it first. There are numerous perennial and seasonal seeps and springs that provide good water in the canyon. Contact the BLM for an update on water availability. Since campsites at the canyon's springs are heavily used, solitude seekers will want to tank up at springs, then move on to more secluded sites.

Since you will be walking in the Paria River and crossing it countless times, in waters ranging from ankle-deep to shin-deep, proper footwear is critical for an enjoyable hike. Your feet will be wet from start to finish (see **Backcountry Essentials**, page 8).

Peak use periods in the wilderness occur during Easter Week, in April and May, with a secondary peak in October. During those times, the few campsites between the Paria Narrows and the Mecca of Big Spring are frequently occupied. The concentration of campers and the amplifying effect of the canyon walls can degrade the qualities of quiet and solitude. To reduce your impact while visiting Paria Canyon, camp in previously used sites whenever possible. Remember that it is better to concentrate your use on an already impacted site rather than spreading your impact into pristine areas where vegetation is intact and only natural processes of erosion occur. And it is important to be a good neighbor. Be sure to pack out your used toilet paper. You can see the tragic results of a toilet paper fire at the mouth of Bushhead Canyon, where 14 acres were charred on July 4, 1997.

The trail begins at the road end, leading toward the Paria River between the walk-in campground and toilets. You quickly reach the trailhead register, then pass through a fence via a hiker's maze. A sign just beyond advises that the hiking route is in the river bed, and you then drop down to your first ford of the river, a stream about the size of a modest creek. Initially the shadeless route follows the broad floodplain of the river, studded with rabbitbrush, tamarisk, and thorny mounds of Russian thistle (tumbleweed).

The canyon steadily grows more confined and you will be forced to cross the river repeatedly. The Paria River carves through soft gray clay beds throughout much of its upper course between the Bryce Valley and the White House Trailhead. Thus its waters are always gray and cloudy, and you can't see the bottom to determine its depth. After 2 miles, the canyon briefly opens up and soon thereafter you pass beneath a pair of high-voltage power lines spanning the canyon, then enter the Paria Canyon–Vermilion Cliffs Wilderness. You pass an inviting campsite beneath the partial shade of scattered cottonwoods after 3 miles, too soon to be useful unless you started late in the day. Another camping area lies on the bench east of the river 0.5 mile ahead. These are the last places to camp until you reach the confluence with Buckskin Gulch, about 4 miles ahead.

After 4.5 miles the canyon walls close in and the river is funneled into the Paria Narrows. Cross-bedded cliffs of Navajo Sandstone rise 400 to 800

Paria Canyon—White House Trailhead to Lees Ferry

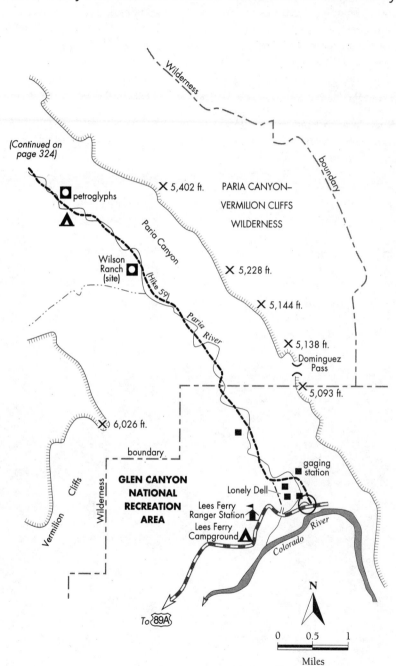

(Continued on page 324)

Wilderness

boundary

petroglyphs

X 5,402 ft.

PARIA CANYON–
VERMILION CLIFFS
WILDERNESS

Paria Canyon

Wilson
Ranch
(site)

(Hike 59)

X 5,228 ft.

X 5,144 ft.

Paria River

X 5,138 ft.
Dominguez
Pass

X 5,093 ft.

X 6,026 ft.

boundary

Vermilion Cliffs

Wilderness

GLEN CANYON
NATIONAL
RECREATION
AREA

gaging
station

Lonely Dell

Lees Ferry
Ranger Station

Lees Ferry
Campground

Colorado River

To 89A

N

0   0.5   1

Miles

feet above the narrows. The sculpted walls are shaded in red and salmon hues and decorated with patches brown desert varnish and black cliff-wash rich in manganese. In this resistant, massive sandstone, downcutting of drainages proceeds at a faster rate than canyon widening, thus Navajo Sandstone canyons tend to be deep yet narrow.

From the beginning of the narrows to about mile 15, you will spend most of your time wading in the river. The river bed is generally sandy and occasionally cobble-strewn. During average flows the crossings and wading are trouble-free. The canyon is remarkably straight through the narrows to the confluence with Buckskin Gulch, with only a few minor bends. Slide Rock, a prominent slump block fallen from the canyon wall, funnels the river beneath its "arch" 0.5 mile above the confluence. When you reach the confluence after 7.2 miles, you can continue down-river, though few hikers pass up the chance to explore Buckskin Gulch. There are campsites on a sandy bench about 0.5 mile up Buckskin, but if you're here during a period of heavy use, those few sites, the most heavily used in the canyons, may be occupied.

Since competition for scarce campsites is high in this narrow part of the upper canyon, plan your trip with flexibility in mind. Get an early start and you will have a greater chance of finding an available campsite during your first day in the canyon. Once you pass beyond Big Spring after 12.3 miles, you have a much better chance of finding that perfect campsite and enjoying it in solitude.

Camping in Lower Paria Canyon.

Just below the confluence you enter Arizona, and another two bends down-canyon and about 0.6 mile lead you to another campsite, though many hikers continue to the better sites and springs that lie ahead. At 9.4 and 9.9 miles are good campsites located next to springs which provide a good flow most of the time. The sites between here and Buckskin Gulch are the best choice for your first night in the canyon.

By now the canyon averages 400 to 500 feet deep, and at mile 10 it begins to describe a series of tight meanders that continue for another 8 miles. Great slickrock amphitheaters with cliffs vaulting over the river bed appear around the next several bends of the canyon. You cover a lot of ground to gain little lateral distance down the canyon.

After 11.2 miles you pass a *rincon*, or abandoned meander of the river bed. Three more prominent rincons are passed in the following 6 miles. The river once followed those meanders, but the inexorable process of downcutting has left the meanders high and dry above the present, straighter river channel. Big Spring, at 12.3 miles, is a popular destination for both round-trip and through hikers alike. This reliable spring provides the greatest discharge in the canyon, rich hanging gardens, and good campsites on the bench north of the river. Big Spring, or the amphitheater at 14.7 miles, offers a reasonable destination for your second day in the canyon.

Tank up here and, if the campsites are occupied, hike 0.6 mile down-canyon to another good campsite. The canyon ahead continues to curve back and forth in a long series of deeply incised meanders, leading generally northeast beneath 600-foot, often overhanging, sandstone cliffs. You'll spend the better part of the next 3 miles walking in the water. There are few places to camp along this stretch, and there are very few seasonal springs. After 14.7 miles you pass a campsite opposite a magnificent amphitheater, where the vaulted ceiling rises 650 feet overhead. A seasonal seep in the amphitheater may provide enough water to top off your water bottles.

After 15 miles the canyon gradually begins to open up, with low sandy terraces flanking the river and supporting a scattering of cottonwood groves, and occasional boxelder trees, their verdant foliage contrasting with the stark sandstone cliffs rising 600 feet above. Soon the river begins a final series of tight meanders, and a boulder jam at 16.2 miles presents one of the few obstacles in Paria Canyon. For about 0.5 mile, you'll be picking your way slowly through the boulder field. Beware of deep pools in the river along this stretch.

Save for occasional petroglyphs, campsites, and hikers' footprints, and a few eroded uranium mining roads in the extreme lower part of the canyon, there is little evidence of human activity in this remote canyon. Indeed, the canyon was seldom visited until it was discovered by modern-day back-packers. One notable exception is the Judd Hollow Pump, an obvious arti-fact located at the riverside, adjacent to the last major rincon at 17.4 miles. The pump was originally brought into the canyon in 1939 by cattlemen who intended to pump water to their stock that grazed on the dry, sandy Paria

Navajo Sandstone flanks Paria Canyon for 21 miles.

Plateau. The pump was moved to its present location in 1949, where it was tested for the first and only time, then abandoned.

About 0.6 mile and four bends below the pump at 18 miles, you reach the first of several good campsites leading to Shower Spring, 4 miles ahead. The canyon floor grows increasingly wider as you proceed, with sandy, cottonwood-studded benches flanking the canyon. At 18.4 miles you pass a reliable spring and a campsite shown in the BLM's hiker's guide, though there are many more seeps issuing from the porous Navajo Sandstone, and more campsites ahead than the BLM maps would suggest.

After 19.1 miles you reach the tremendous slickrock amphitheater of The Hole. You may find a seasonal flow of water here and there are several good campsites, beyond the reach of most round-trip hikers, that provide a greater potential for solitude. The route ahead involves less wading and more walking on segments of trail across sandy benches between river crossings. Beyond The Hole, the river turns to the south for nearly 1 mile, and the deep gorge of Wrather Canyon opens up ahead. There are several fine, but dry, campsites at the mouth of Wrather Canyon at 20.4 miles, but no camping is permitted inside that canyon to preserve its delicate riparian environment. Any one of the many campsites between the Judd Hollow Pump and Wrather Canyon is a good place to pass your third night in Paria Canyon.

Don't miss the rewarding side trip up the canyon to Wrather Arch, the largest span in the Paria River drainage. A well-worn path leads upcanyon, gaining 600 feet of elevation to the arch. Cottonwood, box elder, and a ribbon of other riparian growth hugs the banks of the intermittent stream that flows through Wrather Canyon.

About 1 mile below Wrather Canyon, the red sandstone of the Kayenta Formation emerges at river level, and the character of the canyon begins a notable transformation ahead. You'll likely hear the rain of Shower Spring before you see it emerging from the east canyon wall at the Navajo-Kayenta interface at 22 miles. Some hikers miss Shower Spring since it is well hidden behind a mantle of vegetation. A good campsite lies opposite the spring, one of the last best sites in the canyon.

At Shower Spring, you are about 16 miles from Lees Ferry, a very long one-day trek. If you are taking the recommended five days to complete the trip and passing your third night at Shower Spring, you will want to spend two more days en route to Lees Ferry. Perhaps the best choice of campsites to pass your final night are located at either end of the so-called High Water Route, at 28 and 30.25 miles, respectively. That will leave 8 to 10 miles of hiking on your last day.

Beyond Shower Spring, slopes and terraces composed of the Kayenta Formation flank the river, with convoluted Navajo slickrock rising to the canyon rims, now 1,200 to 1,400 feet above. Only three bends and 0.8 mile below the spring, the Moenave Formation emerges, also a reddish brown ledge former that is not easily distinguishable from the Kayenta. The canyon remains confined by towering cliffs as you continue, and the river is funneled between low cliff bands and ledges. At 25.2 miles, the last reliable spring adjacent to the river issues from the east canyon wall, and it is easy to miss if you're not looking for it. Bush Head Canyon, 1.2 miles ahead, also contains a good spring, and offers your last chance to tank up for the long, dry trek to Lees Ferry.

The river cuts into the colorful Chinle Formation at 25.5 miles, and ahead the canyon becomes much wider. At this point you will be following a poor to fair boot-worn trail that follows the right (south) side of the river for nearly 5 miles ahead, the longest stretch of dry hiking in Paria Canyon. After 26.4 miles Bush Head Canyon opens up to the south. The once-pleasant campsites at the canyon mouth are now surrounded by charred vegetation, the result of an out-of-control toilet paper fire. Burning toilet paper may be an acceptable practice in wetter environments, but in the desert, it often leads to tragic results. Heed the wilderness regulations for Paria Canyon and pack out used toilet paper.

Not only does the canyon grow wider below Bush Head Canyon, it grows deeper, as well. Cliffs of Moenave, Kayenta, and Navajo rocks soar 2,000 feet skyward. The soft clay beds of the Chinle Formation afford a poor foundation for the cliffs above. As the river cuts into the Chinle rocks the canyon becomes deeper, and as the cliffs above crumble, the gorge grows wider. Huge sandstone blocks fallen from the cliffs above begin to choke the river channel, and by Mile 28, the so-called High Water Route avoids this tangle of boulders and deep water holes by traversing talus slopes above the south banks of the river. The river bed is passable if the water is low and no recent floods have occurred.

You'll pass the first of three final campsites at the beginning of the route, which is actually a good, though rocky, trail. Shortly after the trail returns to the canyon bottom, you pass the second campsite, situated beneath a lone, gnarled cottonwood, at 30.25 miles. The canyon ahead is an interesting change of pace from the nearly 30 miles of slickrock gorge that lies behind you. In its lower reaches, the Paria courses through a classic desert canyon. Here you can see the canyon in its entirety, from the boulder-strewn river to the canyon rims more than 2,000 feet above, spanning a colorful array of rock formations that record 35 million years of natural history, ranging from lakes, streams, and broad floodplains, to vast deserts of drifting sand.

Beyond the campsite, you begin crossing the river once again, though crossings are widely separated by long stretches of well-worn trail traversing sandy benches. At 31.5 miles, on a barren Chinle bench on the north side of the river, there are several sandstone boulders decorated with a profusion of petroglyphs. On the backside of one boulder you will find that most of the ancient carvings are upside down. Another boulder perched on the slope above the trail features some fine bighorn sheep carvings. Unfortunately, modern graffiti has been added to the boulder by thoughtless vandals.

You'll pass the last good campsite in a small grove of cottonwoods just beyond the next river crossing below the petroglyphs. The view back up the canyon reveals Spire 5475, an especially striking landmark soaring 1,000 feet above its base on the south wall of the canyon. The way ahead is fully exposed to the sun, crossing wide benches where four-wing saltbush, arrow-weed, shadscale, and prickly pear cactus dominate. Tamarisk occasionally fringes the river banks, sharing space with the tall, thorny gray shrubs of Russian olive. Notice the light gray stems of arrow-weed, and you'll see that most are straight, slender with little taper, and somewhat rigid. These stems were valuable to native inhabitants for use as arrow shafts, hence the name.

Shortly before Mile 33, old 1950s uranium prospector's roads begin to appear, carving through the Chinle slopes south of the river. Above the Chinle, vast dune fields reach one mile south from just above the river banks to the foot of the canyon's 1,800-foot cliffs. The canyon reaches its deepest point in this area, with an elevation difference of 2,700 feet between the rims and the river. At Mile 33 the canyon bends south, and soon thereafter you pass the faint remains of the Wilson Ranch, first homesteaded in 1918. All that remains today are the foundation of the original cabin, and a corral. A thicket of tamarisk and cottonwood fringe the site, nurtured by seepage labeled as springs on the topo map. Don't expect to fill your water bottles here. At the next bend below Wilson Ranch you'll spy the dark portals of one of several old uranium mines in lower Paria Canyon.

About 1.5 miles below Wilson Ranch, the low sandstone cliff of the Shinarump Conglomerate, the bottom layer of the Chinle sequence, emerges at river level. The high slickrock saddle of Dominguez Pass notches the rim on the southeastern skyline. As you leave the Shinarump cliff behind, you follow the river as it carves a corridor through the thinly-bedded, chocolate brown cliffs of the Moenkopi Formation. Here, the craggy triad of the Echo Peaks, first scaled by members of John Wesley Powell's 1869 Colorado River Expedition, appear ahead. These towering peaks will be your guide for the remainder of the journey.

The valley floor briefly becomes more confined after entering the realm of the Moenkopi, but soon the walls recede and broad benches once again embrace the river. You'll know you are entering what was once an outpost of civilization when first you pass the rusting remains of an old car, then an abandoned cabin, and finally a sturdy plank corral that is still used today by ranchers who graze their cows along the lower Paria. At this point you'll notice that the towering Vermilion Cliffs have turned southward, marching off toward the distant Marble Platform.

You reach the trail register about 200 yards beyond the corral, and about 0.2 mile farther, a sign points to "Lonely Dell" and "Trailhead Parking." Follow the trail up to the Lonely Dell Cemetery, and just beyond it, adjacent to the rusting hulk of an old truck and Picture Window Cabin, an orange post with an arrow points down a road to the left. An alternative way to the trailhead is to walk through Lonely Dell for about 0.1 mile to the paved road, then turn left and follow the road for 0.4 mile to the large parking area.

The cabins of Lonely Dell are well worth a visit. After you reach your trailhead, drive down to the small parking area signed for Lonely Dell, pick up a copy of the self-guiding trail pamphlet, and take a step back in time as you explore this once lonely outpost that the operators of famous Lees Ferry called home.

Turn left onto the road just beyond the cemetery and cross the shrub-dotted clearing, the site of John D. Lee's orchard in the 1870s. From the road's end, 0.25 mile from the cemetery, ford the river one last time opposite the Paria River gauging station, then follow the trail southeast along the tamarisk-fringed banks of the river. When the bench pinches out, the trail mounts a steep, rocky slope, 20 to 30 feet directly above a bend in the river. The trail is badly eroded on this slope, so proceed with caution. This may be the most dangerous part of the hike, but the exposure lasts for only a few yards.

The final several hundred yards of the trail passes above the Lees Ferry River Ranger Station, and ends at the north end of the long-term parking lot, thus ending a long and rewarding journey.

Appendix A: For more information

Note: Land management agencies and emergency contacts are listed at the end of each regional introduction in the *For more information* section.

Arizona Strip Interpretive Association
345 Riverside Drive
St. George, UT 84770
(435) 628-4491
fax (435) 673-5729

Canyonlands Natural History Association
3031 South Highway 191
Moab, UT 84532
(435) 259-6003
(800) 840-8978
fax (435) 259-8263

Dixie Interpretive Association (Escalante Interagency visitor center)
755 West Main
Escalante, UT 84726
(435) 826-5499

Escalante Outfitters
310 West Main
P.O. Box 570
Escalante, UT 84726
(435) 826-4266
fax (435) 826-4388
(Books and maps available via mail order)

Glen Canyon Natural History Association
P.O. Box 581
Page, AZ 85040
(520) 645-3532

Southern Utah Wilderness Alliance (SUWA)
1471 South 1100 East
Salt Lake City, UT 84125
(801) 486-3161

Willow Creek Books and Coffee
263 South 100 East
Kanab, UT 84741
(435) 644-8884
(Books and maps available via mail order)

Appendix B: Further Reading

Geology

Baars, Donald, *The Colorado Plateau, A Geologic History*. New Mexico: University of New Mexico Press, 1983.

Barnes, F. A., *Canyon Country Arches and Bridges*. Salt Lake City: Wasatch Publishers, 1987.

Barnes, F. A., *Canyon Country Geology*. Salt Lake City: Wasatch Publishers, 1978.

Hintze, Lehi F., *Geologic History of Utah*. Provo, Utah: Department of Geology, Brigham Young University, 1975.

Rigby, J. Keith, *Northern Colorado Plateau*. Dubuque, Iowa: Kendall/Hunt Publishing Co., 1976.

Stokes, William Lee, *Geology of Utah*. Salt Lake City: Utah Museum of Natural History, University of Utah, and Utah Geological and Mineralogical Survey, Department of Natural Resources, 1986.

History

Abbey, Edward, *Desert Solitaire: A Season in the Wilderness*. New York: Ballantine Books, 1968.

Crampton, C. Gregory, *Standing Up Country: The Canyon Lands of Utah and Arizona*. Salt Lake City: Peregrine Smith Books, 1983.

Frost, Kent, *My Canyonlands*. New York: Abelard-Schuman, 1971.

Jones, Dewitt, and Linda S. Cordell, *Anasazi World*. Portland, Oregon: Graphic Arts Center Publishing Co., 1985.

Lavender, David, *One Man's West*. Doubleday and Company, Inc., 1956.

Matlock, Gary, *Enemy Ancestors, The Anasazi World With a Guide to Sites*. Northland Press, 1988.

Powell, Allan Kent, *San Juan County, Utah: People, Resources, and History*. Salt Lake City: Utah State Historical Society, 1983.

Powell, J. W., *The Exploration of the Colorado River and its Canyons*. New York: Dover Press, 1961.

Schaafsma, Polly, *The Rock Art of Utah*. Cambridge, Mass.: Harvard University, Peabody Museum of Archaeology and Ethnology, 1971.

Weaver, Donald E., *Images On Stone, The Prehistoric Rock Art of the Colorado Plateau*. Flagstaff, Arizona: Museum of Northern Arizona, 1984.

Natural History

Andersen, Bernice A., *Desert Plants of Utah*. Utah State University, Cooperative Extension Services.

Elmore, Francis H., *Shrubs and Trees of the Southwest Uplands*. Tucson, Arizona: Southwest Parks and Monuments Association, 1976.

Fischer, Pierre C., *70 Common Cacti of the Southwest*. Tucson, Arizona: Southwest Parks and Monuments Association, 1989.

Peterson, Roger Tory, *A Field Guide to Western Birds*. Boston: Houghton Mifflin, 1961.

Udvardy, Miklos D. F., *The Audubon Society Field Guide to North American Birds, Western Region*. New York: Alfred A. Knopf, 1977.

Welsh, Stanley L., and N. Duane Atwood, Sherel Goodrich, Larry C. Higgins, editors, *A Utah Flora*. Provo, Utah: Brigham Young University, 1987.

Appendix C: Hiker Checklist

Hiking in the Glen Canyon region requires ample planning, and one of the first steps to being well prepared is packing the right equipment. Don't overburden your pack with too much equipment and unnecessary items; bring only what you really need. Scan the checklist below before your trip into the canyon country to ensure you haven't forgotten an essential item.

- [ ] Backpack
- [ ] Day pack
- [ ] Extra pack straps
- [ ] Water bottles (1 to 2 quart Nalgene bottles are best)
- [ ] Collapsible bucket (for settling silty water)
- [ ] Water filter (with brush to clean in the field)
- [ ] Pocket knife
- [ ] Hiking poles (1 or 2)
- [ ] Foam or self-inflating sleeping pad
- [ ] Sleeping bag (or sheet, or sleeping bag liner for summer)
- [ ] Tent, stakes, ground sheet and/or tarp
- [ ] Sunglasses (with UV protection)
- [ ] Sunscreen (with a SPF of 15 or greater)
- [ ] Backpack stove, fuel bottle (full)
- [ ] Signal mirror
- [ ] First-aid kit
- [ ] Medication: prescriptions, anti-inflammatory, and/or pain medication
- [ ] Knee and/or ankle wraps (neoprene is best)
- [ ] First-aid tape
- [ ] Moleskin, Second Skin
- [ ] Band-Aids, bandages
- [ ] Aspirin (or other pain medication)
- [ ] Lip balm
- [ ] Toothbrush, toothpaste
- [ ] Toilet paper
- [ ] Lightweight trowel
- [ ] Boots (well broken-in)
- [ ] Camp shoes or sandals
- [ ] Extra shirt
- [ ] Extra underwear
- [ ] Extra socks

- [ ] Hiking socks; wool outer, polypropylene or nylon liner
- [ ] Parka (synthetic pile works best)
- [ ] Sweater
- [ ] Pants
- [ ] Hiking shorts
- [ ] Swimsuit
- [ ] Rain gear (Gore-tex or similar fabric that is both waterproof and windproof)
- [ ] Biodegradable soap, small towel
- [ ] Cookware, cup, pot handle, pot scrubber
- [ ] Spoon and fork
- [ ] Matches in waterproof container
- [ ] Insect repellent
- [ ] Nylon tape or duct tape
- [ ] Pack cover
- [ ] Nylon stuffsacks, and 20- to 30-pound test fishing line (for hanging food)
- [ ] Topo maps
- [ ] Zipper-lock bags (for packing out trash and used toilet paper)
- [ ] Enough food, plus a little extra
- [ ] Watch
- [ ] Compass
- [ ] Binoculars
- [ ] Thermometer
- [ ] Camera, film, lenses, filters, lens brush and paper
- [ ] Small sewing kit
- [ ] Notebook, pencils
- [ ] Field guidebooks
- [ ] Water
- [ ] Backcountry Use Permit (where required)

Add the following for winter travel:
- [ ] Gaiters
- [ ] Instep crampons
- [ ] Wool or polypro cap or balaclava
- [ ] Space blanket
- [ ] Layers of warm clothing
- [ ] Sleeping bag with a rating of at least 0 degrees F.
- [ ] Waterproof/windproof clothing
- [ ] Mittens or gloves
- [ ] Thermal underwear (wool or polypropylene)

Appendix D: Glossary of terms

alcove: a cave-like hollow in a canyon wall.

amphitheater: a very large concave hollow in a canyon wall.

bay: a small **amphitheater**.

boulder jam: where a canyon is blocked by a mass of boulders fallen from the canyon walls.

butte: smaller than a **mesa**, and isolated from a mesa by erosion.

chockstone: a rock or boulder wedged into a narrow canyon.

dome: a smooth, rounded mass of **slickrock**, often resembling a pertified sand dune.

dugway: a road or trail carved into a cliff or steep slope.

hoodoo: spires of resistant rock sculpted by erosion.

mesa: segments of a larger flat surface known as a plateau, and isolated by erosion, usually bounded by cliffs.

mushroom rocks: a common form of **hoodoo**.

narrows or slot: a constriction in a canyon.

perennial (as in a spring or wildflower): lasting throughout the year.

pitch: a climbing term describing the vertical distance between segments of the climb.

plunge pool: a pool at the bottom of a pouroff, often scoured deeply into the canyon bottom by powerful floodwaters plunging over a pouroff.

pouroff: a dry waterfall in a drainage.

sand slide: a steep slope of soft sand.

seepline: a line of seepage on a canyon wall, usually supporting the specialized plant community of hanging gardens.

slickrock: smooth, bare sandstone, ranging from vertical to horizontal.

wash: the streambed or drainage, usually dry, in the bottom of a canyon.

Index

Page numbers in italic type refer to maps.
*Page numbers in **bold** type refer to photos.*

About the Author

Ron Adkison, an avid hiker and backpacker, began his outdoor explorations at age six. After more than 30 years of hiking, he has logged more than 8,000 trail miles in ten western states. He has walked every trail in this guide to provide accurate, firsthand information about the trails, as well as features of ecological and historical interest. When he's not on the trail, Ron lives on the family's mountain ranch in southwest Montana, and with the help of his wife, Lynette, and two children, Ben and Abbey, raises sheep and llamas.

Ron shares his love and enthusiasm for wild places in this, his ninth guidebook.

Other FalconGuides by Ron Adkison: *Hiking California, Hiking Grand Canyon National Park, Hiking Washington, Hiking Wyoming's Wind River Range, Beast Easy Day Hikes Grand Canyon, Best Easy Day Hikes Grand Staircase–Escalante and the Glen Canyon Region.*

FALCON®

get
FALCON GUIDED

■ *To order any of these books, check with your local bookseller
or call FALCON® at **1-800-582-2665**.*
Visit us on the world wide web at:
www.falconguide.com

FALCON®

get
FALCON GUIDED

BEST EASY DAY HIKES SERIES

Beartooths
Canyonlands & Arches
Best Hikes on the Continental Divide
Glacier & Wateron Lakes
Grand Staircase-Escalante and the Glen Canyon
    Region
Grand Canyon
North Cascades
Olympics
Shenandoah
Yellowstone

12 SHORT HIKES SERIES

Colorado
Aspen
Boulder
Denver Foothills Central
Denver Foothills North
Denver Foothills South
Rocky Mountain National Park-Estes Park
Rocky Mountain National Park-Grand Lake
Steamboat Springs
Summit County
Vail

California
San Diego Coast
San Diego Mountains
San Francisco Bay Area-Coastal
San Francisco Bay Area-East Bay
San Francisco Bay Area-North Bay
San Francisco Bay Area-South Bay

Washington
Mount Rainier National Park-Paradise
Mount Rainier National Park-Sunrise

■ *To order any of these books, check with your local bookseller*
or call FALCON® at 1-800-582-2665.

Visit us on the world wide web at:
www.falconguide.com

FALCON®

get FALCON GUIDED

Scenic Driving Guides

Scenic Driving Alaska and the Yukon
Scenic Driving Arizona
Scenic Driving the Beartooth Highway
Scenic Driving California
Scenic Driving Colorado
Scenic Driving Florida
Scenic Driving Georgia
Scenic Driving Hawaii
Scenic Driving Idaho
Scenic Driving Michigan
Scenic Driving Minnesota
Scenic Driving Montana
Scenic Driving New England
Scenic Driving New Mexico
Scenic Driving North Carolina
Scenic Driving Oregon
Scenic Driving the Ozarks including the
    Ouchita Mountains
Scenic Driving Texas
Scenic Driving Utah
Scenic Driving Washington
Scenic Driving Wisconsin
Scenic Driving Wyoming
Back Country Byways
National Forest Scenic Byways
National Forest Scenic Byways II

Historic Trail Guides

Traveling California's Gold Rush Country
Traveling the Lewis & Clark Trail
Traveling the Oregon Trail
Traveler's Guide to the Pony Express Trail

Wildlife Viewing Guides

Alaska Wildlife Viewing Guide
Arizona Wildlife Viewing Guide
California Wildlife Viewing Guide
Colorado Wildlife Viewing Guide
Florida Wildlife Viewing Guide
Idaho Wildlife Viewing Guide
Indiana Wildlife Vewing Guide
Iowa Wildlife Viewing Guide
Kentucky Wildlife Viewing Guide
Massachusetts Wildlife Viewing Guide
Montana Wildlife Viewing Guide
Nebraska Wildlife Viewing Guide
Nevada Wildlife Viewing Guide
New Hampshire Wildlife Viewing Guide
New Jersey Wildlife Viewing Guide
New Mexico Wildlife Viewing Guide
New York Wildlife Viewing Guide
North Carolina Wildlife Viewing Guide
North Dakota Wildlife Viewing Guide
Ohio Wildlife Viewing Guide
Oregon Wildlife Viewing Guide
Tennessee Wildlife Viewing Guide
Texas Wildlife Viewing Guide
Utah Wildlife Viewing Guide
Vermont Wildlife Viewing Guide
Virginia Wildlife Viewing Guide
Washington Wildlife Viewing Guide
West Virginia Wildlife Viewing Guide
Wisconsin Wildlife Viewing Guide

■ *To order any of these books, check with your local bookseller*
or call FALCON® at **1-800-582-2665**.

Visit us on the world wide web at:
www.falconguide.com

FALCON®

Discover the Thrill of Watching Wildlife.

 The Watchable Wildlife® Series

Published in cooperation with Defenders of Wildlife, these high-quality, full color guidebooks feature detailed descriptions, side trips, viewing tips, and easy-to-follow maps. Wildlife viewing guides for the following states are now available with more on the way.

Alaska	Massachusetts	Ohio
Arizona	Montana	Oregon
California	Nebraska	Tennessee
Colorado	Nevada	Texas
Florida	New Hampshire	Utah
Idaho	New Jersey	Vermont
Indiana	New Mexico	Virginia
Iowa	New York	Washington
Kentucky	North Carolina	West Virginia
	North Dakota	Wisconsin

Watch for this sign along roadways. It's the official sign indicating wildlife viewing areas included in the Watchable Wildlife® Series.

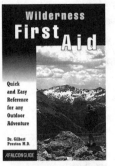

WILDERNESS FIRST AID

By Dr. Gilbert Preston M.D.
Enjoy the outdoors and face the inherent risks with confidence. By reading this easy-to-follow first-aid text, all outdoor enthusiasts can pack a little extra peace of mind on their next adventure. *Wilderness First Aid* offers expert medical advice for dealing with outdoor emergencies beyond the reach of 911. It easily fits in most backcountry first-aid kits.

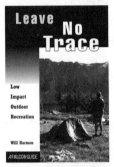

LEAVE NO TRACE

By Will Harmon
The concept of "leave no trace" seems simple, but it actually gets fairly complicated. This handy quick-reference guidebook includes all the newest information on this growing and all-important subject. This book is written to help the outdoor enthusiast make the hundreds of decisions necessary to protect the natural landscape and still have an enjoyable wilderness experience. Part of the proceeds from the sale of this book go to continue leave-no-trace education efforts. The Official Manual of American Hiking Society.

BEAR AWARE

By Bill Schneider
Hiking in bear country can be very safe if hikers follow the guidelines summarized in this small, "packable" book. Extensively reviewed by bear experts, the book contains the latest information on the intriguing science of bear-human interactions. *Bear Aware* can not only make your hike safer, but it can help you avoid the fear of bears that can take the edge off your trip.

MOUNTAIN LION ALERT

By Steve Torres
Recent mountain lion attacks have received national attention. Although infrequent, lion attacks raise concern for public safety. *Mountain Lion Alert* contains helpful advice for mountain bikers, trail runners, horse riders, pet owners, and suburban landowners on how to reduce the chances of mountain lion-human conflicts.

Also Available
- ***Wilderness Survival*** • ***Reading Weather*** • ***Backpacking Tips***
- ***Climbing Safely*** • ***Avalanche Aware***

To order check with your local bookseller or
call FALCON® at **1-800-582-2665.**
www.falconguide.com